The Cambridge Companion to Rhythm

One of the defining aspects of music is that it exists in time. From clapping to dancing, toe-tapping to head-nodding, the responses of musicians and listeners alike capture the immediacy and significance of the musical beat. This Companion explores the richness of musical time through a variety of perspectives, surveying influential writings on the topic, incorporating the perspectives of listeners, analysts, composers, and performers, and considering the subject across a range of genres and cultures. It includes chapters on music perception, visualizing rhythmic notation, composers' writings on rhythm, rhythm in jazz, rock, and hip-hop. Taking a global approach, chapters also explore rhythmic styles in the music of India, Africa, Bali, Latin America and the Caribbean, and Indigenous music of North and South America. Readers will gain an understanding of musicians' approaches to performing complex rhythms of contemporary music, and revealing insights into the likely future of rhythm in music.

RUSSELL HARTENBERGER is a percussionist with both Nexus and Steve Reich and Musicians. He is Emeritus Professor at the University of Toronto, author of *Performance Practice in the Music of Steve Reich*, editor of *The Cambridge Companion to Percussion*, and composer of numerous works for percussion.

RYAN MCCLELLAND is Professor of Music Theory at the University of Toronto. His research interests include rhythmic-metric theory, Schenkerian analysis, and performance studies. In addition to articles on these topics in journals including *Music Analysis* and *Music Theory Spectrum*, he has published a book on the scherzos of Johannes Brahms.

Cambridge Companions to Music

Topics

The Cambridge Companion to Ballet
Edited by Marion Kant

The Cambridge Companion to Blues and Gospel Music
Edited by Allan Moore

The Cambridge Companion to Choral Music
Edited by André de Quadros

The Cambridge Companion to the Concerto
Edited by Simon P. Keefe

The Cambridge Companion to Conducting
Edited by José Antonio Bowen

The Cambridge Companion to Eighteenth-Century Music
Edited by Anthony R. DelDonna and Pierpaolo Polzonetti

The Cambridge Companion to Electronic Music
Edited by Nick Collins and Julio D'Escriván

The Cambridge Companion to the 'Eroica' Symphony
Edited by Nancy November

The Cambridge Companion to Film Music
Edited by Mervyn Cooke and Fiona Ford

The Cambridge Companion to French Music
Edited by Simon Trezise

The Cambridge Companion to Grand Opera
Edited by David Charlton

The Cambridge Companion to Hip-Hop
Edited by Justin A. Williams

The Cambridge Companion to Jazz
Edited by Mervyn Cooke and David Horn

The Cambridge Companion to Jewish Music
Edited by Joshua S. Walden

The Cambridge Companion to the Lied
Edited by James Parsons

The Cambridge Companion to Medieval Music
Edited by Mark Everist

The Cambridge Companion to Music in Digital Culture
Edited by Nicholas Cook, Monique Ingalls and David Trippett

The Cambridge Companion to the Musical, third edition
Edited by William Everett and Paul Laird

The Cambridge Companion to Opera Studies
Edited by Nicholas Till

The Cambridge Companion to Operetta
Edited by Anastasia Belina and Derek B. Scott

The Cambridge Companion to the Orchestra
Edited by Colin Lawson

The Cambridge Companion to Percussion
Edited by Russell Hartenberger

The Cambridge Companion to Pop and Rock
Edited by Simon Frith, Will Straw and John Street

The Cambridge Companion to Recorded Music
Edited by Eric Clarke, Nicholas Cook, Daniel Leech-Wilkinson and John Rink

The Cambridge Companion to the Singer-Songwriter
Edited by Katherine Williams and Justin A. Williams

The Cambridge Companion to the String Quartet
Edited by Robin Stowell

The Cambridge Companion to Twentieth-Century Opera
Edited by Mervyn Cooke

Composers

The Cambridge Companion to Bach
Edited by John Butt

The Cambridge Companion to Bartók
Edited by Amanda Bayley

The Cambridge Companion to the Beatles
Edited by Kenneth Womack

The Cambridge Companion to Beethoven
Edited by Glenn Stanley

The Cambridge Companion to Berg
Edited by Anthony Pople

The Cambridge Companion to Berlioz
Edited by Peter Bloom

The Cambridge Companion to Brahms
Edited by Michael Musgrave

The Cambridge Companion to Benjamin Britten
Edited by Mervyn Cooke

The Cambridge Companion to Bruckner
Edited by John Williamson

The Cambridge Companion to John Cage
Edited by David Nicholls

The Cambridge Companion to Chopin
Edited by Jim Samson

The Cambridge Companion to Debussy
Edited by Simon Trezise

The Cambridge Companion to Elgar
Edited by Daniel M. Grimley and Julian Rushton

The Cambridge Companion to Duke Ellington
Edited by Edward Green

The Cambridge Companion to Gershwin
Edited by Anna Celenza

The Cambridge Companion to Gilbert and Sullivan
Edited by David Eden and Meinhard Saremba

The Cambridge Companion to Handel
Edited by Donald Burrows

The Cambridge Companion to Haydn
Edited by Caryl Clark

The Cambridge Companion to Liszt
Edited by Kenneth Hamilton

The Cambridge Companion to Mahler
Edited by Jeremy Barham

The Cambridge Companion to Mendelssohn
Edited by Peter Mercer-Taylor

The Cambridge Companion to Monteverdi
Edited by John Whenham and Richard Wistreich

The Cambridge Companion to Mozart
Edited by Simon P. Keefe

The Cambridge Companion to Arvo Pärt
Edited by Andrew Shenton

The Cambridge Companion to Ravel
Edited by Deborah Mawer

The Cambridge Companion to the Rolling Stones
Edited by Victor Coelho and John Covach

The Cambridge Companion to Rossini
Edited by Emanuele Senici

The Cambridge Companion to Schoenberg
Edited by Jennifer Shaw and Joseph Auner

The Cambridge Companion to Schubert
Edited by Christopher Gibbs

The Cambridge Companion to Schumann
Edited by Beate Perrey

The Cambridge Companion to Shostakovich
Edited by Pauline Fairclough and David Fanning

The Cambridge Companion to Sibelius
Edited by Daniel M. Grimley

The Cambridge Companion to Richard Strauss
Edited by Charles Youmans

The Cambridge Companion to Michael Tippett
Edited by Kenneth Gloag and Nicholas Jones

The Cambridge Companion to Vaughan Williams
Edited by Alain Frogley and Aiden J. Thomson

The Cambridge Companion to Verdi
Edited by Scott L. Balthazar

Instruments

The Cambridge Companion to Brass Instruments
Edited by Trevor Herbert and John Wallace

The Cambridge Companion to the Cello
Edited by Robin Stowell

The Cambridge Companion to the Clarinet
Edited by Colin Lawson

The Cambridge Companion to the Guitar
Edited by Victor Coelho

The Cambridge Companion to the Harpsichord
Edited by Mark Kroll

The Cambridge Companion to the Organ
Edited by Nicholas Thistlethwaite and Geoffrey Webber

The Cambridge Companion to the Piano
Edited by David Rowland

The Cambridge Companion to the Recorder
Edited by John Mansfield Thomson

The Cambridge Companion to the Saxophone
Edited by Richard Ingham

The Cambridge Companion to Singing
Edited by John Potter

The Cambridge Companion to the Violin
Edited by Robin Stowell

The Cambridge Companion to Rhythm

Edited by
RUSSELL HARTENBERGER
University of Toronto

RYAN MCCLELLAND
University of Toronto

CAMBRIDGE
UNIVERSITY PRESS

CAMBRIDGE
UNIVERSITY PRESS

University Printing House, Cambridge CB2 8BS, United Kingdom

One Liberty Plaza, 20th Floor, New York, NY 10006, USA

477 Williamstown Road, Port Melbourne, VIC 3207, Australia

314–321, 3rd Floor, Plot 3, Splendor Forum, Jasola District Centre, New Delhi – 110025, India

79 Anson Road, #06–04/06, Singapore 079906

Cambridge University Press is part of the University of Cambridge.

It furthers the University's mission by disseminating knowledge in the pursuit of education, learning, and research at the highest international levels of excellence.

www.cambridge.org

Information on this title: www.cambridge.org/9781108492928
DOI: 10.1017/9781108631730

First published 2020

A catalogue record for this publication is available from the British Library.

Library of Congress Cataloging-in-Publication Data
Names: McClelland, Ryan C. editor. | Hartenberger, Russell, editor.
Title: The Cambridge companion to rhythm / edited by Russell Hartenberger, Ryan McClelland.
Description: [1.] | New York : Cambridge University Press, 2020. | Series: Cambridge companions to music | Includes bibliographical references and index.
Identifiers: LCCN 2019060082 (print) | LCCN 2019060083 (ebook) | ISBN 9781108492928 (hardback) | ISBN 9781108730129 (paperback) | ISBN 9781108631730 (epub)
Subjects: LCSH: Musical meter and rhythm–History. | Musical meter and rhythm. | Musical analysis. | Music–Psychological aspects.
Classification: LCC ML437 .C36 2020 (print) | LCC ML437 (ebook) | DDC 781.2/2–dc23
LC record available at https://lccn.loc.gov/2019060082
LC ebook record available at https://lccn.loc.gov/2019060083

ISBN 978-1-108-49292-8 Hardback
ISBN 978-1-108-73012-9 Paperback

Contents

Figures

Tables

Music Examples

Notes on Contributors

MATTHEW BUTTERFIELD is Associate Professor of Music at Franklin & Marshall College, where he teaches courses in jazz and blues history, songwriting, and music theory. He received his bachelor's degree in music from Amherst College and earned his Ph.D. from the University of Pennsylvania. His research focuses on jazz rhythm, with a specific emphasis on the elusive rhythmic phenomenon known as "swing." His current work concerns the history of this term in relation to African American music and the process of its racialization in the first few decades of the twentieth century.

DANIEL CAMERON is a cognitive neuroscientist and a trained percussionist and drummer. His research investigates the perception of musical rhythm, including cross-cultural differences, development in infancy and childhood, and the neural mechanisms that underlie rhythm's rich relationship with human life. He has degrees in percussion performance and cognitive neuroscience and is currently a postdoctoral fellow at McMaster University.

TREVOR DE CLERCQ is Associate Professor in the Department of Recording Industry at Middle Tennessee State University, where he coordinates the musicianship curriculum and teaches coursework in audio theory and music technology. His research focuses on the ways in which contemporary popular music departs from traditional theoretical frameworks developed primarily within the context of common-practice-era music, especially as shown through computational and corpus methods. His *Nashville Number System Fake Book*, which includes charts for 200 acclaimed country songs, was published in 2015. He holds a Ph.D. in music theory from the Eastman School of Music.

NICK COLLINS is Professor in the Durham University Music Department with strong interests in artificial intelligence techniques applied within music, computer and programming languages as musical instrument, and the history and practice of electronic music. He has performed as composer-programmer-pianist and codiscian, from algoraves to electronic chamber music. Many papers and much code and music are available from www.composerprogrammer.com.

ALAN DODSON is Assistant Professor of Music Theory at Mount Allison University and previously taught at the University of British Columbia, where he was a founding member of the UBC Rhythm Research Cluster. His analytic case studies on rhythm in recorded music have appeared in *Intersections: Canadian Journal of Music*, *Journal of Music Theory*, *Music Analysis*, *Music Performance Research*, *Music Theory Online*, and *Music Theory Spectrum*. He is currently preparing an annotated translation of Heinrich Schenker's *lessonbooks* from the 1920s for *Schenker Documents Online*.

JESSICA GRAHN is Associate Professor at the Brain and Mind Institute and Department of Psychology at the University of Western Ontario (Western). She has degrees in neuroscience and piano performance from Northwestern University and a Ph.D. from Cambridge University in the neuroscience of music. Her research specializes in rhythm, movement, and cognition.

RUSSELL HARTENBERGER is Professor Emeritus and former Dean of the Faculty of Music, University of Toronto. He has been a member of both Nexus and Steve Reich and Musicians since 1971. His compositions include *The Invisible Proverb*, *Telisi Odyssey*, *Magic Time*, *Requiem for Percussion and Voices*, and *Eagles*, and his arrangements include *Moondog Suite* and *Persian Songs* with Iranian classical vocalist Sepideh Raissadat. He is author of *Performance Practice in the Music of Steve Reich* and editor of *The Cambridge Companion to Percussion*. In 2017 he was awarded the Leonardo da Vinci World Award of Arts by the World Cultural Council.

GRETCHEN HORLACHER writes on issues of musical rhythm and meter in the music of Igor Stravinsky, Béla Bartók and Steve Reich, and music-choreographic relations. She is the author of *Building Blocks: Repetition and Continuity in Stravinsky's Music* and co-editor (with Severine Neff and Maureen Carr) of *The* Rite of Spring *at 100*, which received the Ruth A. Solie Award from the American Musicological Society. She is Professor of Music Theory at the Jacobs School of Music at Indiana University.

JAMES KIPPEN is Professor Emeritus of Ethnomusicology at the Faculty of Music, University of Toronto. He studied *tabla* with Afaq Hussain of Lucknow, and his book *The Tabla of Lucknow* examined the musical lives of hereditary drummers in a city once famous for its opulent culture. His interests lie in the history of rhythm and drumming in India, and he analyses manuscripts and early printed works in various Indian languages. His book *Gurudev's Drumming Legacy* is a detailed reconstruction of repertoire and rhythmic theory in the context of rising nationalism and musical institutionalization in the early twentieth century.

HARALD KREBS is Distinguished Professor at the University of Victoria and head of theory at its School of Music. He was President of the Society for Music Theory in 2011–13 and is a fellow of the Royal Society of Canada. His monograph *Fantasy Pieces: Metrical Dissonance in the Music of Robert Schumann* won the Society for Music Theory's Wallace Berry Award. His research on Josephine Lang (1815–80) led to the book *Josephine Lang: Her Life and Songs* (co-authored with Sharon Krebs), and to two editions of songs by Lang. Krebs's recent work focuses on expressive declamation in the German *Lied*.

DAVID LOCKE is Professor in the Music Department at Tufts University. An ethnomusicologist, his research interests include music-cultures of Africa, documentation and musical analysis of traditional African music, relationship of music and dance, and new contexts for roots traditions. Author of three books on African music, two online monographs, numerous scholarly articles, and the African chapter in *Worlds of Music* textbook, he is also the founder of the Agbekor Society, a Boston-based group for African performance.

PETER MANUEL has researched and published extensively on musics of India, the Caribbean, Spain, and elsewhere. His several books include *Caribbean Currents: Caribbean Music from Rumba to Reggae, Cassette Culture: Popular Music and Technology in North India*, and *Tales, Tunes, and Tassa Drums: Retention and Invention in Indo-Caribbean Music*. He has also produced three documentary videos, including *Tassa Thunder: Folk Music from India to the Caribbean*. Formerly an amateur performer of sitar, jazz piano, flamenco guitar, and highland bagpipes, he teaches ethnomusicology at John Jay College and the Graduate Center of the City University of New York.

RYAN MCCLELLAND is Professor of Music Theory at the University of Toronto and also serves as Associate Dean, Academic & Student Affairs in the Faculty of Music. His research interests include rhythmic-metric theory, Schenkerian analysis, and performance studies. He has published on these subjects in journals including *Music Analysis* and *Music Theory Spectrum*, as well as in essay collections devoted to Brahms and to

Schubert. He has published two books: *Brahms and the Scherzo* and *Analysis of 18th- and 19th-Century Musical Works in the Classical Tradition* (co-authored with David Beach).

KRISTINA F. NIELSEN is Assistant Professor of Musicology at Southern Methodist University. Her research focuses on the performance of Indigenous music in the Mexican American diaspora, Indigenous cultural revitalization movements, and the development of *danzas de conquista* in colonial-era Mexico. She has contributed to *Flower World: Music Archaeology of the Americas*, and her book reviews have appeared in *The Journal of the Royal Anthropological Institute* and *Ethnomusicology*.

MITCHELL OHRINER is Assistant Professor of Music Theory at the University of Denver where he teaches core music theory courses, modal counterpoint, pedagogy, and non-major courses on hip-hop as well as the psychology of preference for music genres. His research on computational music analysis and rap music is detailed in the monograph *Flow: The Rhythmic Voice in Rap Music*. Other writings can be found in *Music Theory Online, Empirical Musicology Review, The Journal of New Music Research*, and *The Oxford Handbook of Music Theory Concepts*.

DAVID ROBERTSON is a conductor, artist, and thinker who occupies some of the most prominent platforms in the worlds of opera, orchestral music, and new music. He has served in numerous artistic leadership positions, including with the St. Louis and Sydney Symphony Orchestras, and, as a protégé of Pierre Boulez, the *Ensemble InterContemporain*. He appears regularly with The Metropolitan Opera, Royal Concertgebouw Orchestra, *Bayerischen Rundfunk*, New York Philharmonic, and with major orchestras and in leading opera houses internationally. Robertson is the recipient of numerous awards and serves as Director of Conducting Studies and Distinguished Visiting Professor at The Juilliard School.

STEVEN SCHICK is a percussionist, conductor, and author who has commissioned more than 150 works, many of which are standard repertoire for percussionists. Schick founded the percussion group red fish blue fish – now celebrating its twentieth anniversary – and was the original percussionist of the Bang on a Can All-Stars. He is currently music director of the La Jolla Symphony and Chorus and artistic director of the San Francisco Contemporary Music Players. Schick is Distinguished Professor of Music at the University of California, San Diego and holds the Reed Family Presidential Chair in Performance.

ADAM SLIWINSKI has built a dynamic career of creative collaboration as percussionist, pianist, conductor, teacher, and writer. A member of the ensemble Sō Percussion since 2002, Adam has performed at venues around the world. He is co-director of the Sō Percussion Summer Institute, an annual intensive course on the campus of Princeton University. He has taught in residencies and masterclasses at more than 100 conservatories and universities in the United States and internationally. Along with his colleagues in Sō Percussion, Sliwinski is Edward T. Cone performer-in-residence at Princeton University. He holds the Doctor of Musical Arts degree from Yale University.

LESLIE TILLEY is Associate Professor of Music at the Massachusetts Institute of Technology. She received her Ph.D. in ethnomusicology at the University of British Columbia, carrying out fieldwork in Bali, Indonesia. She is particularly interested in exploring analytic approaches to world musics and has published in *Ethnomusicology*, *The Springer Handbook of Systematic Musicology*, and the *Current Research in Systematic Musicology* volume *Computational Phonogram Archiving*. Her book *Making It Up Together: The Art of Collective Improvisation in Balinese Music and Beyond* considers collective processes of improvisation across genres and cultures, using close analyses of diverse Balinese practices to establish broad analytic concepts and frameworks.

Acknowledgments

Many friends and fellow musicians have provided substantial assistance in preparing this volume. In particular, we would like to thank Kate Brett and Eilidh Burrett of Cambridge University Press. Kate encouraged us to pursue the topic of rhythm and contributed valuable advice in the initial stages of the book. As our manuscript wound its way to a finished product, Eilidh gently kept us on track with her sage advice. Several people were helpful to us in the initial stages of this book. Jeff Packman and Danielle Robinson gave advice on the book's structure and guided us in the direction of authors for specific chapters. Likewise, Tara Browner and Michael Tenzer provided valuable suggestions that were extremely helpful.

From Russell Hartenberger:

I want to thank the sixteen musicians from both Canada and Brazil whose clapping hands appear on the cover of this book. I especially want to thank my wife, Bonnie Sheckter, for her design of the cover as well as her help in creating jpegs, tiffs, photoshopping images, and other technical matters. But most importantly, I want to thank Bonnie for her personal support and encouragement throughout the entire project.

As a percussionist, I have always been intrigued by rhythm, however, several musicians have been particularly significant in opening my mind and ears to the greater world of rhythm. James Kippen has long been my "rhythm whisperer" in giving me advice on both scholarly and performative aspects of rhythm, and I will forever be in his debt for his friendship and mentorship. While I was a graduate student at Wesleyan University, Abraham Adzenyah (Ghana), Ramnad V. Raghavan (South India), Sharda Sahai (North India), Prawotosaputro and Sumarsam (Indonesia) introduced me to the rhythms of their individual cultures and showed me that rhythm and percussion could be the foundation of musical structure and performing ensembles. In 1971, I met composer Steve Reich and began performing with his ensemble. Steve's imaginative use of rhythm in his compositions demonstrates that rhythm and percussion can be prominent elements in Western music as well as non-Western music. When I asked him about this, Steve said, "... there is an old tradition of this kind of rhythmic counterpoint [in Africa] ... and in Bali. And more importantly, percussion and the music generated by percussion as the dominant voice – there's a tradition for that; you're not all by yourself. Go, both in terms of the contrapuntal structure of the music and the instrumentation of the music. This is a solid well-trodden path; there's a path and there's got to be a future."

From Ryan McClelland:

My academic interest in the study of rhythm stems from my days as a graduate student at Indiana University, where Gretchen Horlacher, Marianne Kielian-Gilbert, and Frank Samarotto in particular guided my work on rhythm in the music of Johannes Brahms. Since coming to the University of Toronto in 2004, I have had the privilege several times to offer a seminar on rhythm for our graduate students, and I would like to acknowledge the contributions of these students to my understanding of rhythm and to its role in music of various genres, styles, and traditions. I am fortunate to be part of a lively music research environment at the University of Toronto, and I have profited in ways too numerous to articulate from the insights and encouragement of my colleagues. The fact that I can still find some time for research since I have entered into academic administration is a debt I owe to the administrative staff at the University of Toronto, particularly Faculty of Music Registrar Nalayini Balasubramaniam.

Much of my research in rhythm over the past decade has been supported by grants from the Social Sciences and Humanities Research Council of Canada (SSHRC), and I wish to acknowledge that support. I also want to thank my parents for their early and steadfast commitment to my musical education, my childhood piano teachers for stressing excellence in both execution and interpretation, and Jackie for her love, humor, and encouragement.

Introduction

RUSSELL HARTENBERGER AND RYAN MCCLELLAND

One of the defining aspects of music is that it exists in time. From clapping to dancing, toe-tapping to head-nodding, the responses of musicians and listeners alike capture the immediacy and significance of the musical beat. *The Cambridge Companion to Rhythm* explores the richness of musical time through a variety of perspectives, surveying influential writings on the topic, incorporating the perspectives of listeners, analysts, composers, and performers, and considering the subject across a range of genres and cultures.

The choice of the term *rhythm* – and what we mean by it – requires some explanation. Some authors, especially those focusing on Western art music composed since 1700, proffer a narrow definition of rhythm as the durations of sounds and distinguish it from the recurrent pattern of strong and weak beats known as meter. In other words, these authors understand meter and rhythm as separate concepts and one does not subsume the other. We do not intend rhythm in this narrow sense and instead use it as the best single-word option for referring to "musical time" or "temporal organization of music." Indeed, in common parlance, English-speaking musicians use rhythm in this way, whereas terms such as *pulse*, *beat*, *meter*, or even *groove* cannot possess this degree of generality. And among English-language scholars, those who write on the music of cultures from around the world often employ *rhythm* as the shorthand term for "musical time" (e.g., African rhythm).

Books on rhythm generally fall into two categories. The first consists of theoretical treatises that explore fundamental concepts and propose methodologies for analysis. The second consists of in-depth studies of the rhythmic language of a particular composer or repertoire. In both categories, the books emphasize specialization rather than a general overview of rhythm. The majority of writings on rhythm appear either in article format or as one chapter in a book that explores a particular composer or repertoire from a variety of musical parameters. *The Cambridge Companion to Rhythm* provides an overview of rhythmic theory and analysis, demonstrates the significance of rhythm in multiple musical traditions, and offers an entry point toward more specialized writings on these topics.

This volume is organized in six parts. Part I, "Overview of Rhythm," provides an orientation to the topic of rhythm. Ryan McClelland reviews rhythmic concepts that recur in many of the essays in this volume and draws attention to the principal theoretical studies of rhythm in the Western art music tradition. Drawing on a wide range of studies in music psychology, Daniel Cameron and Jessica Grahn explore perceptual, cognitive, and neural aspects of rhythm. Their chapter considers relationships between rhythmic stimuli and beat/meter perception, the role of listener attention, and correspondences between rhythm and movement.

Although rhythm unfolds in time and is only fully experienced through performance, scholarship has – until relatively recently – shown a propensity to privilege the analysis of written texts, namely scores, over aural ones. We have organized this volume to address matters of performance in Part II, "Performing Rhythm." Drawing principally on research from the past two decades, Alan Dodson surveys innovations in the visualization of rhythm that move beyond traditional score notation. Dodson shows how these new approaches provide a clearer understanding of rhythmic nuances and thereby reveal insights into patterns in expressive timing, relationships of expressive timing to various aspects of musical structure, and dimensions of performance such as pacing and momentum. Musicians are faced with a variety of rhythmic issues in the performance of contemporary music, and the next three chapters, written by two accomplished performers and a conductor who is an advocate for new music, provide insight into the methods they use to solve rhythmic problems in these genres. Steven Schick discusses mental and physical techniques that can be used in performing complex rhythms accurately and musically with examples from the music of Brian Ferneyhough, Josh Levine, Roger Reynolds, Morton Feldman, Karlheinz Stockhausen, Gérard Grisey, Michel Gordon, and others. In minimalist, pulse-based music, musicians must learn to deal with extensive repetition, additive rhythmic phrases, metric and perceptual ambiguity, and other concepts and techniques that are new to Western music performance. Russell Hartenberger describes the performance techniques necessary to perform this music confidently, with special reference to the music of Philip Glass, Steve Reich, Terry Riley, and Frederic Rzewski. In orchestras and chamber ensembles of today, conductors are required to develop techniques that manage new rhythmic issues. David Robertson provides an overview of rhythmic development in orchestral music and discusses the techniques he uses in conveying rhythmic precision while leading mixed ensembles of musicians.

Part III, "Composing with Rhythm," offers some perspectives on how composers in the Western art music tradition have deployed rhythm for expressive purposes or to expand their musical language. The first two chapters demonstrate the significance of rhythm to common-practice tonal music (i.e., music composed between c. 1700 and c. 1910) and to post-tonal music (i.e., music composed since c. 1910). Harald Krebs explores expressive uses of rhythm in setting texts in German lieder from the late eighteenth and nineteenth centuries. Drawing on the songs of Joseph Haydn, Franz Schubert, Fanny Hensel, Felix Mendelssohn, Robert Schumann, Clara Schumann, and Hugo Wolf, Krebs elucidates the expressive potential of rhythm at local and larger levels of musical structure, both within the vocal melody and the piano part. Gretchen Horlacher explores the breakdown in periodicity that typifies many works composed in the twentieth century. Through close readings of excerpts from the music of Béla Bartók, Igor Stravinsky, Aaron Copland, and Olivier Messiaen, Horlacher demonstrates how these composers moved the rhythmic languages they inherited, much as they did with their more widely discussed innovations in pitch organization. While the chapters by Krebs and Horlacher are written from the listener-analyst perspective, the following chapter captures the perspectives of several composers in their own words. In a review of writings on rhythm by Henry Cowell, Olivier Messiaen, Béla Bartók, Carlos Chávez, John Cage, Elliott Carter, and Steve Reich, percussionist Adam Sliwinski compares the words of these composers with his own ideas of rhythm and meter.

The significance of rhythm in Western popular music is widely acknowledged; it is often the defining feature of a genre and the subject of lively debates among players, listeners, and especially dancers. Part IV, "Rhythm in Jazz and Popular Music," opens with Matthew W. Butterfield's chapter on the central, but elusive, concept of swing in jazz. Exploring the historical origins of the term and the influence of ragtime on early jazz, Butterfield exposes the complexity of swing and suggests how recent research in microtiming offers new insights into it. Trevor de Clercq explores typical rhythmic structures of rock music. Beginning from reflections on the meaning of "the beat" in rock music, de Clercq then explores rhythmic organization at larger levels and also interactions between melody and established drum patterns. In the final chapter of Part IV, Mitchell Ohriner turns to contemporary hip-hop. Through close study of several tracks from Kendrick Lamar's 2017 album *DAMN.*, Ohriner demonstrates the complexity and irregularity of drum patterns compared with rock music. Ohriner also shows a range of microtiming scenarios for rap syllables with respect to the established underlying grid.

Part V, "Rhythm in Global Musics," probes the rhythmic techniques and their meanings in a range of cultures. The selection of musical traditions reflects the greater amount of extant scholarship on rhythm in the music of certain cultures, the heightened role of rhythm in particular traditions, and a view toward representing multiple continents. Rhythm permeates nearly all the musical cultures of Africa and one of the most intriguing of these genres is the West African drumming ensemble music of the Ewe people of Ghana. David Locke describes the musical rhythm of the Agbadza songs in Ewe music and examines the cultural connections that are a part of much African music. The classical music of India, both in the North (Hindustani) and the South (Karnatak) have highly developed rhythmic systems based on tala cycles. James Kippen explores the structure of Indian rhythm and how styles have evolved over the centuries. The cyclic construction of the gamelan orchestras of Indonesia is the foundation for one of the most sophisticated rhythmic systems in the music of the world. In her chapter, Leslie Tilley surveys the rhythmic system of Balinese gamelan and its connections to Western music in the compositions of Colin McPhee, Benjamin Britten, and Steve Reich. With roots in West Africa and Europe, the rhythms of Latin American and Caribbean music permeate popular music in the West. Peter Manuel provides an overview of many of these musical genres, including salsa, Afro-Cuban music, Jamaican reggae, reggaeton, tango, rumba, and mambo. Indigenous cultures in North and South America have a variety of ways of expressing rhythm to enhance their heritages. Drums, rattles, and singing bring to life their ritual ceremonies, while dance embodies rhythm and makes it discernible. In the final chapter of Part V, Kristina F. Nielsen examines the cultural heritage of music and dance in Indigenous American cultures.

Part VI, "Epilogue," consists of a single chapter in which Nick Collins looks at the possible directions for future rhythmic development in music with a discussion of computer time/computer-generated rhythm, artificial intelligence, programmed musical composition, and other innovations.

The eighteen chapters in *The Cambridge Companion to Rhythm* cover many facets of rhythm including analysis, performance, history, perception, and cultural connections. We recognize that we could easily create a second volume on different rhythmic topics with an equivalent number of chapters. Our hope in presenting this volume is that it may provide the reader with a greater understanding of the significance of rhythm in all music, and that the diversity of rhythmic usage in music throughout the world is, in fact, a fascinating common thread among cultures and traditions.

PART I

Overview of Rhythm

1 | Rhythm in Western Music

Concepts and Literature

RYAN MCCLELLAND

Although each chapter in this book has a distinct focus, there are many concepts that recur. This is especially true for Chapters 2–12, which explore various aspects of Western music. The present chapter introduces some of these recurrent ideas for readers less familiar with rhythmic terms and surveys significant recent theoretical contributions to the study of rhythm in Western music. The interested reader can find more comprehensive overviews of rhythmic theory in two essays by William E. Caplin and Justin London in *The Cambridge History of Western Music Theory*.[1]

As noted in the Introduction, the present volume takes the term *rhythm* to refer to the temporal organization of music. Writers on time in Western music, however, frequently use the term *rhythm* in a more circumscribed manner to refer specifically to the durations of sound events. A repeating sequence of durations might be referred to as a rhythmic pattern, for instance. In this sense, rhythm is a property of a wide range of styles from Medieval plainchant to common-practice tonal music to the plethora of compositional languages present in the past hundred years. Within most Western music since the late Medieval period, there is also a sense that the individual rhythmic events occur in relation to a regular underlying pulse, typically referred to as the beat. And, moreover, those beats are not perceived to be of equal strength but have a recurrent pattern of strong and weak beats called meter. Meter is a feature of some music from the late Medieval period, is found in virtually all music from the Renaissance to the start of the twentieth century, and is present in most – but by no means all – music from the past hundred years. Meter offers a way of measuring musical time that is distinct from chronometric time; its patterned regularity, or periodicity, provides a framework that coordinates individual sound events, or rhythm.

The origin of rhythm, in the sense of durations of sound events, is clear enough: sounds begin and end, and this physical property is directly observable in the same way that pitch (frequency) and volume (amplitude) are. Meter, on the other hand, cannot be ascribed to a discrete component of sound. Yet, for the most part, listeners immediately respond to meter, such as by coordinating a pattern of dance steps or clapping on particular – rather than all – beats. What are the musical features that allow listeners to infer meter from the aural input? This is a complex question that music psychologists and music theorists have wrestled with, but it is the latter body of scholarship on which I draw below.

Meter and Metric Dissonance

A detailed and highly influential treatment of the musical factors that create meter is found in Fred Lerdahl and Ray Jackendoff's *A Generative Theory of Tonal Music*.[2] Lerdahl and Jackendoff present a series of preference rules. These include preferences for similar musical content to receive parallel metric placement and for the onset of long events to fall on stronger beats. Long events refer not only to extended rhythmic durations but also to a variety of other parameters, such as the length of a dynamic level, pattern of articulation, or harmony. For common-practice Western art music and genres such as jazz and rock, changes of harmony are often the most significant factor in the projection of strong beats. In addition, the pitch onsets within the bass line itself, at least in many styles, tend to occur on strong beats.

As a demonstration of meter in common-practice tonal music, consider an excerpt from a string quartet by Haydn (shown in Example 1.1) and

1.1 Haydn, String Quartet in C Major, Op. 74, No. 1, III, mm. 49–60

try to auralize it without paying attention to the notated $\frac{3}{4}$ meter and the barlines. In the first seven measures, observe the placement of long durations (half notes and dotted half notes) in the second violin and viola. Although moving in consistent quarter notes, the cello also outlines a three-beat pattern owing to the lower register of every third pitch. Moreover, when the lowest note departs from the pitch C and the harmony moves to predominant and then dominant, these changes coordinate with the established triple meter.

Now consider the music that begins in the excerpt's eighth measure. The repeated melodic-rhythm pattern in the first violin outlines a two-beat pattern. The sudden shift to this contrasting thematic material, reinforced by the *forzando* marking, suggests a strong-weak (rather than weak-strong) identity for these two-beat units, as does the placement of long durations in the second violin. For two measures, the music projects a duple grouping of beats, namely, $\frac{2}{4}$ meter. One could argue that a composer writing after 1900 might have notated a change from $\frac{3}{4}$ meter to $\frac{2}{4}$ meter for these two measures, and that the aural effect here is a change in meter completely akin to that which can occur between the large sections of a common-practice tonal work, such as a ternary or rondo form. The prevalent view, however, is that the established metric context informs our understanding of short passages that project a different meter. In other words, the duple grouping of beats in these two measures is not heard as fully stable but rather as an unstable intrusion that subsequently resolves. The phenomenon of duple grouping of beats, usually across a two-measure span, within a triple-meter context is frequently encountered, and is referred to as hemiola. In Baroque music it even has a typical formal function as preparation for a cadential arrival. I will return to the formal function of the hemiolic measures in the Haydn excerpt below, but for now it suffices to observe that the harmonic changes in the excerpt's last two measures re-establish triple meter and bring the phrase to a satisfactory tonal – and metric – conclusion.

During the past two decades, many authors have applied the terminology of consonance and dissonance familiar from theories of pitch organization to the domain of meter. The most extensive development of this analogy is found in Harald Krebs's book on the music of Robert Schumann.[3] Krebs outlines two types of metric dissonance: grouping dissonance and displacement dissonance. In a grouping dissonance, one or more layers in the music projects a grouping of beats that is non-congruent with that of the prevailing meter. The hemiola described above is the simplest instance of grouping dissonance, as it involves a switching between triple and duple grouping at the level of the beat. More complex grouping dissonances might involve a switching between quadruple and triple grouping, for instance. The number of textural layers involved in the grouping dissonance, as well as the particular musical parameters that cause it to arise, give grouping dissonances a variety of intensities.

Displacement dissonance involves one or more textural layers that shift the strong beat from its expected location. For instance, in a triple meter dynamic accents or placement of harmonic changes might make the second or third beat of the notated meter – the prevailing metric consonance – sound as the strong beat in the meter. As with grouping dissonance, displacement dissonance can involve the entire musical texture or only particular layers and can thereby seem to be stronger or weaker. Consider the initial pair of phrases from the first movement of Haydn's Symphony No. 104, shown in piano reduction in Example 1.2.

At the start of the excerpt, strong beats in the meter are articulated through the placement of long durations in the melody and the harmonic changes at the moments corresponding to the downbeats of the first, third, and fourth measures. The lack of rhythms faster than the eighth note suggests the beat is the notated half note (as does Haydn's cut-time, or 2/2, meter signature to the reader of the score). The metric organization is duple with no ambiguity as to the location of the strong beats. In the fifth measure, the alto voice (played by the second violins) has a series of half-note durations displaced by a quarter note from the strong beats. Compared to the grouping dissonance in the string quartet excerpt, the displacement dissonance here is much weaker and in no way makes the location of the strong beats unclear. (And for a listener thoroughly familiar

1.2 Haydn, Symphony in D Major, No. 104, I, mm. 17–33 (piano reduction)

with eighteenth-century style, the sense of displacement dissonance is very minimal since the dislocation of this layer arises through the contrapuntal technique of the suspension.) Many writers would simply refer to this alto line as syncopated, although the term *syncopation* can also be used for the singular placement of the onset of a long duration on a weak beat. In the excerpt's second phrase (shown on the second line of Example 1.2), the fifth and sixth measures exhibit a somewhat stronger displacement dissonance owing to the participation of two voices (played by the second violins and cellos) and the placement of these voices in the bottom of the texture.

Hypermeter

To this point, I have written almost exclusively about the level of meter referred to as the beat or tactus, that is, the level to which most listeners would respond bodily through finger- or toe-tapping and to which most conductors would coordinate their gestures. Yet, at least in music of the eighteenth and nineteenth centuries, the sense of strong and weak ascribed to beats within a meter also operates on larger (i.e., slower) levels of the metric hierarchy. The annotations on Example 1.2 include Arabic numerals, and these represent a type of meter. A widespread, but not pervasive, view among music analysts is that all of the measures marked "1" have a strength, or metric accent, analogous to the first beat in $\frac{4}{4}$ meter.[4] This strength is articulated by changes in melodic design and harmony. Meter above the level of the notated meter is referred to as hypermeter, the unit corresponding to a complete cycle of hyperbeats as a hypermeasure, and the first beat of a hypermeasure as a hyperdownbeat.

Hypermeter is less consistently periodic than is meter. One scenario where hypermetric irregularity frequently occurs is when a cadential arrival simultaneously functions as the beginning of the next phrase. In Example 1.2, the first phrase spans eight measures, concluding on the dominant harmony. The second phrase, which is parallel in construction, heads to a cadence on tonic harmony in its eighth measure. However, the arrival is marked by the sudden onset of a new dynamic and the entrance of the winds, brass, and timpani. The melodic idea that begins at this point initiates the next phrase, meaning that the measure has a dual function in the passage's phrase organization. Hypermetrically, a measure that was initially weak (a fourth hyperbeat) is reinterpreted as strong (a hyperdownbeat); this is shown by the 4 = 1 annotation.[5] Phrase overlap, or elision, can occur without hypermetric reinterpretation, and hypermetric irregularities can arise in other situations.

Let's return to the string quartet excerpt in Example 1.1 and consider its hypermetric structure; the reading shown, with which I concur, is adapted from William Rothstein's book *Phrase Rhythm in Tonal Music.*[6] The Arabic numerals convey quadruple hypermeter, stemming from melodic parallelism (compare measures 1 and 5 of the excerpt). The hemiolic passage begins where the fourth hyperbeat of the second hypermeasure is expected, and it also replaces the expected cadential arrival on tonic harmony. From the perspective of phrase structure, the hemiolic measures expand the phrase by delaying the cadence; adopting Rothstein's terminology, they can be understood as a parenthetical insertion in the phrase structure owing to the degree of contrast they exhibit with the surrounding music. The theoretical question that arises is whether they cause hypermeter to be inoperative or whether they suspend hypermeter temporarily. In the view of Rothstein and many other authors, a parenthetical insertion does not preclude the continuation of hypermeter; in fact, some analysts contend that lengthier parenthetical insertions can even have their own independent surface hypermeter while the underlying hypermeter is held in abeyance until the end of the parenthetical insertion. This view stretches the extent to which periodicity can be withheld without losing the temporal foundation of hypermeter. It asserts that hypermeter is more dependent upon the influence of phrase organization and the distinct qualia of hyperbeats than upon the measuring of duration.

The idea that hypermeter can exist in the absence of strict periodicity has led theorists to debate the extent to which meter is operative at levels above the notated measure. For Lerdahl and Jackendoff, meter is a "relatively local phenomenon" that, in tonal music, often extends "from one to three levels . . . larger than the level notated by barlines, corresponding to regularities of two, four, and even eight measures."[7] Theorists influenced by the hierarchical understanding of pitch organization posited by Heinrich Schenker, such as Carl Schachter, William Rothstein, and Frank Samarotto, typically view meter as still operative on slightly deeper levels (i.e., levels corresponding to sixteen or thirty-two measures). Of course, the number of hypermetric levels present depends somewhat on the nature of the music; a piece with exceedingly regular phrase structure or harmonic rhythm – such as a waltz or march – is more readily interpreted in this manner. In other cases, a greater degree of abstraction is required, as higher levels of meter are correlated with significant tonal arrivals and assumed models of underlying periodic phrase structure beneath surface-levels expansion (or, less frequently, contractions). Very few authors posit the existence of hypermeter at the larger levels of form (i.e., beyond thirty-two measures) owing to the extreme deviations from periodic beats, but one notable instance is Jonathan Kramer in his book *The Time of Music.*[8]

Positing multiple levels of hypermeter asserts that meter has a quality not unlike the physical property of inertia, that is, once established meter has considerable inherent stability and independence from the individualities of the musical foreground. In other words, when events that induce the perception of metric accents occur at unexpected moments, the ongoing meter and hypermeters have a resilience that allows them to continue. Some recent authors have questioned this separation of meter from the details of the musical surface, either on phenomenological or cognitive grounds, or both. Informed by research in music cognition, Justin London suggests that meter has a "temporal envelope" whose "upper limit is around 5 to 6 seconds."[9] London demonstrates how the constraints on human temporal perception can explain the prevalence of certain meters at various tempi, as the shortness of subdivisions of beats and the length of hyperbeats move toward perceptual thresholds. The latter perhaps explains the rarity of triple hypermeters, besides an aesthetic preference for the symmetry and balance of duple construction.[10] From a phenomenological perspective, Christopher Hasty has offered the strongest critique of what I have called metric inertia, arguing for the role of rhythmic durations in creating "projected potentials" that are realized or denied depending on whether an immediately successive event begins at the expected moment in time.[11] Hasty's approach invites close hearing of the music and demands constant renewal of meter through the durations of events and their identities as beginnings, continuations, or anacruses. For Hasty, meter is not fundamentally about levels of beats in proportional relationships but about different configurations of rhythmic events whose particularities can make two passages with the same notated meter have quite different temporal characteristics, and in Hasty's view these features are metric, as opposed to rhythmic.

Given the competing claims in contemporary music theory about the nature of hypermeter, one might wonder about the validity of the concept and whether there is any evidence that composers of common-practice tonal music were sensitive to hypermetric considerations. There are clear indications that some composers were cognizant of hypermeter, at least for one or two levels above the notated meter. Explicit notation of hypermeter is exceedingly rare, but there are examples. The most famous occurs in the scherzo of Beethoven's Ninth Symphony where he writes *ritmo di tre*

1.3 Liszt, *Mephisto Waltz*, No. 1, mm. 1–9

battute and *ritmo di quattro battute* to show shifts between triple and quadruple hypermeter. A less well-known instance is found in the Mephisto Waltz No. 1 where Liszt uses Arabic numerals to indicate quadruple hypermeter in a manner exactly parallel to the analytic annotations on the examples above, as shown in Example 1.3.[12] Moreover, Liszt notates a measure of rest before the music begins. Somewhat more commonly encountered is a notated measure of rest at the end of a movement or work to complete a hypermeasure; an early instance of this happens at the end of the first movement of Beethoven's Piano Sonata in A Major, Op. 2, No. 2.

Perhaps the strongest support for the idea of hypermeter comes from pieces in fast tempi where the notated downbeats are perceived as beats. In these instances, the perceived meter is not the notated one but rather a hypermeter; given that there is some subjectivity involved in deciding which level of meter corresponds to the heard meter, most analysts simply employ the terms *meter* and *hypermeter* with respect to notation. Many nineteenth-century scherzo movements are notated in $\frac{3}{4}$ meter but proceed at a sufficiently fast tempo where the downbeats of consecutive measures are perceived as beats in a larger, usually quadruple, meter. The scherzo from Beethoven's Ninth Symphony mentioned above is exceptional in that this larger meter shifts back and forth between triple and quadruple organization; typically, the larger meter remains quadruple throughout, albeit sometimes with playful moments of dislocation when the hyperdownbeat shifts (generally by two notated measures), as in the scherzo from Beethoven's Seventh Symphony. Outside of the scherzo repertoire, a clear instance where the notated meter is not the perceived meter occurs in the first movement of Beethoven's Fifth Symphony, shown in reduction in Example 1.4. Instead of coordinating their gestures with the notated 2/4 meter, conductors uniformly show a larger quadruple pattern that spans four notated measures. This leads to a moment of metric crisis in the development section when Beethoven fragments the thematic material until the winds and brass play isolated chords in rapid alternation with ones sounded by the strings, and the clarity of four-measure units dissolves.

1.4 Beethoven, Symphony No. 5, I, mm. 6–21

Meter in Post-tonal Music

In music written since 1900, metric structure has become much more varied, not unlike the broadening in pitch organization beyond common-practice tonality. The degree of metric periodicity found in music throughout the eighteenth and nineteenth centuries waned, except in many genres of popular music, where – due, at least in part, to the connection to dance – metric periodicity remains present. In fact, popular genres are distinguished as much by their characteristic beat, or groove, as by features of melodic, harmonic, or formal organization. Often these characteristic elements are recurrent rhythmic patterns or established norms for using particular instruments to articulate meter, as in the rock drum kit.

While some genres of Western popular music, such as progressive rock, moved away from multiple levels of duple (and less frequently triple) meter, it was in the art-music tradition where the most consistent break from metric periodicity occurred. The present chapter cannot survey all of the rhythmic innovations of the past century; rather, it outlines some of the most significant ones and their implications for thinking about rhythm.

Throughout the eighteenth and nineteenth centuries, meter consists of equally spaced beats that are organized in a duple or triple grouping, depending on whether one or two weak beats fall between adjacent strong beats. Except for unmeasured pieces, such as some Baroque keyboard preludes, there are very few exceptions to the principle of equally spaced, or isochronous, beats. The most famous exception is the second movement of Tchaikovsky's Symphony No. 6 ("Pathétique"), composed in 1893, where instead of a triple-meter scherzo (or waltz) a lively movement in 5/4 meter occurs. Quintuple meter consists of both duple and triple grouping of beats, either consistently (as recurring 2+3 or 3+2), or with variable patterning of the duple and triple groupings. In either case, a larger periodicity results, and the sense of meter remains clearly intact. Very occasional instances of septuple meter can be found before the twentieth century, yet in these instances composers stuck to the convention of notated duple and triple measures. Two examples occur in the music of Brahms: his piano variations on a Hungarian song (Op. 21, No. 2) and the slow movement of his Piano Trio in C Minor, Op. 101; in the former work, a consistent alternation of notated $\substack{3\\4}$ and $\substack{4\\4}$ measures occurs, while in the later one each notated $\substack{3\\4}$ measure is followed by a pair of $\substack{2\\4}$ measures. In the piano variations the folk inspiration of the asymmetrical meter is explicit, but in the piano trio movement the transparent melody-and-accompaniment texture, slow harmonic rhythmic, and simple harmonies invoke folk music (as depicted by nineteenth-century composers).

The folk impetus behind asymmetrical meters remains explicit in much of the music of the early twentieth century, most notably that of Bartók and Stravinsky. While much of Bartók's music features consistent use of an asymmetrical meter such as $\substack{5\\8}$ or $\substack{7\\8}$, some of his works and many of Stravinsky's present a more trenchant challenge to the sense of meter through the use of rapid changes of notated meter, often referred to as mixed meter (e.g., a succession of four measures with $\substack{3\\8}$, $\substack{5\\8}$, $\substack{2\\4}$, and $\substack{3\\8}$ notated meters). Most often, mixed-meter passages maintain a consistent beat or subdivision – usually the eighth note – and the way those beats group into a meter or the subdivisions group into beats changes unpredictably. Frequently, such passages are based around a short melodic cell that recurs in slightly varied forms that render it longer or shorter, and the onset of each of its iterations is generally an important reference point for feeling the temporal organization. Passages with such a high degree of metric irregularity raise several theoretical questions: How much deviation from periodic accentuation can a listener relate to a periodic underlying metric grid? At what point does the notated meter become best conceived as an element of the score that communicates compositional organization and helps performers synchronize with one another but does not have much connection with listener perception? When does a sense of beat and meter dissolve into a tracking of periodic pulses? Music theorists have offered a variety of perspectives on these questions; perhaps most influential is Hasty's *Meter as*

Rhythm, which has broad applicability even in music with little periodicity due to its continual engagement with local durations and their potential for replication. Hasty's approach compels the analyst to engage temporally with music, however complex its rhythmic design, as seen in his discussion of music by Anton Webern, Elliott Carter, and Stefan Wolpe.

Besides a greater range of possibilities within the domain of rhythm, art music of the past century has also seen changing relationships between rhythm and other musical parameters. Returning once again to Stravinsky, I would point out that passages with mixed meter and additive rhythmic construction are not his only rhythmic innovations. Equally new are passages built upon three or more independent rhythmic layers, each repetitive, sometimes composed of an exactly repeating ostinato and sometimes an irregularly recurring figure. A clear example is the first of Stravinsky's *Three Pieces for String Quartet* where the cello and viola have an ostinato that repeats after seven quarter notes, violin I has an ostinato that repeats after twenty-three quarter notes, and violin II has an irregularly recurring four-note interjection. Similar layered textures occur in Stravinsky's *Rite of Spring*, composed at nearly the same time, often building to a thick texture involving the entire orchestra. In such passages, one layer is often sufficiently prominent to exert its metric identity on the texture as a whole, but the distinction between the rhythmic profile of individual lines and the effect of the overall musical texture begins to breakdown. This permeability between the parameters of rhythm and texture became of considerable interest to composers in the middle of the twentieth century, such as in the ensemble and orchestral works of György Ligeti in the 1960s and 1970s.

In eighteenth- and nineteenth-century music, rhythmic-metric design and pitch structure are closely intertwined but have different organizational principles. Composers of the twentieth century experimented with importing techniques familiar from the domain of pitch into the realm of rhythm, such as mid-century approaches known as integral, or multi-parametric, serialism. The transformations of transposition, retrograde, inversion, and retrograde inversion applied to twelve-tone pitch rows by Schoenberg were adapted to rhythm, albeit in different ways, by composers including Pierre Boulez, Karlheinz Stockhausen, and Milton Babbitt.

Meter and Meaning

Music exists in time, and rhythm is therefore an inherent property, however it is organized and perceived. Rhythm also plays an important role in the communication of expressive meaning in a wide range of music. For instance, fast rhythms might convey excitement or agitation, a rhythmic pattern might reflect some aspect of the lyrics in a texted work, or a rhythmic figure might reference a musical topic. Or rhythm might produce a visceral response such as when the bass groove re-enters at a beat drop in electronic dance music. In closing, I will explore a few more abstract ways that rhythmic design can create meaning.

In my research on the music of Brahms, I have observed several instances where thematic material undergoes rhythmic transformation during the course of a movement or work, typically leading from a less stable initial state to a more stable one.[13] This might involve a theme whose metric or hypermetric structure is initially unclear or incorporates metrically dissonant elements and that later recurs in a more stable or metrically consonant version. This type of large-scale thematic process is not unique to Brahms's music, although it occurs with greater frequency than in the music of many other composers. Moreover, I have suggested that large-scale changes in metric or hypermetric structure can have significant meaning even when they occur in the absence of shared thematic content.[14] Similarly, through his use of "metrical maps," Krebs tracks changes in the types of metric dissonances in pieces, and has coined terms to reflect intensification and de-intensification (e.g., tightening and loosening; surfacing and submerging).[15] These global processes, although less celebrated than tonal procedures such as modulation, can shape the overall expressive impact of a work. In the music of the past century, and especially as composers have written more about their own practices, certain rhythmic techniques have been developed for particular expressive purposes, such as Messiaen's deployment of repeating rhythms and symmetrical rhythms to project qualities of timelessness and contemplation. The following chapters offer perspectives on the possibilities for rhythm to convey meaning in addition to its role as a structural component of musical design.

Endnotes

1 W. Caplin, "Theories of Musical Rhythm in the Eighteenth and Nineteenth Centuries," and J. London, "Rhythm in Twentieth-Century Theory," in T. Christensen (ed.), *Cambridge History of Western Music Theory* (Cambridge University Press, 2002), 657–94 and 695–725.

2 F. Lerdahl and R. Jackendoff, *A Generative Theory of Tonal Music* (MIT Press, 1983).

3 H. Krebs, *Metrical Dissonance in the Music of Robert Schumann* (Oxford University Press, 1999).

4 Besides Lerdahl and Jackendoff, theorists who view hypermeter as having essentially the same accentual properties as meter include Carl Schachter, William Rothstein, and the author of the present chapter; see C. Schachter, "Rhythm and Linear Analysis: Aspects of Meter," *Music Forum*, 6 (1987), 1–59; W. Rothstein, *Phrase Rhythm in Tonal Music* (New York: Schirmer Books, 1989). Writers who view larger levels of meter as less similar to meter include Christopher Hasty and Justin London, as will be explored later in this chapter.

5 This example is cited in the discussion of phrase elision and hypermeter in Lerdahl and Jackendoff, *A Generative Theory*, 57–8.

6 Rothstein, *Phrase Rhythm*, 88–9.

7 Lerdahl and Jackendoff, *A Generative Theory*, 21 and 99.

8 J. Kramer, *The Time of Music: New Meanings, New Temporalities, New Listening Strategies* (New York: Schirmer Books, 1988).

9 Justin London, *Hearing in Time: Psychological Aspects of Musical Meter*, 2nd ed. (Oxford University Press, 2012), 27.

10 For examples of triple hypermeter see S. Rodgers, "Thinking (and Singing) in Threes: Triple Hypermeter and the Songs of Fanny Hensel," *Music Theory Online*, 17.1 (2011).

11 Christopher Hasty, *Meter as Rhythm* (Oxford University Press, 1997).

12 I would like to acknowledge Robert Rival for bringing this example to my attention.

13 R. McClelland, "Brahms and the Principle of Destabilised Beginnings," *Music Analysis*, 28 (2009), 3–61.

14 See, for instance, my analysis of the F–A–E scherzo in *Brahms and the Scherzo* (Aldershot: Ashgate, 2010).

15 Krebs, *Fantasy Pieces*.

2 Perception of Rhythm

DANIEL CAMERON AND JESSICA GRAHN

Introduction

Music is an essentially temporal experience, and the temporal structures by which music unfolds are critical to listeners' aesthetic, emotional, and behavioral responses. Music is perceived at multiple related timescales, from notes to measures to phrases. In our usage, *rhythm* refers to the absolute timing of individual notes or sounds, *beat* refers to the perceived regular pulse that listeners tend to feel and synchronize their movements with, and *meter* is the repeating cycle of beats, often a pattern of variable salience (composed of stronger and weaker beats). The beat tends to be steady or theoretically isochronous (evenly spaced), although human performance of music inevitably adds temporal variability, via both musical intention (e.g., *rubato*, expressively stretching and compressing the beat rate) and natural performance dynamics (e.g., due to the limits of temporal precision of human movements). Importantly, beat and meter perception can differ between listeners, relating to factors such as musical context, expertise, cultural experience, or cognitive processes such as attention.

In this chapter we discuss perceptual, cognitive, and neural aspects of musical rhythm: the relationships between rhythmic stimuli and beat and meter perception, the influence of a listener's attention and experience, and the interesting correspondences between musical rhythm and movement. We also discuss the instantiation of musical rhythm in the brains of listeners, and what we may learn from rhythm perception across non-human species.

Perception of Rhythm, Beat, and Meter

The perception of beats tends to arise in humans when they hear musical rhythms, usually as one level, termed the *tactus*, in a hierarchical metric structure.[1] Beats arise at specific, regularly spaced positions in a rhythm, and tone onsets "on the beat" are perceived as more salient than onsets of surrounding tones. Once the perception of ongoing beats is established, beats can be perceived even when no tone onset occurs, as well as in silence. Povel and Essens demonstrate that certain temporal grouping structures influence the perceived salience of individual notes in a rhythm, guiding beat and meter perception.[2] They show that when notes are isolated – the second in a group of two, or the first or last in groups of three or more – they are perceived as more salient, or subjectively accented. When subjectively accented notes occur at regular intervals, beats are perceived at the rate and cyclic positions that align with the most subjective accents. This model is limited to assessing perception for isolated rhythms out of the musical context, rather than capturing the ongoing and dynamic perception that occurs for real music, but it is an important empirical demonstration of how *hearing* rhythm leads to *perceiving* beat and metric structure.

A critical aspect of beat and meter perception is that they are not direct products of a rhythmic stimulus, but are active psychological phenomena, and, as such, they depend on internal processes in the listener's mind and brain.[3] One demonstration of the internal contributions to rhythm perception is that humans tend to perceive an isochronous stream of identical sounds as having alternating strong and weak notes – the "tick tock" phenomenon.[4] As a rhythmic stimulus becomes more complex than isochrony (e.g., musical rhythms, which tend to have inter-onset intervals that vary in duration), the subjectivity of perception also becomes more evident and more complex, and the malleability and heterogeneity of perception across listeners becomes evident. That is, despite listening to the same rhythmic stimulus, different listeners may experience different beat and meter perception, in relation to multiple interacting factors, such as their cognitive state during listening (e.g., whether or not they are attending to the rhythm), their familiarity (i.e., cultural experience) with rhythms, and whether or not they have musical training.

The flexible nature of rhythm perception – that perception is not strictly a product of the rhythmic stimulus – has been shown in brain responses of listeners. The "tick tock" perception of a metronomic sequence has been found to relate to neural responses occurring after individual sounds: responses to odd-numbered sounds were stronger than those to even-numbered sounds.[5] Another study had listeners impose a march or waltz metric structure on a metronomic sequence by imagining an emphasis on either every second or every third note. The results showed distinct signals in the electroencephalogram (EEG) of listeners corresponding to not only the rate of the metronome but also to the rate of the imagined metric emphasis.[6] Other researchers had listeners imagine an emphasis on one of two notes in a repeating rhythm consisting of two notes and a rest, all having the same durational value. Brain responses in listeners increased in strength due to the imagined emphasis.[7] These studies show neural activity corresponding to perception that is generated internally, rather than strictly by the stimulus, although they do not indicate *how*, or by what mechanisms, these internal contributions to perception occur.

Rhythm and Movement

From a biological perspective, perhaps the most notable thing about musical rhythm is that it elicits movement from human listeners. Moving to musical rhythm is one of the most convincingly universal aspects of music. This movement tends to be synchronized to the regularities in the rhythms and is enjoyable, perhaps explaining why humans have been spontaneously synchronizing movements to music since the time of our ancient ancestors.[8] In most cultures, music and dance evolved together, and even today, there are cultures that do not have separate words for music and dance.[9] Moving to music occurs spontaneously, without training, at a young age. For example, infants make a greater number of rhythmic movements when they hear music, or even steady drumbeats, although these movements are not synchronized to the beat.[10] Synchronization ability emerges in some children by age three or four, and later for many other children.[11]

Musical Features That Influence Movement

In the scientific study of music perception, the term *groove* has been used to refer to the quality of music that makes an individual listener want to move.[12] Music that is rated as high in groove elicits more spontaneous movements than music that is low in groove, even when listeners are instructed to remain still.[13] Some acoustic and musical factors are known to influence groove: a strong repetitive beat and a high density of sound events between beats are associated with more groove.[14] Other factors that influence groove include emotional responses to the music, preferred tempo, enjoyment, and familiarity.[15] Groove and enjoyment ratings tend to be correlated.[16] Groove has also been related to neural activity: rhythms that were rated as having more groove tended to elicit greater neural entrainment (see below), although this relationship was only observed for rhythms that were human-performed rather than computer-synthesized.[17]

The way individuals move to music reflects their perception of its hierarchical metric structure.[18] Vertical torso movements and side-to-side arm movements tend to occur at the beat rate, whereas other movements, such as shoulder rotation and side-to-side body sway, occur at slower metric rates (every two or four beats).[19] The energy to move a body part depends on size and distance from the center of mass; thus, it is natural to select slower metric levels for body parts that require more energy.[20]

Music also affects non-dancing movements such as walking.[21] For example, even when walking in synchrony to music that is at the same tempo, walking speed fluctuates, influenced by other musical features such as loudness or pitch patterns.[22] Perceived groove, and to a lesser extent, familiarity, also increases walking speed.[23] Although spontaneous synchronization to music can occur during certain activities, such as running[24] or dancing, it does not necessarily occur during walking. For example, when walking to music on a treadmill, only participants who were explicitly instructed to synchronize actually did so.[25] Similarly, another study found that participants walking to music outside did not spontaneously synchronize.[26]

Movement and Its Relationship to Rhythm Perception

Moving to rhythm can alter how that rhythm is perceived. In one influential study, two groups of seven-month-old infants were bounced to the same rhythm, but one group was bounced every second beat, and the other group was bounced every third beat.[27] After the bouncing, infants could choose to listen to different versions of the rhythm by triggering different speakers with their gaze: rhythms listened to longer were considered preferred. Infants preferred rhythm versions that were accented consistently with how they had been bounced: infants bounced every two beats preferred rhythms with accents every two beats, and infants bounced every three beats preferred rhythms accented every three beats. In another study, when adults bent at the knee to every second or every third beat while hearing the same ambiguous unaccented rhythm, they later reported that an accented rhythm that matched their bounce rate was more familiar.[28] Thus, the perception of metric structure is altered by how our bodies have moved to that rhythm.

Simply tapping along with a beat in rhythm can influence how quickly and accurately the beat is perceived. Tapping along at the beginning is most helpful for rhythms in which the beat is not obvious.[29] The tapping-induced improvement may result from greater attention to the beat caused by tapping, or from the extra feedback about the beat timing provided by the taps. Tapping along with the beat can improve perception even after tapping has stopped. In one study, participants tapped with an isochronous sequence, and then judged whether a final tone was "in time" with the previous part of the sequence or not.[30] Tapping to the initial sequence led to better accuracy than did listening alone, even when tapping stopped before the final tone. Tapping aided percussionists more than musical novices when making the judgments.[31] Thus, overall, tapping aids beat perception and timing accuracy, but musical experts have greater tapping-induced timing benefits.

Interestingly, some rhythmic features of music overlap with rhythmic features of movement. For example, when music slows down, the deceleration dynamics are similar to those observed when runners slow to a stop.[32] In addition, one of the most popular tempos in a database of contemporary Western music is very similar to the preferred walking rate of most humans: around 2 hertz (Hz), or 120 beats per minute.[33]

Musical Rhythm in the Brain

Neuroscientific studies of musical rhythm aim to understand the links between the human experience of musical rhythm and the functions and activity of the brain. While neural correlates of rhythm have led to fascinating findings, it is notable that we lack a truly robust and reliable brain marker of beat perception – a neural signal that, when detected, indicates the listener is perceiving a beat. Rather than a measure of brain activity that can tell us exactly what is happening in the mind of the listener, two of the most prominent branches of research in the neuroscience of rhythm inform us about both how musical rhythm exerts its effects on human listeners, and about fundamental mechanisms in brain function. These are the involvement of the brain's motor system and of neural oscillations.

Musical Rhythm and the Brain's Motor System

Perhaps unsurprisingly, given the strong behavioral relationships between music and movement, there is strong evidence that rhythm and beat perception cause activity in the brain's motor system. Motor areas, including premotor cortex and the cerebellum, respond during passive listening to music, according to a recent analysis of forty-two functional magnetic resonance imaging (fMRI) studies.[34] As discussed below, rhythmic aspects of the music, rather than melodic or timbral aspects, appear to drive these motor responses.

Links between music and movement may arise in part through very basic brain mechanisms. For example, simply hearing a tone can change the excitability (how likely a neuron is to fire) of motor neurons in the spine.[35] Musical rhythms also change the excitability of the motor system. One study found greater motor system excitability for rhythms with a strong beat than a weak beat,[36] and another study found greater motor excitability for high groove music compared to low groove music, although only in musicians, not in non-musicians.[37]

Higher-level motor areas also respond to rhythm. Hearing musical rhythm, even when no movement is made, activates brain areas that control movement, including the supplementary motor area, premotor cortex, cerebellum, and basal ganglia.[38] Certain motor areas, such as the supplementary motor area and basal ganglia, appear to respond more to regular rhythms that give rise to a clear sense of the beat compared to rhythms that do not.[39] Other motor areas, such as the cerebellum, respond more to irregular rhythms that do not induce a beat.[40] Research with different neurological patient populations supports this dissociation: basal ganglia function is compromised in patients with Parkinson's disease, and they also have a deficit in detecting changes in beat-based rhythms, but not non-beat-based rhythms.[41] In contrast, patients with cerebellar degeneration have deficits in tasks using non-beat-based rhythms, but not beat-based rhythms.[42] Finally, consistent with a role in beat perception, basal ganglia activity does not correlate with the speed of the beat that is perceived,[43] and instead is most active for sequences with rates around 500–700 milliseconds (ms),[44] the range in which beat perception is also maximal.[45] Therefore, the basal ganglia are most responsive to regularity at the rate that best induces a sense of the beat. Overall, these studies support the idea that different motor areas underlie perception of rhythms, and especially rhythms that elicit beat perception.

An important part of understanding the neural mechanisms of rhythm and beat perception is not just which brain areas are active, but how these different brain areas communicate with each other. Communication can be indexed by "functional connectivity," which measures correlations in activity between two brain areas over time. When correlations between two brain areas increase, communication is thought to be greater. Connectivity between brain areas changes based on the type of rhythm being listened to. When listening to beat-based rhythms, compared to non-beat-based rhythms, the connectivity increases between the basal ganglia and cortical motor areas (supplementary motor cortex, premotor cortex), as well as between the basal ganglia and auditory cortical areas.[46] Thus, rhythm and beat perception increase communication within motor networks, and between auditory and motor networks. This may be because we automatically try to link our auditory perception of the rhythm with a potential motor response, even when we have no intention of actually moving.[47]

Thus, auditory and motor areas are important to perceiving a rhythm and feeling the beat. Feeling the beat (compared to hearing rhythms without a beat) increases activity in a subset of these motor areas, including the basal ganglia and supplementary motor area. Motor and auditory areas also exhibit greater functional connectivity during perception of the beat. A potential mechanism for this connectivity may be through oscillatory responses, which are not directly measurable with fMRI, but can be measured with EEG or magnetoencephalography (MEG).

Musical Rhythm and Neural Oscillations

Neural interactions between auditory and motor areas during beat perception may be accomplished by oscillations. Neural oscillations are fluctuations in the excitability of neural populations, and are a fundamental brain mechanism that allows neural activity within and across brain regions to synchronize, coordinating their processing. Neural oscillations occur at different rates, or frequency bands. Two frequency bands have been associated with rhythm perception: the delta band (1–3 Hz), which spans the rates at which the beat is perceived[48] and is associated with temporal prediction,[49] and the beta band (15–30 Hz), which is associated with the motor system[50] and also with temporal prediction.[51] Delta- and beta-band neural oscillations appear to support important functions during rhythm perception; moreover, the two bands appear to interact during perception of rhythms, possibly in service of temporal predictions and/or communication between auditory and motor systems.[52]

Neural oscillations synchronize, or entrain, with auditory rhythms. For example, beat-rate oscillations (which are usually in the delta band) appear to entrain to the perceived beat during rhythm perception.[53] Entrainment of delta-band oscillations in musicians have also been associated with groove in human-performed (but not computer-synthesized) musical rhythms[54] and with cross-cultural differences during musical rhythm perception.[55] Musicians have greater beta-band entrainment during music perception than do non-musicians.[56] Entrainment of neural oscillations to the beat causes greater neural responsiveness for stimuli on the beat than off the beat, which may be the mechanism underlying improved perception of on-beat compared to off-beat sounds.[57]

Oscillations in the beta band are associated with motor functions, and modulations of the strength of beta oscillations have also been associated with beat perception.[58] For example, an above-mentioned study measured oscillatory neural responses evoked by a repeating rhythmic pattern consisting of two tones followed by a rest.[59] While undergoing MEG to measure neural oscillatory responses, listeners imposed a mental accent on either the first or second tone. Beta-band responses were stronger for the tone that was mentally accented, corresponding to the perceived beat, despite both tones being acoustically identical. In isochronous auditory sequences, beta power peaks just prior to the onset of each tone, but not when the sequence timing is random and unpredictable,[60] suggesting that beta-band activity may index the expectation of a regular beat. Consistent with the fMRI studies described above, beta power in these studies appears to originate from both auditory and motor brain areas, including premotor cortex, supplementary motor area, and cerebellum.

Other Influences on Rhythm and Beat Perception

Rhythm perception can change with the listener's cognitive state, depending on, for example, whether or not they are attending to the rhythm, and different listeners can perceive the same rhythm differently, depending on cultural experience or musical training.

Attention

Attention is one cognitive mechanism by which listeners' internal states contribute to perception of musical rhythms. An overarching theory, Dynamic Attending Theory, posits that rhythm perception is mediated by fluctuations in attention that synchronize with (or entrain to) the metrically salient positions in the rhythm – aligning closely to the theory that beat and meter perception arise from the interactions between neural oscillations.[61] Evidence that dynamic attention underlies perception of rhythm comes in the form of greater perceptual sensitivity to events that occur in temporal positions that are strongly predicted by the temporal structure of the preceding sequence, such as "on-beat" tones.[62]

Attention is also related to the hierarchical aspect of musical rhythm perception: listeners can focus attention on a rhythmic stimulus or can rather perceive a rhythm more passively, and attention can alter perception. Attention seems required to perceive the beat when it is indicated only by temporal structure, particularly for complex rhythms,[63] whereas volume changes that mark the beat in a rhythm can induce beat perception without a listener attending.[64] One neural study of attention and rhythm perception compared brain responses to individual tones that perturbed either the rhythmic or metric structure of a perceived rhythm. Brain responses occurring approximately 100–150 ms after the perturbation were observed after rhythmic perturbations regardless of whether or not listeners were attending to the rhythm, whereas they occurred for metric perturbations only when listeners were attending to the rhythm.[65] This indicates that perceiving metric structure may require more cognitive engagement, enabled by attention, than perceiving the rhythm itself. Another study used a similar method and found that brain responses were sensitive to metric structure only when listeners were attending to the rhythm, but responses were sensitive to the beat regardless of attention.[66]

Cultural Experience of the Listener

Musical rhythms differ across cultures, as has been widely documented in the field of ethnomusicology. Besides cultural differences in rhythmic structures, ethnomusicologists have also documented cultural differences in the perception of rhythm, and recent attention to cultural variability from a cognitive science perspective has empirically validated the influence of culture on rhythm perception. Cultural differences in rhythm perception have been shown in children as young as four months old. One study showed that American infants prefer rhythms with a regular meter to those with an irregular meter, while Turkish infants did not have the same bias, presumably related to their exposure to the irregular meters found in Turkish music.[67] Another study found that Japanese and American participants differed in their perception of how sequences of alternating short and long tones were grouped. American listeners had a strong tendency to group the pattern as "short–long," while Japanese listeners did not have a tendency for one grouping over the other, and were much more likely than American listeners to identify the sequence as "long–short."[68] Comparing two cultures directly, another study found that North American and East African listeners had greater accuracy in tapping the beat to rhythms if the rhythms were based on culturally familiar musical rhythms, and that East African participants tended to use a greater range of metric levels as the tapped beat compared to North Americans.[69] Moreover, these two cultural groups were found to have different patterns of neural entrainment to rhythms – East Africans tended to have greater entrainment to the fastest metric beat rate and North Americans to the slowest.[70]

A recent line of research has used a novel, iterative rhythm reproduction paradigm to demonstrate that cultures vary in the underlying perceptual biases that listeners bring to rhythm perception. Listeners hear and then synchronize their tapping with repeating, rhythmic, three-interval sequences. Their taps are converted to a sound sequence that they hear and synchronize their tapping to again, and this process is repeated five times. Over time, the participants' tapping stabilizes, with fairly accurate synchronization, and the intervals that are produced at this stage are thought to reveal perceptual biases of the listener – the time intervals that are most expected, familiar, and easy to tap. This paradigm has demonstrated cultural differences, for example that American and native Amazonian (Tsimané) listeners differ in their rhythm perception biases.[71] Some stable patterns were the same for Westerners and Tsimané (e.g., 1:1:1), but there were other patterns stable for Tsimané and not Westerners (e.g., 1:2:2), and for Westerners but not Tsimané (3:3:2).

Musical Training of the Listener

Unsurprisingly, musical training is associated with better ability to perceive and produce rhythms, and to synchronize to the beat of rhythms or rhythms themselves.[72] However, neuroimaging studies show mixed findings with respect to brain activity related to musical training and rhythm perception. Studies have found that while performing a rhythm discrimination task, musicians have greater activity in motor regions of the brain compared to nonmusicians, despite not having superior performance on the discrimination task,[73] as well as greater communication between auditory and motor brain regions when listening to rhythms during a rating task.[74] However, another study found that active motor regions during a rhythm synchronization task did not differ in their degree of activation between musicians and nonmusicians but, rather, other frontal brain regions associated with more general cognitive function were more active for musicians.[75] A different study found that some motor regions are less active in people with more musical training.[76] A series of studies on differences in brain structure between early- and late-trained musicians (those beginning training before and after seven years of age, respectively) showed that early-trained musicians performed better on a rhythmic synchronization task,[77] had greater connectivity in the corpus callosum – the primary white matter tract connecting right and left hemispheres[78] – and greater gray matter volume in the premotor cortex.[79]

Rhythm Perception in Non-human Species

One topic of recent interest is whether non-human animals have beat perception and synchronization abilities.[80] This interest was spurred by Snowball, a dancing cockatiel that bobs its head to certain music.[81] Snowball, however, only synchronizes for brief "bouts," and only when the tempo is close to its preferred rate. Moreover, visual cues (e.g., from Snowball's handler) enhance performance. In terms of other species, there is some evidence that budgerigars, bonobos, chimpanzees, and elephants may be able to synchronize to simple stimuli, such as isochronous metronome tones.[82] The most convincing non-human example of synchronization comes from a head-bobbing California sea lion named Ronan. Ronan synchronizes head-bobs not only with isochronous metronome tones, but also to music, even music she has never heard before.[83] Interestingly, Ronan can re-synchronize quickly when the rhythm contains an error, such as a sudden timeshift to an earlier or later phase of the beat, and the timecourse of her correction for the error looks similar to humans.[84]

Evolutionarily, non-human primates are closer to humans than sea lions or songbirds. However, they don't appear to spontaneously synchronize to auditory or musical sequences, although other timing abilities are similar to humans. For example, when reproducing single time intervals, rhesus macaques and humans are equally accurate. However, humans are more accurate when synchronizing with metronome sequences and also when continuing movements at the same rate after the metronome tones stop.[85] Moreover, during synchronization, macaques often tap just after tone onset, whereas humans tend to tap with, or even slightly ahead of, metronome tones. Macaques are not entirely insensitive to auditory regularities, however. For example, macaques showed behavioral evidence of awareness (changes of gaze and facial expressions) when timing was altered in isochronous, but not irregular sequences.[86] Similarly, unexpected tone omissions from isochronous sequences elicited mismatch negativity (MMN) brain responses in EEG, similar to humans. However, humans also showed larger MMN responses when the omissions were "on" rather than "off" the beat, whereas the macaques' responses did not show this distinction, suggesting they were not perceiving the beat. Overall, therefore, monkeys appear to be able to perceive regularity, particularly in simple isochronous sequences, but are less able to perceive beats in more complex rhythms, and less accurate when synchronizing movements.[87]

There are currently two main theories of the underlying neural requirements for beat perception across species. The vocal learning hypothesis suggests that beat perception occurs in species that are vocal learners, which alter their vocalizations in response to environmental input. Vocal learning is mediated by neural connections between auditory input and vocal motor output centers, and this circuitry is proposed to underlie the capacity for beat perception.[88] Parrots are vocal learners,[89] as are humans, bats, cetaceans, seals, elephants, songbirds, and hummingbirds. The second theory suggests that the degree of neural structural connection between auditory and motor areas in a species correlates with rhythmic and beat perception abilities.[90] Rhesus macaques have limited auditory-motor connections and have basic timing skills such as producing single time intervals,[91] whereas chimpanzees have more auditory-motor connections and have shown some capacity for spontaneous synchronization.[92] However, neither of the theories explains the existence of beat perception in animals that are neither primates nor vocal learners, such as Ronan the sea lion.[93]

Conclusion

Cognitive and neuroscientific research informs us of fundamental aspects about the perception of musical rhythm. Musical rhythm's unique characteristics – that it elicits perception of a steady beat and hierarchical metric structure, that it elicits movement and pleasure from human listeners, that it is both universal and culturally specific, and that it is essentially uniquely human – relate to the cognitive and neural processing of these particular sound sequences. Perceiving rhythmic sounds in a musical way (e.g., beat and meter perception) is an active process, conducted in the minds and brains of listeners, dependent on attention, memory, a neural system that also controls our movements, and neural activity that oscillates in time with the regularities we hear, feel, and move to. Future research, involving more sophisticated neuroimaging methods, or incorporating genetic techniques, holds promise for furthering our understanding of humans' special relationship with rhythm.

Endnotes

1 G. W. Cooper and L. B. Meyer, *The Rhythmic Structure of Music* (University of Chicago Press, 1963).

2 D. J. Povel and P. Essens, "Perception of Temporal Patterns," *Music Perception*, 2 (1985), 411–40.

3 J. London, *Hearing in Time: Psychological Aspects of Musical Meter* (Oxford University Press, 2004).

4 T. L. Bolton, "Rhythm," *American Journal of Psychology*, 6 (1894), 145–238; R. Brochard, D. Abecasis, D. Potter, R. Ragot, and C. Drake, "The 'Ticktock' of Our Internal Clock: Direct Brain Evidence of Subjective Accents in Isochronous Sequences," *Psychological Science*, 14 (2003), 362–6; R. Parncutt, "A Perceptual Model of Pulse Salience and Metric Accent in Musical Rhythms," *Music Perception: An Interdisciplinary Journal*, 11 (1994), 409–64.

5 Brochard et al., "The 'Ticktock.'"

6 S. Nozaradan, I. Peretz, M. Missal, and A. Mouraux, "Tagging the Neuronal Entrainment to Beat and Meter," *Journal of Neuroscience*, 31 (2011), 10234–40.

7 J. R. Iversen, B. H. Repp, and A. D. Patel, "Top-Down Control of Rhythm Perception Modulates Early Auditory Responses," *Annals of the New York Academy of Sciences*, 1169 (2009), 58–73.

8 B. Nettl, "An Ethnomusicologist Contemplates Universals in Musical Sound and Musical Culture," in N. L. Wallin, B. Merker, and S. Brown (eds.), *The Origins of Music* (Boston, MA: Bradford, 2000), 463–72.

9 J. Lewis, *A Cross-Cultural Perspective on the Significance of Music and Dance to Culture and Society Insight from BaYaka Pygmies* (Cambridge, MA: MIT Press, 2013).

10 M. Zentner and T. Eerola, "Rhythmic Engagement with Music in Infancy," *Proceedings of the National Academy of Sciences*, 107 (2010), 5768–73.

11 T. Eerola, G. Luck, and P. Toiviainen, "An Investigation of Pre-Schoolers' Corporeal Synchronization with Music," in *Proceedings of the 9th International Conference on Music Perception and Cognition* (2006), 472–6; J. D. McAuley, M. R. Jones, S. Holub, H. M. Johnston, and N. S. Miller, "The Time of Our Lives: Life Span Development of Timing and Event Tracking," *Journal of Experimental Psychology*, 135 (2006), 348.

12 G. Madison, "Experiencing Groove Induced by Music: Consistency and Phenomenology," *Music Perception*, 24 (2006), 201–8.

13 P. Janata, S. T. Tomic, and J. M. Haberman, "Sensorimotor Coupling in Music and the Psychology of the Groove," *Journal of Experimental Psychology*, 141 (2012), 54.

14 G. Madison, F. Gouyon, F. Ullén, and K. Hörnström, "Modeling the Tendency for Music to Induce Movement in Humans: First Correlations with Low-Level Audio Descriptors across Music Genres," *Journal of Experimental Psychology: Human Perception and Performance*, 37 (2011), 1578.

15 Janata et al., "Sensorimotor Coupling"; Madison et al., "Modeling"; J. Stupacher, M. J. Hove, G. Novembre, S. Schütz-Bosbach, and P. E. Keller, "Musical Groove Modulates Motor Cortex Excitability: A TMS Investigation," *Brain and Cognition*, 82 (2013), 127–36.

16 Janata et al., "Sensorimotor Coupling"; Madison et al., "Modeling."

17 D. J. Cameron, I. Zioga, J. P. Lindsen, M. T. Pearce, G. A. Wiggins, K. Potter, and J. Bhattacharya, "Neural Entrainment Is Associated with Subjective Groove and Complexity for Performed but Not Mechanical Musical Rhythms," *Experimental Brain Research*, 237 (2019), 1981–91.

18 B. Burger, M. R. Thompson, G. Luck, S. Saarikallio, and P. Toiviainen, "Influences of Rhythm- and Timbre-Related Musical Features on Characteristics of Music-Induced Movement," *Frontiers in Psychology*, 4 (2013), 183.

19 P. Toiviainen, G. Luck, and M. R. Thompson, "Embodied Meter: Hierarchical Eigenmodes in Music-Induced Movement," *Music Perception*, 28 (2010), 59–70.

20 Toiviainen et al., "Embodied Meter."

21 M. Leman, D. Moelants, M. Varewyck, F. Styns, L. van Noorden, and J. P. Martens, "Activating and Relaxing Music Entrains the Speed of Beat Synchronized Walking," *PLoS ONE*, 8 (2013), e67932; L. A. Leow, T. Parrott, and J. A. Grahn, "Individual Differences in Beat Perception Affect Gait Responses to Low- and High-Groove Music," *Frontiers in Human Neuroscience*, 8 (2014), 811; L. A. Leow, C. Rinchon, and J. Grahn, "Familiarity with Music Increases Walking Speed in Rhythmic Auditory Cuing," *Annals of the New York Academy of Sciences*, 1337 (2015), 53–61.

22 Leman et al., "Activating and Relaxing."

23 Leow et al., "Individual Differences"; Leow et al. "Familiarity with Music."

24 E. Van Dyck, B. Moens, J. Buhmann, M. Demey, E. Coorevits, S. Dalla Bella, and M. Leman, "Spontaneous Entrainment of Running Cadence to Music Tempo," *Sports Medicine-Open*, 1 (2015), 15.

25 C. Mendonça, M. Oliveira, L. Fontes, and J. Santos, "The Effect of Instruction to Synchronize over Step Frequency while Walking with Auditory Cues on a Treadmill," *Human Movement Science*, 33 (2014), 33–42.

26 M. Franěk, L. van Noorden, and L. Režný, "Tempo and Walking Speed with Music in the Urban Context," *Frontiers in Psychology*, 5 (2014), 1361.

27 J. Phillips-Silver and L. J. Trainor, "Feeling the Beat: Movement Influences Infant Rhythm Perception," *Science*, 308 (2005), 1430.

28 J. Phillips-Silver and L. J. Trainor, "Hearing What the Body Feels: Auditory Encoding of Rhythmic Movement," *Cognition*, 105 (2007), 533–46.

29 Y. H. Su and E. Pöppel, "Body Movement Enhances the Extraction of Temporal Structures in Auditory Sequences," *Psychological Research*, 76 (2012), 373–82.

30 F. Manning and M. Schutz, "'Moving to the Beat' Improves Timing Perception," *Psychonomic Bulletin & Review*, 20 (2013), 1133–9.

31 F. C. Manning and M. Schutz, "Trained to Keep a Beat: Movement-Related Enhancements to Timing Perception in Percussionists and Non-Percussionists," *Psychological Research*, 80 (2016), 532–42.

32 A. Friberg and J. Sundberg, "Does Music Performance Allude to Locomotion? A Model of Final Ritardandi Derived from Measurements of Stopping Runners," *Journal of the Acoustical Society of America*, 105 (1999), 1469–84.

33 H. G. MacDougall and S. T. Moore, "Marching to the Beat of the Same Drummer: The Spontaneous Tempo of Human Locomotion," *Journal of Applied Physiology*, 99 (2005), 1164–73.

34 C. L. Gordon, P. R. Cobb, and R. Balasubramaniam, "Recruitment of the Motor System during Music Listening: An ALE Meta-Analysis of fMRI Data," *PLoS ONE*, 13 (2018), e0207213.

35 S. Rossignol and G. M. Jones, "Audio-Spinal Influence in Man Studied by the H-reflex and Its Possible Role on Rhythmic Movements Synchronized to Sound," *Electroencephalography and Clinical Neurophysiology*, 41 (1976), 83–92.

36 D. J. Cameron, L. Stewart, M. T. Pearce, M. Grube, and N. G. Muggleton, "Modulation of Motor Excitability by Metricality of Tone Sequences," *Psychomusicology: Music, Mind, and Brain*, 22 (2012), 122.

37 J. Stupacher et al., "Musical Groove."

38 J. L. Chen, V. B. Penhune, and R. J. Zatorre, "Moving on Time: Brain Network for Auditory-Motor Synchronization Is Modulated by Rhythm Complexity and Musical Training," *Journal of Cognitive Neuroscience*, 20 (2008), 226–39; J. A. Grahn and M. Brett, "Rhythm and Beat Perception in Motor Areas of the Brain," *Journal of Cognitive Neuroscience*, 19 (2007), 893–906; J. A. Grahn and J. B. Rowe, "Finding and Feeling the Musical Beat: Striatal Dissociations between Detection and Prediction of Regularity," *Cerebral Cortex*, 23 (2013), 913–21.

39 Grahn and Brett, "Rhythm and Beat Perception"; J. A. Grahn and J. B. Rowe, "Feeling the Beat: Premotor and Striatal Interactions in Musicians and Non-musicians during Beat Perception," *Journal of Neuroscience*, 29 (2009), 7540–48; S. Teki, M. Grube, S. Kumar, and T. D. Griffiths, "Distinct Neural Substrates of Duration-Based and Beat-Based Auditory Timing," *Journal of Neuroscience*, 31 (2011), 3805–12.

40 M. Grube, F. E. Cooper, P. F. Chinnery, and T. D. Griffiths, "Dissociation of Duration-Based and Beat-Based Auditory Timing in Cerebellar Degeneration," *Proceedings of the National Academy of Sciences*, 107 (2010), 11597–601; Teki et al., "Distinct Neural Substrates."

41 D. J. Cameron, K. A. Pickett, G. Earhart, and J. A. Grahn, "The Effect of Dopaminergic Medication on Beat-Based Auditory Timing in Parkinson's Disease," *Frontiers in Neurology*, 7 (2016),19; J. A. Grahn and M. Brett, "Impairment of Beat-Based Rhythm Discrimination in Parkinson's Disease," *Cortex*, 45 (2009), 54–61.

42 Grube et al., "Dissociation."

43 Chen et al., "Moving on Time."

44 A. Riecker, D. Wildgruber, K. Mathiak, W. Grodd, and H. Ackermann, "Parametric Analysis of Rate-Dependent Hemodynamic Response Functions of Cortical and Subcortical Brain Structures during Auditorily Cued Finger Tapping: A fMRI Study," *NeuroImage*, 18 (2003), 731–9.

45 P. Fraisse, "Perception and Estimation of Time," *Annual Reviews in Psychology*, 35 (1984), 1–36.
46 Grahn and Rowe, "Feeling the Beat."
47 Chen et al., "Moving on Time."
48 Parncutt, "Perceptual Model."
49 M. J. Henry and B. Herrmann, "Low-Frequency Neural Oscillations Support Dynamic Attending in Temporal Context," *Timing & Time Perception*, 2 (2014), 62–86.
50 A. K. Engel and P. Fries, "Beta-Band Oscillations – Signalling the Status Quo? *Current Opinion in Neurobiology*, 20 (2010), 156–65; R. Salmelin and R. Hari, "Spatiotemporal Characteristics of Sensorimotor Neuromagnetic Rhythms Related to Thumb Movement," *Neuroscience*, 60 (1994), 537–50.
51 L. H. Arnal, "Predicting 'When' Using the Motor System's Beta-Band Oscillations," *Frontiers in Human Neuroscience*, 6 (2012), 225; T. Fujioka, L. J. Trainor, E. W. Large, and B. Ross, "Internalized Timing of Isochronous Sounds Is Represented in Neuromagnetic Beta Oscillations," *Journal of Neuroscience*, 32 (2012), 1791–1802.
52 L. H. Arnal, K. B. Doelling, and D. Poeppel, "Delta–Beta Coupled Oscillations Underlie Temporal Prediction Accuracy," *Cerebral Cortex*, 25 (2014), 3077–85; K. B. Doelling and D. Poeppel, "Cortical Entrainment to Music and Its Modulation by Expertise," *Proceedings of the National Academy of Sciences*, 112 (2015), E6233–42.
53 Nozaradan et al., "Tagging the Neuronal Entrainment"; S. Nozaradan, I. Peretz, and A. Mouraux, "Selective Neuronal Entrainment to the Beat and Meter Embedded in a Musical Rhythm," *Journal of Neuroscience*, 32 (2012), 17572–81.
54 Cameron et al., "Neural Entrainment."
55 D. J. Cameron, "The Neural Mechanisms of Musical Rhythm Processing: Cross-Cultural Differences and the Stages of Beat Perception" (Ph.D. dissertation, University of Western Ontario, 2016).
56 Doelling and Poeppel, "Cortical Entrainment."
57 D. Bolger, J. T. Coull, and D. Schön, "Metrical Rhythm Implicitly Orients Attention in Time as Indexed by Improved Target Detection and Left Inferior Parietal Activation," *Journal of Cognitive Neuroscience*, 26 (2014), 593–605; M. R. Jones and P. Q. Pfordresher, "Tracking Melodic Events Using Joint Accent Structure," *Canadian Journal of Experimental Psychology*, 51 (1997), 271–91.
58 Engel and Fries, "Beta-Band Oscillations"; Salmelin and Hari, "Spatiotemporal Characteristics."
59 Iversen et al., "Top-Down Control."
60 Fujioka et al., "Internalized Timing."
61 M. R. Jones and M. Boltz, "Dynamic Attending and Responses to Time," *Psychological Review*, 96 (1989), 459–91; E. W. Large and M. R. Jones, "The Dynamics of Attending: How People Track Time-Varying Events," *Psychological Review*, 106 (1999), 119.

62 M. R. Jones, H. Moynihan, N. MacKenzie, and J. Puente, "Temporal Aspects of Stimulus-Driven Attending in Dynamic Arrays," *Psychological Science*, 13 (2002), 313–19; Large and Jones, "Dynamics of Attending"; H. Quené and R. F. Port, "Effects of Timing Regularity and Metrical Expectancy on Spoken-Word Perception," *Phonetica*, 62 (2005), 1–13.

63 H. L. Chapin, T. Zanto, K. J. Jantzen, S. J. Kelso, F. Steinberg, and E. W. Large, "Neural Responses to Complex Auditory Rhythms: The Role of Attending," *Frontiers in Psychology*, 1 (2010), 224.

64 F. L. Bouwer, T. L. Van Zuijen, and H. Honing, "Beat Processing Is Pre-Attentive for Metrically Simple Rhythms with Clear Accents: An ERP Study," *PLoS ONE*, 9 (2014), e97467.

65 E. Geiser, E. Ziegler, L. Jancke, and M. Meyer, "Early Electrophysiological Correlates of Meter and Rhythm Processing in Music Perception," *Cortex*, 45 (2009), 93–102.

66 Bouwer et al., "Beat Processing."

67 G. Soley and E. E. Hannon, "Infants Prefer the Musical Meter of Their Own Culture: A Cross-Cultural Comparison," *Developmental Psychology*, 46 (2010), 286–92.

68 J. R. Iversen, A. D. Patel, and K. Ohgushi, "Perception of Rhythmic Grouping Depends on Auditory Experience," *The Journal of the Acoustical Society of America*, 124 (2008), 2263–71.

69 D. J. Cameron, J. Bentley, and J. A. Grahn, "Cross-Cultural Influences on Rhythm Processing: Reproduction, Discrimination, and Beat Tapping," *Frontiers in Psychology*, 6 (2015), 366.

70 Cameron, "Neural Mechanisms."

71 N. Jacoby and J. H. McDermott, "Integer Ratio Priors on Musical Rhythm Revealed Cross-Culturally by Iterated Reproduction," *Current Biology*, 27 (2017), 359–70.

72 C. Drake, "Reproduction of Musical Rhythms by Children, Adult Musicians, and Adult Nonmusicians," *Perception & Psychophysics*, 53 (1993), 25–33; Chen et al., "Moving on Time"; J. A. Grahn and D. Schuit, "Individual Differences in Rhythmic Ability: Behavioral and Neuroimaging Investigations," *Psychomusicology: Music, Mind, and Brain*, 22 (2012), 105.

73 Grahn and Brett, "Rhythm and Beat Perception."

74 Grahn and Rowe, "Feeling the Beat."

75 Chen et al., "Moving on Time."

76 Grahn and Schuit, "Individual Differences."

77 J. A. Bailey, R. J. Zatorre, and V. B. Penhune, "Early Musical Training Is Linked to Gray Matter Structure in the Ventral Premotor Cortex and Auditory–Motor Rhythm Synchronization Performance," *Journal of Cognitive Neuroscience*, 26 (2014), 755–67.

78 C. J. Steele, J. A. Bailey, R. J. Zatorre, and V. B. Penhune, "Early Musical Training and White-Matter Plasticity in the Corpus Callosum: Evidence for a Sensitive Period," *Journal of Neuroscience*, 33 (2013), 1282–90.

79 Bailey et al., "Early Musical Training."
80 P. Cook, A. Rouse, M. Wilson, and C. Reichmuth, "A California Sea Lion (Zalophus californianus) Can Keep the Beat: Motor Entrainment to Rhythmic Auditory Stimuli in a Non Vocal Mimic," *Journal of Comparative Psychology*, 127 (2013), 412; A. D. Patel, J. R. Iversen, M. R. Bregman, and I. Schulz, "Experimental Evidence for Synchronization to a Musical Beat in a Nonhuman Animal," *Current Biology*, 19 (2009), 827–30; A. Schachner, T. F. Brady, I. M. Pepperberg, and M. D. Hauser, "Spontaneous Motor Entrainment to Music in Multiple Vocal Mimicking Species," *Current Biology*, 19 (2009), 831–6.
81 Patel et al., "Experimental Evidence"; Schachner et al., "Spontaneous Motor Entrainment."
82 E. W. Large and P. M. Gray, "Spontaneous Tempo and Rhythmic Entrainment in a Bonobo (Pan paniscus)," *Journal of Comparative Psychology*, 129 (2015), 317; Y. Hattori, M. Tomonaga, and T. Matsuzawa, "Spontaneous Synchronized Tapping to an Auditory Rhythm in a Chimpanzee," *Scientific Reports*, 3 (2013), 1566; A. Hasegawa, K. Okanoya, T. Hasegawa, and Y. Seki, "Rhythmic Synchronization Tapping to an Audio–Visual Metronome in Budgerigars," *Scientific Reports*, 1 (2011), 120; Schachner et al., "Spontaneous Motor Entrainment."
83 A. A. Rouse, P. F. Cook, E. W. Large, and C. Reichmuth, "Beat Keeping in a Sea Lion as Coupled Oscillation: Implications for Comparative Understanding of Human Rhythm," *Frontiers in Neuroscience*, 10 (2016), 257; Cook et al., "California Sea Lion."
84 Rouse et al., "Beat Keeping."
85 W. Zarco, H. Merchant, L. Prado, and J. C. Mendez, "Subsecond Timing in Primates: Comparison of Interval Production between Human Subjects and Rhesus Monkeys," *Journal of Neurophysiology*, 102 (2009), 3191–202.
86 E. Selezneva, S. Deike, S. Knyazeva, H. Scheich, A. Brechmann, and M. Brosch, "Rhythm Sensitivity in Macaque Monkeys," *Frontiers in Systems Neuroscience*, 7 (2013), 49.
87 H. Merchant and H. Honing, "Are Non-Human Primates Capable of Rhythmic Entrainment? Evidence for the Gradual Audiomotor Evolution Hypothesis," *Frontiers in Neuroscience*, 7 (2014), 274.
88 A. D. Patel, "Musical Rhythm, Linguistic Rhythm, and Human Evolution," *Music Perception*, 24 (2006), 99–104.
89 Patel et al., "Experimental Evidence."
90 Merchant and Honing, "Non-Human Primates."
91 H. Merchant, O. Pérez, W. Zarco, and J. Gámez, "Interval Tuning in the Primate Medial Premotor Cortex as a General Timing Mechanism," *Journal of Neuroscience*, 33 (2013), 9082–96.
92 Hattori et al., "Spontaneous Synchronized Tapping."
93 Cook et al., "California Sea Lion."

PART II

Performing Rhythm

3 Visualizing the Rhythms of Performance

ALAN DODSON

Traditional staff notation provides a quantized view of musical time: rhythm symbols place each note at a fixed position within a metric framework consisting of integer multiples and fractions of the beat. This familiar representation of rhythm conceals the temporal elasticity of music in performance, including the nuances of *tempo rubato* in Western art music as well as the distinctive rhythmic irregularities in other musical traditions, such as the unequal or "swung" eighth-note subdivisions of jazz and blues and the speech-like rhythms of hip hop and other genres of groove-based music. To promote a clearer understanding of such rhythmic practices, collectively known as *expressive timing* or *microtiming*, several new methods of visualizing rhythm have been proposed over the past century, both in the context of Western art music – the focus of this chapter – and in other contexts.

I begin with some historical background on rhythm notation and a discussion of some pioneering studies of expressive timing from the twentieth century. Next, I turn to scholarly literature published since 2000 that offers novel illustrations of expressive timing alongside sensitive remarks on the motion qualities of Western art music in performance. I conclude by proposing a new visualization strategy for recordings that deviate from the notational meter, with examples from piano recordings by Ignacy Paderewski, Guiomar Novaes, and Claude Debussy.

The figures and examples for this chapter are given on a supplementary webpage: www.rptm.ca/essays/vrp

Beginnings

The idea of showing proportional, integer-related durations through the shapes of the notes on the page can be traced back to the thirteenth-century treatise *Ars cantus mensurabilis* ("The Art of Measured Song") by Franco of Cologne.[1] This was a watershed moment in the history of Western music, because proportional notation freed composers from their former reliance on a limited set of stock rhythmic formulas, the rhythmic modes of the *ars antiqua*, and opened new possibilities for rhythmic flexibility, complexity, and innovation. Since the time of Franco, proportional rhythmic symbols have been used in all of the leading systems of music notation in the West, from the mensural notation of the late Middle Ages and Renaissance to the modern notation that emerged in the seventeenth century and remains in common use today.

There is no denying that proportional rhythmic notation presents a simplified image of musical time, because the durations in actual performances rarely form integer relationships with each other. Aware of this limitation, some scholars began seeking new, performance-sensitive representations of rhythm by the early twentieth century.[2] Among these, the most influential was Carl E. Seashore, a pioneering figure in the field of music psychology who assembled a research team at the University of Iowa during the 1920s and 1930s to analyze commercial recordings and live performances. One of the main goals of Seashore's work, summarized in his 1938 textbook on the psychology of music, was to demystify the artistic dimensions of performance, which he equated with "deviation from the fixed and the regular: from rigid pitch, uniform intensity, *fixed rhythm*, pure tone, and perfect harmony."[3] Seashore sought a practical visual representation of these artistic deviations, and his solution is a graphic format that he calls the "performance score."[4] Figure 3.1 is his performance score showing measure-level durations in two renditions of the beginning of Chopin's Polonaise in A Major, Op. 40, No. 1, as performed in the lab by the concert pianist Harold Bauer.[5]

This graph maps the relationship between two aspects of musical time. The horizontal axis shows what we might call "score time"; it divides the performance into discrete increments based on the barlines in the score, a *chain* of units of time that are conceptually equal to each other.[6] The vertical axis shows these units' duration in "clock time," which can be thought of as a continuous timescale, a free-flowing *stream* of musical time. In this type of graph, the changes in vertical position from measure to measure represent expressive timing. Duration is the inverse of tempo, so downward slope means acceleration and upward slope deceleration.

Bauer was asked to play through the entire passage twice with the same expression, and this figure is meant to show that he could do that rather well. The main expressive features here are a "phrase arch" – that is, an acceleration followed by a deceleration – within mm. 1–8, another phrase arch in mm. 9–16, and an acceleration all the way through mm. 17–24.

To give a clearer sense of what the performance score represents, Multimedia example 3.1 includes an excerpt from another recording of the A-major Polonaise from the 1930s, along with my own Seashore-style analysis. The recording is by Artur Rubinstein, who repeats mm. 1–8 as prescribed in the score but does not repeat mm. 9–24.[7] To track Rubinstein's recording, I located measure onsets in Sonic Visualiser, a widely used, open-source performance analysis program.[8] Like Bauer's performance in the lab, Rubinstein's recording has a clear phrase arch in mm. 1–8 as well as a ritardando in m. 16, but in place of Bauer's eight-bar phrase arch in mm. 9–16, Rubinstein gives a pair of four-bar phrase arches that reflect this material's antecedent-consequent design. Another difference is that Rubinstein has a further phrase arch in mm. 17–24 when the opening material returns, in place of Bauer's race-to-the-finish-line accelerando.

Some might object that this performance score misrepresents the musical experience, because our attention may very well be drawn to expressive features in the recording that are not shown in the graph. For example, we might be struck by certain rhythmic details *within* the measure, such as the elongated eighth notes and the compressed sixteenths, as well as certain details of dynamic accentuation, not to mention the wrong notes in the repeat of the opening phrase. Why aren't these features shown in the graph? Seashore would not deny their importance or discourage us from exploring them empirically, but he places a premium on the clarity that can be obtained when variables are isolated. Because the graphs discussed above only show durations at the measure level, they draw our attention to phrase-level patterns that are subtle but nonetheless readily audible and, moreover, musically meaningful given their close correspondence to the phrase structure of the composition and their stability across repeated performances. For these reasons, I find it helpful to avoid thinking of these graphs as representations of the overall effect or "essence" of a performance. Instead, I prefer to think of them as lenses or filters that draw attention to certain expressive features that the analyst considers meaningful.

After Seashore's retirement in 1946, a second wave of empirical performance analysis began to emerge in the 1960s and continued into the 1980s and 1990s.[9] New technologies such as MIDI and the personal computer greatly facilitated this type of research. Most empirical studies from this period echo Seashore in equating performance expression with measurable deviations from exact regularity, and they often feature graphs that closely resemble Seashore's performance scores. Innovation during this period lay mostly in the development of new theoretical models that map aspects of musical structure onto patterns gleaned from performance data. Among these *generative* models of performance, as they came to be known, the one cited most often in recent literature is Neil Todd's computational model of phrase arching, the expressive device we observed in the timing graphs discussed above.[10] The model represents phrase arching as sets of nested parabolic curves, and it encompasses both expressive timing and variations in loudness (Figure 3.2).[11] The embedding depth of each curve is proportional to the unit's hierarchical position in the grouping structure, which is itself modeled through the rule system given in Fred Lerdahl and Ray Jackendoff's *Generative Theory of Tonal Music.*[12] The model predicts that the changes in tempo and dynamics at section boundaries will be more extreme than those at phrase boundaries within a section, which will in turn be more extreme than those at subphrase boundaries within a phrase. As supporting evidence, Todd provides graphs of timing and dynamics from performances by professional pianists, with patterns similar to those predicted by the model (see the broken lines in Figure 3.2).

In a thoughtful review of Todd's work, Luke Windsor and Eric Clarke compare human and computer-generated recordings of a Schubert Impromptu and conclude that the model does not provide a complete explanation of how pieces are performed but may nonetheless be useful as a general expressive baseline or norm against which the nuances of a particular performance can be interpreted.[13] This could be described as a deductive (theory-driven) approach to performance analysis. Bruno Repp offers a complementary inductive (data-driven) approach in a series of corpus studies from the 1990s.[14] Here models are extracted from large sets of performance data through statistical methods (mainly averaging and principal components) and are then used as frames of reference for the interpretation and comparison of individual recordings.

In addition to this work by music psychologists, some historical research involving empirical methods of performance analysis began to emerge in the 1990s. One especially noteworthy contribution in this vein is José Bowen's 1996 article on tempo fluctuation in recordings of orchestral music from the Classical and Romantic eras.[15] Bowen tracked the tempo by tapping along on a computer keyboard while listening to recordings, a more efficient but less accurate method than those used by music psychologists.[16] Bowen presents the tempo data in a series of graphs, again mainly in the style of Seashore's performance scores but now at several levels of scale, proceeding from entire movements to individual phrases. He uses this data to support some rather broad interpretive claims about historical trends in performance practice over the course of the twentieth century and about the performing styles of several well-known conductors.

For example, he shows that the tempos within the first movement of Tchaikovsky's Sixth Symphony have become more extreme over time (Figure 3.3),[17] but he also points out that the earlier recordings tend to have wide tempo fluctuations within each section, citing as a prime example the Concertgebouw Orchestra's 1937 recording conducted by Willem Mengelberg (Multimedia example 3.2).[18] Within the latter recording, Bowen highlights a series of three rather extreme phrase arches, beginning in m. 100, as well as a high level of tempo volatility from the beginning of the exposition to the first climax at m. 38.

Another tapping study from the mid 1990s, an essay by Nicholas Cook on Wilhelm Furtwängler's recordings of Beethoven's Ninth Symphony, forged a connection between empirical performance analysis and the discourse of music theory: Cook shows several correspondences between Furtwängler's interpretation and the analysis in Heinrich Schenker's monograph on the Ninth Symphony, which Furtwängler knew well.[19] This sort of disciplinary cross-fertilization was a hallmark of research by scholars associated with the Centre for the History and Analysis of Recorded Music (CHARM), of which Bowen and Cook were founding members. First established at the University of Southampton in 1994, within a decade CHARM grew into a multi-institutional enterprise that hosted a series of international interdisciplinary conferences during the first decade of this century.

Recent Innovations

Over the past twenty years, partly as an outcome of CHARM and other related initiatives, the empirical literature on rhythmic aspects of performance has continued to flourish. During this period, traditional timing graphs have continued to appear routinely in performance analysis contributions, for instance in my own work on prolongational boundaries and metric dissonance in recorded music, and in writings on performing style and expression by Daniel Leech-Wilkinson and Dorrotya Fabian.[20] However, several new types of analytic figures have also been proposed, often in conjunction with observations about subtle qualities of motion that arise from interactions between performing nuances and aspects of grouping and meter. To illustrate this recent trend, I'll now turn to some musical examples from five representative publications, all of which deal with recordings of nineteenth-century music for solo piano. (This repertory has probably been emphasized because piano note onsets are percussive and therefore relatively easy to locate in a sound file, and because *tempo rubato* tends to be more prominent in recordings of music from the nineteenth century as compared to other periods.)

In a 2012 essay on three recordings of the first movement of Beethoven's "Moonlight" Sonata, Elaine Chew superimposes curved arrows on timing graphs to show what she calls "high-level phrase arcs" (Multimedia example 3.3).[21] Chew's conception of the phrase arch phenomenon differs fundamentally from Todd's, because she does not invoke Lerdahl and Jackendoff's rule system, whose input consists of compositional features such as melodic parallelism and cadence.[22] Instead, her conception of the phrase rests entirely on expressive timing: for Chew, a "performed phrase" is simply a segment of the recording that begins and ends with minima in the timing graph.[23] She compares the rhythmic effect of different recordings by considering the relationship between these performed phrases and the metric notation within the first fifteen measures, showing that Daniel Barenboim and Maurizio Pollini slow down at the barlines, whereas Artur Schnabel does so only at formal boundaries marked by cadences. Chew notes that prior to these cadence points, "the consistent ebb and flow across the bar lines creates a sense of continuity, perhaps a clue as to how [Schnabel] creates these long, long lines."[24] The arrow notation in Multimedia example 3.3a highlights the high-level performed phrases in Schnabel's recording. In a follow-up study, Chew considers the formal implications of the high-level phrase arcs in other recordings. For example, she describes the differences between Schnabel's and Pollini's interpretations (Multimedia example 3.3b) in the following way:

> While Schnabel's [recording] draws a long line to the first modulation, to E major, Pollini's long line is reserved for bars 5 through 15. This suggests that Pollini may have heard the first four bars as an introduction, after which the long line begins and stretches to the downbeat of bar 15, which is the cadence in b minor.[25]

Thus Chew's annotated tempo graphs point not only to differences in performing style, but also to different ways of hearing the succession of formal functions in this passage.[26]

Phrasing hierarchy is also the subject of an article on recordings of Chopin's Mazurkas by Mitchell Ohriner, who builds on the traditional timing graph in two ways.[27] As a first approximation, he uses simple annotations to show how different performances resolve a grouping ambiguity in different ways: in Multimedia example 3.4, the third beat of m. 24 in the Mazurka in C Major, Op. 24, No. 2, can be heard either as (a) the ending of a group that begins in m. 21 or (b) the beginning of a group that ends in m. 28.[28] Recordings by Frederic Chiu and Vladimir Ashkenazy tip the balance one way or the other. Furthermore, at the measure level (not shown here), Chiu accelerates in m. 25 but Ashkenazy does not, so there is also a difference in the salience of different levels of the grouping hierarchy in these two performances, as shown through the boldfacing in Multimedia example 3.4c.[29]

The second method involves using an algorithm to describe grouping similarities and differences within a large set of recordings at three levels of scale. As shown in Multimedia example 3.5, the segments of a timing graph are translated into *durational contours*, that is, ordered sets that represent the durations within the segment as integers from 0 (the shortest unit) to n–1 (the longest unit), where n is the number of units.[30] Next, a contour reduction algorithm checks for *group-final lengthening* (GFL) – that is, a slow ending – at the 2-, 4-, and 8-measure levels, in reference to a hypothetical grouping structure of (2+2)+(2+2) measures.[31] The algorithm omits the midsized duration within a rolling 3-unit window, and this process is repeated recursively until the contour cannot be reduced further. Only contours that reduce to a pattern of decelerating throughout (<01>), or accelerating and then decelerating (<102> or <201>) are considered GFL-reflective. The results are displayed visually as a set of boxes that are either thick or thin, indicating the presence or absence of GFL. Multimedia example 3.6 shows the results for 6 of the 29 recordings of the C-major Mazurka that Ohriner analyzes with this method.[32]

Because the reference structure is the same for all recordings, the second method is less sensitive to fine grouping boundary differences than the first, but it can nonetheless reveal more fundamental differences in the pacing of the recordings. For example, it shows that Brailowsky's recording differs from both Chiu's and Ashkenazy's insofar as it lacks GFL at the four-bar level, giving it a markedly different feel from the other two. (Multimedia example 3.6 includes an excerpt from the Brailowsky recording.) The basic idea here is that the hypothetical (2+2)+(2+2) pattern exists in reality only to the extent that its constituent parts are performed in a GFL-reflective way. In this sense Ohriner's approach (like Chew's) offers a less deterministic representation of grouping than earlier generative approaches grounded in Lerdahl and Jackendoff's rule system.

Meter rather than grouping forms the framework for a new visualization strategy proposed in a paper by Olivier Senn, Lorenz Kilchenmann, and Antoine Camp, who prepared a note-by-note durational analysis of the first four measures in Martha Argerich's recording of Chopin's Prelude in E Minor (Multimedia example 3.7).[33] In this case, units at various levels of the metric hierarchy – measures, half-measures, beats, and beat subdivisions – are represented in both the horizontal and the vertical axis, resulting in a series of nested squares.[34] The left and right hands are tracked separately, and asynchronies at points aligned in the score are shown as positive or negative integers in the middle of the graph, between the two streams of nested squares. Performance expression is multileveled, and it is very helpful to be able to survey several levels of activity at a single glance. This hierarchical representation is thus a significant advance over the traditional timing graph, which tracks durations on only one level of scale at a time, typically the measure or beat level.

Senn et al. point out some recurring patterns in the Argerich recording: the second half-measure is consistently longer than the first, there are consistent "melody leads" (i.e., the melody notes begin a few milliseconds before the chords), and there are beat- and subdivision-level ritardandos into the first three barlines as well as the midpoint of m. 4.[35] The authors describe the overall effect of these patterns as follows: "Argerich seems to make a new effort to gain some speed with each new bar (hence the faster first halves), but this effort is lost [and] as the bar progresses, the tension relaxes and the music seems to stagnate."[36] From the loose fit between Argerich's performed durations and the rhythmic notation, Senn and his co-authors offer this musical narrative-in-miniature as a speculative "inverse interpretation" that is presented "strictly from the listener's point of view."[37] This is a preliminary study of modest scope, limited to four measures from one recording.[38] However, it has the special distinction of having inspired several creative applications, in the form of a series of compositions by the American composer Richard Beaudoin. In these compositions, the durations in the score are derived from various nested-squares performance analyses, including the one in Multimedia example 3.7.[39]

Some other recent studies have explored phrase-level patterns of dynamics as well as expressive timing. Jörg Langner and Werner Goebl explore interaction between these two domains of performance expression through innovative "performance worm" animations involving a string of overlapping discs in a space defined by tempo on the horizontal axis and loudness on the vertical.[40] Multimedia example 3.8 demonstrates this approach through an analysis of a recording of Chopin's Etude in E Major, Op. 10, No. 3, by the pianist Mauricio Pollini.[41] As noted above, Todd's generative model suggests that both tempo and dynamics tend to increase and decrease in arch-shaped patterns over the course of a phrase. If the dynamic and tempo arches were congruent, then one would expect the performance worm to move diagonally most of the time, first to the northeast and then to the southwest. However, Langner and Goebl observe that in many recordings, such as the Pollini recording in Multimedia example 3.8, the tempo tends to increase before the dynamic level in the approach to a phrase's climax, and counterclockwise patterns are prevalent overall.[42] Though based on a relatively small sample of recordings, this observation suggests a possible refinement of our understanding of phrase arching. Follow-up studies have sought further recurring patterns of motion in the tempo-loudness space, including performer-specific patterns as well as generic patterns, through artificial intelligence models.[43]

Dynamic and temporal aspects of phrase arching are explored in a different way by Nicholas Cook in the chapter on recordings of Chopin's Mazurkas that forms the centerpiece of his broad-ranging book on performance analysis, *Beyond the Score: Music as Performance*.[44] Cook presents the data in the form of "scape plots" in which beat-level data are represented at the base of a triangle and adjacent beats' values are averaged recursively at higher levels, as shown schematically in Figure 3.4.[45] The loudness triangle is inverted and aligned with the timing triangle along the base, creating a diamond shape overall, and the numerical information is color-coded in such a way that flame-like patterns emerge at the loudest and slowest points in an excerpt. Multimedia example 3.9a is Cook's analysis of a recording that he describes as a textbook example of phrase arching, namely Heinrich Neuhaus's recording of Chopin's Mazurka in C-sharp Minor, Op. 63, No. 3.[46] Through graphs of several other recordings of this piece, Cook demonstrates that the technique of phrase arching, though prevalent since the Second World War (especially among Russian-trained pianists), was less widely used in the first half of the twentieth century, when a more rhetorical and improvisatory style of performance prevailed. In Ignaz Friedman's recording (Multimedia example 3.9b), for instance, Cook hears a "focus on moment-to-moment expression" arising from features such as the unusually long opening upbeat and abrupt changes of tempo and articulation later in the excerpt.[47] Thus Cook uses his flaming diamond graphs to support the argument that phrase arching is a historically and culturally specific practice, not a universal or "hard-wired" psychomotor phenomenon, as Todd's model and other generative models seem to imply.

Despite their sharp differences in design, all of the recent examples I have surveyed help bring into focus musically meaningful patterns that might otherwise escape our notice, as well as the qualitative effects that these patterns help to generate. Like Seashore's performance scores, then, these new types of graphs can be thought of as analytic lenses or filters that help us reach a clearer understanding of the music we are actually hearing, as distinct from the music we read on the page. Another way in which these new graphs resemble Seashore's performance scores is that they use the notational meter – the beats and measures shown in the score – as a frame of reference: durations are tracked at the level of the notated beats, and measure numbers are shown either on the horizontal axis (Chew, Ohriner, Cook), at the top of the nested squares (Senn et al.), or on the face of the performance worm (Langner and Goebl). In my view, this is not problematic in the particular examples surveyed above, because these beats and measures can easily be heard and felt in these recordings. However, reliance on the metric notation limits the generalizability of these analytic approaches, because many other recordings do not conform to that notation – especially those by performers trained at the beginning of the twentieth century, a period when many musicians and critics railed against the "tyranny of the barline."[48] I consider the variations in meter within such non-literalist recordings to be a distinct type of "artistic deviation from the regular" – in other words, a special type of performance expression.

Visualizing Metric Variation in Performance

Let's consider two versions the opening of Chopin's Mazurka in A Minor, Op. 17, No. 4, one recorded by Ignacy Paderewski in 1923 and the other by Guiomar Novaes in 1954.[49] According to the score (Multimedia example 3.10a), this excerpt consists of eight bars in triple meter, grouped as 4+4.[50] Timing graphs of the two recordings are very similar (Multimedia example 3.10b), and the corresponding timescape graphs are nearly identical (Multimedia example 3.10c).[51] However, these illustrations conceal some fundamental differences between the recordings in the domain of *experiential meter*, by which I mean the meter felt by the listener, as opposed to the meter represented in the score.[52] To get at these differences, I will borrow some concepts and analytic symbols from Christopher Hasty's *Meter as Rhythm*, which casts meter not as a structure or schematic framework but instead as a dynamic, emergent aspect of the listening experience.[53] Hasty represents experiential meter through static images, but I will instead use animations in an effort to represent more directly the temporal qualities that the theory describes, an approach suggested in John Roeder's review of

Meter as Rhythm.[54] I created Multimedia example 3.11–3.15 using Adobe Animate, a multimedia computer animation program.

For Hasty, the basis of the experience of meter is *projection*, the feeling that once a duration has been articulated, it will immediately be reproduced: after hearing two sounds, we expect a third sound at a specific future moment (Multimedia example 3.11a).[55] A *complex projection* occurs when a long projection is coordinated with two or more shorter projections (Multimedia example 3.11b),[56] and within a complex projection, the *dominant beginning* (|) launches a projection that remains active for more than one beat, while a *continuation* (\) initiates a shorter projection between two dominant beginnings.[57]

One of the benefits of Hasty's analytic notation, as compared to traditional metric symbols like time signatures and barlines, is that it allows for more subtlety and flexibility in tracking changes of meter. Hasty defines three types of metric change relevant to the excerpts discussed below: *denial* occurs when a timespan does not fulfill its projected duration and instead launches a new projection that is considerably shorter or longer than the one before it (Multimedia example 3.12a),[58] *deferral* happens when an extra continuation postpones a dominant beginning and therefore alters the metric type, for instance by shifting from duple to triple meter (Multimedia example 3.12b),[59] and *interruption* occurs when the ending of a projected duration is pre-empted by a new, early beginning (Multimedia example 3.12c).[60]

Hasty's own analyses center on *compositional* applications of these processes of metric change, mainly in music from the twentieth century, and he uses scores rather than recordings as his objects of analysis. I often hear these same metric processes when listening to recordings of earlier, common-practice repertoire, including the Paderewski and Novaes excerpts discussed above, to which I now return.[61]

Multimedia example 3.13a shows the variations in meter that I hear in the Paderewski excerpt.[62] Up to the boundary of the introduction and theme, I hear a projection of triple meter without anacrusis. This triple meter is so well established that I feel a fifth downbeat during the sustained chord that begins in the fourth experiential measure, but the mazurka theme enters before this fifth measure is completed – a clear case of interruption. A further complication occurs during the first three beats of the theme, which Paderewski plays as weak–strong–weak. This can be heard either as a syncopation or an anacrusis in its local context, but once the theme's second downbeat is articulated the ambiguity resolves in favor of syncopation. From that point on, I hear an unambiguous triple meter until the end of the excerpt.

Multimedia example 3.13b maps the hypermeter in Paderewski's recording, which is equally flexible. Although a potential for duple hypermeter can be sensed throughout the excerpt, this potential is fully realized only toward the end.[63] Duple hypermeter is ubiquitous in Romantic piano music, so we might reasonably expect it at the outset of the recording. Instead, the second hyperdownbeat is deferred until the sustained chord at the end of the introduction, which gives the fourth experiential measure a much stronger sense of "beginning" than the third, and suggests that the recording begins with *triple* hypermeter. This effect is enhanced by the increased tempo and rhythmic activity leading up to the sustained chord, which bring a sense of anacrusis, of into-the-beginning. However, the projection of this triple hypermeter is interrupted by the entry of the mazurka theme, which itself projects the duple hypermeter expected from the outset.

In Novaes's recording, I hear a fundamentally different metric process involving a shift from duple to triple meter at the surface level (Multimedia example 3.14a). Duple meter is projected throughout the introduction, and the triplet figure near the end of the introduction sounds like a *quarter-note* triplet, not an eighth-note triplet as in Paderewski's recording and in the score. This quarter-note triplet foreshadows a shift from duple to triple meter at the beginning of the theme, and the ritardando that surrounds the triplet helps smooth out this metric transition. In conjunction with this ritardando, a shift from duple to triple hypermeter can also be discerned in the introduction (Multimedia example 3.14b). The accents on the first and fifth chords of the introduction project duple hypermeter, and the triplet figure defers the next hyperdownbeat until the sustained chord. Then, as in Paderewski's recording, this triple hypermeter is interrupted by the entry of the mazurka theme, which itself projects duple hypermeter throughout.

The Paderewski and Novaes example show some ways in which an investigation of experiential meter may shed light on distinctive and meaningful patterns that would be obscured in an analysis framed by the notational meter. To demonstrate this approach further, I will now turn to a more metrically intricate passage from Debussy's 1913 piano roll recording of his piece *D'un cahier d'esquisses* ("From a Sketchbook") as reissued on CD.[64] The passage includes a cadenza that features two gong-like bass notes, each of which is followed by a rapid ascending passage and a short melodic fragment. The cadenza is preceded by a short transition and followed by a coda.[65] Multimedia example 3.15a maps the metric fluctuations that I hear in this excerpt.

A clear and continuous tactus can be felt throughout the excerpt, but the underlying (measure-level) projections are considerably less clear and continuous: a slow duple meter is established at the outset, but two processes of metric change, namely, denial and deferral, can be traced within the cadenza. Because of the slow tempo, these processes do not bring as much tension as the interruptions and deferrals in the Paderewski and Novaes recordings. Instead, they bring a subtle ebb and flow of metric determinacy over the course of the excerpt.

The melodic fragment after the cadenza's initial gong stroke includes an extra continuation ("weak beat") that defers the next downbeat until the second gong stroke. This establishes a potential *triple* meter, but when the melodic fragment returns soon after the second gong stroke, its rhythm is altered in such a way that the gesture now encompasses four beats instead of three. The result is that the tentative triple meter recedes from our field of awareness,[66] and the referential duple meter is restored.

By the end of the excerpt, the tempo has become slow enough to undermine the duple meter, which seems to dissipate shortly after the coda begins. However, there is a feeling of rhythmic continuity between the tactus pulses of the cadenza and the triple measures of the coda. In other words, there seems to be a transition from a slow duple to a moderate triple meter toward the end of the excerpt, similar to what happens in the Novaes excerpt discussed above.

The score and recording are again quite remote from each other in this case. The cadenza is mostly unmeasured in the score (Multimedia example 3.15b), and one of its main focal points in the recording, the second gong stroke, is altogether absent.[67] A few beats later, at the beginning of the coda, the score indicates a change from $\substack{6\\8}$ to $\substack{6\\4}$ meter, as well as a tactus shift (dotted quarter = quarter), indicating that the coda should proceed at only one-third the tempo of the previous $\substack{6\\8}$ measures – a dramatic discontinuity in comparison to the seamless connection heard in the recording.

These animations provide a new way to visualize and interpret the nuances of rhythm and timing in recordings that lack a consistent metric framework. As such, they fill a gap in the literature surveyed in Parts I and II of this chapter. Further applications might explore recordings of Gregorian chant and other types of monophonic singing in free rhythm, as well as free-flowing instrumental music like the unmeasured keyboard preludes of the French baroque. These are just a few of seemingly endless possibilities for research in performance analysis, a field that will surely continue to grow and develop as new technologies become available in the years ahead – thereby helping to further expand our appreciation and understanding of the rhythms of performance.

Figures and Multimedia examples for Chapter 3

These figures appear on the website www.rptm.ca/essays/vrp

3.1 Timing in the opening of Chopin's Polonaise in A Major, Op. 40, No. 1, performed by Harold Bauer (Seashore, *Psychology of Music*)
3.2 Graphs of human and computer-generated performance expression:
  (a) Timing in an excerpt from Haydn's Sonata in E-flat Major, Hob. XVI/49 (Todd, "A Computational Model of Rubato")
  (b) Loudness in an excerpt from Chopin's Prelude in F-sharp Minor, Op. 28, No. 8 (Todd, "The Dynamics of Dynamics")
3.3 Average tempos in various recordings of the first movement of Tchaikovsky's Symphony No. 6 in B Minor, Op. 74 (Bowen, "Tempo, Duration, and Flexibility")
3.4 Generalized scape plot design (Sapp, "Computational Methods")

These multimedia examples appear on the website www.rptm.ca/essays/vrp

3.1 Timing in the opening of Chopin's Polonaise in A Major, Op. 40, No. 1, performed by Artur Rubinstein
3.2 Timing in the first movement of Tchaikovsky's Symphony No. 6 in B Minor, Op. 74, performed by the Concertgebouw Orchestra conducted by Willem Mengelberg (Bowen, "Tempo, Duration, and Flexibility")
3.3 Timing and high-level phrase arcs in the opening of Beethoven's "Moonlight" Sonata, Op. 27, No. 2
  (a) performed by Artur Schnabel (Chew, "About Time")
  (b) performed by Artur Schnabel (top half) and Maurizio Pollini (bottom half) (Chew, "From Sound to Structure")
3.4 Timing and grouping in an excerpt from Chopin's Mazurka in C Major, Op. 24, No. 2 (Ohriner, "Grouping Hierarchy and Trajectories of Pacing")
  (a) performed by Frederic Chiu
  (b) performed by Vladimir Ashkenazy
  (c) effects of performance strategies upon grouping structure
3.5 Durational contour in Chopin's Mazurka in C-sharp Minor, Op. 63, No. 3, performed by Stanislav Bunin (Ohriner, "Grouping Hierarchy and Trajectories of Pacing")
3.6 Group-final lengthening in six recordings of Chopin's Mazurka in C Major, Op. 24, No. 2 (Ohriner, "Grouping Hierarchy and Trajectories of Pacing")

3.7 Timing and notational meter in the opening of Chopin's Prelude in B Minor, Op. 28, No. 4, performed by Martha Argerich (Senn et al., "Expressive Timing")
3.8 Timing and dynamics in Chopin's Etude in E Major, Op. 10, No. 3, performed by Maurizio Pollini (Langner and Goebl, "Visualizing Expressive Performance")
3.9 Timing and dynamics in the opening of Chopin's Mazurka in C-sharp Minor, Op. 63, No. 3 (Cook, *Beyond the Score*)
  (a) performed by Heinrich Neuhaus
  (b) performed by Ignaz Friedman
3.10 Timing and notational meter in the opening of Chopin's Mazurka in A Minor, Op. 17, No. 4
  (a) score
  (b) timing graphs of two recordings, performed by Ignacy Paderewski and Guiomar Novaes
  (c) scape plots of the two recordings
3.11 Animations for projection, as described in Hasty's *Meter as Rhythm*
  (a) simple
  (b) complex
3.12 Three types of metric change discussed in Hasty's *Meter as Rhythm*
  (a) denial
  (b) deferral
  (c) interruption
3.13 Experiential meter in the opening of Chopin's Mazurka in A Minor, Op. 17, No. 4, performed by Ignacy Paderewski
  (a) preliminary analysis (two levels)
  (b) full analysis (three levels)
3.14 Experiential meter in the opening of Chopin's Mazurka in A Minor, Op. 17, No. 4, performed by Guiomar Novaes
  (a) preliminary analysis (two levels)
  (b) full analysis (three levels)
3.15 Experiential and notational meter in the cadenza from Debussy's *D'un cahier d'esquisses*
  (a) performed by the composer
  (b) score

Endnotes

1 This innovation and its cultural significance are discussed in A. W. Crosby, *The Measure of Reality: Quantification and Western Society, 1250–1660* (Cambridge University Press, 1997), 151–63.

2 These newer representations are based on the measurement of musical durations in "clock time," a practice whose origins in the eighteenth and early nineteenth centuries are discussed in M. R. Grant, *Beating Time and Measuring Music in the Early Modern Era* (Oxford University Press, 2014), 127–34 and 183–208.

3 C. E. Seashore, *Psychology of Music* (New York: McGraw-Hill, 1938), 29, emphasis added. For further details on Seashore's contributions, see A. Gabrielsson, "The Performance of Music," in D. Deutsch (ed.), *The Psychology of Music*, 2nd ed. (San Diego: Academic Press, 1999), 527–32.

4 Seashore, *Psychology of Music*, 21–2.

5 Ibid., 246.

6 The "chain" and "stream" analogies are borrowed from C. Seeger, "Prescriptive and Descriptive Music-Writing," *The Musical Quarterly*, 44 (1958), 185.

7 A. Rubinstein, *Fryderyk Chopin: Polonaises (Selections) [and] Andante spianato and Grande polonaise brilliant*, Naxos 8.110661, 2000, track 5 (recorded December 1934). Unfortunately, recordings of Bauer's performances in the lab are not available.

8 C. Cannam, C. Landone, and M. Sandler, "Sonic Visualiser: An Open Source Application for Viewing, Analysing, and Annotating Music Audio Files," in *Proceedings of the ACM Multimedia 2010 International Conference* (New York: ACM Publications, 2010), 1467–8. See also N. Cook and D. Leech-Wilkinson, *A Musicologist's Guide to Sonic Visualiser* (https://charm.rhul.ac.uk/analysing/p9_1.html), accessed September 26, 2019.

9 Gabrielsson, "Performance of Music," 532–79; Gabrielsson, "Music Performance Research at the Millennium," *Psychology of Music*, 31 (2003), 225–37.

10 N. Todd, "A Model of Expressive Timing in Tonal Music," *Music Perception*, 3 (1985), 33–58; Todd, "A Computational Model of Rubato," *Contemporary Music Review*, 3 (1989), 69–88; Todd, "The Dynamics of Dynamics: A Model of Musical Expression," *Journal of the Acoustical Society of America*, 91 (1992), 3540–50.

11 Todd, "Computational Model," 77; Todd, "Dynamics of Dynamics," 3549.

12 F. Lerdahl and R. Jackendoff, *A Generative Theory of Tonal Music* (MIT Press, 1983), 345–52.

13 L. Windsor and E. Clarke, "Expressive Timing and Dynamics in Real and Artificial Musical Performances: Using an Algorithm as an Analytical Tool," *Music Perception*, 15 (1997), 127–52. The human and computer-generated recordings discussed in this article are available in N. Cook, *Beyond the Score: Music as Performance* (Oxford University Press, 2013), companion website (www.oup.com/us/beyondthescore), media examples 3.08 and 6.02, accessed September 26, 2019.

14 Among his many publications in this vein, the most widely cited is B. H. Repp, "Diversity and Commonality in Music Performance: An Analysis of Timing Microstructure in Schumann's 'Träumerei,'" *Journal of the Acoustical Society of*

America, 92 (1992), 2546–68. See also C. E. Cancino-Chacón, M. Grachten, W. Goebl, and G. Widmer, "Computational Models of Expressive Music Performance: A Comprehensive and Critical Review," *Frontiers in Digital Humanities*, 5, No. 25 (2018), 1–23.

15 J. A. Bowen, "Tempo, Duration, and Flexibility: Techniques in the Analysis of Performance," *Journal of Musicological Research*, 16 (1996), 111–56.

16 Ibid., 130. Bowen estimates his method's margin of error at 60 ms, as compared to 10 ms for Seashore's and Repp's methods. Of these authors, only Repp provides data to justify his estimate (Repp, "Diversity and Commonality," 2551).

17 Bowen, "Tempo, Duration, and Flexibility," 137.

18 Ibid., 140 (graph) and 142 (discussion).

19 N. Cook, "The Conductor and the Theorist: Furtwängler, Schenker and the First Movement of Beethoven's Ninth Symphony," in J. Rink (ed.), *The Practice of Performance: Studies in Musical Interpretation* (Cambridge University Press, 1995), 105–25.

20 A. Dodson, "Performance, Grouping, and Schenkerian Alternative Readings in Some Passages from Beethoven's 'Lebewohl' Sonata, Op. 81a," *Music Analysis*, 27 (2008), 107–34; Dodson, "Metrical Dissonance and Directed Motion in Paderewski's Recordings of Chopin's Mazurkas," *Journal of Music Theory*, 53 (2009), 57–94; D. Leech-Wilkinson, *The Changing Sound of Music: Approaches to Studying Recorded Musical Performance* (London: CHARM, 2009), https://charm.rhul.ac.uk/studies/chapters/intro.html, accessed September 27, 2019; D. Fabian, "Commercial Sound Recordings and Trends in Expressive Music Performance: Why Should Experimental Researchers Pay Attention?" in D. Fabian, R. Timmers, and E. Schubert (eds.), *Expressiveness in Music Performance: Empirical Approaches Across Styles and Cultures* (Oxford University Press, 2019), 58–75; D. Fabian, *A Musicology of Performance: Theory and Method Based on Bach's Solos for Violin* (Cambridge: Open Book Publishers, 2015), https://openbookpublishers.com/htmlreader/978-1-78374-152-6/main.html, accessed September 27, 2019.

21 E. Chew, "About Time: Strategies of Performance Revealed in Graphs," *Visions of Research in Music Education*, 20 (2012), 13.

22 See note 13. Chew's performance-centered definition of phrase also diverges sharply from the two prevailing views of phrase in music theory today, which remain grounded entirely in compositional features: W. Rothstein, *Phrase Rhythm in Tonal Music* (New York: Schirmer, 1989), 3–15; W. Caplin, *Classical Form: A Theory of Formal Functions for the Instrumental Music of Haydn, Mozart, and Beethoven* (Oxford University Press, 1999), 260, note 5.

23 Chew, "About Time," 8.

24 Ibid., 9.

25 E. Chew, "From Sound to Structure: Synchronising Prosodic and Structural Information to Reveal the Thinking behind Performance Decisions," in C. MacKie (ed.), *New Thoughts on Piano Performance: Research at the Interface*

between Science and the Art of Piano Performance (London: London International Piano Symposium Publications, 2016), 143–4.

26 The relationship between performance and alternative readings of formal function is discussed more fully, though without performance analysis graphs or data, in J. Schmalfeldt, *In the Process of Becoming: Analytical Perspectives on Form in the Early Nineteenth Century* (Oxford University Press, 2011), 118–21.

27 M. S. Ohriner, "Grouping Hierarchy and Trajectories of Pacing in Performances of Chopin's Mazurkas," *Music Theory Online, 18.1* (2012).

28 Ibid., ¶ 7.

29 Ibid., ¶ 8.

30 Ibid., ¶ 16.

31 Ibid., ¶ 15 and ¶ 22. When successive durations are too close to be differentiated aurally, the second iteration is pruned, so mm. 37–38 in Figure 3.8 will reduce to <102>, making it GFL-reflective. Ohriner admits that the algorithm is not able to recognize the contour in mm. 33–34 as GFL-reflective because it has a sawtooth pattern. This is a limitation of the methodology.

32 Ibid., ¶ 22.

33 O. Senn, L. Kilchenmann, and A. Camp, "Expressive Timing: Martha Argerich Plays Chopin's Prelude Op. 28/4 in E Minor," in A. Williamon, S. Pretty, and R. Buck (eds.), *Proceedings of the International Symposium on Performance Science 2009* (Utrecht: European Association of Conservatoires, 2009), 110.

34 A similar graphic format was used several years earlier in a study of piano roll recordings: H. Gottschewski, "Graphic Analysis of Recorded Interpretations," *Computing in Musicology*, 8 (1992), 95.

35 Senn et al., "Expressive Timing," 110.

36 Ibid., 111.

37 Ibid., 108.

38 A further four measures are analyzed in a follow-up study: O. Senn, L. Kilchenmann, and A. Camp, "A Turbulent Acceleration into the Stretto: Martha Argerich Plays Chopin's Prelude Op. 28/4 in E Minor," *Dissonance*, 120 (2012), 31–5.

39 This compositional approach is discussed more fully in R. Beaudoin and A. Kania, "A Musical Photograph?" *Journal of Aesthetics and Art Criticism*, 70 (2012), 115–27. The "microtiming" page on Beaudoin's website (www.richardbeaudoin.com/microtiming) includes a complete list of works for which nested-squares analyses served as a compositional resource.

40 J. Langner and W. Goebl, "Visualizing Expressive Performance in Tempo-Loudness Space," *Computer Music Journal*, 27 (2003), 69–83.

41 https://iwk.mdw.ac.at/goebl/animations.html, accessed September 22, 2019.

42 Langner and Goebl, "Visualizing Expressive Performance," 72.

43 Summarized in G. Widmer and W. Goebl, "Computational Models of Expressive Music Performance: The State of the Art," *Journal of New Music Research*, 33 (2004), 210–12.

44 Cook, *Beyond the Score*, 126–223.
45 C. Sapp, "Computational Methods for the Analysis of Musical Structure" (Ph. D. dissertation, Stanford University, 2011), 96. (Sapp, a CHARM Research Fellow, collaborated with Cook on the Mazurka project discussed in *Beyond the Score*.)
46 Cook, *Beyond the Score*, 198 (color version from online supplement).
47 Ibid., 189 (graph, color version from online supplement) and 190 (quotation).
48 See, for example, D. G. Mason, "The Tyranny of the Bar-Line," *The New Music Review and Church Music Review*, 9 (1909–10), 31–3.
49 J. I. Paderewski, *Paderewski Plays Chopin, Volume II*, Pearl GEMM CD9397, 1990, track 10 (recorded May 1923); G. Novaes, *Guiomar Novaes: Chopin Mazurkas*, Vox PL7920, 1954, track 4.
50 *Friedrich Chopins Werke* (Leipzig: Breitkopf and Härtel [1879]), vol. 3, 22.
51 I created Figure 3.14c using an online scape plot tool (www.mazurka.org.uk/software/online/scape/) after tracking the recordings at the beat level in Sonic Visualiser.
52 This term was coined in R. S. Parks, "Structure and Performance: Metric and Phrase Ambiguities in the Three Chamber Sonatas," in J. R. Briscoe (ed.), *Debussy in Performance* (Yale University Press, 1999), 280.
53 C. Hasty, *Meter as Rhythm* (Oxford University Press, 1997).
54 J. Roeder, Review of *Meter as Rhythm* by C. Hasty, *Music Theory Online*, 4.4 (1998), paragraph 2.4.
55 Hasty, *Meter as Rhythm*, 84–86.
56 Ibid., 106.
57 Ibid., 104.
58 Ibid., 88–89.
59 Ibid., 133–35.
60 Ibid., 87–88.
61 Others have drawn extensively on Hasty's work in analyses of jazz, popular music, and world music recordings. Two recent examples: N. Murphy, " 'The Times They Are A-Changin' ': Flexible Meter and Text Expression in 1960s and 70s Singer-Songwriter Music" (Ph.D. dissertation, University of British Columbia, 2015), esp. 40–49 and 121–201; J. Roeder, "Formative Process of Durational Projection in 'Free Rhythm' World Music," in R. Wolf, S. Blum, and C. Hasty (eds.), *Thought and Play in Musical Rhythm* (Oxford University Press, 2019).
62 This analysis builds on some observations in Dodson, "Metrical Dissonance and Directed Motion," 65–66.
63 I attribute this feeling of a potential hypermeter mainly to the fast tempo and repetitive rhythm in the recording. My expectation of *duple* hypermeter is surely conditioned by the stylistic norms of Romantic piano music in general, and of Chopin's Mazurkas in particular.

64 C. Debussy, *Claude Debussy: The Composer as Pianist*, Pierian 001, 2000, track 14 (recorded November 1913). This recording is explored more fully in A. Dodson, "'So Free as to Seem Improvised': Rhythmic Revisions and Kinetic Form in Debussy's Recording of *D'un cahier d'esquisses*," in T. Popovic (ed.), *Claude Debussys Aufnahmen eigener Klavierwerke* (Stuttgart: Steiner Verlag, forthcoming).

65 For an overview of the form, see R. Howat, *Debussy in Proportion: A Musical Analysis* (Cambridge University Press, 1983), 138–9.

66 Hasty describes this type of attenuation process to be a weak form of denial because in such cases "it is not at all clear 'when' the projected potential . . . becomes exhausted." Hasty, *Meter as Rhythm*, 89.

67 C. Debussy, *D'un cahier d'esquisses*, first edition (Brussels: Schott, 1904).

4 | A Percussionist Understands Rhythm in Five Essays of Exactly 1,000 Words Each Not Including Titles and Subtitles

STEVEN SCHICK

Rhythm as a relational language that reflects the tension between an event and its surrounding temporal context. There are no complex rhythms. The difficulty of maintaining rhythms whose ratios feature large denominators.

Imagine that you are sitting on a grassy slope near a cliff rising above the sea. In the distance, an approaching cloud formation threatens rain. You wait, lost in thought. The first raindrop surprises you. How do you react?

Does the first drop feel cold or heavy? Do you feel at one with nature, or are you more concerned with the future of your cashmere sweater? Do you feel inspired? Annoyed? Or, do you shake your head in exasperation and mutter, "That drop is late!"

The last question almost certainly doesn't come to mind. Concepts like early or late – the lingua franca of rhythm – rely not just on a single event, but upon the relationship between that event and an external, often communal, temporal context. Temporal context, whether it is sensed, conducted, or intoned on a metronome, establishes an expectation in timing such that we can say whether a note (or raindrop) is early, late, or right on time; downbeat, upbeat, or syncopate. In particular, those terms of rhythmic art describe the tension inherent in expectation and make the difference between playing a rhythm and merely articulating a point in time.

So, the mastery of rhythm – if mastery is the right word for something that is primarily felt rather than measured – lies in the intelligent management of the tension inherent in expectation. This is a truly complex feat, involving ears, mind, and muscles in a feedback loop that is both prognosticative (Is this the right moment to play?) but also retrospective (Was I early or late, and do I need to adjust so the next note will arrive when I want it to?). If playing even a single note on time is this complex, then this musician refuses to accept a term like *complex rhythm* (since all relationships and therefore all rhythms are complex). And though I have been tasked to comment on complex contemporary rhythms in these pages, I will begin by observing that there is no qualitative difference in complexity between playing triplets (a ratio of 3:2 faster than the unity value of the surrounding temporal context) and a seemingly more difficult rhythm like 7:5.

So, instead of focusing on words like *complexity*, let's examine the *quality of tension* between an event and its surrounding temporal context. At its most basic level, this is unproblematic. A note that arrives on time or a succession of notes that adheres exactly to an ongoing pulse can be thought of as "unity," or 1:1. Set your metronome on 100 and play along at the same speed. You are at unity. A succession of notes that moves 50 percent faster than unity reaches a speed of 3:2, or 150 beats per minute. In the relational language of rhythm, we call them triplets. A ratio of 4:3 produces a speed of a bit more than 133, but most musicians would know this better as a sequence of dotted notes. Broadly speaking, the higher the denominator of the fraction when reduced to its simplest form, the greater the relational distance from unity values and the greater the amount of temporal (and therefore rhythmic) tension produced. The point here is not to mystify the rhythms we know by parsing them as ratios – please continue to think of triplets as such rather than as the polyrhythm 3:2 – but to demystify them. If everything is a ratio, then, in principle, 1:1 is not fundamentally more complex than 15:7, but simply describes a different quality of tension relative to a given unity value.

Or you might wish to think in harmonic terms: a triplet has the same relationship to rhythmic unity that a perfect fifth has to its root. The sequence of dotted rhythms has the same ratio as a perfect fourth. This might be useful if, the next time you struggle with a rhythm like 15:8, you think of it as a just-tuned major seventh – nearly but not quite at unity.

"Tuning rhythms" can be a useful strategy because arriving early to a downbeat is like playing sharp. Simply play the rhythm a little "flatter" (or later, if you will) and you'll be right. And, like intonation, there are many versions of correctness. A just-tuned major third above C will be fourteen cents lower than a tempered major third. Both are thirds, but they behave differently in context. A just-tuned third feels settled to me, while a high seventh – a favorite for leading tones everywhere – seems skittish, unsatisfied. Triplets, quintuplets, and backbeats have many of the same variations of behavior, though in the rhythmic space, we think of these small variations in rhythmic behavior not as intonation but rather as "feel." Imagine these distinctions as the difference between a Charlie Watts backbeat resting firmly in the pocket of a groove and an edgy, spring-loaded David Lang rhythm.

Understanding rhythms as ratios – and therefore as the creation and management of rhythmic tension – provides a useful strategy in performance. A performer who sees a 7:5 in a musical score might start by conceiving of it as 1.4 times faster than unity speed. (Simply divide 7 by 5 on your calculator.) If you already know how to play triplets (1.5 times faster than unity value) and you can manage dotted eighth notes (1.3 times faster), then 7:5 slides neatly in between.

Here the difficulty is not so much *finding* but *maintaining* the rhythm. It is fairly easy to see why. If you play 1:1, every note you play aligns with the external template and is completely supported by the rhythmic pulse you are counting to yourself. A value of 3:2 means that you align with the unity pulse every other note – still well supported. If you play 7:5, that means you align only every five notes; 13:7 aligns only every seven notes, and so on. The longer the cycle, the more chance there is to drift between points of alignment. And, for a musician wishing to explore these kinds of ratios, the more important it becomes to internalize cycles of varying lengths.

Learning in cycles. The pan-rhythmic spectrum. The transaction between the firmness of cycles and the fluidity of rhythms.

Ratios provide a simple means to understand the speed of a rhythm. But they are less useful in actual musical performance, unless relative speed is the only criterion. See Ben Johnston's *Knocking Piece* (1962), for example. However, in much contemporary music, rhythmic speed aligns with or rubs against a temporal cycle.

The relationship between cycle (the extent to which the underlying external temporal context can be seen to have recurring patterns) and any given musical event that inflects it (the placement of a note on strong or weak beats) is what most people think of as rhythm. Your hard-partying cousin raises a fist during his wedding dance because a musical event (Van Halen power chord) aligns with a nodal point in the musical cycle (end of the solo; beginning of the verse). The coincidence is powerful and synesthetic: alignment between rhythmic event and cycle produces both a (potentially dangerous) muscular response and a zap of euphoria.

Powerful experiences in rhythm release powerful emotions. But no one is moved by the correct execution of 7:5. We are moved because the perception of cycles is deeply embedded in the human psyche. And, when we hear or play a rhythm that excites, transgresses, or clarifies a cycle, strong emotion often results. In a moment of profound connection with my father, I remember walking with him out onto the plowed black earth of our Iowa farm, quickly sniff the warming spring air, and in one of the greatest examples of rhythmic improvisation I have seen, say, "It's time to plant." He was like a great jazz musician with his metronome set on $\frac{1}{525,600}$.

Human beings, migrating birds, and animals with memory all feel deeply the long cycles of sun and moon; of mating season and endocrine system. We know that the good movies usually come out in December, and we understand the inevitability of D major at the end of Beethoven's Ninth Symphony. We intuit the cyclical architecture of tragedy when Anna Karenina meets Vronsky at a train station after someone has thrown herself to the tracks and then, several hundreds of pages later, is herself crushed by a train.

These are powerfully felt cycles. But unarticulated cycles, like all balanced systems, create no heat. To make art, cycles must be articulated by events, which parse them on a human scale. Note that large planting/harvest cycles consist of multiple mini-cycles of cultivation, detasseling, and irrigation. D major returns many times in sub-articulations of Beethoven's Ninth before we arrive at the final cadence. Articulation of large cycles through deliberate rhythmic interventions is the trade of all good artists and farmers.

It's a complex process, because even identical points of time function very differently as rhythm depending on the quality of a given musical event. Take the thousand-plus downbeats in our Beethoven symphony. On one level, they're equal – each is theoretically the strongest beat of the measure. But a downbeat at an important change of harmony, or another marked by a timpani *fortissimo* (note how often these are simultaneous) is not just a different sound than a less profiled downbeat; it is also a different rhythm. Musical texture, sonic weight, harmony, and intonation comprise a non-temporal component of rhythm. And, since a rhythmic event is a point of inflection within a temporal cycle, variations in the vibrancy of that inflection create not just different sounds but also, in essence, different rhythms. The resulting "pan-rhythmic" spectrum, whereby texture also functions as rhythm, rhythm as intonation, polyphony as harmony, and so forth, extrapolates the relational tension between cycle and event to include sound, impact, and emotion.

To practice hearing cycles and not just points-in-time, examine the first measure of Brian Ferneyhough's *Bone Alphabet* (1992). An upper line consisting of 64th notes and dotted 32nd notes provides a duple template – cycle, if you will – against which is heard a syncopated line at $\frac{10}{12}$ of the duple speed. Two learning strategies come to mind: (1) create a composite grid on which all notes of both rhythmic strands can be found (see the discussion below of verticality) or (2) reconceive the lower line at a tempo which is $\frac{10}{12}$ of the basic speed. If the duple line is at MM54, then the 10:12 line is at 45. But neither a flattened composite that results from the first strategy, nor an unproblematized restatement of rhythm as tempo captures any of the relational tension between a pre-existing rhythmic cycle and an activation of that cycle through rhythmic events.

Try first hearing the repeated 10:12 phrase as the cycle of two dotted eighths. Set your metronome on 36, the speed of the dotted eighth, and then sing the line against it. As you do so, sense not just the speed of the rhythm but also where it feels grounded as downbeat within the cycle and where it is forwardly directed, like an upbeat. You will begin to hear not just speed but also the tension of a rhythm against its cycle. Now play only the first beats of the two cycles (eighths and dotted eighths) and hear how the asymmetrically overlaid cycles create temporal tension even before you add the details of the rhythms themselves. Try to retain this underlying sense of cycle when you play the entire rhythm in final performance.

Two interstitial topics: We use the term *cycle* because of its profound extra-musical associations. However, we'll now refer to cycles when they are expressed in musical time as *meter.*

Second, the relationship between cycle and rhythm is fundamentally transactional: the cycle is fixed and repetitive while the rhythms within it are malleable and interchangeable. Cycles don't change to accommodate rhythms; it's the reverse. To explore, I am giving this chapter a rigid temporal architecture – five essays of exactly 1,000 words each – within which to express a fluid set of ideas. Weighing whether to discard something in order to add something else, I feel the tension of transaction and see that this project, like so much in life, is fundamentally rhythmic.

Anchoring and surging in polyrhythmic lines. Cyclical and non-cyclical polyrhythms. The beauties of guessing. A solution in behavior.

Every rhythm is a polyrhythm. Even a simple pulse is tied to an underlying sense of time and creates a polyrhythm of 1:1. With more interesting polyrhythmic lines – ones with higher denominators – the principle is the same. And, whether points of coincidence between rhythm and underlying pulse are proximate (1:1, in which every note aligns with its underlying pulse) or distant (10:12 which aligns every 12 beats), every polyrhythm functions both vertically and horizontally. Verticality anchors the polyrhythm to its underlying pulse; horizontality describes temporal surges within the rhythmic line and creates tension within the line.

When two rhythms occupy the same period of time – what I'll call a *cyclical polyrhythm* since both rhythms are anchored to the same cycle – verticality is straightforward. In Example 4.1, the indication 10:12 means that twelve 64th notes (or three 16ths) are divided simultaneously into

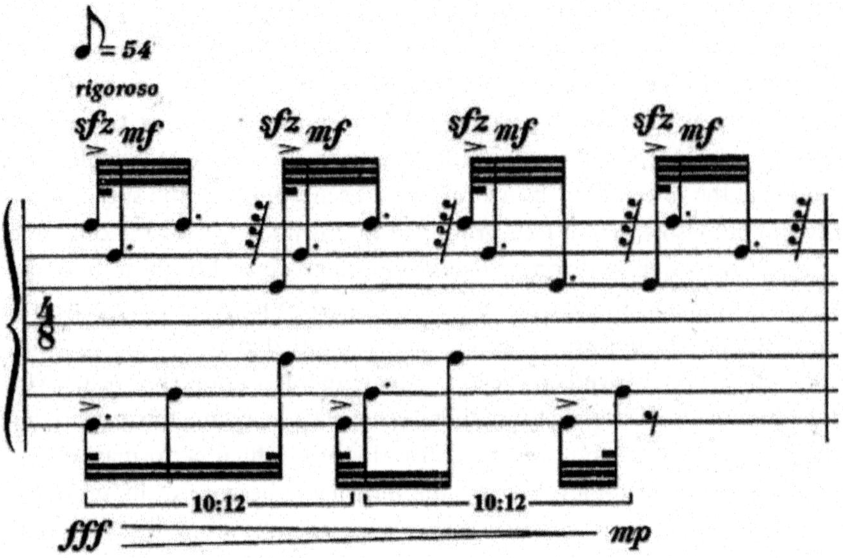

4.1 Ferneyhough, *Bone Alphabet*, m. 1.

divisions of 12 (in the upper line) and 10 (in the lower line) subdivisions. To locate both 10:12 lines, multiply 10 and 12 to create a grid of 120. Then make two groupings of the 120 points: one every 10 units and another every 12, dividing the 120 into 12 and 10 equal parts, respectively. Every note in both rhythms can be found on this grid. Note that in a grid this large, I number the beats starting with zero, so that major subdivisions fall on 10, 20, 30, and so on, rather than 11, 21, 31.

Some polyrhythmic lines are not multiple divisions of the same period. See Example 4.2, from *Bone Alphabet* for a polyrhythm that does not have identical beginning and ending points. By contrast to Example 4.1, this is a *non-cyclical polyrhythm*. The lower 6:7 line begins its second cycle on the eighth 64th note of the measure, while the upper line begins its second cycle on the ninth 64th note. Without aligned cycles, the simple grid described above does not work. One could design a very large grid in which each line relates to a third, unstated, line – in this case a 64th note subdivision. But the grid would be so large as to be unusable. In a further complication, the 4:3, a *nested polyrhythm* within the 6:7, adds another layer to the creation of a grid.

The solutions here are effective but not exacting. First, I view the nested 4:3 rhythm not as a new rhythm, but as a *surge* in a preexisting one. Play the 6:7 rhythm as a straightforward sextuplet at tempo 46 ($\frac{6}{7}$ of 54), and

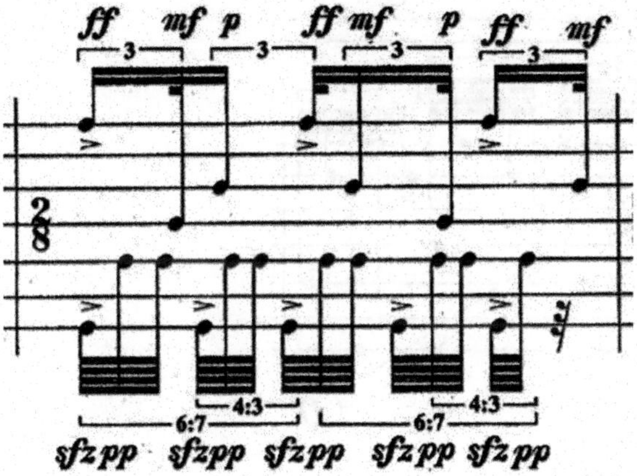

4.2 *Bone Alphabet*, m. 2.
Used with kind permission of C. F. Peters Corp., Henmar Press

then play a simple 4 over the last three notes. It should feel like an inflection of the sextuplet – a surge.

The next step is the correlation of the upper and lower lines – 6:7 and triplets. A global grid that reconciles the two is not possible, so I start by guessing (which is a vastly underutilized strategy in calculating rhythms!). I start with the more detailed line, in this case 6:7, and guess where the triplets might fall. A workable "first draft" of vertical alignments comes quickly. Then, I fine-tune by ear: I toggle mentally between the two lines as I practice the composite and test, by ear, whether the triplets sound accurate, and whether the 6:7 rhythm still has the right kind of surge.

Does guessing feel too irrational an approach for such a seemingly rational problem? For me, precisely how a guess is constructed is of critical importance. If my guess is based upon a secure sense of the rightness of each individual line, and if it accounts for meter in such a way that the tension with a basic pulse(s) (here 54 and 46) inheres in the polyrhythm, then it works very well. A guess like this is how we play the correct rhythm at the beginning of Beethoven's Fifth Symphony, or how we might play the groove at the top of "Ticket to Ride." But as Ronald Reagan said, "Trust and verify." Make a recording or ask for help from a colleague to determine how well you have guessed.

Sometimes the ebbs and flows of nested polyrhythms feel more like variations of behavior than musical performance. Note Example 4.3, measure 7, also from *Bone Alphabet*. The $\frac{1}{8}$ measure is now at tempo 46 – a metric modulation prepared by the 6:7 polyrhythm in measure 2. The

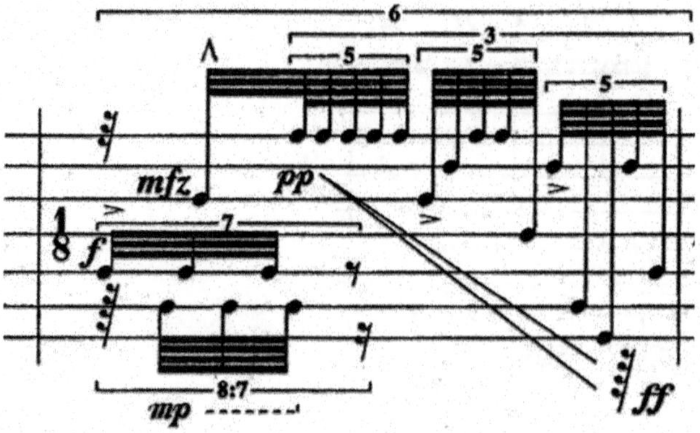

4.3 *Bone Alphabet*, m. 7.
Used with kind permission of C. F. Peters Corp., Henmar Press

outermost polyrhythm subdivides the measure into six parts with a speed of six times faster than the eighth note (thus MM276). The second polyrhythm layer takes the last four sextuple values and divides them into three, slowing their speed to MM207. Practically, this is not unmanageable: simply count two beats at MM276 and switch for three beats to 207. The quintuplets at MM207 produces a final tempo of MM1035 for the individual notes. Percussionists can test their hand speed by playing 32nd notes at tempo 130. That's very close to the limits of playability, especially given that those notes cover the entirety of the seven-instrument set-up.

But there are problems. My conversion of a triply nested polyrhythm into tempo tells you how fast to play, but it doesn't help you coordinate the lower nested polyrhythm, a fascinating simultaneity of 8:7 and 7:8. And it runs contrary to my repeated insinuations that rhythm is always expressed by a tension between rhythm and an underlying pulse. And, with three nested polyrhythms, two of which increase the speed of the basic pulse, and a third (the sextuple marking) that slows the pulse, what reasonably should we consider as the basic pulse: 46? 207? 1035?

So, let's try this as *behavior*. The sextuple subdivision – the one that slows the pulse – might feel grounded, *pesante*, restrained. Perhaps this is how you play the very first upper staff *mfz* note. By contrast, the fast quintuple subdivisions might feel mercurial, light, or capricious. Remember the panrhythmic spectrum. Rhythm is more than simple location in time; it's behavior, transaction, and tension. A deft solution is always one in which rhythmic and metric parameters are supported in performance by involving texture, weight, and timbre.

Rephrasing Rhythm

At the 60 percent point of this essay, I wonder what I have offered to our conversation about rhythm. We've spoken of rhythm in transactional terms as the tension between an underlying pulse, cycle, or meter and its surface inflections. We touched on the panrhythmic spectrum, whereby rhythm is expressed in both temporal and non-temporal terms. We engaged in some problem solving with cyclical and non-cyclical polyrhythms, and discussed the temporal ebb and flow embedded within nested polyrhythms. But surely you could have figured these things out for yourself!

And, while this is important prefatory material, none of it touches the fundamental concept that rhythm is the musical product of the interface between mind, body, and sound. If that's a definition so broad as to be useless, I take comfort from centuries of musical thinkers who have felt similarly, from Pythagoras, who expressed rhythm as universal and interdependent harmonies, to Karlheinz Stockhausen, whose seminal comments in *Vier Kriterien der Elektronischen Musik* (1973) speak to the relationship between rhythm and tone and annotate one of his most memorable musical moments: the dizzying seven-octave descent of a complex tone and its ultimate dissolution into rhythm in the extraordinary *Kontakte* (1959).

What is clear from Pythagoras, Stockhausen, and others is that rhythm is a physical state of musical material, standing in relation to tone, form, and texture just as ice is a physical state of water related to vapor and liquid water. For many mid-century modernists, searching not just for *an* answer but for *the* answer, treating rhythm as an inseparable component of an inclusive musical continuum was the brave new world. Their vision was a unified temporal field consisting of regular or irregular oscillations, perceived at the upper end of frequency as pitch and at the lower end as form. Rhythm falls in between. They proposed that serial technique, the great equalizer in the realm of pitch, could be applied to rhythm (as *time-point technique* in the language of East Coast Americans) and to form (as *Moment Form* in Stockhausen's nomenclature.)

At its best, rhythmic serial technique provided the mechanics of permutation, in which variations were rooted in a single source code that created consistency. If all rhythms were related to the same set, then they were, by definition, related to each other. (If A=B and B=C, then A=C.) For this listener, this creates a powerful sense of organicity and inevitability in Olivier Messiaen's modal approach to rhythm, but in lesser composers often produces an unappealing uniformity. As tantalizing as a grand unified theory of rhythm might seem, it often fails for the same reason it's not possible to swim in steam. The fundamental material may be the same, but a change of state necessitates a change in usage.

So, we are left with a *koan*: rhythm consists of the same stuff as pitch and form, and comprises with them the pitch-form continuum. But boundaries of rhythm are delimited by perception, which firmly distinguishes it from pitch and form. Take a pitch and gradually slow the speed of the oscillations until we hear discrete impulses. We call this rhythm. And, getting slower yet, soon we can no longer tell whether or not the oscillations are equal. We call this form. On the fast end of the spectrum, our rhythmic sense is limited by the speed of cognition and on the slower end by the capacity of memory.

If rhythm is a property of human perception, then Pythagoras's search for the cosmic origins of music was partly in vain. This also means that our delight at Gérard Grisey's musical rendering of the regular rhythms of distant pulsars in *Le noir de l'étoile* (1990) celebrates not the universality of pulse in the cosmos but the miraculous ability of a human listener to track patterns in time. It turns out that the music of the spheres is really music of the ears.

Most rhythmic patterns fall on the slow side of the spectrum between pitch and form. Even the fastest moments in virtuosic piece like *Bone Alphabet* fall short of the range of audible tone. (A stroke speed of 1035, on the border of playability, is a meager 17.25 cycles per second, not usually audible to humans.) On the slow end of the spectrum, we can track a regular pulse up to a period of around eight seconds (in an utterly unscientific self-study). Here, questions of expectation and foreshadowing, repetition and reformulation emerge. This is the poetry of rhythm: Have we heard this before? When do we expect the next impulse? And, depending on whether this satisfies or derails expectations, what emotional or artistic impact results?

So, rhythm – or at least our perception of it – is ultimately a quality of memory. This works in the aesthetic as well as psycho-acoustic realm. The reason a reassigned downbeat in a Beethoven Scherzo (see practically every symphony!) surprises us lies in memory. We recognize and *remember* the downbeat and then are surprised when it is reassigned. (Beethoven's method adds stress to a weak beat and when he is sure we perceive that as the downbeat, he shows us the true downbeat.) If we did not remember – and consequently develop an expectation – we could not be surprised.

The language of memory – corporeality, aurality, and the creation of and deviation from pattern – is also the language of rhythm. So "rephrasing" rhythm as an aspect of memory leads us gratefully away from the calculations of nested polyrhythms and the anxiety that even very fine musicians feel when faced with thorny non-cyclical polyrhythms. Even though I have made thousands of such calculations and still see the value of accurate solutions to complicated rhythmic problems, I argue that rephrasing rhythm as memory aligns us, as performers, with the mindset of listeners. It informs the late pieces of Morton Feldman, where forgetting is poignant, and governs the vocal/instrumental works of Roger Reynolds and Georges Aperghis. Each contains "complex rhythms," but viewing rhythm as memory, each offers music on a human scale and with human rewards.

Rhythm as Memory

In the last decade of his life, Morton Feldman composed the longest and most evocative pieces of his career. Musicians are advised to know all three of the late trios for flutes, piano and percussion, but to this performer his *For Philip Guston* (1984) is the most beautiful. On the level of rhythm, it is also his most complex. Measures occupy equal physical space, but because the meters are different in each part, vertical alignment rarely equals simultaneity. Without significant calculations, the performers frequently do not know with what notes in the other parts they are to align.

In the age-old trade-off between reading and memory – think of the amount of music and literature committed to memory in the Ancient World due to the lack of written texts – if you cannot track points of alignment by reading the score, you must necessarily remember them. Thus, maintaining the correct rhythmic relationship with your partners in *Guston* means that tempo must be internalized (memorized as an inner

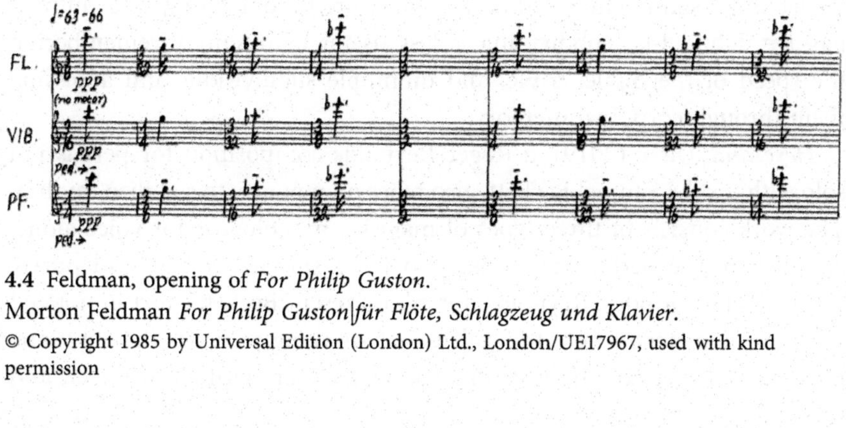

4.4 Feldman, opening of *For Philip Guston*.
Morton Feldman *For Philip Guston|für Flöte, Schlagzeug und Klavier*.

click-track) and rhythm converted scrupulously to physicality (memorized as corporeal impulse). For the percussionist, the $\frac{3}{32}$ note has a shorter stroke than the $\frac{3}{8}$. We know that stroke length varies in response to dynamics and the surface quality of the instrument to be played. But in *For Philip Guston*, where the dynamics are fixed and low, and the instruments, aside from the chimes, do not require radically different stroke types, the corporeal memory of striking is a nearly exact map of rhythm.

In Michael Gordon's *XY* (1998), also from the percussion repertory, corporeal memory works similarly in the service of rhythmic accuracy. If you are having trouble with your 6:5, try holding the stick playing quintuplets at a height that is $\frac{6}{5}$ greater than the sextuplet stick. Then play with the same stroke speed. Other instrumentalists and vocalists will devise their own versions of these mechanical strategies.

On the level of form, we engage a different sort of rhythmic memory. Major points of arrival in tonal forms are so far apart that composers tag them with memorable characteristics – a burst of instrumental color or a memorable theme. However, in *For Philip Guston*, such markers are largely absent, and with a duration of nearly five hours, even the performers can forget where they are in the form. In Feldman, the poetry of remembering is contradictory: on the local level the execution of rhythm is a matter of remembering the speeds of notes, but on a global level the received sense of form is often the product of forgetting.

Note the "irrational meters" in Josh Levine's *Four Places, Many More Times* (2011). By irrational, we refer to measures that contain subdivisions that do not add up exactly to the denominator of the time signature. Measure 134 in Example 4.5 is four quintuplets in length. Measure 138 is $\frac{2}{3}$ of a half note. Ferneyhough and many others would name these measures as a $\frac{4}{10}$ measure and $\frac{2}{6}$ measure, respectively. (There are ten eighth-note quintuplets in a measure; four of them make a $\frac{4}{10}$ measure. A quarter-note triplet is a "sixth note" – thus a $\frac{2}{6}$ measure.) Conducting this difficult passage, I find that subdividing is less useful than simply remembering the speed of the duple, triple, and quintuple subdivisions and accessing them through corporeal memory.

Here and There (2019), a Roger Reynolds composition for percussion solo with text by Samuel Beckett, also relies on memory to stabilize rhythm. The work consists of three types of material: monologues for voice alone, arias where the performer speaks and plays simultaneously, and purely instrumental episodes. Reynolds doesn't represent Beckett's text in notated rhythms or meters – here the cadence of speaking provides the rhythmic template. Conversely, the instrumental passages are written in meter, and

4.5 Levine, from *Four Places, Many More Times.*
Used with kind permission of the composer, Josh Levine

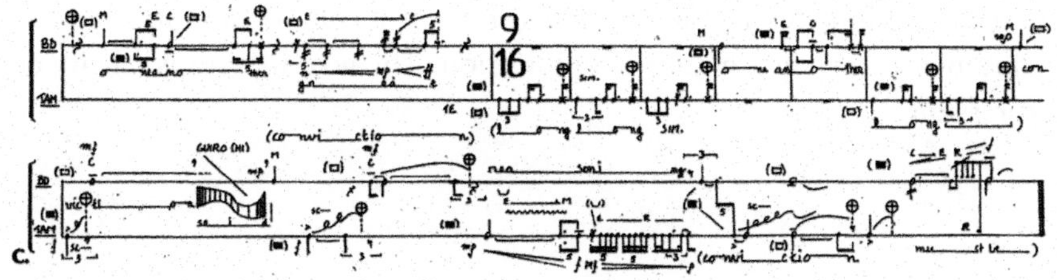

4.6 Reynolds, from *Here and There.*
Used with kind permission of C. F. Peters Corp., Henmar Press

in these moments Reynolds ingeniously provides light cursive writing below rhythms. These words (unspoken in performance) are drawn from the Beckett text, and provide the rhythmic architecture of the instrumental passages. In order to remember the rhythms, just remember the text! (See Example 4.6.)

An ideal performance of *Here and There* melds words with music in a fertile in-between world (*zwischen immer und nie*, "between always and never," to use the words of novelist André Aciman). So rhythmic sense, like everything in the piece, is rooted in the memory of both words and sounds.

In practice, I found I could quickly solidify the rhythm of the text, which then served as a platform not just for consistency of delivery but also as a rhythmic template for the rest of the piece. Text became the "memory palace" of *Here and There*: a place where the linkage between spoken word and instrumental sounds is stabilized by a shared temporal memory.

Here and There was a recent confirmation, but we intuit that many rhythmic problems are really memory problems. You can play 16th notes at MM60 without the need for a calculator because you have done so repeatedly. You *remember* not only how fast they are, but also the quality of tension between them and the underlying pulse. You might have difficulty with 13:5, because you have comparatively little experience with that rhythm. You have not yet memorized it. In its many guises, memory is an organizing principle: in an ethical life (see St. Thomas) or as the way we know what to buy at the store (see Hermann Ebbinghaus's studies in the degradation of short term-memory). But memory achieves a kind of apex moment in the execution of rhythm in which corporeal, aural, mechanical, and even visual modes of memory collude.

Temporal tension directs the utility of both memory and rhythmic sense toward the future. Memory is not about the past any more than rhythm is about the present. Both require that we metabolize past and present time to give direction to the future. Whether that future is remembering a wedding toast or the impetus to lift a mallet (or bow) to play a note in a nested quintuplet is merely a matter of application. The goal in both is felicity of expression.

5 A Different Kind of Virtuosity

RUSSELL HARTENBERGER

My first encounter with what has come to be known as minimalist music was at a rehearsal of Steve Reich's iconic composition, *Drumming*, in his downtown New York City loft in the early spring of 1971. Reich was still composing the piece and was teaching it to the assembled musicians by rote. Two pianists, a woodwind player, and Reich – the only one of the four with percussion training – were playing on a line of eight stand-mounted bongo drums and striking them with wooden timbale sticks. Normally, drummers play on one pair of tightly tuned bongos with their hands and they hold the drums between their knees, so I was surprised to see four pairs of bongos, tuned to precise pitches, being played in this manner. However, my surprise turned to curiosity, and even a touch of bewilderment, when I watched and heard what they were playing on these drums.

Two players built up a rhythmic pattern one attack at a time, and once a full, coherent pattern was established, chaos ensued. Out of the confusion of seemingly wild and random stick attacks an intriguing composite pattern emerged. When this new rhythmic combination was established, a third player entered playing patterns that created melodic fragments on four pitched drums. Reich, who was the only person not playing bongos, began singing similar melodic phrases into a microphone placed near the drums using vocables that imitated the attack sound of sticks on bongos.

I was intrigued by this music, to say the least, and agreed to join the nascent Steve Reich and Musicians ensemble. At this point in my musical life I had completed two degrees in classical percussion performance and was enrolled in the Ph.D. program in World Music at Wesleyan University. My classical music training had not prepared me for the new concepts that I began to experience in the Reich ensemble, but I soon noticed similarities between Reich's musical ideas and the African, Indian, and Indonesian music I was studying at Wesleyan. I realized that in order to perform this new musical style successfully, I would have to merge my facility in classical music performance with the skills that I was beginning to develop in my world music lessons; in fact, my definition of virtuosity evolved to include proficiency in these techniques. As a result, my view of virtuosic performance in pulse-based music grew to incorporate pulse, time feel/inner pulse, repetition, endurance, concentration, metric/perceptual ambiguity, rhythmic expressivity, and an enhanced sense of ensemble. In this chapter, I will describe how each of these components is essential in developing virtuosity in the performance of pulse-based music.

Pulse

An element that has become a distinctive structural component in Western classical music in the past fifty years is pulse – specifically, pulse independent of meter. Terry Riley's *In C* (1964), the composition that jump-started the minimalist movement, is performed with a pianist pulsing on the instrument's top two Cs throughout the piece. *In C* is made up of fifty-three modules of varying length through which performers move at their own pace. Robert Carl, in his book *Terry Riley's In C*, explains that the "major stumbling block" in early rehearsals for the piece "was rhythm; as soon as the divergence of modules began, it became difficult to maintain a common tempo or metric reference point, and the work fell apart." Steve Reich was a participant in these rehearsals and Carl quotes Reich as saying, "once a drummer always a drummer, I said we kind of need a drummer here, but since drums would be inappropriate, what about use the pianos; so Jeanie [Brechan] played some high Cs just to keep us together, and Terry said, 'Let's give it a try' or something like that, and we tried it and *voila* everyone was together." Carl concludes, "And so the Pulse was born."[1]

Reich began including a pulse in his own compositions, and other composers followed suit. To delineate the pulse, Reich used various instruments: maracas in *Four Organs* (1970) and later in *Tehillim* (1981); a pulse clave in *Music for Pieces of Wood* (1973); combinations of pulse played on marimbas, xylophones, pianos, strings, winds, voices, and maracas in *Music for 18 Musicians* (1976); and even the handles of percussion mallets tapped together in portions of *Sextet* (1984) and *The Desert Music* (1984). Reich continues to employ a pulse in his compositions, both explicitly and implicitly, including the appropriately named *Pulse* written in 2015. Two other prominent composers who began writing pulse-based music in the 1960s and 1970s are Philip Glass, who used repeated arpeggiated figures and an additive rhythmic process in his early compositions to outline a steady pulse, and John Adams, who used pulsing, repetitive cell structures in his solo piano work *Phrygian Gates* (1977) and placed the pulse in the wood block in his orchestral work *Short Ride on a Fast Machine* (1986).

Classical musicians are not generally trained to play strict pulse-based music. Orchestral players, for example, develop an association with pulse from the historical development of the repertoire and learn to adjust regular attacks in music according to conductors' motions, the amorphous attacks of entire sections of strings, the varied articulation of wind and brass players, and the more precise attacks of harp, piano, and percussion instruments. Although *In C* was written for a large chamber ensemble rather than a symphony orchestra, the performers face the same problem of creating a unified approach to attack placement and ensemble coherence. However, musicians who perform *In C* have the additional issue of achieving this amid a web of overlapping rhythmic patterns. The person who plays the upper two Cs on the piano keyboard throughout *In C* must keep the pulse as steady as possible while being swayed by other players as they wind their way through the work's fifty-three modules. This responsibility is not unlike that of a jazz drummer and bass player working together to outline a rhythmic grid while soloists improvise freely but with a constant sense of the pulse. The pianist in the Riley work has no one else with whom to maintain a steady pulse and must rely on some internal mechanism to keep playing regularly for an hour or more.

Time Feel/Inner Pulse

At a rehearsal of Steve Reich's *Six Pianos* (1973) for a 2007 concert in Toronto, pianist Gregory Oh, who was playing the piece for the first time, remarked to percussionist Bob Becker, who had played it many times with the Reich ensemble, "How can you play with such steadiness but appear so motionless?" Becker replied, "Because I have a sense of inner pulse." Inner pulse is something we can all develop and is an ability that is essential in the performance of pulse-based music. Becker was trained as a classical musician and like most percussionists has played forms of pulse-based music in various non-orchestral formats. His sense of inner pulse was heightened, however, by his experiences with West African drumming and North Indian *tabla* drumming.

West African drumming ensemble music is structured around a cyclic rhythmic pattern played on an iron bell. The twelve-unit cycle of the most commonly used bell patterns can be felt with a steady pulse of 1, 2, 3, 4, 6, or 12, although the drummers, singers, and dancers generally perform with a pulse sense of four within the twelve-unit cycle in order to stay together and have a unified feel. Ghanaian master drummer Abraham Adzenyah, the West African drum teacher at Wesleyan with whom both Becker and I studied, used the terms *hidden beat* and *invisible conductor* to describe the performance subtleties that are required to play this music correctly. The hidden beat is the inner pulse that is felt communally by all the performers, and the invisible conductor (one of my favorite descriptive phrases) is the time feel sense that is generated in the music.

Tabla drummers of North India, as well as their counterparts in South India, use an additive, or sometimes subtractive, system of rhythmic construction in creating complex mathematical rhythmic patterns. These rhythms are played within a *tala* cycle that establishes a structural framework for the music. The inner pulse for these drummers is an inviolable sense of the *tala* cycle, and their rhythms are placed within and across the cycles. Philip Glass first experienced Indian music when he worked with Ravi Shankar on a soundtrack for the film *Chappaqua* in Paris in the mid-1960s; he later visited India and studied with *tabla* master Alla Rakha. This introduction to a new way to view rhythm had a significant impact on Glass's early musical output. Although he did not adopt the concept of *tala*, Glass did incorporate the idea of cyclic structure in his music. His systematic use of additive rhythms is most clearly seen in *1+1* (1968) and *Two Pages* (1969). In the score of *1+1*, Glass wrote two rhythmic units: (a) two sixteenth notes and an eighth note, and (b) an eighth note. In his instructions in the score, he stated that "*1+1* is realized by combining the above two units in continuous, regular arithmetic progressions." In *Two Pages*, Glass wrote two, three, and four eighth-note groupings with varying numbers of repeats. Wes York, in an analysis of *Two Pages* in his essay "Form and Process" (1981), writes, "Ultimately, the structure of *Two Pages* can be understood as first, the exposition and juxtaposition of two sets of opposing processes, and then, the coordination of all shapes which both emerge from, and reflect back on, those processes. . . . With respect to the various processes at work one finds two types which are responsible for creating motion and change within the composition. One of these is a subtractive process; the other is additive."[2]

In *Les Moutons de Panurge* (1969), composer Frederic Rzewski uses the additive/subtractive process to the extreme. The piece begins with any number of musicians playing the notated score in a sequence of 1, 1-2, 1-2-3, 1-2-3-4, and so on until reaching note 65. They repeat the complete cycle of 65 notes, then begin subtracting notes from the beginning: 2 through 65, 3 through 65, 4 through 65, and so on until reaching 65 alone. Even though Rzewski allows for errors on the part of the musicians in sequencing the notes, he is clear that a pulse must be established and maintained by all players.

In the works of Glass and Rzewski described above, there is no explicit pulse played by any instrument and the success of the performance depends on a sense of pulse felt by the performers. While expertise in non-Western music is not an imperative for Western musicians attempting to play these compositions, a familiarity with the additive process provides a level of comfort in keeping a steady pulse while navigating the requirements of the scores. As with Becker in his performance of *Six Pianos*, experience with non-Western music and the sense of inner pulse in the midst of a quilt-work of pulse options helps Western-trained classical musicians play pulse-based music with confidence.

Jazz is also primarily a pulse-based music, and great jazz musicians have this same sense and control of inner pulse. Drummer Kenny Clarke was influential in creating the bebop form of jazz. He changed the style of jazz drumming by moving the basic cymbal pattern from the hi-hat cymbal to the ride cymbal, thus freeing his left hand to play fills on the snare drum. He then played syncopated accents on the bass drum instead of delineating each beat of the meter, thereby creating a flow to the music. Prior to Clarke's innovations, jazz drummers played the bass drum on every beat so the other musicians could hear where the time was in each measure. Clarke's random bass drum bombs, as they were called, and his ride cymbal rhythm, obscured the sense of barline and created a feeling of longer phrases stretching over several measures at a time. Clarke was able to create this flow by keeping a sense of time in his head when he played. In an interview with Helen Oakley Dance in 1977, Clarke remarked that musicians in his band complained and said, "Kenny keeps breakin' up the time. Why doesn't he keep four beats on the bass drum?" Clarke replied, "If you're playing, the tempo should be in your head. Don't depend on me. Depend on yourself. Because if you're playing music, the tempo you're playing in is in your head."[3]

Steve Reich has often said he admired Clarke's time feel and that he tries to achieve this same feel in his own music. In a conversation with me in 2003, Reich explained, "That feeling of time and time sense is getting it 'right' which might show up on an oscilloscope as 'slightly wrong.' A lot of very good players lack that magic because they are very concentrated on being right . . . some people have that quality of magic in their playing and others just don't – but you know it when you hear it."

Time feel is an essential ingredient in the performance and appreciation of jazz as well as in many kinds of pulse-based music. A performer's ability to control attack placement in relation to a steady pulse becomes an expressive element in the music. When an ensemble has a unified time feel, it can create the lilting sense of "magic time" that Reich admires.

Repetition

In her book titled *On Repeat: How Music Plays the Mind*, Elizabeth Hellmuth Margulis writes, "In a famous essay, [Gilles] Deleuze references [David] Hume to the effect that 'repetition changes nothing in the object repeated, but does change something in the mind which contemplates it.' Deleuze identifies repetition as a phenomenon well-suited to exposing the elements that the mechanisms of perception bring to an experience over and above the elements that literally exist in the world." Margulis continues, "Since two iterations are never precisely repetitions in their deepest essence – they're composed of different atoms or occur at different time points – it is perception that abstracts both a relationship of shared identity and a relationship of difference. At a minimum, a repeated element will sound different from its initial presentation by virtue of coming later and having been heard before."[4]

In the music of Adams, Glass, Reich, Riley, and Rzewski, repeating the same pattern for a long period of time can be perceptually interesting for the player, but it is also fraught with challenges. For the performer, nothing should change in the pattern that is to be repeated because it is the musician's job to present a soundscape that allows something to change in the mind of the listener who contemplates the music. The performer is the facilitator, and as such must find a way to control muscle memory in order to articulate each repetition similarly, yet keep mental control.

In West African drumming, musicians who play the drum and bell parts that form the accompaniment to the master drum, singers, and dancers repeat their patterns for extremely long stretches of time. At a harvest festival celebration in a Ga village near Accra during the summer I spent in Ghana in 1971, I witnessed two bell players playing the same interlocking pattern throughout the night (although the two original players were relieved by others as the hours passed). But even under normal performance circumstances, a Ghanaian drummer might repeat the same pattern for an hour or more.

Abraham Adzenyah instructs his students to move their bodies in order to transmit the right feeling while playing repeated patterns on the drums. He also teaches them to hear checkpoints in the music so they know how to recover if their mental control falters and they stray from their patterns. These same instructions apply to the performance of repetitive, pulse-based Western music. The performers must first repeat the assigned pattern until muscle memory begins to take over. Body movements, in this case, cannot be excessive, but subtle motions can be utilized to facilitate muscle memory. Once the pattern is secure, the players can expand their sonic perception to hear connections between the patterns they are playing and other patterns that they hear; in particular, the players can locate points of coincidence in the composite pattern relationships. These checkpoints add security by indicating where to get back on track if a mistake is made.

Early minimalist music moves from event to event, so performers are relieved of the necessity of counting numbers of repeats; they have to know the overall structure of the piece and then pay attention as the process unfolds. This frees their minds from the restriction of keeping track of the number of repeats and allows them to become immersed in the musical details of the performance style. The performers learn to play their patterns as evenly as possible to enable listeners to hear a seemingly unchanging stasis in different ways. In other words, the listeners' minds are allowed, and in fact encouraged, to hear something change.

Endurance

This repetition of the same pattern for several minutes creates an endurance problem for the performers. String players are accustomed to playing almost continuously throughout an hour-long symphony, chamber piece, or solo work. However, in this conventional kind of music they vary their musical patterns, dynamics, articulation, and other musical expressions. Shem Guibbory, violinist in the early rehearsals and performances of *Music for 18 Musicians*, said:

> The violin repertoire is nothing if not virtuosic. It's virtuosic in terms of quantity of notes, the variety of expression, vastness of registers - full four octaves - articulation with the bow, double stops, scores of issues. But with [Reich's] music ... the requirements were for repetition. ...To make my violin part happen within the group ... and with the power that you guys in the percussion could deliver, I had to develop an incredible efficiency of motion and the ability to let my spirit sustain it throughout the entire work.[5]

Audrey Wright, a violinist commenting on her preparation to play *Music for 18 Musicians* for the first time, said she did not realize "how physically and psychologically demanding it would be, nor how rewarding. With my violinist mentality, I originally scanned the score thinking, 'OK, this is long. But playing some sustained fourths here, a few pages of repeated eighth notes there, and catching a bass clarinet cue once in a while is a piece of cake compared to a Mahler symphony.' . . . As it turns out, it is not a piece of cake." Wright continued:

> One of the greatest challenges as a violinist playing *Music for 18 Musicians* is the physical endurance required of playing repeated eighth notes, ostinato figures, and sustained double-stops. The repeated eighth notes, which can last for up to roughly ten minutes, are like a marathon for the bow arm. These eighth notes are written as double-stops rather than single notes, so it is not only a challenge to produce the same clear tone on down- and up-bows when playing up to tempo, but to keep that tone consistent throughout the dynamic *crescendos* and *decrescendos* which occur over and over like waves. In order to work up bow stamina and consistency for this, I practiced scales and double-stop scales with this stroke for the week leading up to the first rehearsal with an overall goal of continually releasing tension from my right shoulder, elbow, and hand. In this way, I was able to build up the strength I'd need in my bow arm to play this music without muscling through and forcing the sound.[6]

Other string players, wind players, and vocalists have commented on the need to prepare for the physical demands of Reich's music. Even the seemingly simple maraca parts in Reich's compositions create endurance issues. In *Four Organs*, *Music for 18 Musicians*, and *Tehillim*, the maraca player is the pulse-keeper in the ensemble for long periods of time and must play strongly with the maracas placed high in the air in order to produce the desired volume. Gary Schall, who was the regular maraca player in the Reich ensemble, said that prior to performances of these pieces he practiced maracas thirty minutes a day for a month in order to develop stamina.

In playing Reich's music and West African drumming, I use something I call energy-shifting, a technique I developed from practicing yoga postures and doing breathing exercises. I find that it is necessary to have a certain amount of tension while playing in order to produce a strong, centered sound, especially when I have to generate this sound with consistency over long periods of time. In order to prevent tension buildup, I keep up the necessary energy by shifting the tension around in my body. For example, if I feel tension mounting in my wrists, I concentrate on releasing the tightness by focusing my breathing in that area and allowing my arms or another part of my body to absorb the tension. By practicing this technique, I developed the ability to energy-shift quickly and easily.

Musicians often make small changes in technique to help their endurance. Stephanie Chua, a pianist in a 2018 performance of Reich's *Six Pianos* in Toronto, told me that to help with relaxation she uses fingerings that force her to change positions in the middle of a pattern. Sometimes it is a very small physical change like Stephanie made that enables performers to endure long periods of repetition of the same pattern and thus heighten their ability to concentrate on musicality.

Concentration

Repeating a pattern for long periods of time requires physical adaptation, but the hypnotic state it induces in listeners creates a concentration problem for performers. I often find myself succumbing to a trance-like state while playing *In C, Music for 18 Musicians*, *Drumming*, and other pulse-based compositions. In order to enjoy this sensation and still maintain my sense of equilibrium, I use techniques I learned while playing in West African drum ensembles. First, I determine the placement of the general "one" of the ensemble or the beginning of the most audible phrase, and I place my part accordingly. I then relate the pattern I am playing to other patterns that are easily discernible. Finally, I find checkpoints in the music that are easy to detect so I can return to my proper rhythmic alignment if I happen to stray off course. When these elements are in place, I feel secure enough to allow my mind to enjoy the mesmerizing aspects of the music. I rely on my muscle memory to perform the many repetitions of my pattern, but I periodically check in mentally to make sure I am playing correctly.

Commenting on his concerns in performing Reich's *Six Pianos*, Gregory Oh said, "The challenge for the performer is managing two states of being: one must be conscious of the notes, the precision of the notes and the time and pacing and fitting in, while simultaneously suppressing any thoughts of control or ego. Rather than 'Just Do It,' it's more like 'Just Let It Happen.' The biggest danger in this piece is getting in one's own way."[7]

To keep from "getting in one's own way," some performers may find that practices such as yoga, tai chi, or meditation are helpful in developing the ability to concentrate. These disciplines train their practitioners to block out unnecessary thoughts and focus on breathing and staying grounded. However, it is important for the performers to maintain awareness of the form of the compositions. It is incumbent on the musicians to hear and understand the progression of events in order to move from one section to the next in proper sequence. All these factors are important in maintaining concentration when performing music that frequently shifts the player's sense of perception.

Metric/Perceptual Ambiguity

In his performing directions that accompany the score to *In C*, Riley states, "The group should aim to merge into a unison at least once or twice during the performance. At the same time, if the players seem to be consistently too much in the same alignment of a pattern, they should try shifting their alignment by an eighth note or quarter note with what's going on in the rest of the ensemble." This shift of eighth-note alignment occurs early in the piece in modules 4 and 5. Each of the modules consists of three ascending eighth notes, E, F, G, but module 4 is an eighth rest followed by the three eighth notes and module 5 begins with the three eighth notes followed by an eighth rest. In his instructions, Riley further encourages this ambiguity when he says, "Each pattern can be played in unison or canonically in any alignment with itself or with its neighboring patterns. One of the joys of IN C is the interaction of the players in polyrhythmic combinations that spontaneously arise between patterns. Some quite fantastic shapes will arise and disintegrate as the group moves through the piece when it is properly played." Riley's intentional pulse displacement allows the listener (and performer) to hear the same composite patterns differently.

A rhythm by itself can be intriguing, but when it is heard against a pulse or another rhythm it can become metrically ambiguous. The metric implications of standard notation in Western music, such as strong impulse at the beginning of a measure, are replaced by options for the listener. Rhythmic groupings and pulse placement are created by the listener, allowing the same music to be heard differently as the listener's mind changes its perceptual vantage point. David Locke, author of the chapter on rhythm in West African music in this volume, coined the term *Gestalt* flip to describe the sensation of hearing a rhythmic pattern one way in relation to a pulse and then changing perception of the same pattern to hear it a new way in relation to a different pulse.

Reich's use of canons played on like instruments creating interlocking composite patterns makes it problematic for the musicians to tell who is playing the parts that they hear. This is especially true in *Drumming* when players facing each other across bongo drums see their sticks moving in conjunction with their playing partner but can have trouble determining whose sticks are making which sounds. Leslie Tilley, in her chapter on Balinese gamelan in this book, describes a similar effect in Balinese gamelan playing when she writes, "Many non-Balinese musicians are first drawn to Balinese music … because of a distinctly Balinese brand of interlocking, where a melody or rhythm is seamlessly shared between two or more performers such that the resultant composite is a single, smooth strand of music. One often cannot discern which musician has performed which note in an interlocking passage; the perceptual effect is of a group of musicians each playing the entire passage in perfect synchrony, much faster than humanly possible."[8]

In the *amadinda* xylophone music of Uganda, musicians play separate patterns on either side of a twelve-note xylophone, alternating their attacks. To achieve the virtuosity required, both players feel their pulses as downbeats. In *Music for 18 Musicians*, an on-beat and off-beat pulse is played for most of the composition by pianos, marimbas, and xylophones. Philip Bush, who played in the Reich ensemble for many performances of *Music for 18 Musicians*, was the pianist who played the off-beat pulse. He told me that in order to play the pulse consistently, he had to (*Gestalt*) flip his sense of pulse so that he felt that his off-beat pulse was on the beat. Consequently, Bush heard the entire composition in a parallel universe from most other people.

In Indian music, rhythmic sequences are overlaid across *tala* cycles and inserted within *tala* cycles. The juxtaposition of the irregularity of these rhythms against the regularity of a cycle creates metric ambiguity. Glass uses the process of additive rhythms to create an unexpected conflict with the usual regularity of expectation in Western music. The metric intrigue in all these genres creates perceptual ambiguity for the listener that is first unsettling, but then becomes aesthetically satisfying.

Rhythmic Expressivity

In his book *Repeating Ourselves: American Minimal Music as Cultural Practice*, Robert Fink writes that in the early days of minimalism, critics such as Donal Henahan and Harold Schonberg (in the *New York Times*), Samuel Lipman, and Christopher Lasch described the music as a kind of social pathology.[9] Pwyll ap Siôn, in his article "Moving Forward, Looking Back," notes that "German critics also seized upon other aspects [of Reich's music], including what they identified as the music's mimetic representation of industrial production and machine-like processes. Worse still, some went further and accused Reich of creating a form of musical fascism that 'suppressed social criticism and manipulated the listener's emotions.'"[10]

One of the implications of this criticism was that minimalist composers were dictating every aspect of the music and that the performers had no room for expression or creativity. The reality within the composer-based ensembles of Riley, Glass, Reich, and others was that the performers not only had input into the composition of the music, but they also established the expressiveness and feel of this pulse-based music.

Riley spent much of his early career as a pianist playing ragtime, blues, and jazz. He also visited Morocco where he heard traditional *maqamat* music. All these types of music use improvisation and Riley's music allows for the sense of improvisation that characterizes these various musical styles. In six paragraphs of instructions that accompany *In C*, Riley outlines ways the performers can improvise their way through the composition.

Glass's early ensemble was made up primarily of electric keyboards, woodwinds, strings, and voices. The nature of the attack of these instruments and voices gives Glass's music a less precise rhythmic feel, but still imbues the music with a time feel that is different from that of more traditional classical music.

Reich taught *Drumming* to the percussionists in his ensemble by rote, demonstrating each part until the players learned the patterns and where the patterns fit into the ensemble. Once the percussionists, all of whom were classically trained, learned the music and had an idea of Reich's stylistic approach, they developed a rhythmic nuance, time feel, and sense of centered sound that became the identifying characteristic of Reich's music. This rhythmic expression had its basis in classical training but added elements from other pulse-based music including music of Africa, India, Indonesia, and jazz. As Reich's compositional output increased to include strings, winds, and additional vocalists, the other musicians imitated the percussionists' sound and feel. A detailed description of the early rehearsals and development of the performance style for *Drumming* and other early Reich works can be found in my book *Performance Practice in the Music of Steve Reich.*[11]

Attack placement is an essential element in giving feeling to any music, but it is of critical importance in playing rhythms expressively in pulse-based music. Musicians often talk about playing behind the beat, in the middle of the beat, or ahead of the beat, and some musicians instinctively place their attacks in one of these ways, giving their performance a certain style or character. Other musicians are able to alter their attack placements according to the musical expression they wish to convey. Regardless of which of these ways the interpretation of attack is deployed by musicians who are performing pulse-based music, the aim should be to have a unified sense of feel from the entire ensemble.

Sense of Ensemble

When the minimalist composers' ensembles were created, they rehearsed compositions for long periods of time before the premieres. Rehearsals of *Drumming*, for example, took place weekly for nearly a year prior to the first performances. The lengthy rehearsal periods gave the musicians an opportunity to develop the techniques that resulted in a distinctive sound with a unified time feel in the music. The structure of the music and the inner communication that was required to perform it helped create a bonding experience in the ensembles and create a sense of purpose and community. Steven Schick, in his book *The Percussionist's Art*, says:

Beyond pointing to a model of cultural coexistence, *Drumming* also demonstrates a new way of musical interaction within a chamber ensemble. This is simple to describe: no one leads *Drumming*. In fact, nowhere else in the entire chamber music repertoire for percussion is there an example of such a mutually dependent and communally reinforced musical structure. Stewardship of the piece is a group concern, progressing as one player after another completes his or her specific task(s) from building up to phasing to playing resultant patterns. . . . The great parable of this music – that the health and vitality of the whole is tied to the health and vitality of the smallest of its parts – requires the presence of human beings who need each other and who make space for each other.[12]

Robert Carl describes the sense of ensemble in Terry Riley's composition this way:

In C provides a delicate balance between the individual and the group. . . . It demands of its players a high degree of individual responsibility. No matter how many performers participate, they must *listen* carefully to one another for the performance to have any chance of success. . . . The music is the result of a group decision, but each entity retains its separate character and autonomy. . . . Indeed, one can look at the piece as an exercise in anarchy, though of the most benign and constructive form. . . . But *In C* is also very much a product of *community*. That act of listening implies that all the players devote themselves to the greater good of the piece, that they not only listen to their interaction with immediate neighbors but also hear the influence of their actions on the total work. One must listen *out* to the edges of the piece as one plays and adjust decision-making to the amorphous but real will of the collective.[13]

The ensembles that were created by Riley, Reich, and Glass in the 1960s and 1970s brought a new approach to the performance of contemporary music and resulted in tightly knit groups that were well rehearsed. The composers and musicians combined to develop a special sound and feel to the compositions that allowed the musicians to have a sense of ownership as important contributors to the final product. The sense of community that Schick and Carl mention helped the performers and composers establish the techniques that formed the basis of the new virtuosity.

Conclusion

The techniques I have described are not, individually, exclusive to the performance of pulse-based music, but collectively they form a performance practice that requires a different kind of virtuosity than has been a part of the traditional training of a Western classical musician. Now, more than fifty years since the premiere of *In C*, second and third generations of musicians are assimilating these techniques into their musical development, and gradually this different kind of virtuosity will become standard practice for musicians who have an interest in rhythm and a desire to play pulse-based music.

Endnotes

1 R. Carl, *Terry Riley's In C* (Oxford University Press, 2009), 44.
2 W. York, "Form and Process," in R. Kostelanetz (ed.), *Writings on Glass: Essays, Interviews, Criticism* (New York: Schirmer Books/London: Prentice Hall International, 1997), 61, 63.
3 K. Clarke, Interview with Helen Oakley Dance, Paris, September 9, 1977 (Jazz Oral History Project, Institute for Jazz Studies, Rutgers University, Newark, NJ).
4 E. H. Margulis, *On Repeat: How Music Plays the Mind* (Oxford University Press, 2014), 34–5.
5 S. Guibbory, Interview with author (July 13, 2015).
6 A. Wright, Email correspondence (June 12, 2014).
7 G. Oh, in Ludwig van Toronto, October 2, 2018. Article by Hye Won Cecelia Lee. Online arts journal.
8 L. Tilley, "The Draw of Balinese Rhythm," in R. Hartenberger and R. McClelland (eds.), *The Cambridge Companion to Rhythm* (Cambridge University Press, 2020), Chapter 15.
9 R. Fink, *Repeating Ourselves: American Minimal Music as Practice* (University of California Press, 2005), 19.
10 S. Gopinath and P. ap Siôn (eds.), *Rethinking Reich* (Oxford University Press, 2019).

11 R. Hartenberger, *Performance Practice in the Music of Steve Reich* (Cambridge University Press, 2016).

12 S. Schick, *The Percussionist's Art: Same Bed, Different Dreams* (University of Rochester Press, 2006), 241.

13 Carl, *Riley's In C*, 7–8.

6 Conducting Rhythm

DAVID ROBERTSON

The great conducting teacher Hans Swarowsky told his students at Vienna's Academy of Music and Performing Arts that a conductor has only three jobs: start the piece, make any changes within it, and finish it. Indeed, certain elements of time keeping would seem to render that task in conducting rather simple.

At its most basic level, a conductor's gestures convey, through a repeated, patterned series of pulses with the hands and arms, a visual counterpart to the rhythmic structure of the score that the musicians hear as they play. While this information can be helpful to those who are playing, it is often crucial to those in a group who may be looking at bars of rest, as it helps them confirm the passage of musical time, including when they may be called upon to rejoin the musical discourse.

Here is the question anyone who sees a conductor is likely to ask: How do the gestures of a conductor help musicians stay in place? In the vast majority of cases, musicians usually have in front of their eyes only their own lines to play in a piece for ensemble or orchestra. Thus, at the first reading of a piece, players start creating in their minds a virtual score that resides in their memory. This virtual score is constructed from what they hear in relation to what they play and to a conductor's clear, consistent indication of the beats in the piece. This process, usually done in rehearsal, helps the players assess securely whether the other parts they hear are before, after, or coincide with what they play. For the conductor, determining what will be most important in gestural terms has to do with allowing the players to make the best, most accurate virtual score in their minds. The better musicians understand what their colleagues are doing, the more flexibility and interpretative liberty they obtain.

In scores before the early 1800s, the rhythmic organization for most Western concert music did not really require such a time beater; performances could be led from the first violin chair or from the keyboard. While some notable exceptions existed, Beethoven's Fifth Symphony being a good example, to be played properly, most compositions had few major changes that would need a conductor.

However, early into the new century composers such as Berlioz, Schumann, and Mendelssohn were writing works that enjoyed the possibilities in expanding the size of larger instrumental groups, combined with a less strictly organized rhythmic pulse. As a well-known example, performing the opening measures of Berlioz's *Symphonie Fantastique* without a conductor's help in the shaping of how all the players interpret time's flow would be a major challenge. It is certainly possible, but a good deal of rehearsal will be consumed in an activity that is vastly simpler with a good conductor. And this is before any consideration of the musicians being in an acoustic where transparent hearing is not possible.

Such demanding scores led to the rise of conducting as a profession during the nineteenth century. Romantic composers' interests in explorations of varying moods, often within a single piece of music, meant that a conductor could be called upon to negotiate quite a number of changes in a short period of time. As an example, the second movement of Rimsky-Korsakov's *Scheherazade* begins with a small cadenza for solo violin and harp, followed by a recitative-like melody for bassoon and divided bass section. Rimsky-Korsakov continues to develop this material while adding new ideas expressed in different meters and speeds.

Before the nineteenth century, rubato was a way of using rhythm where two parts could float in freedom as long as they came back together at some point. The classic rule of thumb was that, for a pianist, the right hand steals time (forward or backward) without the left hand being aware of anything amiss. Starting with the Romantic composers, rubato might be viewed as a structural device, that is to say, within-phrase tempo variation could be applied as a way of changing or influencing the arc of the piece on a larger scale. This kind of rubato might not be connected within a bar or bars, but rather used to delineate one part in a work that has great tempo freedom in contrast with other parts that are more strict. The second movement of Tchaikovsky's Fifth Symphony is a good example, as the composer sets up a first section where melodic material and even the opening harmony respond to the tempo of *Andante Cantabile, con alcuna licenza* by being flexible even before the many printed indications of *animando*, *ritenuto*, *sostenuto*, *animato*, and the like. This is contrasted by a second section where a tempo indication of *Moderato con anima* and an unwavering series of regular syncopations in the accompaniment make it clear that rubato is to be put aside. Indeed, this section ushers back in the motto of the work, itself of a rhythmic quality unrelenting in its steadiness. In this way, for Tchaikovsky, the desired tempo indications that include rubato actually serve a formal as well as an expressive purpose.

Nineteenth-century opera was a major driver in the importance of the conductor's role. The addition of ever larger groups of soloists, choruses, and dancers created a compelling need for the conductor to be able to present the passage of time and its changes visually to the performers. The dramatic narrative began to evolve away from opera as a collection of scenes that might contain widely different expressive material presented with quite wide-ranging musical means. While some earlier composers such as Mozart had been expanding numbers in their operas for expressive purposes (the finales of acts two and four of *The Marriage of Figaro*, or the finale of Act One of *The Magic Flute* come to mind), the division between separate numbers as a way to articulate a story becomes much less rigid. Opera composition transforms from a set of scenes into a flowing narrative with wide ranging musical means to express the many moods and situations succeeding each other without interruption. The wink in Swarowsky's eye is evident when one considers just how challenging "making any changes" could be.

At the dawn of the twentieth century, the influence of rhythm's importance in Western art music was being felt through an increasing number of challenging scores. Composers were using syncopation, complex meter changes, and polyrhythms in their experiments with freeing up musical time. Dance choreography was also pushing against the traditional boundaries set by traditional ballet. While Stravinsky's *Rite of Spring* is held up as the poster child for this newer, complex use of rhythm, works such as Debussy's *Jeux*, Schoenberg's *Five Pieces for Orchestra*, Webern's *Six Pieces for Orchestra*, Ravel's *Daphnis and Chloe*, Ives's *Three Places in New England*, and Grainger's *The Warriors* all demand a very organized mind and clear hand to be played well.

After the First World War, the number and variety of rhythmic explorations continued to increase. The influence and incorporation of jazz elements, ethnomusicological research into both European and non-European folk musics, as well as the type of experimental ideas put forward in Henry Cowell's book *New Musical Resources*, which imagines a future of superimposed speeds and time signatures, led to a perplexing set of challenges that might face a conductor when encountering a new score.

Following 1945, with the continued experimental ideas of the composers who came of age during this period such as Boulez, Maderna, Stockhausen, Berio, Cage, Nono, Carter, Xenakis, and Birtwistle, among many others, conductors might be forgiven for approaching a new score with a certain amount of trepidation. The technical demands of works by these composers might require a unique rhythmic approach for every new opus.

What is one to do, for example, at the end of Carter's *Double Concerto* where the two different groups play in $\frac{4}{4}$ and $\frac{9}{8}$ simultaneously? Personally, in preparing this passage, I worked for several months to beat four equal beats with my left hand while hearing all the music in the $\frac{9}{8}$ group in my head, followed by conducting three equal beats with my right hand while hearing all the $\frac{4}{4}$ musical material in my head. The trick was then to put these two beat patterns together simultaneously and flexibly (no mean feat in a bilaterally symmetrical body!) while imagining the whole in one's inner ear. As a small footnote, it also meant making a copy of all the pages of the score and putting them on one enormous sheet of music so that I didn't have to turn pages!

With the rhythmic choices available to composers today, it is often helpful for the conductor to have a few rules of thumb to help make decisions when encountering a new score for the first time. In a practical sense, the rhythm of most scores will be roughly divided, from the conductor's point of view, into two categories: (1) the use of a pulse with a certain degree of regularity that is subdivided into various groupings, as in *Modulations* by Gérard Grisey or (2) a small duration used as the basis for combinations of different bar lengths, as seen throughout *Tehillim* by Steve Reich. The reality, however, is quite often a combination of these two approaches in addition to any tempo flexibility that may be required. Hence a piece might require a conductor to beat what appear to be simple time signatures, but within those bars some players are playing seven notes in the time of three while others may have a syncopated rhythm of five against four. This is the sort of approach one might find in a score by György Ligeti. In another score, there could be combinations of successive bars with alternating lengths of $\frac{7}{16}$, $\frac{3}{8}$, $\frac{2}{4}$, $\frac{11}{16}$, and so on, as seen in works by Australian composer Brett Dean.

A number of composers have developed quite sophisticated uses of tempo changes in close succession and of superimposed tempi to give the effect of music that moves at several speeds at once. Elliott Carter's metric modulation is one example in which an underlying subdivision of, say, five sixteenth notes on one side of a barline equaling four triplet eighth notes on the other, keeps the change of speed in a mathematical relationship. Karlheinz Stockhausen developed a scale of tempo that would be parallel to a scale of tones by dividing the speeds of 60 and 120 beats per minute into twelve discrete gradations, equivalent to the twelve semitones within an octave. This allows him in his composition *Inori*, for example, to have a tempo that switches up or down with an immediacy equivalent to the change of pitch. This is why, in that score, the three beats in a bar for the conductor may require three quite different speeds. It also accounts for the raised eyebrows of musicians when encountering 63.5 as a metronome marking.

Thomas Adès uses a system of metric time signatures to denote the different speeds of notes and bars in his scores that at first glance may appear confusing. In traditional notation we use a fraction such as $\frac{5}{4}$ to indicate that the length of that bar is five quarter notes long. Each one of those quarter notes could be combined or subdivided to make for larger or smaller units of half notes, eighths, or sixteenths within the bar. But those units also could be parsed differently. If we combine the last two quarters into a half note and then subdivide that into triplets, we have a bar of three normal quarters followed by three triplet quarters. Adès used the value and speed of the last three notes to write them out as "sixth" notes (notes whose speed is a relation of six in the time of four) and our so our familiar $\frac{5}{4}$ could be written out as $\frac{3}{4}+\frac{3}{6}$. This may require some explanation in rehearsal when players are confronted with a series of times signatures of $\frac{1}{6}$, $\frac{2}{4}$, $\frac{3}{8}$, $\frac{2}{4}$, $\frac{2}{6}$, $\frac{4}{4}$ as found in the third movement of Adès's *Asyla*. It is, however, simply a very practical way to notate the idea of metric modulation on a smaller time scale and becomes intuitive quickly.

Sometimes the requirement is to stay exactly synchronized with an electronic component, as in *Désintégrations* by Tristan Murail, or a visual element, as in *Three Tales* by Steve Reich. This degree of precision and alignment with other clock sources necessitates the use of a click track in which a series of audible clicks is fed to the conductor via headphones. Indeed, it is not unusual in the realm of soundtrack recordings for film that an entire group of musicians has a click given to them directly on headphones while they play. In this studio setting, it might appear that the conductor no longer needs to fulfill the duties of a timekeeper, but it glosses over an important fact. Conductors work with their own bodies to create a personal language in which they are able to express the quality and feeling of the rhythms to be played while they are also providing the regular pattern of the time signature and speed of the tempo. This is, thankfully, not something that the click will ever accomplish on its own and is an essential part of unifying any performance of music, with or without a click provided.

Thus, even when it seems like one might simply replace the timekeeper with a machine of some sort, the conductor's job returns, in a very real sense, back to Professor Swarowsky's adage and demonstrates how, ironically in a purely aural medium, a conductor visually embodies time.

PART III

Composing with Rhythm

7 Expressive Rhythm and Meter in the German Lied

HARALD KREBS

It is not surprising that many discussions of the eighteenth- and nineteenth-century German Lied have centered on harmony and tonality; given its modest extent and relative textural simplicity, the Lied is eminently suitable for the exploration and explication of complex harmonic devices and unusual tonal techniques.[1] The opportunity to connect harmony and tonality to text expression lends an additional attraction to the pitch-based analysis of Lieder. Many a classroom has been enlivened by discussions of a composer's imaginative deployment of particular harmonic and tonal techniques to reflect or underline aspects of the given poetic text.

Numerous recent writings about the Lied have revealed that composers brought various rhythmic and metric features into play as well for the purposes of text expression.[2] In the present chapter, I provide examples of text-expressive durational devices from the eighteenth and nineteenth centuries, beginning with local rhythmic details and progressing toward larger-scale durational structure. Throughout this chapter, all translations are my own.

Durational Details

We can understand some aspects of the expressive function of duration in Lieder by considering how it functions in speech. Pauses between words contribute significantly to expressive speech. They can indicate agitation or passion by lending an utterance a breathless quality, or they can suggest fatigue, reluctance or hesitation – that is, some physical or emotional obstacle in verbal fluency. An utterance unbroken by pauses, on the other hand, is likely to strike listeners as confident, controlled, and serene. The pacing of an utterance, whether or not it is punctuated by pauses, also contributes to its expressive quality. A generally languid pace creates a calm mood, whereas a quick pace suggests excitement or impatience. A consistent pace creates a sense of emotional equilibrium; a sudden change of pace, however, be it an acceleration or a deceleration, denotes an influx of emotion – a surge of excitement, or a moment of introspection. A surprising change of pace in speech might also have a humorous effect. Frequent changes of pace within an extended utterance are likely to create a sense of instability and volatility.

Composers mobilize all of these rhythmic features of speech within their songs, and use them to express their interpretation of the meaning and the emotional content of a poem. The piano part can participate in such rhythmic expression. Robert Schumann's Lieder, for instance, contain passages in which an established accompaniment pattern is abruptly accelerated by the use of tuplets. In the final song of his Op. 90 ("Requiem"), Schumann slows the micropulse of his accompaniment pattern from the predominant sixteenth notes to triplet eighths at m. 31 ("Seid Fürsprecher . . ."), returns to sixteenth notes at m. 35 (with a brief foreshadowing of this return during the piano interlude at m. 33), then increases the pace to quintuplet sixteenths at m. 41 (Example 7.1a). The increase in speed suggests the mounting ecstasy of the soul as it ascends into Heaven.[3] Josephine Lang (1815–80) uses a change of pace in the piano part in a more comical manner at the end of her early song "Der Schmetterling." In the final measures (Example 7.1b), the fluttering triplet-eighths that have dominated the song unexpectedly yield to pairs of normal

7.1a R. Schumann, "Requiem," Op. 90, No. 7, mm. 39–42

7.1b Lang, "Schmetterling," Op. 8, No. 1, ending

eighths. This gesture, which always elicits a chuckle from the audience, contributes subtly to the musical reflection of the unpredictable flight pattern of members of the order *Lepidoptera*.

It is in the vocal lines of Lieder, however, that the expressive function of small-scale rhythmic phenomena can most clearly be demonstrated. Just as pauses and changes of pace in speech express the emotions behind an utterance, changes of duration and pacing in the vocal rhythm of a song – in other words, the panoply of devices included in the declamation of a song text – have a profound expressive effect.[4] Pioneers of the Lied were already aware of the expressive potential of declamatory rhythm. Carl Zelter's strophic setting of Goethe's "Mitternacht" (1818), whose vocal line the poet greatly admired for its "variety of movement, of pauses, and intake of breath," contains excellent examples.[5] With rhythms that change from strophe to strophe, Zelter responds to rhythmic details of the poetry as well as to aspects of its meaning. In mm. 6–7 (Example 7.2a), a rest followed by sixteenth notes sets off the parenthetical "nicht eben gerne" (not at all gladly) from the preceding elongated words "ging ich" (I walked), and in m. 8 the shortening of the durations at Goethe's charming repetition of the adjective "small" vividly suggests the littleness of the boy who is walking with trepidation near a cemetery by night. In mm. 14–15 (Example 7.2b), the melismatic thirty-second notes coinciding with the poet's mention of the stars – these are the only such notes in the song – are another effective rhythmic gesture; the many short notes that fill a long duration form an audible analogy to the visual image of innumerable pinpricks of light within a large expanse.

Equally expressive small rhythmic details exist in the vocal lines of later generations of Lied composers. Even the small elongation resulting from the placement of a dot can have an expressive impact. In Josephine Lang's song "Die Schwalben" (Example 7.3), one would expect the dot placement in the second half of m. 7 to match that of the first half, both because we

7.2a Zelter, "Um Mitternacht," mm. 4–8, vocal line

7.2b "Um Mitternacht," mm. 13–15, vocal line

7.3 Lang, "Die Schwalben," Op. 10, No. 2, mm. 4–8, vocal line

7.4a Haydn, "Lob der Faulheit," mm. 15–24, vocal line

7.4b R. Schumann, "Aufträge," Op. 77, No. 5, mm. 1–4, vocal line

7.4c Wolf, "Storchenbotschaft," m. 35

expect an established pattern to be repeated without change, and because durational accents commonly occur on strong beats. Lang, instead, places the dot on the second eighth note of the second group of three eighths, thereby moving the durational accent to an unexpected location. This rhythmic surprise contributes to the evocation of the erratic flight of swallows.

Example 7.4 shows three vocal lines in which the surprising placement of rests has a humorous effect. In Haydn's setting of Lessing's "Lob der Faulheit" ("Praise of Sloth"), the rests suggest a torpor so intense that it inhibits speech, or an utterance interrupted by yawns. Robert Schumann's use of rests in the vocal line of "Aufträge" conjures up a more specific (and more comical) image of the protagonist than does de la Motte Fouqué's poem on its own; the rhythm of this line makes us imagine a person who is somewhat out of shape and who huffs and puffs as he attempts to catch up to a swiftly moving brook or dove to press upon it his messages to his

7.5a Hensel, "Suleika" (1836 setting), mm. 3–8, vocal line

7.5b "Suleika," mm. 30–35, vocal line

beloved. In "Storchenbotschaft," Wolf dramatizes the shepherd's horrified realization that he is about to become the father of twins by interrupting his question to his avian guests with unexpected hesitations. Had Wolf stayed with the even eighth notes with which the vocal rhythm of the song begins, the humorous effect would have been lacking.

In "Suleika" (1836), Fanny Hensel delivers the same melody in a rest-ridden and "rest-less" manner. In the two initial strophes, every fourth bar includes an eighth-note rest (Example 7.5a); the breathless, agitated effect that these rests produce is appropriate for the first portion of the poem, which is dominated by Suleika's longing for her distant beloved. In the final strophe (Example 7.5b), Hensel smoothes out the vocal line by eliminating the rests; the "rest-less" line sounds much more restful, calm, and confident – which is appropriate, since the latter portion of the poem refers hopefully to an impending reunion.

I conclude my discussion of small-scale rhythmic expression with an example of a declamatory detail from Hugo Wolf's famous miniature, "Das verlassene Mägdlein." Mörike's poem begins with the following lines:

Früh wann die Hähne krähn
Eh die Sternlein verschwinden . . .
(Early in the morning when the cocks crow,
Before the stars disappear . . .)

The declamation at the beginning of Hugo Wolf's setting plods along in relatively slow note values, matching the listless, lethargic state of the maiden; the occasional single sixteenth notes do not appreciably affect the overall slowness of the declamation. Had he set the second line exactly as Mörike wrote it, Wolf would have run into a problem at the two adjacent unstressed syllables, "-lein ver-": there would have been no option but to write two quick notes in a row (see Example 7.6a) – a minute, yet significant disruption of the prevailing slow declamatory pace, and therefore of the mood of the opening. Wolf's solution to this problem was to

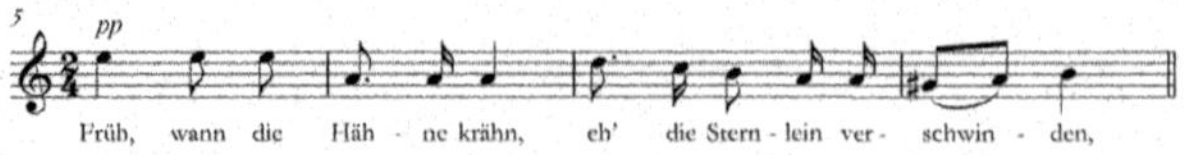

7.6a Wolf, "Das verlassene Mägdlein," mm. 5–8, vocal line, with Mörike's original text

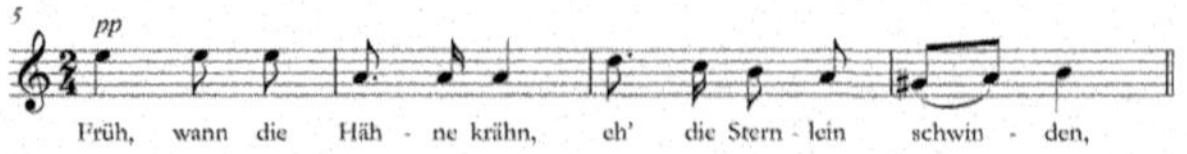

7.6b The same passage with Wolf's altered text

alter Mörike's word "verschwinden" (disappear) to the virtually synonymous "schwinden" (fade); the elimination of the second of the adjacent weak syllables enabled him to avoid the rhythmic disruption (Example 7.6b).[6]

Larger-Scale Text-Expressive Durational Devices and Techniques

The preceding example shows a composer who was normally respectful of the poet's art tampering with the semantic and rhythmic content of a poem for the sake of faithfulness to its emotional content. If we investigate declamatory rhythm from a larger-scale standpoint, we discover that across wider expanses of vocal lines, too, Lied composers are often willing to distort the rhythm of a poem in order to do justice to its emotional content. In the vocal lines of a number of the songs discussed earlier, the overall rhythm does not move at the steady pace that the poetic rhythm would suggest; instead, the vocal rhythm is irregular and unpredictable, such that relatively long durations alternate with spurts of quick motion. In each case, these irregularities are not haphazard, but have an expressive purpose.

The poem of Schumann's "Aufträge," for instance, would suggest an uninterrupted flow until the period at the end of the fourth line; Example 7.7 shows a translation of the rhythm of the poem into the expected even note values. Schumann, however, not only inserts the aforementioned rests (at the end of each poetic line), but also elongates syllables in an unpredictable manner (compare Example 7.4b). For example, he stretches the initial stressed syllables of the words "wenig," "Welle," and "Liebste," and spaces all of the syllables of the third line farther apart than those of earlier lines. All of his rhythmic decisions make sense in relation to various aspects of the poem. The pauses at the ends of the first and second lines correspond to the punctuation. The elongations in the second line express the idea of waiting ("warten"). Those in the third and fourth lines serve to emphasize

7.7 R. Schumann, "Aufträge," opening, expected vocal rhythm

7.8 Hensel, "Suleika," beginning of 1825 setting, vocal line

the importance of the message that is to be conveyed, and the intensity of the protagonist's feelings for the "*Lieb*ste," respectively.

Similar observations can be made about Hensel's "Suleika" of 1836. Again, the poem suggests a steady pace, without pauses. In 1825, Hensel composed a setting of the poem in which the declamation adhered to this steady pace (Example 7.8); in this example, the even spacing of the asterisks (which denote stressed and strongly stressed syllables), demonstrates the steadiness of the pace.[7] In the new vocal rhythm that Hensel created for her setting of the same poem in 1836 (refer to Example 7.5), she alternated sustained and quick notes, such that stressed syllables were unevenly spaced and some poetic feet were compressed. The later song thereby gained a restless, agitated quality that the earlier setting did not possess, and that more successfully matched the mood of the poem, which deals mainly with unfulfilled longing and the suffering caused by separation.[8]

Changes in declamatory rhythm between sections often contribute to text expression in Lieder. When a poem alternates between two speakers while remaining perfectly regular in rhythm, a composer may render these speakers' sections distinct from each other by using different declamatory schemata (to use Yonatan Malin's terminology), a contrast between regularity and irregularity, or other contrasting devices.[9] Wolf's "Herr, was trägt der Boden hier" (from the *Spanisches Liederbuch*) consists of a dialogue between a human and Christ; the former interlocutor asks questions, and Christ answers. As is clear from the rising pitch level (compare the first and third questions – Examples 7.9a and 7.9c) and the addition of the designation "schmerzlich" (painfully) at the second question (Example 7.9b), Wolf interprets the questions as becoming increasingly agonized, with Christ's answers remaining calm and comforting throughout. Wolf uses

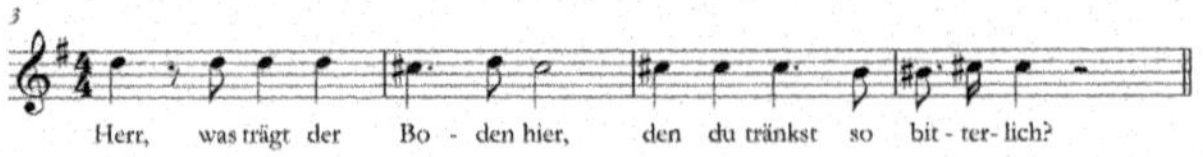

7.9a Wolf, "Herr, was trägt der Boden hier," mm. 3–6, vocal line

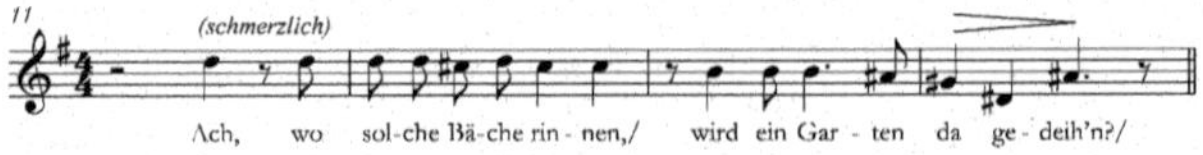

7.9b "Herr, was trägt der Boden hier," mm. 11–14, vocal line

7.9c "Herr, was trägt der Boden hier," mm. 19–22, vocal line

declamatory rhythm in addition to the aforementioned devices to distinguish the two interlocutors.

The poem is perfectly regular in rhythm (trochaic tetrameter, with pauses at the ends of lines). Wolf adheres to this declamatory regularity in all of Christ's speeches; the trochaic tetrameter of the poem and the pauses at line ends are perfectly audible in Wolf's vocal rhythm in these sections. The first of the human questions (Example 7.9a) also begins in a regular fashion, and pauses at line ends are present – but the final word of the question, "bitterlich" (bitterly), is accelerated; we expect the same rhythm as that used at the end of the first line (m. 4), but Wolf presents a diminution of this rhythm, such that the second line ends slightly earlier than expected. In the second and third questions (Examples 7.9b and 7.9c), Wolf takes the acceleration much farther, replacing many of the slow note values that predominate in the earlier question and in Christ's answers with eighth notes. He also injects a substantial amount of irregularity in the form of fluctuations between fast and slow note values (see mm. 11–13 and 20–21), and some surprising syncopations (see mm. 13, 20, and 21). The expected pauses between lines, still present in the first question, are minimized in the second question (a mere eighth rest separates the two lines – see mm. 12–13) and are completely eliminated in the third question (see m. 21). Thus, across this remarkable Lied, declamation contributes not only to the characterization of the two interlocutors, but also to the representation of the gradually changing emotional state of the human speaker.

In his early song "Ferne," Felix Mendelssohn constructs a large-scale, expressive process that includes "bad" declamation, that is, accentuation of an unstressed syllable. The first two stanzas, which deal with the absence of

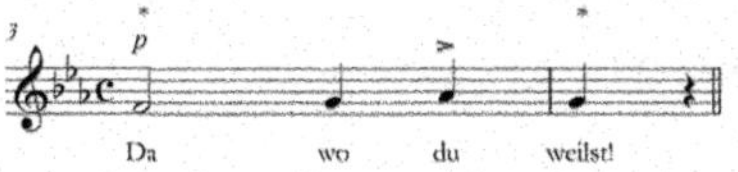

7.10a Mendelssohn, "Ferne," Op. 9, No. 9, mm. 3–4, vocal line

7.10b "Ferne," mm. 27–28, vocal line

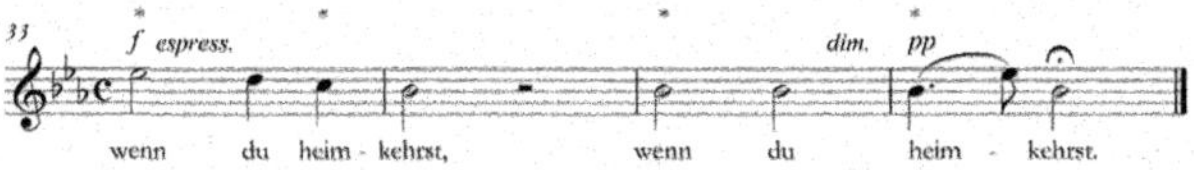

7.10c "Ferne," mm. 33–36, vocal line

the beloved person, end with the refrain "Da wo du weilst" (where you tarry). In the third stanza, which is about the homecoming of the beloved, the poet changes the refrain to "Wenn du heimkehrst" (when you return home). As a comparison of Examples 7.10a and 7.10b reveals, the stress patterns of the refrains differ – "stressed-unstressed-unstressed-stressed" and "stressed-unstressed-stressed-unstressed," respectively. The melodies to which Mendelssohn sets the refrains begin with a rhythm that works well for the "stressed-unstressed" succession that initiates both refrains. The third and fourth syllables of the two refrains, however, have opposite stress patterns. Mendelssohn's refrain rhythm, which fits "Da, wo du weilst" like a glove, clashes violently with the normal pronunciation of the word "heimkehrst" in the final refrain (which should be "*heim*kehrst," not "heim*kehrst*").

The end of the song (Example 7.10c) clarifies the expressive purpose of the unorthodox declamation. Mendelssohn states the refrain "wenn du heimkehrst" twice more to conclude the song. In the first of these statements, he uses the same anomalous declamation that occurred earlier in the song. He then provides a new melody and rhythm for the final reiteration; he elongates the second syllable of the refrain ("du"), such that it fills up a measure and such that the syllable "heim-" is pushed forward into the next and final measure. Thus, this stressed syllable, after being uncomfortably perched on a weak fourth beat, is *brought home* to a downbeat at the end of the song. With this moving resolution of his declamatory dissonance, Mendelssohn turns an apparent flaw into an expressive virtue.

The next example, besides demonstrating text-expressive declamation, also contains another durational device that usually reaches beyond the

7.11a R. Schumann, "Schlaraffenland," Op. 79, No. 6, mm. 11–16

7.11b "Schlaraffenland," mm. 1–6, vocal line

momentary, namely, metric dissonance.[10] When setting poems that exhibit two levels of stress (there are many such poems), composers normally place the strongest stresses on downbeats. Example 7.11a, however, shows an excerpt from Robert Schumann's *Songbook for Young People*, Op. 79, in which the strongest stresses (shown by double asterisks) are, in several adjacent measures, placed on a weaker beat. The resulting effect of displacement of the metric duple layer is reinforced by various musical accents – registral accents in mm. 11–15, durational accents in mm. 13–16, and dynamic accents in mm. 11–12.

The first six measures of the same song (Example 7.11b) illustrate another type of conflict against the notated duple meter: the dynamic and durational accents, which coincide with the beginnings of a repeated melodic idea, create a three-quarter-note layer that is much more clearly audible than the notated meter.[11] Why would Schumann include so much metric conflict in this apparently simple and jolly song? Jon Finson has suggested that Schumann's inclusion in Op. 79 of numerous poems by the passionate republican Hoffmann von Fallersleben constitutes a political statement on the composer's part. One could go even further by considering how Schumann might have interpreted the content of this particular poem in the light of contemporaneous events in Germany. It describes in great detail a Utopia that is, however, inaccessible (the final stanza states, "keiner kam hinein" – nobody was able to enter!). Schumann might have connected this poem to the failed revolution of 1848; there had been much hope that the repressive monarchic systems of Germany could be replaced by a republic, but this hope had been dashed by the time Schumann was working on his Op. 79 in 1849. The metric conflicts in this song could be Schumann's admittedly cagey way of alluding to the political tensions of his time.

Both types of metric conflict described above – the association of a metric layer with a displaced version of that same layer (displacement dissonance), or the association of a metric layer with an incongruent, conflicting layer (grouping dissonance) – are common text-expressive devices in Lieder. Low-level (that is, relatively quickly moving) grouping dissonances, usually of the type that I label G3/2 (where duple and triple divisions of the same timespan coexist), often occur in settings of poems that describe the minuscule motions of natural phenomena. In Hensel's unpublished song "Geheimniß" (Example 7.12a), the conflict created in the piano part by duple sixteenth notes grouped into threes by a complete neighbor-note pattern conjures up the rustling of leaves in the forest.[12] In Clara Schumann's "Geheimes Flüstern" (Example 7.12b), the persistent dissonance between the duple and triple grouping of the steady sixteenth notes similarly alludes to the "secret whispering" in the forest. In Wolf's "Um Mitternacht" and "Nachtzauber" (Examples 7.12c and 7.12d), the grouping dissonances beautifully evoke the subtle sounds of the night; the rippling of wellsprings, mentioned in both poems, was likely the specific inspiration for the dissonances. In these songs, the metric layers are clearly announced by the vocal lines (and in "Nachtzauber," also by the bass); the "antimetrical" layers – the duple grouping of the eighth-note pulse in the former song, and the triple organization of the metric four-sixteenth groups in the latter – are created by pitch repetition.[13]

7.12a Hensel, "Geheimniß," mm. 1–4

7.12b C. Schumann, "Geheimes Flüstern," Op. 23, No. 3, mm. 1–13

7.12c Wolf, "Um Mitternacht," mm. 1–3

7.12d Wolf, "Nachtzauber," mm. 1–2

7.13 R. Schumann, "Lust der Sturmnacht," Op. 35, No. 1, mm. 1–9

In the piano part of "Um Mitternacht," low-level displacement dissonance plays a role as well; one might expect the C♯ octaves in the left hand to appear on the downbeat and on alternate eighth pulses thereafter – but Wolf brings in this octave an eighth pulse later, so that in each left-hand pair, the second eighth note rather than the first carries a density accent and a registral accent. The opening of "Nachtzauber" exhibits a larger-scale displacement: the longest notes (durational accents) in the left hand occur not on downbeats, where they would reinforce the notated meter, but on third beats. In both songs, then, displacement adds its mite to the evocation of the numerous minute, uncoordinated sounds that one hears outdoors at night.

Displacement dissonance can, of course, be used separately for expressive effect. In the first song of Schumann's Justinus Kerner cycle, Op. 35 (Example

7.14a Schubert, "Der blinde Knabe," mm. 1–2

7.14b "Der blinde Knabe," recomposition of mm. 1–2

7.13), persistent low-level displacement dissonance contributes to the representation of the turmoil of a storm. On this surface-level displacement, Schumann superimposes a larger one: the *sforzandos* at the ends of even-numbered measures create a layer that conflicts strongly with the layer of that duration determined by the notated two-measure groups. This dissonance may be intended to suggest sudden gusts of wind projecting above the general roar of the storm. Both the small- and the larger-scale displacements likely refer not only to the natural storm, but also to the storms of passion that rage indoors.[14]

My final examples of text-expressive metric dissonance come from a song by Franz Schubert, who was extraordinarily adept at constructing expressive metric conflicts. The piano part of "Der blinde Knabe" (Example 7.14a) is filled with subtle displacement dissonance. In numerous four-sixteenth-note groups, the lowest notes in the left hand and the highest in the right hand (i.e., the registral accents) appear not on the first, but on the second sixteenth. Furthermore, the low-pitched staccato taps in the left hand frequently appear on third beats rather than on downbeats, resulting in a higher-level displacement.[15] Example 7.14b shows a hypothetical piano part without these displacements; how bland and uninteresting it is in comparison with Schubert's version! What might the displacement dissonances mean in relation to the poem? Surely they refer in some way to the blind boy's condition – but the *dis*placement should not be interpreted as standing for *dis*ability. The protagonist, though referring to himself as "a poor, blind boy," does not consider himself pitiable, and is happy in

7.14c "Der blinde Knabe," mm. 18–21

spite of his lack of sight. The subtle displacement in this song could better be understood merely as an acknowledgment of the boy's non-alignment with the norm – of his different abilities and spiritual qualities.[16]

A passage associated with a strong assertion of the boy's difference includes a powerful grouping dissonance. Just before m. 17, the boy declares that he knows nothing of the rising and setting of the sun, and in mm. 17–24 he says, "I create day and night for myself; while I sleep and play, my inner life smiles radiantly for me." During this description of the boy's individual reckoning of time, Schubert spaces the staccato taps in the bass *five* quarter notes apart (see Example 7.14c); the five-layer conflicts strongly against the metric four-layer which, though not clearly articulated during the dissonant passage, has been prominent in the earlier portion of the song.

Metric dissonance, as I define it, is based on the interaction of regular layers. But metric irregularity can also be found in German Lieder – and it can effectively express aspects of the meaning of a text. Example 7.15 is a complete song by the critic and composer Felix Draeseke (1835–1913). The song is notated in $\frac{3}{4}$ time, but it is difficult to hear and perform it in accordance with that meter. The numbers above the music show how I actually hear the meter. I have placed "1's" at points that are strongly accented by parameters such as poetic stress, dynamics, harmonic change, duration, and contour. In m. 2, for instance, the notated third beat sounds more like a downbeat because of the poetic stress ("*wohl*vertraute"), the dynamic accent created by the *crescendo*, and the registral accent resulting from the upward leap. In m. 3, the second beat sounds like a downbeat because it is coordinated with a poetic stress ("*Flie*der"), with the resolution

7.15 Draeseke, "Die Stelle am Fliederbaum," Op. 26, No. 5

of the preceding dominant seventh chord, with a durational accent in the piano part, and with a suspension (a dissonance associated with a metric accent). There are similar rationales for later downbeat placements in my analysis.

The notated meter is actualized at several points (in mm. 1, 8, 11–13, 17–22, and 26–29); Draeseke provides enough such passages to provide a foil for the various metric disruptions. Some of these disruptions involve displacement of the three-quarter-note layer (by one beat at mm. 3–4, 6–7 and 15–16, by two beats at mm. 30–31). Even more prevalent are passages in which perceived downbeats are two beats apart, resulting in grouping dissonance (G3/2); this dissonance first appears close to the beginning (mm. 2–3), recurs frequently throughout, and is featured at the very end of the song. Mere acknowledgment of these metric dissonances, however,

7.15 (*cont.*)

does not do justice to the flexibility of the meter. How far removed is this $\frac{3}{4}$ from the normal succession of groups of three beats! Draeseke's avoidance of the familiar aspects of this meter expresses the theme of the poem. This $\frac{3}{4}$ meter, deprived of its customary, comfortable regularity, and overgrown with unpredictable incursions of conflicting metric layers, stands for the unrecognizability of a place that one knew long ago, and to which one has returned after a long absence.

Text-Expressive Hypermeter

I conclude with a consideration of hypermeter – meter above the level of the barline. Hypermeter, which most frequently involves groups of four bars, might seem to have less potential for expression than the devices mentioned earlier. Indeed, four-bar hypermeter on its own has little such potential. When this common large-scale meter, however, is associated with a displaced "shadow meter," or when hypermeter becomes irregular or ambiguous, a link between the resulting structures and a given poem may well become apparent.[17] Josephine Lang's songs contain numerous examples of hypermetric expansions (i.e., elongations beyond an established four-bar duration) that serve to emphasize powerful words and important textual themes.[18] In Robert Schumann's late songs (as opposed to his early ones, in which hypermeter is usually straightforward and therefore not expressive), there are examples of superpositions of non-aligned hypermeters in the vocal line and the piano part (in several of the Lenau settings, Op. 90), of hypermetric ambiguity (see "Tief im Herzen," Op. 138, No. 2), and of pervasive hypermetric irregularity that is ultimately resolved into regularity (see the Mignon song "So lasst mich scheinen," Op. 98a, No. 9). The superpositions of non-aligned hypermeters in Op. 90 relate to the conflicts between lovers referred to in the given poems. The deep-level ambiguity in the superficially simple song "Tief im Herzen" suggests the topic of the poem: pain concealed beneath a calm surface. The hypermetric irregularity in the Mignon song is associated with lines that describe Mignon's manifold trials and tribulations; resolution into regular four-bar hypermeter occurs at the end, where Mignon looks forward to the untroubled, serene state to which she shall accede after her imminent death.[19]

In "Suleika," Fanny Hensel follows a hypermetric strategy similar to that of Robert Schumann in the Mignon song. I mentioned earlier that the first portion of "Suleika" is dominated by restless longing for an absent lover, which yields at the end to the confident expectation of the assuagement of the longing. Hypermetric structure plays a significant role in the musical representation of this emotional shift. Most of the song is written in three-bar hypermeter.[20] Toward the end, however, Hensel moves smoothly into four-bar hypermeter, which, since it sounds more stable, matches the greater emotional stability of the protagonist that is implied at the end of the poem (Example 7.16). The resolution into four-bar hypermeter was less clear in an earlier version of the song; although the vocal line already ended with four-bar hypermeter in that version, the postlude consisted of only three tonic-prolonging measures, which could have been heard as reinstating the initial three-bar hypermeter. In a revision of the ending in this autograph, Hensel added a fourth measure to the postlude (m. 44), thereby reinforcing the vocal ending's four-bar hypermeter.[21]

We have seen that composers of the German Lied mobilize many aspects of rhythm and meter, from the local to the large scale, in order to

7.16 Hensel, "Suleika" (1836 setting), ending

assist in the expression of the meaning of a poetic text. I do not pretend that this chapter has exhausted the rhythmic or metric devices that they invoke for this purpose, but I hope at least to have illuminated some aspects of the creativity and ingenuity with which they compose expressively with rhythm and meter.

Endnotes

1 See, for example, H. Krebs, "Alternatives to Monotonality," *Journal of Music Theory*, 25 (1981), 1–16; D. Stein, *Hugo Wolf's Lieder and Extensions of Tonality* (University of Michigan Press, 1984); D. Stein and R. Spillman, *Poetry into Song: Performance and Analysis of Lieder* (Oxford University Press, 1996), 105–40; W. Everett, "Deep-Level Portrayals of Directed and Misdirected Motions in Nineteenth-Century Lyric Song," *Journal of Music Theory*, 48 (2004), 25–68.

2 Yonatan Malin's work is significant in this regard; see "Metric Dissonance and Music-Text Relations in the German Lied" (Ph.D. dissertation, University of Chicago, 2003); *Songs in Motion: Rhythm and Meter in the German Lied* (Oxford University Press, 2010). Stein and Spillman provide a concise summary of ways

in which rhythm and meter function expressively in Lieder; see *Poetry into Song*, 166–90. The expressive function of rhythm and meter in Brahms's songs has attracted a lot of attention; see, for example, D. Rohr, "Brahms's Metrical Dramas: Rhythm, Text Expression and Form in the Solo Lieder" (Ph.D. dissertation, Eastman, 1997); R. Cohn, "Complex Hemiolas, Ski-Hill Graphs and Metric Spaces," *Music Analysis*, 20 (2001), 313–21; W. Lau, "The Expressive Motivation of Meter Changes in Brahms's Lieder" (Ph.D. dissertation, University of Oregon, 2015); H. Platt, "Temporal Disruptions and Shifting Levels of Discourse in Brahms's Lieder," in S. Murphy (ed.), *Brahms and the Shaping of Time* (University of Rochester Press, 2018), 49–79; J. Miyake, "Phrase Rhythm and the Expression of Longing in Brahms's 'Gestillte Sehnsucht,' Op. 91, No. 1," *Brahms and the Shaping of Time*, 83–109. My own recent writings have also focused on the text-expressive function of rhythm and meter; relevant publications are cited in the various sections of this chapter.

3 I thank pianist Hartmut Höll for drawing my attention to this passage during one of his master classes at the Musikhochschule in Karlsruhe; his words were, "It is as if sixteenth notes are no longer enough [to express the ecstasy]."

4 My most recent publications have dwelt on this aspect of rhythm; see, for example, "Fancy Footwork: Distortions of Poetic Rhythm in Robert Schumann's Late Songs," *Indiana Theory Review*, 28 (2010), 67–84; "Motion and Emotion: The Expressive Use of Declamatory Irregularity in the Lieder of Richard Strauss," *Music Theory and Analysis*, I (2014), 5–37; "Expressive Declamation in the Songs of Johannes Brahms," *Brahms and the Shaping of Time*, 13–48.

5 Goethe to Zelter, Jena, March 19, 1818. Translated by Lorraine Byrne Bodley, *Goethe and Zelter: Musical Dialogues* (Farnham: Ashgate, 2009), 241.

6 By making this change, Wolf ironed out a rhythmic irregularity that Mörike deliberately created to set up a folk-like (*volkstümlich*) atmosphere; see L. L. Albertsen, *Mörikes Metra* (Flensburg: Futura Edition, 1999), 21–22.

7 The asterisk notation is adapted from the work of the linguist Morris Halle and his colleagues; see, for example, N. Fabb and M. Halle, *Meter in Poetry: A New Theory* (Cambridge University Press, 2008).

8 I have discussed the earlier, unpublished setting in detail in "Working with Words: Revisions of Declamation in Fanny Hensel's Song Autographs," *The Songs of Fanny Hensel* (Oxford University Press, forthcoming). It is located in the Mendelssohn Archive of the *Deutsche Staatsbibliothek Preußischer Kulturbesitz* in Berlin (MA Ms. 35, p. 18; dated May 5, 1825).

9 Malin's analysis of Brahms's "Liebestreu," Op. 3, No. 1, describes the manifold rhythmic and metric distinctions between the utterances in a mother/daughter dialogue; see *Songs in Motion*, 154–8.

10 For a detailed discussion of the theory of metric dissonance, see H. Krebs, *Fantasy Pieces: Metrical Dissonance in the Music of Robert Schumann* (Oxford University Press, 1999).

11 Jon Finson points out that the song begins with "three-measure units"; see "Schumann's Mature Style and the 'Album of Songs for the Young,'" *Journal of Musicology*, 8 (1990), 242. The three-bar hypermeter, played off against the more "normal" four-bar hypermeter in the second half of the song, is another durational feature that lends a subtle tension to this apparently simple song. The text-expressive function of hypermeter is discussed in the final section of this chapter.

12 The autograph of "Geheimniß" is located in the Mendelssohn Archive of the *Deutsche Staatsbibliothek Preußischer Kulturbesitz* in Berlin (MA Ms. 35, p. 57; dated July 12, 1826).

13 Another example of low-level grouping dissonance representing minute motions in nature is Josephine Lang's "Auf dem See in tausend Sterne," Op. 14, No. 6, in which triplet eighth notes in both hands are consistently grouped in pairs; the specific referent here is the shimmer of sunlight on the surface of a lake. Yonatan Malin has discussed this example in "Metric Dissonance and Music-Text Relations in the German Lied," 246–52; he also discusses metric dissonances in Wolf's "Um Mitternacht" (267–72). I provide additional examples of the association between low-level grouping dissonance and nature in "Functions of Metrical Dissonance in Schubert's Songs," *Musicological Explorations*, 14 (2014), 5–7.

14 A low-level displacement similar to that in Schumann's song occurs in Wolf's Mörike setting "Begegnung"; in that song, too, the displacement relates to an emotional as well as a natural storm. I provide several additional examples of associations between displacement dissonance and passion in "Text-Expressive Functions of Metrical Dissonance in the Songs of Hugo Wolf," *Musicologica Austriaca*, 26 (2007), 131–3. In Brahms's "Meine Liebe ist grün," Op. 63, No. 5, too, consistent low-level displacement dissonance contributes to the expression of overwhelming passion. For a different, albeit related, interpretation of the text-expressive function of displacement dissonance, see Y. Malin, "Metric Displacement Dissonance and Romantic Longing in the German Lied," *Music Analysis*, 25 (2006), 251–88.

15 Mezzo-soprano Mitsuko Shirai, known as the "First Lady of the German Lied," suggests that the low-pitched staccato notes represent the tapping of the blind boy's stick (personal communication). Graham Johnson makes the same point in his discussion of "Der blinde Knabe" in *Franz Schubert: The Complete Songs*, vol. 1 (Yale University Press, 2014), 308–12. Johnson refers to the metrical disorientation in the opening figure as "a tonal analogue for blindness via the workings of the ear" (310).

16 I have proposed a similar interpretation of the pervasive displacements in Schubert's "Harfenspieler," D. 480, and in *Winterreise*; see "Functions of Metrical Dissonance in Schubert's Songs," 11–12 and 16–22. For examples of scholarship on disability and music, see B. Howe, S. Jensen-Moulton, N. Lerner, and J. Straus (eds.), *The Oxford Handbook of Music and Disability Studies* (Oxford University Press, 2015).

17 The term *shadow meter* appears in W. Rothstein, “Beethoven with and without *Kunstgepräng*,” *Beethoven Forum*, 4 (1995), 186–93. This essay is one of the first in which the text-expressive potential of hypermeter is discussed.

18 See H. Krebs, “Hypermeter and Hypermetric Irregularity in the Songs of Josephine Lang,” in D. Stein (ed.), *Engaging Music: Essays in Music Analysis* (Oxford University Press, 2005), 28–9, for examples of the underlining of particular words via hypermetric elongation. Additional examples of expressive hypermeter are discussed in H. Krebs and S. Krebs, *The Life and Songs of Josephine Lang* (Oxford University Press, 2007), 32, 91, 118–23, and 143.

19 For analyses of hypermeter in these and other late songs by R. Schumann, see H. Krebs, “The Expressive Role of Rhythm and Meter in Schumann’s Late Lieder,” *Gamut* 2, (2009), Special Feature – A Music-Theoretical Matrix: Essays in Honor of Allen Forte (Part I), 267–98. (https://trace.tennessee.edu/gamut/vol2/iss1/9/), accessed September 10, 2019; “Meter and Expression in Robert Schumann’s Op. 90,” in R. Kok and L. Tunbridge (eds.), *Rethinking Schumann* (Oxford University Press, 2011), 183–205.

20 Stephen Rodgers has drawn attention to the presence of three-bar hypermeter in this and other songs by Fanny Hensel; see “Thinking (and Singing) in Threes,” *Music Theory Online*, 17.1 (2011).

21 The earlier version is found in Hensel’s autograph booklet MA Ms. 45, on page 26; like most of Hensel’s autographs, this booklet is held in the Mendelssohn Archiv at the *Deutsche Staatsbibliothek Preussischer Kulturbesitz* in Berlin.

8 Rhythm in Post-tonal Music

A Modernist Primer

GRETCHEN HORLACHER

Post-tonal Rhythm's Legacy

Composers coming of age in the early twentieth century inherited from the Western European art tradition at least two ways to articulate temporality, both dependent on the highly organized language of tonality and a vocabulary of proportionally related durations (whole notes, half notes, quarter notes, etc.). This musical time evokes an ordered, continuous flow – a sense of moving forward toward a goal, one where complexity arises from possible diversions in an ongoing flow and a pattern of metric accent. The temporal identities are determined by their placement within a phrase and within a hierarchical, fundamentally periodic series of beats, measures, and hypermeasures; for example, a chord may occur on a beat within a measure and (often) a hypermeasure, and also at the beginning, middle, or end of a phrase.

This kind of temporality is highly dependent on tense. An event may occur not only before others, but also in the past, making its identity malleable: we may anticipate its identity before it happens, adjust its identity as it happens, and again reconsider it once it is over. In other words, while we often think of time as an arrow, it reaches forward with a strong reference to its own earlier movements. This evolution of identity relies in large part on our sensations of regularity: when phrases have typical lengths and metric accentuation proceeds periodically, these modes of articulation permit deviations such as phrase expansion and syncopation. In Western musical notation, flow is shown in the left-to-right display of musical scores, and the articulation of that flow is generally represented with durational symbols, time signatures, and barlines. These symbols form a reasonably accurate guide to time's articulation into discrete durations and groups of durations, and to the generally periodic accentuation of meter, measurements that can be perceived across small spans of time and larger ones. Our sense of rhythm is intimately connected to our experiences of bodily movement, especially our abilities to perceive and anticipate regularly occurring beats.[1]

As Western tonal music became increasingly chromatic, the regularities of Western tonal temporality began to break down. Additionally, composers were increasingly aware of music outside of Western Europe, and of scientific and psychological ideas about time and sequence that questioned a simple relationship of cause and effect. The relatively simple relationship between rhythmic notation (as indicated via scores) and its perception no longer held as composers wrote music whose phrase boundaries, phrase rhythm, and metric identities became much less regular. In the following close readings of four musical excerpts (by Bartók, Stravinsky, Copland, and Messiaen), I will demonstrate a number of ways in which post-tonal music stretches, and even breaks, concepts and practices associated with Western European tonal art music as it forges new, modernist temporalities which match and make possible new pitch organizations.

Bartók's Hybrid Composition

Let's begin with Example 8.1a, a short piano piece from Book IV of the collection *Mikrokosmos* by Béla Bartók, finished in 1939. This collection of

8.1a Bartók, "Bulgarian Rhythm" (*Mikrokosmos* #113).

*) Eventuell Fingersatz 2 statt 3, siehe Einzelanmerkungen / Possibly fingering 2 instead of 3, see Detailed Notes
Possiblement doigté 2 au lieu de 3, voir Notes Détaillées

8.1a *(cont.)*

153 short piano solos, organized in six books of increasing difficulty, was written with a pedagogical aim: to teach piano skills while it also introduced Eastern European folk practice and more "modern" melodies, harmonies, and rhythms to players.[2] A particularly challenging skill in #113 is learning to play in $\frac{7}{8}$, the "Bulgarian Rhythm" referenced in the piece's title.[3]

This piece is notated entirely in what is commonly called an "asymmetric" meter – $\frac{7}{8}$ – because seven cannot give rise to a single longer pulse of either two or three eighths. Notice that the opening alternation of B♭and G♯ in mm. 1–3 groups the constant eighth pulsations into a pattern of 2+2+2+1, and Bartók beams the eighths in the left hand in 2+2+3 throughout the piece. This inequality undoubtedly arose from Bartók's long and thorough study of Eastern European folk music, and the particular irregularities given here, along with the speedy articulation of the eighths, suggest that the piece uses an "aksak" rhythm.

8.1b $\frac{8}{8}$ and cut-time recompositions of m. 4

8.1c Durational reduction of first phrase

"Aksak" can be translated as limping, slumping, or stumbling, apt words whose qualities become especially evident when compared to the more typically common-practice $\frac{8}{8}$ and cut-time re-compositions given in Example 8.1b. Even so, a critical feature of this piece's irregularity is its periodic repetition of $\frac{7}{8}$ and the steadiness of its internal patterns. These emerging pitch and durational patterns align with László Vikárius's conception of hybridity in art music, where meaning and comprehension arise in reference both to folk tradition and European tonal practice. Example 8.1c presents mm. 1–3 and mm. 4–6 in the manner of Carl Schachter's durational reductions, where both durational and pitch patterns combine to create an emerging profile for $\frac{7}{8}$ from a series of continuous eighths, to one of 2+2+2+1, to one of 4+3, a periodic succession of long-short. The reduction proceeds from top to bottom on the three staves in Example 8.1c, and to the right of the top staff is a simple sketch showing pitch priority. This reduction derives both from Western tonal art music and the chromatic vocabulary used by Bartók.

The 4+3 reading is potentially metric, in that we may experience two beats, the first of which is stronger than the second (or in the language of metric theorist Christopher Hasty, is a dominant beginning followed by a continuation) and the second of which is interrupted just a little too soon by a return of the first.[4] The tempo of the piece reinforces this reading. Music cognition researchers recognize a "sweet spot" for a tactus that lasts somewhere around 60 beats per minute (600 milliseconds [ms]); at the notated tempo, a quarter lasts about 292 ms (pretty short for a tactus), a half note lasts 584 ms (about right), and a dotted eighth lasts 438 ms (on the short side).[5] At the given tempo, a duple meter whose second beat is a little shorter than expected includes a repeating sequence of durations 584+438 ms.[6]

This metric reading draws our attention to a common trait of early modernist music, the possibility of an uneven tactus, that is, a beat whose value can vary within a certain durational range. Justin London describes these kinds of meters as non-isochronous, noting that they are extremely common in non-Western folk repertories, and that they commonly feature continuous articulations at the "sub-tactus" level (here the repeating eighths), because their continuous repetitions helps one recognize and "absorb" the irregularity. London argues that because the degree of inequality between 3 and 4 is small – in mathematical terms, 3 and 4 are a maximally even division of 7 – they can be recognized as non-isochronous, functional beats within a measure.[7] Hasty might focus more on the sensation of interruption we may feel when the return of material comes an eighth early, and also on our ability to feel the equality of a duration spanning seven eighths as a measure, helping us to anticipate when a new beginning may occur next.[8] A recording of the piece made by Bartók meticulously observes the right-hand phrasing, whose span across the measure and staccato markings accent the notated downbeat. He also emphasizes the inequality of beats with a slight lean in the left hand from each measure's final G♯ into the subsequent downbeat A.[9]

The phrase rhythm of a passage such as this may also be characterized as hybrid. While the four-bar model associated with Classical-era pieces did not remain as powerful in later nineteenth-century tonal music, the rhythms of proportion, the pacing of harmonic change, and tonal motion toward a cadence still define the temporality of phrases. Table 8.1 diagrams the formal shape of the piece, identifying an introduction and coda and functional labels and cadences for each of the four phrases. When the opening B♭and G♯ converge on A, a symmetric center as well as the consonant fifth above D, the introductory mm. 1–3 elide into the

Table 8.1 Formal diagram of "Bulgarian Rhythm"

Measures:	
1–4	Three-bar introduction; overlaps into m. 4
4–8	Exposition; initial five-bar shape with cadence at third bar (m. 6) and external expansion
9–14	Sequential development; repeats five-bar phrase rhythm with an open cadence at m. 11
15–19	Further sequential development with same phrase rhythm and another open cadence
20–24	Closing phrase: returns to cadence from m. 6 at its third bar (m. 22)
25–30	Coda: returns to introduction, extending it to the five-bar length in the main body of the piece

expository first phrase, enduring through mm. 4–8. This phrase cadences in the manner of a perfect authentic cadence as the melody descends through a D-minor arpeggiation in mm. 5–6 (see the sketch on Example 8.1c for more detail), resting upon D halfway through m. 6. The latter half of that measure through m. 8 is (using William Rothstein's terms for phrase rhythm) an external expansion, reinforcing the arrival of D.[10] Notice that the cadence in this five-bar phrase arrives at its halfway point, a modernist take on a more typical model of expanding a four-bar phrase with a single bar of external expansion.

The second phrase, from mm. 9–14, follows suit, arriving at its cadence at m. 11, and resting on the dissonant C until m. 14; its melodic sequence of mm. 4–6 marks it as developmental, and its harmonically open cadence promises additional phrases of similar shape and temporality. In fact, Bartók provides two more five-bar phrases, the second of which closes fully on the lower D. The composer enhances closure with a six-bar coda taken from the introduction, this time holding the A until the end of the piece.

My more general point is that while the rhythmic features of this piece – its metric and formal temporality – vary from Western tonal art practice, they are highly dependent on its models. Its exceptional features include a tactus that may have a variable length (within limits, an issue developed below), and phrases whose internal rhythm may follow different paths, even if their durations are proportionally related. Given these irregularities, different listeners and performers may reach different interpretations, originating in their familiarity with Western tonal traditions, Eastern European folk music, and preferences for regularity more generally.

The Limits of Irregularity: Stravinsky's *Rite*

The next example stretches concepts of phrase and meter even further. Like the Bartók example above, Igor Stravinsky's ballet the *Rite of Spring* also derives some of its irregular rhythmic and pitch features from folk music (in this case from Russia), filtered through his Modernist habits.[11] Stravinsky's music is often associated with repeating short, fragmental melodies whose frequent alternations create a series of contrasting blocks. The challenges to rhythm as measurable flow can be severe: How can we engage with continual interruption? Is there any order amidst the seeming chaos?[12]

The dance entitled "Glorification of the Chosen One," from the second part of Stravinsky's *Rite of Spring*, whose opening is given in Example 8.2a (in the two-piano version of the *Rite*) and in Example 8.2b (in a format explained below), demonstrates this considerably more complicated rhythmic vocabulary. In this portion of the dance, the Chosen One – the virgin who is sacrificed for the good of the community by dancing herself to death – has been identified, and stands in the middle of a circle of maidens who honor her with extreme, repetitive leaps.[13] This dance is preceded at R103/2 by the repetition of a chord eleven times (marked by the very rare time signature $\substack{11\\4}$), whose quarter-note pulsation is a backdrop to "Glorification."

What follows this pulsation are two varied "blocks" of material, a main motive called "A" and a vamp figure, whose initial appearances are bracketed on Example 8.2a. "A" is an alternation of a harmonized bass pitch A and a fragmental, chromatic melody that ascends and descends via step to and from G, often notated in $\substack{5\\8}$ bars. The vamp consists of an alternation in quarter notes of a bass line and its accompaniment in upper voices. The format of Example 8.2b lays out one possible segmentation of the first fifteen measures in a manner I've described elsewhere as an "ordered succession," a term meant to capture the tension between the "radical" discontinuous successions of a block form and the residues of continuity in how blocks proceed and are ordered. [14]

This passage is considerably more complex, and more irregular, than the Bartók excerpt. The sensation of "stop-and-start" endures throughout the excerpt: just when we manage to entrain to a pulse, it fails to continue. The first iteration of motive A at R104 features the germ of the irregularity: we immediately experience two different versions of a beat, both arising from the same fundamental tonal convention; when a harmonized chord with a clear bass note is followed by an upper-voice response, we typically

8.2a Stravinsky, opening of "Glorification of the Chosen One," two-piano version.

8.2a (*cont.*)

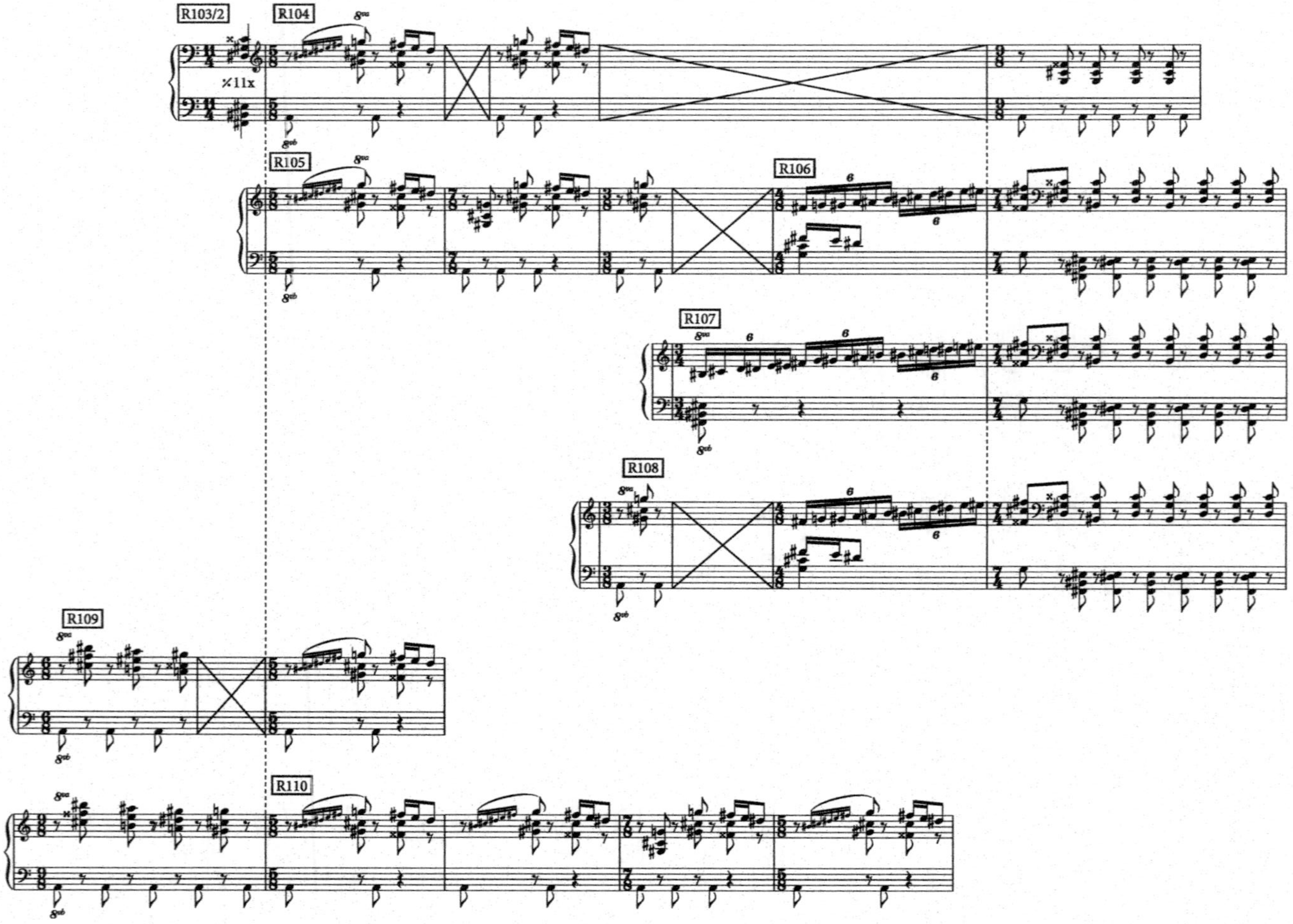

8.2b Ordered succession of R104–R110

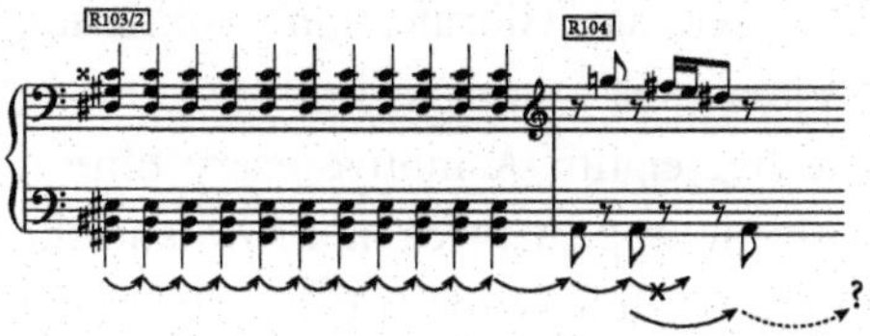

8.3a Quarter-note pulse leading to the start of the dance

8.3b Motive A's $\frac{5}{8}$ bar

assign the start of a beat to the bass note.[15] In the first measure of "Glorifications," this pattern first lasts two eighths, and then three eighths, reflected in the $\frac{5}{8}$ meter signature. The second notated measure repeats the 2+3 pattern.[16]

The inequality within each measure, a 2+3 modernist take on a "boom-chick" pulsation, interrupts the flow of its melody in its successive returns, as the two possible recompositions of Example 8.3 demonstrate. Example 8.3a attempts to capture the bumpy feeling with the first notated measure of the dance (R104), given the preceding quarter-note pulsations. However, given the quick tempo, Example 8.3b demonstrates how we may continue from R104 into R104/3, more attuned to the completion of two "equal" bars each lasting five eighths.[17] In this second reading, we absorb the duration of five eighths as predictive, and we will expect the third notated measure to begin when it does. In this way, the example mimics the irregularity found in the Bartók example. That third measure of R104, however, returns to the more tonally familiar alternation of upper and lower registers, serving as a "vamp": its lack of melody suggests that we are in a holding pattern, and it lasts long enough to "even out" or replace the earlier measures with a quarter-note pulse. But when the vamp ends at the fourth notated measure (R105), we encounter another bump in the early arrival of the A motive. Notice the unprecedented sounding of two bass note A's one right after the other as R104/3 passes into R105.

This very irregular series of events characterizes Stravinsky's rhythmic practice in his "Russian" period, and serves as a precedent for countless composers whose rhythmic/metric styles reach beyond the maintenance of equal pulsation, even when the shorter durations within of a pulsation are non-isochronous. However, were this passage endlessly chaotic, it would risk losing the listener's interest. In fact, as "Glorification" continues, critical regularities emerge, serving as goal posts and reset buttons. Among them are the exact reiteration of the five-eighth A motive every time it reappears, a predilection for that motive to appear twice in a row, and the likelihood that a quarter-note pulsation will follow the two-bar statement of the motive.

These frequent sensations of disruption become the focal point of a dance based largely on brute repetition: our engagement is enhanced both by the intrusion of events when we don't yet expect them, along with a growing sense of recognition as repetitions accumulate, impressions dependent almost entirely on rhythm. For example, as we enter the "early" return of the motive at R105, we might experience that measure quite differently than we did at R104: we recognize it as a return that plays out as expected, rather than an altered version of a tonal figuration.[18] We may also await another iteration of this foundational measure, as well as the return of the "vamp" figure. Finally, when we hear the vamp move back to the motive, we may also come to hear the completion of a second formal unit, comparing it to the surprisingly typical phrase rhythm of the first three notated measures: in these opening measures, the two equal iterations of the motive are followed by a vamp lasting about the same length, providing a sense of balance.

This extremely "close reading" depends on hearing the passage many times over; yet I argue that its interest arises from the sophisticated interplay of irregular rhythms with more familiar notions of rhythmic/metric regularity. While it would be tedious to continue through the passage in such detail, let me draw attention to a few other tricks Stravinsky has up his sleeves. The second phrase, given by the second system of Example 8.2b, is nearly identical to the first, but one small change has an enormous rhythmic effect. Although two identical iterations of the A motive begin the phrase, the second appears just a quarter note late, having been delayed by a seeming momentary early return to the vamp (R105/2, the first quarter of the $\frac{7}{8}$ bar). It sounds as if the vamp has intruded within motive A, and as a result, this imperfect A must repeat itself a third time (the $\frac{3}{8}$ bar at R015/3) before proceeding to the vamp, albeit it a quarter note too early.[19] The resultant phrase rhythm of this second phrase is a development of the first: beginning as expected, it interrupts motive A at its start (R105/1) and as it tries to finish (R105/3).[20]

Consider also how the passage concludes, from R109 through R110 (the fifth and sixth systems of Example 8.2b). Previously beginning always from G natural, motive A grows! Its new start on B♯ (R109), descends by step to

D♯, passing through seven pitch classes, as if it were filling in a modernist scale. Moving initially off the beat by quarter note, the new melody seems to accelerate to reach its destination; in its second iteration, (final system of Example 8.2b), the scale reaches G seemingly early – without the accompanying chromatic grace notes – before continuing with motive A. What follows is an elongated sequence of motive A, suitable to close the first "period" of the dance: at R110, motive A returns first in its typical two-iteration form, references the $\frac{7}{8}$ version from phrase 2, and then "cadences" into a final $\frac{5}{8}$ repetition.

In the Bartók piano piece, measures are internally irregular, but they consistently repeat a single larger duration. By contrast, across this series of phrases Stravinsky frequently juxtaposes a quarter-note pulse with a dotted-quarter pulse in bars of changing length. Because their motivic content is fixed, however, we can learn to navigate these seemingly unruly rhythms. For example, we learn to recognize the $\frac{5}{8}$ bar (and its extension into $\frac{7}{8}$), taking in their irregular identities. Furthermore, throughout the passage, the return of the "vamp" figure signals counting by quarters, and the return of the motive signals 2+3. We may even distinguish "typical" metric irregularities from atypical surprises. For example, we may experience a jolt when a $\frac{5}{8}$ bar – motive A – is interrupted as it closes (see the $\frac{3}{8}$ bars in the second and fourth systems). The outcome is controlled chaos, a modernist metric practice that enhances Stravinsky's blunt repetitions.

Rhythmic Counterpoint

Example 8.4a is taken from the second movement of Copland's Symphony for Organ and Orchestra (later set for orchestra alone as Symphony No. 1) from 1924. The movement, entitled "Scherzo," is notable for a pervasive motivic figure in the orchestral parts, as bracketed in the clarinet parts of the opening measure. Although the movement is notated in $\frac{3}{4}$, this figure establishes a dotted-quarter pulse; however, where the strongest of the three eighth-note pulses occurs is an open question. Because the two versions of the figure – on D–C and A–G – are offset by an eighth note, the accented eighth can potentially occur on the A that begins the movement, or the G–C fifth, as shown in Example 8.4b. Because C and G occur simultaneously and suggest a resolution from A and D to G and C, the second reading seems more likely. However, accent marks on A, G, and C leave a little room for interpretation, and orchestration and performance choices make both readings viable. Moreover, as we shall see, Copland

8.4a Copland, Symphony for Organ and Orchestra, "Scherzo," opening.

highlights the first reading later in the movement. In fact, this movement underscores a common feature in twentieth-century music, the superimposition and juxtaposition of competing metric organizations where neither reading is primary. This composition from Copland's early period uses metric complication to invoke the character of a modernist scherzo.

8.4b One possible $\frac{3}{8}$ barring of the opening

8.5 Metric challenge and synchronization of oboe melody

In m. 3, an oboe melody begins in synchronization with the A–G figure, adding a D above the A and doubling the C an octave higher. After three iterations it reaches up to the next higher G, but breaks out of the rhythmic ostinato. Its increasingly faster iterations of G push against the dotted-eighth tactus, an effect Copland specifies in his instructions as "senza misuro."[21] At R9 the oboe melody returns to eighths and quarters, as shown on Example 8.5, rebarred in the C-oriented version of $\frac{3}{8}$ so as to help the listener evaluate the pitch structure in a metric context. Notice that it briefly completes the C–G fifth with a triadic E (marked with an asterisk on Example 8.5) but continues in a more dissonant way.[22]

In tonal music, rhythmic challenges to an ongoing periodic pattern are normally heard as syncopations, especially when the stable pattern is in the bass (here, the D–C). For example, in the C-oriented version of $\frac{3}{8}$, we can characterize the A–G iterations as a metric "displacement dissonance" because they replicate the same tactus with a different starting point.[23] In post-tonal music textures like these are often called polyrhythmic, and even polymetric in cases where competing strata set forth more than one potential metric interpretation. For example, when the oboe melody breaks out of the ostinato, it seemingly moves at a different tempo and its metric relationship with the other music is momentarily obscured.

While the evidence for a perceivable polymeter – one where we attend fully to the accentual distinctions and anticipatory features of meter – has been shown to be weak at best, this example does invoke two simultaneous rhythmic strands, neither of which subsumes the rhythmic identity of the other.[24] Especially remarkable is the music spanning Rehearsal 12a through Rehearsal 15, given as Example 8.6. While the orchestral ostinati continue

8.6 Organ melody at R12a

their iterations, organ and first violin alternate a familiar folk tune whose equal durations proceed at two different rates. Notice that at R12a, the organ moves entirely in dotted quarters (notably with a downbeat favoring the ostinato's A), whereas the violin tune proceeds entirely in half notes.[25] The effect is like an off-kilter call-and-response: rather than a continuous

8.7 Violin melody rebarred in $\genfrac{}{}{0pt}{}{4}{4}$

single meter, we hear the alternation of a tactus as it switches between a dotted quarter and a half note, with a possibility of a "multiply metric" overlap between the two sections.[26]

Perhaps because the tune moves in equal values (be those dotted quarters or half notes), because it moves primarily by step, and because the metric organization of the accompanimental ostinato itself has two possible identities, the ostinati almost immediately take on the metric identities of the organ or violin, while each asserts its own meter ($\genfrac{}{}{0pt}{}{6}{8}$ or $\genfrac{}{}{0pt}{}{4}{4}$). Example 8.7 rebars the violin version of the tune in $\genfrac{}{}{0pt}{}{4}{4}$ to highlight this effect; notice that here too the ostinato A appears on a downbeat, and that the descending scale from E down a tenth to C in the accompanying organ part moves in tandem with it, sounding momentarily as syncopated.

Post-tonal composers exploit the spectrum of perceptual possibilities inherent in these textures, from subjecting one line to the metric organization of the other to hearing them as nearly completely separate motions.[27] In this particular example, we are more likely to switch between duple and triple meters, reinterpreting familiar materials with new metric identities, a violation of a tonal metric preference to maintain a metric identity.[28] Other post-tonal composers layer musical strata in ways that suggest near independence, as if two different pieces are playing simultaneously. These pieces reach an important juncture in the efficacy of meter as an organizing rhythmic device; their multiplicity makes them worthy of repeated hearings, and often these dense textures are repeated literally or nearly literally, perhaps demanding from listeners a certain ongoing metric flexibility.

The Precision of Duration

When do rhythmic practices become so irregular that we no longer measure time through counting and phrase rhythm? This is clearly a rhetorical question, for individuals differ not only in their willingness and ability to reference earlier models, but also in what they might experience as

8.8 Messiaen, *Quartet for the End of Time*, VI, opening.

counting. The above analyses lean heavily on one's ability to recognize patterns in order to anticipate subsequent events, but plenty of post-tonal music explores instead a wider diversity of rhythmic styles. In these cases, events that engender one's sense of metric accent – that is, of time "marked for consciousness"[29] – may be too sporadic or irregular to provoke one's anticipation of another such accent. Additionally, while one may apprehend the boundaries of phrases, s/he may not sense motion through them. The next example may serve as a challenge to the measurements of meter and phrase rhythm, although it is highly rhythmically driven.

The opening measures of the sixth movement of Olivier Messiaen's *Quartet for the End of Time* are reproduced as Example 8.8; this reduction of the movement comes from Figure 13 in the composer's 1944 *Technique de mon langage musical* where Messiaen describes in great detail how he conceived of his rhythmic vocabulary.[30] Three of the composer's innovations include "additive and subtractive" rhythms, "non-retrogradable" rhythms, and an isorhythmic technique for creating complex polyrhythms. The notations on Figure 13, including plus signs and identifications of rhythmic motives with letters, point to some of these techniques, each of which provides new opportunities for the measurement of time.

All instruments play this rhythmically complicated melody. The first notated measure begins with a stepwise descent, from F♯ to E in equal eighths. This motive is answered on beat two by a stepwise descent from B♭to A♭, but not before B♭rises by the same distance to C, a sixteenth-note additive rhythm that breaks the pattern of equal eighths and also fills out the emerging whole-tone scale.[31] Messiaen writes that the plus sign under the C indicates it is an "added value," and that is "complicates" motive B.[32] Added values always lengthen a given duration, here by a half, resulting at the given tempo in a very short duration. More generally, added values can elongate any duration as long as it can be quantified proportionally. The wide variety of possible augmentations and diminutions of durations is demonstrated in a table given as his Example 24.[33] Messiaen writes that this

8.9 The interpretation of additive rhythms

practice produces "ametrical" music, but a close examination of the first phrase in Example 8.8 (mm. 1–4) shows a careful, ordered introduction of durations that stretch and interrupt the division of a quarter pulse by two eighths.

In mm. 1–2, the added value appears only in the second notated beat (Messiaen has made beat divisions clear with his beaming), and in both cases the elongation adds a fifth sixteenth to beats that otherwise last a quarter note. As the phrase continues, Messiaen's added values elongate beat 3 (m. 3) and in the final measure of the phrase (m. 4), he elongates the downbeat by two sixteenths and the second beat by one, creating the sole pitch lasting three sixteenths (C).

This tiny addition, creating "beats" of six and five sixteenths, slow down the fourth measure, thereby helping bring the phrase to a cadence on the opening pitch F♯. Messiaen remarks that the added values help create motion through melodies, writing that they enhance the preparation toward an accent, and elongate descents to goal notes.[34] For example, in his Figure 12, given here as Example 8.9, the added sixteenth at the opening (marked A) elongates the ascent up to the accented figure B, and the added sixteenth in the third notated measure (on D♯, marked with letter C) strengthens and elongates the descent down to the E in the next measure. Similarly, Messiaen comments that the elongated C (m. 4, marked by letter A) in Example 8.8 – the only time a pitch lasts three sixteenths in the first phrase – helps "slacken the descents by elongating their penultimate note."[35]

The second phrase in Example 8.8 only complicates the succession of rhythms more, and as the passage continues it seems unlikely that we can actively predict when an eighth note will be extended, especially given that sixteenths are not always added values. From where does our interest in this very intricate rhythmic experience originate? I suggest that we may be more engaged in enjoying the sudden twists and turns of a limited set of durations than in anticipating the return of given patterns; after all, this movement's title references the sounding of seven trumpets signaling the apocalypse, music we might expect to be other-worldly.[36]

8.10 Non-retrogradable rhythms that form a larger isorhythm at Rehearsal F.

Many of the rhythms Messiaen creates with added values are symmetric, or as he calls them, non-retrogradable. Although not all non-retrogradable rhythms form challenges to the creation of traditional meter, those he values most exhibit embedded rhythms based on his principles of augmentation and diminution, and may last more than the necessary three durations it takes to form a non-retrogradable rhythm. In these cases, "all rhythms divisible into two groups, one of which is the retrograde of the other, with a *central common value*, are nonretrogradable."[37] Figure 33 (reproduced here as Example 8.10) from his treatise demonstrates complex examples, including the middle portion of the movement (Rehearsal F) we are studying.

Each of the notated measures is a non-retrogradable rhythm, and like the rhythms that open the movement, these are also carefully ordered, not only within measures, but in the passage as a whole. At first glance we can see that a slower set of durations (three, five, and eight sixteenths) gradually evolves into measures whose non-retrogradable rhythms contain nearly all sixteenths (as shown by the internal subdivisions above each of the seven measures of Example 8.10.) As a consequence, the measures themselves get shorter. The seven-bar pattern is repeated as an isorhythm (notice the repetition of the first measure's rhythm appears as the eighth measure in Figure 33). The sequence of pitches within this complex isorhythm is also patterned: Messiaen repeats a sixteen-pitch class sequence (notice that the D-major triad repeats beginning on the seventeenth duration), and in combination with the longer seven-bar isorhythm, the melody's repetitions are continuously varied by new rhythmic settings.[38]

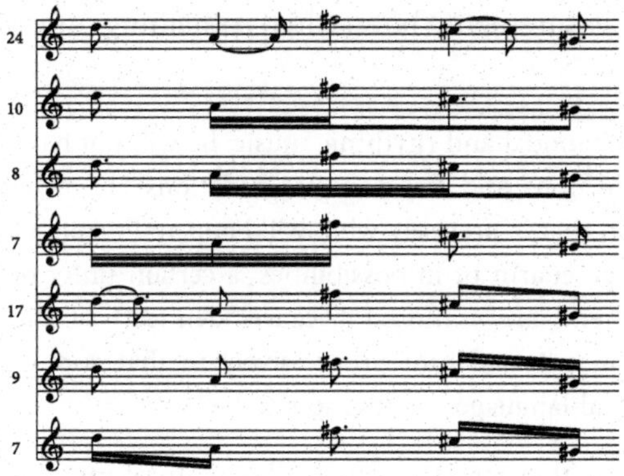

8.11 Rhythmic variations of pitch ostinato.

Hearing the melody return as the isorhythm speeds up and then returns to its slower durations is an exquisite experience of encountering microscopic variations among melodic repetitions while also hearing the pace gradually speed up and then slow down rather suddenly. For example, consider the four durational settings of the opening measure, easily recognizable as a D-major triad followed by two descending leaps of a fourth, given as Example 8.11. The five-note ordered segment is vertically aligned for comparison, and the numbers to the left show how long each segment lasts. Pitches endure from one to eight sixteenths, and successions of sixteenths are common, but no particular pattern emerges. As an idiosyncratic set of durations unfolds, the pace of the pattern speeds up, slows down, and speeds up again, eventually to become nothing but sixteenths (in music not shown here).

Although these practices are interesting unto themselves as compositional techniques, they also affect our experience of temporality in new ways. They create dizzying changes of speed, asking us to enjoy the minute differences between sixteenths and eighths without reference to a continuous pulse, while also shaping our sense of flow across longer spans, from nearly even to bumpy to driven. Remember that four performers play these complicated rhythms in unison and octave doubling, fully exposing their abilities to coordinate precisely with one another; the unending stream of finely graded durations in constant variation requires them to realize in time the exquisite durational differences of one, two, three, or more sixteenth notes.[39] Their efforts are virtuosic, pushing the boundaries of temporal action and perception.

Messiaen frequently wrote that he wanted to invoke mystical, supernatural qualities in his music, suggesting that the appeal of these rhythms lies not in their exact perpetual measurement, but rather something more transcendent:

> Let us think now of the hearer of our modal and rhythmic music; he will not have time ... to inspect the nontranspositions and the nonretrogradations ... to be charmed will be his only desire. And that is precisely what will happen: in spite of himself he will submit to the strange charm of impossibilities: a certain unity of movement (where beginning and end are confused because identical) in the nonretrogradation, all things which will lead him progressively to that sort of *theological rainbow* which the musical language ... attempts to be.[40]

The composer's words border on the ecstatic, especially in invoking the image of a rainbow, a figure whose span is indivisible – without beginning or end. Amidst the unending stream of irregular rhythmic attacks (for this music rarely rests) arises the possibility of a continuity unarticulated by formal breaks. We may recognize returns of the D-major triad as the music begun in Example 8.10 cycles through a meticulously ordered process, and along the way we may also experience sensations of resolution (i.e., pitches E–F and A–B♭as leading tone to tonic) but we likely do not experience clear phrase boundaries or a directed motion through phrases. Instead Messiaen directs us toward the mystical impossibility of an eternal, plentiful time, full of complex, endlessly diverse activity.

The Fullness of Time

In the four preceding analyses I have suggested how composers challenge common methods of measuring rhythm – counting (following metric organization), chunking (marking boundaries of phrases), and comprehending durations (perceiving lengths in proportional relation to one another). The analyses are samples of a much larger set of experimentations too lengthy to cite, and constantly growing. Composers such as Witold Lutoslawski, György Ligeti, John Cage, Steve Reich, and Arvo Pärt help us question the limits of counting and boundary articulation, among many others.[41] Composer and theorist Jonathan Kramer takes a broader view of post-tonal rhythmic novelty in defining more ephemeral categories of musical time, distinguishing between linear and non-linear time, and describing music exhibiting multiply directed, moment, and vertical time. Underlying most of these characteristics is a set of fundamental questions about time as it is experienced simply in the present tense – be that the current moment or an ongoing eternal present – compared to time as experienced as passage – be that the distant past, or simply the preceding seconds. How can we measure "rhythm" in music that breaks or eschews articulations? What are the outer limits of perceiving acceleration and deceleration? How can we experience extreme densities of texture as temporal? How do we experience the passage of time in music characterized by great rhythmic complexity and no fixed temporal referent? Only time will tell.[42]

Endnotes

1 For a good introduction to how we rely on various cognitive time mechanisms for both beat-based rhythms and non-beat-based rhythms, a helpful distinction in post-tonal music, see M. Henry and J. Grahn, "Music, Brain, and Movement," in R. Ashley and R. Timmers (eds.), *Routledge Companion to Music Cognition* (Routledge, 2017), 63–73. For information on music and movement, see also D. Levitin, J. Grahn, and J. London, "The Psychology of Music: Rhythm and Movement," *Annual Review of Psychology*, 69 (2018), 51–75.

2 Malcolm Gillies (*Grove Music Online*, https://doi.org/10.1093/gmo/9781561592630.article.40686, accessed Nov. 14, 2018) writes that these pieces were meant to be learned alongside music from the Western tonal tradition, suggesting a possible reliance on tonal metric practice: "Bartók stressed that his collection did not present a complete 'progressive method', but rather a base to which works by other composers, such as Bach and Czerny, should be added. In a letter to Boosey & Hawkes of 13 February 1940, he explained that he saw *Mikrokosmos* as a bridge leading from his own 20th-century shore to an older one, either through 'centuries-old folk music' or through such typical devices of older art music as canon and imitation."

3 László Vikárius describes "Bulgarian rhythm" as "the continuous employment of an asymmetrical metre throughout a piece, referred to by the Romanian folklorist Constantin Brăiloiu's term as *aksak*, or 'lame rhythm'" (55). He notes that other adjacent pieces in the *Mikrokosmos* such as #115 are meant to introduce how to play $\frac{7}{8}$ in easier contexts; L. Vikárius, "Bartók's Bulgarian Dances and the Order of Things," *Studia Musicologica*, 53 (2012), 55 and 59.

4 C. Hasty, *Meter as Rhythm* (Oxford University Press 1997). For a review of Hasty's book in accessible language, see G. Horlacher, "Review of *Meter as Rhythm* by C. Hasty," *Intégral*, 11 (1997), 181–90.

5 The relationship between tempo and perception of the tactus is discussed in J. London, *Hearing in Time: Psychological Aspects of Musical Meter*, 2nd ed. (Oxford University Press, 2012), Chapter 2.

6 The notated measure would thus last just over a second, a "mensurally determinate" duration, that is, one that can be mentally replicated with a high degree of accuracy, enhancing its metric potential. See Hasty, *Meter as Rhythm*, and Horlacher's review of Hasty. See also S. Arom, "L'aksak: Principes et typologie," *Cahiers de musiques traditionnelles*, 17 (2005), 11–48, where aksak is defined in part by tempo.

7 London, *Hearing in Time*, Chapters 7 and 8. Of course, someone with cultural competence in hearing seven beats as metric may not hear this piece as deriving from a model based on Western art music at all.

8 Multiple ways of hearing this kind of metric irregularity in Bartók's music are considered in G. Horlacher, "Bartók's 'Change of Time': Coming Unfixed," *Music Theory Online*, 7.1 (2001).

9 The recording was issued in 1952 by Columbia as ML 4419 in the "Meet the Composer" series.

10 William Rothstein defines external expansions as additions to the external boundaries of phrases, that is, musical material that precedes the phrase's presentational beginning and musical material that follows its cadence; W. Rothstein, *Phrase Rhythm in Tonal Music* (New York: Schirmer Books, 1989).

11 Richard Taruskin writes voluminously about Stravinsky's modernist take on Russian folklore. For a discussion that focuses specifically on the *Rite*, see Chapter 12 of R. Taruskin, *Stravinsky and the Russian Traditions* (University of California Press, 1996).

12 Debates about the extent to which metric periodicity operates in Stravinsky's music are frequent, and often characterized (using terminology developed by Andrew Imbrie for counting in Beethoven) along a spectrum of conservative to radical, depending on how easily one breaks away from periodic counting; A. Imbrie, "'Extra' Measures and Metrical Ambiguity in Beethoven," in A. Tyson (ed.), *Beethoven Studies* (New York: W. W. Norton & Company, 1973), 45–66. Pieter Van den Toorn, in *Stravinsky and the* Rite of Spring (University of California Press, 1987), describes the debate in Chapters 3 and 4. I attempt to capture aspects of both stances.

13 In an early version of the scenario, Stravinsky writes that the other maidens celebrate her (the Chosen One) in a "boisterous martial dance." See Taruskin, *Stravinsky*, 874 and more generally 860–91. The reader is encouraged to view Millicent Hodson's restoration of Nijinsky's choreography of this dance; one possible link is https://youtu.be/9phS4Piiq2o. It's impossible to know how much this version represents Nijinsky's choices, although Hodson researched available archival evidence extensively. Here, the choreography serves two purposes. First, some of the irregularities in the *Rite* may have arisen as much from bodily rhythm as from musical rhythm (the work was first a ballet before it was a concert piece). Second, seeing dancers repeat movement sequences of variable length, as well as hearing these irregularities, is especially powerful. Analyses that connect the choreographic rhythm with the dance include M. Hodson, *Nijinsky's Crime against Grace: Reconstruction Score of the Original Choreography for* Le sacre du printemps (Stuyvesant, NY: Pendragon, 1997); M. Hodson, "Death by Dancing," in S. Neff, M. Carr, and G. Horlacher (eds.), *The Rite of Spring at 100* (Oxford University Press, 2017), 47–80; and G. Horlacher, "Rethinking Blocks and Superimposition: Form in 'Ritual of the Two Rival Tribes,'" in Neff et al. (eds.), *Rite*, 331–83.

14 G. Horlacher, *Building Blocks: Repetition and Continuity in the Music of Stravinsky* (Oxford University Press, 2011), especially Chapter 2. Although the score is reduced to mostly outer voices (sometimes in octave displacement for ease of reading), all of its measures are present.

15 F. Lerdahl and R. Jackendoff, *A Generative Theory of Tonal Music* (MIT Press, 1983) is often cited as a fundamental text about tonal meter formation. They maintain in one of their metric preference rules that we prefer a metrically stable bass part when other parts contradict it. See especially Chapters 3 and 4.

16 A 3+2 hearing is not impossible, deriving from a sense of the melodic G falling to the F♯. More generally, people may differ in using a bass line or a melodic line as a metric marker.

17 The tempo is unusually marked two tied eighths, *not* one quarter, = 144. Perhaps Stravinsky displayed the tempo by subdividing a quarter into two eighths because the initial core measures last one eighth longer than a quarter; keeping track of the duration of eighths is critical for the performers and conductors.

18 While this analysis has omitted key discussions of pitch structure, it is worth noting that the chordal and melodic configurations also invoke both tonality and a modernist chromaticism as they gain individual, stable identities. The chord mimics a dominant-seventh chord (with A as its root) in its content and spacing, while the melody descends by step through the very familiar Stravinskian 0134 octatonic tetrachord.

19 Notice that while the third iteration of the motive is barred differently ($\frac{5}{8}$ is followed by $\frac{7}{8}$, $\frac{3}{8}$, and $\frac{4}{8}$), motive A is almost always five eighths long. This is one of many examples where notated barring obscures the nature of motivic return in Stravinsky's music. The passage is littered with changes of meter signature, and includes signatures of $\frac{3}{8}$, $\frac{4}{8}$, $\frac{5}{8}$, $\frac{6}{8}$, $\frac{7}{8}$, $\frac{9}{4}$, and $\frac{7}{4}$. Whether these signatures express one's perception of heard meter is open for question, although it's worth noting that $\frac{5}{8}$ appears in seven of the fifteen bars.

20 The quarter-note pulsation of the vamp's second appearance (at the second bar of R106) is *not* interrupted at its end, a small rhythmic detail that demonstrates how significant a duration an eighth note is in this dance.

21 I speculate that the movement is barred in $\frac{3}{4}$ in order to make clear the durations of this accelerating oboe line. Notating these durations in $\frac{3}{8}$ would be nearly impossible. In 1944, Copland wrote about the difficulties of notating rhythmically complicated post-tonal music, noting the possibility that barlines may not always represent "heard" meter, and pointing to the necessity for easily read notation in ensemble music.

22 The reference to Stravinsky's use of ostinato is fairly clear, as described by G. Murchison, *The American Stravinsky: The Style and Aesthetics of Copland's New American Music, the Early Works, 1921–1938* (University of Michigan Press, 2012). She traces how Copland learned about Stravinsky's music via Nadia Boulanger, and how Copland's modernist music in general relies on

post-tonal rhythmic vocabularies. See especially Chapter 2, and analyses of this symphony on 48–53.

23 H. Krebs, *Metrical Dissonance in the Music of Robert Schumann* (Oxford University Press, 1999) generalizes a theory of metric dissonance for tonal music.

24 For a discussion of cognitive evidence for perceiving simultaneous contrasting metric perceptions, see E. Poudrier and B. H. Repp, "Can Musicians Track Two Different Beats Simultaneously?," *Music Perception*, 30 (2013), 369–90. Also pertinent is John Roeder's concept of pulse streams, where superimposed voices with contrasting rhythmic organizations can be tracked in how they support or contrast with one another; J. Roeder, "Interacting Pulse Streams in Schoenberg's Atonal Polyphony," *Music Theory Spectrum*, 16 (1994), 231–49.

25 The tune is taken from the eighteenth-century French folk tune "Au clair de la lune," likely an homage to Nadia Boulanger, with whom he was studying, who arranged the commission of the work and who premiered it on organ with the New York Symphony Orchestra under Walter Damrosch in 1925. This premiere was Copland's first time hearing how his metric effects sounded in his chosen orchestrations.

26 G. Horlacher, "Multiple Meters and Metrical Process in the Music of Steve Reich," *Intégral*, 14 (2000), 1–33, introduces the term "multiple meter" to describe much of Steve Reich's music; the term suggests that we may perceive a piece like *Piano Phase* in more than one meter over multiple repetitions (as opposed to perceiving two meters at the same time).

27 See for example music by Charles Ives, Elliott Carter, and György Ligeti, among others.

28 Lerdahl and Jackendoff, *Generative Theory*, include among their metric preference rules the inclination for metric parallelism.

29 G. W. Cooper and L. B. Meyer, *The Rhythmic Structure of Music* (University of Chicago Press, 1963), 8.

30 For discussions of rhythm, including the use of non-Western music and bird song as rhythmic resources, see O. Messiaen, *Technique de mon langage musical*, John Satterfield (trans.) (Paris: Alphonse Leduc [1944], 1956) and *Traité de rythme, de couleur, et d'ornithologie* (Paris: Alphonse Leduc, 1994).

31 Messiaen identifies the mode of this passage as his mode VI in his modes of limited transposition, in which the whole-tone scale is a subset. Beginning on C, this mode contains C, D, E, F, F♯, G♯, A♯, and B. See Figure 350 in Messiaen, *Technique*.

32 See Messiaen, *Technique*, Chapter 3 and the annotated musical excerpt on page 2 in the musical example for the initial discussion. The brackets on Messiaen's Figure 13 are meant to indicate the "large rhythmic divisions," and appear only with additive durations; Messiaen notably does not call them beats.

33 Added values are described as augmentations and diminutions in Messiaen, *Technique*, 18, and a comprehensive demonstrative table is on page 3 in the

figures chapter. Messiaen's interest in non-Western music, and especially the music of India, is a likely origin for his ideas.

34 See Messiaen, *Technique*, Chapter 3, Section 3 and their related musical examples.

35 Messiaen, *Technique*, 17.

36 See the Bible's Book of Revelations, Chapters 8–11. Messiaen wrote this quartet while in a German prison camp during the Second World War and makes many references to apocalyptic themes.

37 Messiaen, *Technique*, 20, and Chapter 5 more generally.

38 Vincent Benitez describes Messiaen's ideas about time, order, and duration, connecting the composer's ideas about time with his desire for order (including in his serial compositions), and for his reliance on ideas of philosopher Henri Bergson. V. Benitez, "Reconsidering Messiaen as Serialist," *Music Analysis*, 28 (2009), especially 270–73 and Example 2, for a discussion of Messiaen's use of ostinato where measurement and timelessness are both essential elements, and 280–84, for a discussion of how number provides order and Messiaen's exploration of the ideas of Gaston Bachalard.

39 Messiaen's concern with rhythmic order appears also in his geometric approach to music described by J. Hook, "Rhythm in the Music of Messiaen: An Algebraic Study and an Application in the Turangalîla Symphony," *Music Theory Spectrum*, 20 (1998), 97–120.

40 Messiaen, *Technique*, 21.

41 Howard Smither lists a plethora of rhythmically complicated post-tonal works for the first part of the twentieth century, including many examples worthy of further study; H. Smither, "The Rhythmic Analysis of 20th-Century Music," *Journal of Music Theory*, 8 (1964), 54–88.

42 Countless authors have speculated on what an unmeasurable or eternal time might be like. Robert Hatten describes musical "plenitude" as a compositional premise based on "saturation or repleteness"; R. Hatten, *Interpreting Musical Gestures, Topics, and Tropes: Mozart, Beethoven, Schubert* (Indiana University Press, 2004). Jonathan Kramer might use the labels "vertical time" or (drawing from Stockhausen) "moment time"; J. Kramer, *The Time of Music: New Meanings, New Temporalities, New Listening Strategies* (New York: Schirmer Books, 1988).

9 The Concept of Rhythm

Composers in Their Own Words

ADAM SLIWINSKI

What is rhythm? I have not asked myself this question in a long time. Rhythm permeates my life as an ever-present flow of pulses, phrases, counting, and variation. Years of accumulated experience have furnished me with the sense that I know and understand it. Writing this chapter afforded me the opportunity to check in with composers who have deeply affected the way I think about rhythm. As I rummaged through their writings and works, I encountered a variety of perspectives that shook that sense of certainty and led me down multiple paths of inquiry.

The first time this washed over me was when I read an interview with the French composer Olivier Messiaen (1908–92). He wrote, "I feel that rhythm is the primordial and perhaps essential part of music; I think it most likely existed before melody and harmony, and in fact, I have a secret preference for this element. I cherish this preference all the more because I feel it distinguished my entry into contemporary music."[1]

I agree with everything he says here, and I'm delighted that an eminent composer places this much emphasis on rhythm. He even refers to himself as a "Rhythmician" and waxes about the inventiveness of Mozart. Then I encountered this statement: "Schematically, rhythmic music is music that scorns repetition, squareness, equal divisions, and that is inspired by the movements of nature, movements of free and unequal divisions."

This is not what I would have meant by calling something rhythmic. I would have usually characterized music with "free and unequal divisions" as *non*-rhythmic. Also, I am certain that nature contains plenty of repetition. How can Messiaen and I both be so pro-rhythm and mean entirely different things by it? This chapter, stimulated by that paradox, follows my process of reexamining the fundamentals of rhythm through several topics: first, the basic concept of rhythm and its components; then the sub-categories of time, pulse, and meter; and finally how these concepts translate from the page of a score to live performance.

Conceiving Rhythm

The twentieth-century American composer, writer, and teacher Henry Cowell (1897–1965) said this:

In almost any reliable book on harmony, you will find the axiom that the primary elements of music are melody, harmony, and rhythm. If noise were admitted at all, and I doubt if it ever has been, it would unquestionably be classified as part of rhythm. Rhythm is a conception, not a physical reality. It is true that to be realized in music, rhythm must be marked by some sort of sound, but this sound is not in and of itself the rhythm. Rhythmical considerations are the durations of sounds, the amount of stress applied to sounds, the rate of speed as indicated by the movements of sounds, periodicity of sound patterns, and so on.[2]

"Rhythm is a conception, not a physical reality." This sounds like one of those statements in a book on astrophysics that is difficult to wrap one's mind around, such as that "time is a monstrous illusion" (which is true according to Einstein).[3] But it makes sense: rhythms are contextual events, not single objects. The concept always describes more than one sound event. We measure the regularity of those events, and the events have many points of comparison with each other.

Take the concept of accent, a note that receives emphasis. This emphasis exists in relation to notes before and after it. We cannot speak of a single sound, no matter how loud and declamatory, as being accented without knowing what surrounds it. What if that loud note turned out to be the quietest in a succession of louder notes which were still to come? This understanding of the timing and emphasis of more than one sound event depends on us being able to describe how they relate to each other as rhythms. Cowell is lucid when he claims that rhythm is not a physical reality: the sounds themselves *are* a physical reality, but the sense in which they are rhythmic exists as a set of relationships.

Messiaen provides another helpful quote which he attributes to Plato: "Rhythm is the ordering of movement."[4] This definition of rhythm allows us to expand what the word can mean, and it syncs perfectly with Cowell's idea. It also allows us to separate related sub-concepts – pulse, active rhythmic energy – which we often mean when we say something is rhythmic, and to group them as part of the larger idea. The concept of the "ordering of movement" allows us to speak more precisely about what rhythm is and what it does.

If some of this seems abstract, it may help to think visually rather than conceptually. Table 9.1 depicts a timeline with different rhythms written out as evenly spaced boxes. This kind of chart is exactly how modern recording and sequencing software represents music on the screen. For now, we are only concerned with the ordering of sound events and not with any other musical aspects such as pitch, loudness, and so on.

The first element to consider is time, the frame or box. It is an inescapable element for rhythm to exist (more on that later). Wrangling and shaping time

Table 9.1 A variety of different rhythms and pulses presented on a timeline

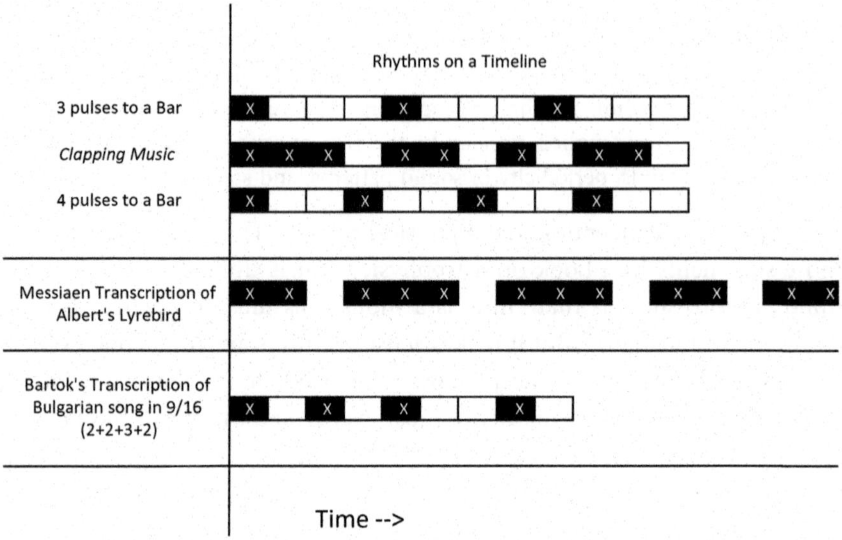

is one of the primary challenges of the performing arts. On this chart, time flows from left to right (as it also does in Western music notation).

Now we can place events and show two characteristics: when they occur, and for how long (duration). If events are repeated and regularly spaced, we have a pulse. Pulse is related to everything we do as humans, most of all the way that our hearts beat throughout our lives. Because of this connection to our bodies, we often say *rhythmic* when we mean *pulsed*. On top of that pulse we can choose to place other sounds that have a perceivable connection to that pulse, such as in Steve Reich's *Clapping Music*, which consists of a pattern of 3–2–1–2. Here, although the events change, the ear and body can hear and feel their relationship to the pulse. The events that occur off the beat we often refer to as syncopations. *Clapping Music* has the potential, common to the Ghanaian music Reich studied, of being interpreted against either three large beats or four, which I have placed on either side of it.

A lot of the work I do as a percussionist is with these two layers (pulse and events perceivably related to the pulse). But Messiaen challenges me to remember that in the process of "ordering movement," this is not the only way things might be. His assertion that rhythm could instead be "movements of free and unequal divisions" reminds me that we might design motives on this grid that are not intended to be heard against a pulse, such as one of Messiaen's own motives inspired by birdsong. When this transcription of an Albert's Lyrebird song is placed on the timeline alongside other more regular rhythms, it doesn't look so different from *Clapping Music*, except that the natural groupings of the birdsong don't refer to regular pulse or meter.[5] Or, the pulse itself could be a smaller connecting thread that creates changing and asymmetric larger beats. This creates music that has both a pulse and continuous variation (and that Messiaen used in pieces like his *Quartet for the End of Time*). In the last part of Table 9.1, transcribed by Béla Bartók (1881–1945) from Bulgarian folk music, a meter of 9 is grouped 2+2+3+2 instead of 3+3+3. Here, each little box represents a small fast pulse that fits into larger groupings.

The speed at which we read or realize these rhythms across the page is the tempo, and this is where Cowell's insight about the conception of rhythm is the clearest: the "ordered movement" passes through time, which is often measured by metrics such as beats per minute, or in older music, quasi-character markings such as *allegro* or *andante*. This means that representing a rhythm on the page can be helpful, but it is incomplete. A breathless scherzo (normally fast music) could conceivably be written in long whole notes, while a slow funeral dirge could be in choppy thirty-second notes, with the right tempo markings. Ultimately, a written score can only go so far in conveying the character of rhythm, which lives in our bodies as we translate the ideas from the page.

Time

> Time seems to me to be the radical dimension of all music.[6] – John Cage (1912–92)

On August 29, 1952, a man walked onto an outdoor concert hall stage in front of an audience in Woodstock, New York, sat down at a piano, and did almost nothing. The pianist was David Tudor, and the nothing was John Cage's silent piece, known as *4′33″*. The composer and journalist Kyle Gann describes that first performance in his book *No Such Thing as Silence: John Cage's 4′33″*, which is devoted to the piece:

> Pianist David Tudor sat down at the piano on the small raised wooden stage, closed the keyboard lid over the keys, and looked at a stopwatch. Twice in the next four minutes he raised the lid up and lowered it again, careful to make no audible sound, although at the same time he was turning pages of the music, which were devoid of notes. After four minutes and thirty-three seconds had passed, Tudor

rose to receive applause – and thus was premiered one of the most controversial, inspiring, surprising, infamous, perplexing, and influential works since Igor Stravinsky's *Le Sacre du Printemps*.[7]

Although it has now been almost seventy years since that premiere, the work still causes uneasiness in the world of concert music. For many in the classical music world, Cage's gesture is best understood as a kind of joke, a winking nod at the idea that "anything is possible."[8] Or it is understood as a rebellious flourish against the staid traditions of the concert hall. The work is simultaneously simpler and more complex: it is about sound and time.

In the 1930s and 1940s, Cage wrote, gathered, and solicited a whole new body of works for percussion instruments that formed the early foundation of repertoire for groups like my quartet Sō Percussion. The insight that drove this activity is that measuring time allows the chaotic noises of the world (i.e., percussion) into the concert hall. Cage set about building compositions for percussion in which musical forms stood apart like a series of bins or containers waiting to be filled by noises. These noises, whether a drum, rattle, or even a blown conch shell, existed in the composition for their own sake rather than as part of a system of argument and development.

In the piece *Third Construction* (1941), Cage pre-composed a structure of twenty-four sections of music, each containing twenty-four measures in $\frac{2}{2}$ time, before filling the piece in with notes. Within those sections, each individual player has their own rhythmic scheme that determines instrumentation and other elements.

Ultimately, *Third Construction* and *4′33″* both grapple with time by creating a container and filling it in. In the case of *Third Construction*, that box is somewhat malleable because it is measured by notes that move relative to tempo. With *4′33″*, the container is limited by measuring against the clock. For me, *4′33″* has become more than a provocative theatrical gesture, or even a reminder to listen to our environment; it is a manifesto on time. Whenever one measures time and sound occurs (whether a musician intends it or not), music happens.

Cage was not the first or only composer to care about the role of time in understanding the nature of rhythm. The writings of the American composer Elliott Carter (1908–2012) feature a categorization of the experience of time formulated by the French composer and theorist Charles Koechlin (1867–1950). I will quote them here as they appear in Carter's writings:

Koechlin's Four Aspects of Time:

1) Pure duration, a fundamental of our deepest consciousness, and apparently independent of the external world: life flows by. . .
2) Psychological time: This is the impression we have of (the above) duration according to the events of our existence: minutes that seem centuries, hours that go by too quickly. . . . That is, duration relative to the circumstances of life.
3) Time measured by mathematical means; all of which depend on visual methods – sand clocks, clocks, chronometers . . .
4) Finally, I would like to talk of "musical time." To us musicians this fact does not present itself as it does to scientists. Auditory time is without a doubt the kind that comes closest to pure duration. However, it appears to have some connection with space in that it seems to us measurable (by ear) and divisible. The divisions embodied in musical note-values (whole-notes, half-notes, etc.) lead to a spatialization of time very different from that (based on vision) which Bergson talks about. Besides, as concerns the measure of this (musical) duration, the role of musical memory possesses and importance that seems to escape many.[9]

I find these categories stimulating and have started using them to help students understand how time management (in the musical sense) affects the quality of their performances. Before examining Carter's use of these concepts, I'd like to discuss how they apply in my own performing and teaching.

Most of a percussionist's life is spent oscillating back and forth between realms number three (mathematical) and number four (musical), but always colliding with number two (psychological). The traditional function of percussionists as timekeepers means that we are constantly measuring and dividing. In drummer/percussionist lingo, we talk about whether other players have "good time" or "steady time." Although these concepts relate to accurately measured time, they also imply judgments of what that drummer's time *feels* like. An important consideration might be whether they play on the "front" (anticipating) or "back" (slightly late) part of the pulse, and whether their playing fits the style of music. These are intuitive, subjective concepts, even though the performer is dividing time as evenly as possible. They involve psychological considerations that aren't always measurable.

A performer's memory of tempo changes as they become more familiar with a piece. I have noticed that when first encountering a complex, new written work, the tempo often seems fast – possibly too fast for me to play.

Over time, as I repeat the passages and my hands learn to predict what comes next, the tempo begins to seem more comfortable. If I go even further and memorize the piece, the material becomes second nature and I naturally will play at a faster tempo without realizing it. In the late stages of this process, I must consult a metronome to convince myself that the marked tempo – which I originally thought fast – isn't too slow. The mathematical tempo hasn't changed at all, which means that my perception of the music has. So even measured music is subject to the vagaries of psychology and perception.

Elliott Carter, in response to the ideas of Pyotr Suvchinsky[10] (1892–1985) and Igor Stravinsky (1882–1971), writes about "chronometric" and "chrono-ametric" time as combining Koechlin's four aspects. Chronometric time is that in which "the sense of time is equivalent to the process of the work," which essentially means that a perceivable rhythmic framework organizes events, while chrono-ametric time "has an unstable relationship between the time of the music and the psychological time that it evokes." He mentions composers like Hadyn, Mozart, and Stravinsky as exemplars of chronometric, while a Wagner opera or Gregorian plainchant might represent the chrono-ametric.[11]

This might seem confusing or overly complicated. Essentially, chronometric time evokes realms three and four (musical time and mathematical time), while chrono-ametric evokes one and two (pure duration and psychological time). In a pop song or Haydn sonata, audible phrase repetitions and divided beats reveal the structure. In Gregorian plainchant or solo Japanese shakuhachi flute playing, states of emotion and expression flow through peaks and valleys. The listener doesn't measure the silence between phrases, and the sense of time passing can become very subjective. The movement known as minimalism (exemplified through the works of Steve Reich, Terry Riley, and Philip Glass) provides both experiences at the same time by constructing vast landscapes of precisely measured music.

With these opposing poles in mind, Carter composed his *Sonata for Violoncello and Piano* (1948) partially as an experiment in combining them. From the very opening of the work (see Example 9.1), the piano marks out regular quarter notes while the cello meanders through long held notes. Carter states his intentions for this work: "Such thinking (which I am not sure I agree with) led me to the idea of the opening of the *Cello Sonata* of 1948, in which the piano, so to speak, presents 'chronometric' time, while the cello simultaneously plays in 'chrono-ametric' time."[12]

9.1 Carter, *Sonata for Violoncello and Piano*, first page.

This way of thinking systematically about time led Carter more deeply into other realms of perception. He devised several "methods of continuous change,"[13] especially the technique known as metric modulation. In metric modulation, an audible element of time sustains from one metric or tempo setting to another, but the context transforms and that element functions in different ways.

A simple example: take quarter notes pulsing at 120 beats per minute, and then abruptly cut the tempo in half to be 60 beats per minute (BPM), with those quarter notes now transformed into eighth notes. The audible rate of speed of those notes is steady over the change, but the musical

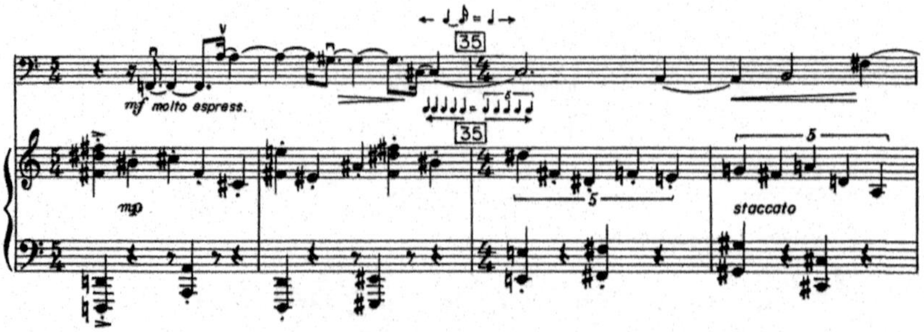

9.2 Carter, *Sonata for Violoncello and Piano*, first metric modulation.

context has transformed to a slower tempo. Another element might now be introduced which is more characteristic of the 60 BPM music, but the connecting thread from the faster tempo provides an aural bridge.

The first instance of this in the *Cello Sonata* is fascinating (see Example 9.2). What we see from measures 33–36 is essentially the same music in which an underlying five-beat pattern in the piano is split in half by the left hand while the cello seems to be playing off the beat. The context for what the cello is doing becomes clear when the metric modulation happens: we now have a $\frac{4}{4}$ measure which is stretched to take up the same amount of time that the $\frac{5}{4}$ took up previously. The former quarter notes are now a five to four polyrhythm over the measure, and the left hand of the piano which was splitting the $\frac{5}{4}$ measure now sits comfortably on beats one and three. Most important, we realize that the previously ill-fitting cello rhythm was a setup for quarter notes after the change.

Pulse

Part of my negative reaction to Messiaen's definition of rhythmic music as that which "scorns repetition" is that I grew up playing music with a steady pulse and frequent repetition. As any skilled drummer knows, pulse is the clay that can be molded to move people's bodies and from which endless cycles of variation, deviation, and return are possible. Over the years I have noticed that composers' feelings about pulse depend greatly upon past musical experiences.

Many European composers of the Second World War generation associated steady pulse with either the marching music of fascist armies or the repeat of gunfire. Avant-garde composition represented an opportunity to make music that was both useless to those repressive forces and rebellious against them. György Ligeti said, "You see, 'avant-garde' music on the whole was a gesture of political resistance. The Nazis proscribed modern art and so did the communists, the latter for a time anyway, then left it in peace but did not support it. My youth was dominated by hatred for Hitler and Stalin and I became an avant-garde, or modern, or experimental composer, for it meant turning against both Nazi and communist cultural policies."[14] In the treatise *Formalized Music,* Iannis Xenakis vividly describes his compositional method in terms of a coalescing uprising and violent military response.[15] Messiaen wrote one of his most famous pieces, the *Quartet for the End of Time*, while a prisoner in a Nazi war camp. His student Pierre Boulez, in a 2008 interview, said of contemporary pop music, "some of it is lively, but the 1–2–3–4 of the rhythms reminds me of marching music."[16]

As a young student, I was puzzled as to why many of these composers insisted on avoiding steady pulse in their music. In my cultural context, pulse was the lifeblood of joy, from Stevie Wonder and the Motown generation to the anthemic pop songs from my childhood in the 1980s; it did not occur to me to associate pulse with negative experiences.

I share this contemporary culture of pulsed music with American composers of other generations such as Steve Reich and Julia Wolfe. In my conversations and public forums with Reich, he often mentions hearing John Coltrane at jazz clubs as a student, and of his love for the playing of the drummer Kenny Clarke. Clarke's ride cymbal playing remains a touchstone for the way Reich wants his own music to feel, which he describes as "floating." He too associated pulse with joy in music.

Over the years I have become more and more interested in how cultural context informs all aspects of musical taste, including pulse. In 1970, Reich wrote, "The pulse and the concept of clear tonal center will reemerge as basic sources of new music."[17] This quote reflects his struggle to assert steady pulse back into concert music. In order to implement his ideas, Reich formed his own ensemble to perform his pulse-based compositions.

In Reich's book, *Writings on Music,*[18] it is surprising how infrequently he talks about rhythm on its own; what appears alongside is usually the word *structure.* For Reich, the use of pulse and repetition stems from a desire to rethink the canvas on which music is painted. In the excerpt from Reich's work *Drumming* in Example 9.3, we see how the opening of the piece teases the possibilities of pulse. The first note on the bongos is assumed by the listener to be a downbeat (the first beat of a metric phrase). As can be seen from following the note-by-note buildup from that first

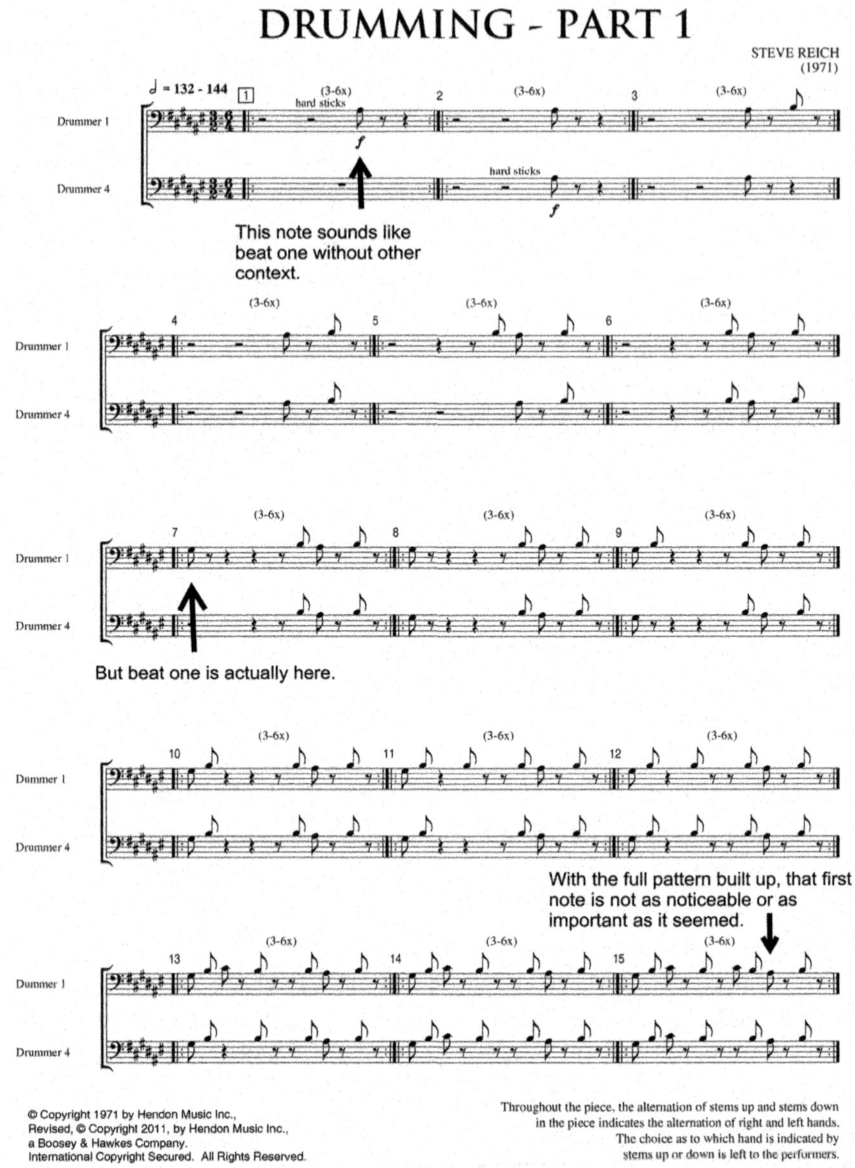

9.3 Reich, *Drumming*, first page.

Drumming by Steve Reich © Copyright 1971 by Hendon Music Inc, a Boosey&Hawkes Company. International Copyright Secured. All Rights Reserved. Reprinted by Permission

measure, this first note is eventually revealed to be the large beat 3 (or 5 of 6) of the phrase. Reich artfully disguises this situation at first, throwing into question our certainty of what it means to hear and feel a beat. Throughout the composition, this prismatic quality manifests at every level.

Henry Cowell's idea of rhythm as a conception and not a fixed object is validated by this example. The single note per measure without the full pattern implies one rhythmic state, but as the audible context around that note changes our concept of its role as a rhythm shifts. The score shows us that this situation existed from the beginning – the note was always on large beat 3. But what we call a rhythm doesn't always have a single identity. This recalls Elliott Carter's concept of metric modulation. A process of transformation that is clear visually in the score might not be evident to the listener, and a skilled composer considers the translation from the page into time and space carefully, exploiting ambiguities for maximum effect.

Another example of steady pulse as a canvas for larger ideas is the piece *Dark Full Ride* by Julia Wolfe. This work is for four drum sets, with the first half performed entirely on cymbals. Wolfe utilizes a common idea from rock drumming: constant sixteenth notes on a closed hi-hat (see Example 9.4).

It is clear from the opening measures that these insistent notes are meant to create an expansive yet measured timescale. We find soon enough that the hi-hat chatter is a premonition of undulating waves and interruptions from other players. Gradually, a new element splashes into the picture and begins to intrude: the open hi-hat, which creates a crashing, sloshy noise that contrasts greatly with the tight "tick" of the closed hi-hat. Eventually, the open sound competes for predominance with the closed sound, toggling back and forth like a switch turning white noise on and off (see Example 9.5). With only these few instruments and their limited capabilities, Wolfe works out these ideas over hundreds of measures. The proportions of the music scramble our perception of time, even though steady pulse is a defining feature of the composition. In this way a composer can enter the realm of "psychological time" even while working with pulse.

Meter

> The laws that regulate the movement of sounds require the presence of a measurable and constant value: *meter*, a purely material element, through which rhythm, a purely formal element, is realized. In other words, meter answers the question of how many equal parts the musical unit which we call a measure is to be divided into, and rhythm answers the question of how these equal parts will be grouped within a given measure. – Igor Stravinsky[19]

9.4 J. Wolfe, *Dark Full Ride*, first page.
Used by kind permission of the composer, Julia Wolfe, and Red Poppy, Ltd

Closely related to pulse is the concept of meter. In ancient Greek poetry, meter was a way of organizing, sequencing, and understanding durations and combinations. For the Greeks, meter involved long and short syllables, while for us in music it refers to the ways in which larger pulses are divided and how they are grouped in regularly recurring patterns.

Béla Bartók was fascinated by the way pulsing rhythm functions, but his perspective was filtered through his knowledge of Central and Eastern European folk music. In his lively essay "The So-Called Bulgarian Rhythm" (1938), Bartók described how he believed classical music would benefit from expanding its metric horizons:

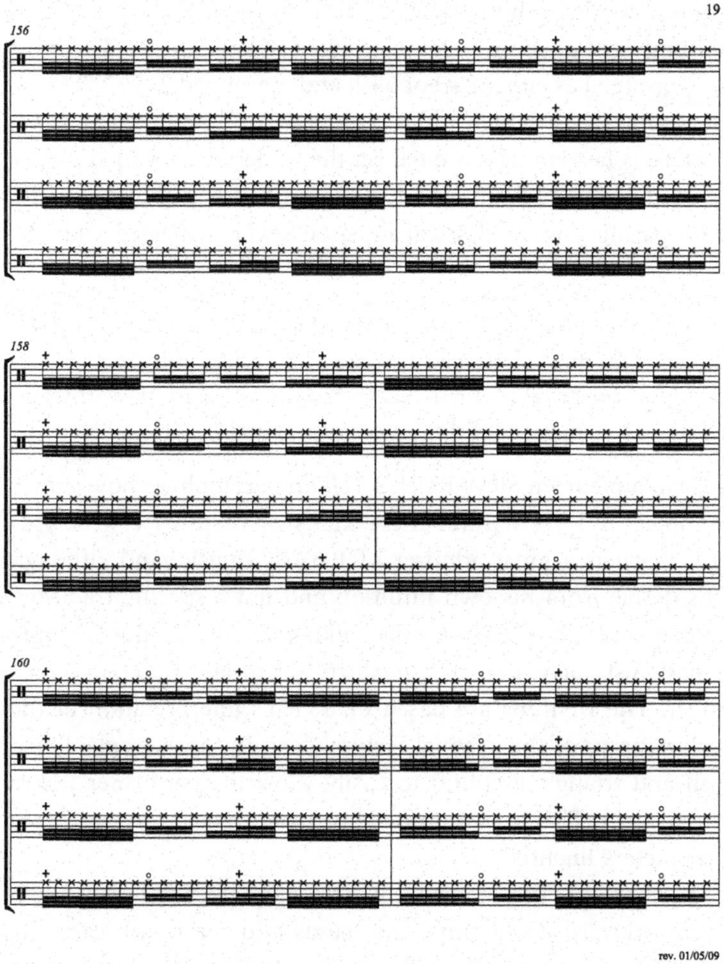

9.5 *Dark Full Ride*, alternation of open and closed hi-hats.
Used by kind permission of the composer, Julia Wolfe, and Red Poppy, Ltd

> The only metres known to ancient European Art music were those divisible into two or threes; that is, in modern terms, 2/4 and 3/4 bars, or their equivalents with the units doubled (half-notes) or halved (eighth-notes) in value. Although I cannot recall any example, it is possible that fleetingly and disguisedly some other kind of rhythmic division occurred here and there, but it is certain that no other kind of time signature was known than these two.[20]

This statement is not historically accurate, but it provides insight into Bartók's mindset about meter and his eagerness to see metric resources expand. Bartók's well-known solution was to explore the folk music of his native Hungary and surrounding areas for inspiration. He was particularly interested in asymmetric rhythms or meters. These are meters with an odd number of pulses which are grouped in larger beats. The most common are $\frac{5}{8}$ grouped as either 2+3 or 3+2, and $\frac{7}{8}$ grouped 2+2+3, 2+3+2, or 3+2+2 (sometimes 7 is thought of as 3+4 or 4+3). These meters, when the smallest pulse is fast enough, are felt on the bigger beats, which means that walking or stepping to them would require a consistently uneven lilt. Bartók was unsparing toward classical musicians who struggled with the concept:

> It is astonishing how helpless orchestral musicians were, not so long ago, when presented with such rhythms. They had become so accustomed to hand-organ-[hurdy-gurdy] like symmetrical rhythms that they could not grasp these rhythms at all, which were so unfamiliar to them, yet so very natural.[21]

The following example from Steve Reich's *Tehillim* exemplifies how simultaneously complex and yet natural these kinds of rhythms can be (see Example 9.6). Reich is a great admirer of Bartók's music, and although these patterns derive from his own intuition and not a specific tradition, they resemble the rhythms Bartók was talking about. In the opening section, percussionists play a small *tambourin* drum and clap to accompany the singer. The rhythms are based on Reich's interpretation of the natural speech patterns of the original Hebrew text. In the example, Reich provides slash and triangle graphics to easily show the performer where twos and threes occur. This is a common shorthand to help the performer read changing meters fluently.

At first, performing the constantly changing meters may seem daunting, even awkward. Over time, the hands and the mind learn the changes and integrate them into a flow. Classical musicians are often astonished at the ease with which percussionists dispatch these rhythms, but Bartók reminds us that the skill of navigating them is acquired through exposure and practice and isn't exclusive to any one musical tradition.

Performance

A composer writes rhythm in the score, and a performer expresses it through the body. The two acts are important and distinctive stages of the process of musical performance. Bartók's exasperation with orchestral musicians' inability to grasp asymmetric rhythms represents a clash of his

9.6 Reich, *Tehillim*, second page.

new compositional ideas with the prevailing performance culture of his time.

Performance culture teaches musicians what rhythm is and how it functions. The players Bartók encountered were not unskilled. Rather, they had been trained in a nineteenth-century performance style combining the supremacy of *bel canto* vocal line with the idea of musical time as a series of emotional and psychological impulses. The exacting subdivisions of pulse that Bartók's music required were unfamiliar to them.

As a student, I had a drum set in my basement where I spent hours imitating, by ear, drummers from my album collection. This ranged from players from famous bands like Ringo Starr or John Bonham, to jazz greats like "Philly" Joe Jones or Tony Williams. While I learned their beats and drum fills, I also labored to make my phrasing and time feel like theirs. When I perform a piece by Steve Reich or John Cage today, I am not consciously imitating these drummers, but I also cannot purge them from my body's memory. Reading about Reich's love for Kenny Clarke's drumming reminds me that I would not want to anyway – each individual musician is a walking bundle of past musical experiences.

Bartók could hardly have expected orchestral musicians to master his rhythmic concepts so quickly. His exasperation stemmed from the fact that an orchestral musician's training did not include those rhythms. Bartók wanted rhythmic performance culture to change as fast as he could write new ideas. But changes in performance culture are counted in generations. What he needed – and eventually got – was an emergent performance culture around his music which would incorporate that skill.

The Mexican composer Carlos Chávez (1899–1978) was preoccupied with this issue. Chávez was fascinated, just as Bartók was, with folk and Indigenous music, which in his case extended to Mexican folk traditions and even to the pre-Colombian culture of the Aztecs. He wrote several works that were thematically tied to that distant past, also incorporating Indigenous percussion instruments.

Chávez and Cowell were very close, and they frequently traded ideas about the vagaries of composition and performance.[22] In his journal article "The Two Persons" (1929), Chávez compares the situation of the plastic vs. time-based arts:

> In contrast with music, see how easy it is to establish the true contact in the case of painting and sculpture. An artist paints a fresco or a sculptor casts a bronze that will stand forever, suffering no integral change. The public for this painting or bronze is anyone who stands and stares at it long enough to experience it with his tactile and visual senses. There is no series of intermediate steps between the two persons.[23]

Music notation helps us preserve works for the future, but not with anything like the exactness of a physical art object. Chávez continues:

It is unnecessary to say how far actual music notation as it now exists falls short of the writing we desire; clearly, it gives no such firm basis on which to build with certainty a duly proportioned performance. It cannot satisfactorily take down, as fixed values, the properties of the different units of sound. And so, of course, in an ensemble there are all sorts of changes in the attributes of each factor. Several performances, taken from identical writings, are always different performances.[24]

As extraordinarily useful as notation is to us in handing down musical ideas, culture does not only survive and transfer through texts. This means that examining rhythm through the eyes of composers who write down scores cannot only dwell on those texts. This is where a skilled performance teacher is most useful: all musical traditions are oral. It is fascinating to explore abstract notions of what rhythms are and how they work, but even composers admit that their efforts to capture it on the page only provide hints and indications of what should happen during performance.

Endnotes

1 O. Messiaen, *Music and Color: Conversations with Claude Samuel* (Paris: Editions Belfond, 1986), 67.

2 H. Cowell, *Essential Cowell: Selected Writings on Music* (Kingston, NY: McPherson & Company, 2001), 250.

3 J. Holt, *When Einstein Walked with Gödel: Excursions to the Edge of Thought* (New York: Farrar, Straus and Giroux, 2018), 16.

4 M. Baggech, "An English Translation of Olivier Messiaen's *Traité de rythme, de couleur, et d'ornithologie*, Volume 1" (Ph.D. Dissertation, University of Oklahoma, 1998), 51.

5 S. Curtis, and H. Taylor, "Olivier Messiaen and the Albert's Lyrebird: From Tamborine Mountain to Éclairs sur l'Au-delà," in J. Crispin (ed.), *Olivier Messiaen: The Centenary Papers* (Newcastle upon Tyne: Cambridge Scholars, 2010), 52–79.

6 J. Cage and D. Charles, *For the Birds* (Boston: M. Boyars, 1995), 43.

7 K. Gann, *No Such Thing as Silence: John Cage's 4′33″* (Yale University Press, 2010), 2–3.

8 J. Cage, *Silence* (Wesleyan University Press, 1961), 162.

9 E. Carter, *The Writings of Elliot Carter* (Indiana University Press, 1977), 344–5.

10 Suvchinsky, a noted Russian theorist and arts patron, wrote a highly regarded article in *La revue musicale* in 1939. Stravinsky cites Suvchinsky in his discussion of the subjective elements of rhythm in his *Poetics of Music* (1942).

11 Carter, *Writings*, 349.

12 Ibid.

13 Ibid.

14 B. A. Varga, *From Boulanger to Stockhausen: Interviews and a Memoir* (University of Rochester Press, 2013), 44.

15 I. Xenakis, *Formalized Music: Thought and Mathematics in Composition* (Hillsdale, NY: Pendragon Press, 1992).

16 P. Culshaw, "Pierre Boulez: 'I was a bully, I'm not ashamed,'" *The Telegraph.* Retrieved from www.telegraph.co.uk/culture/music/classicalmusic/3702982/Pierre-Boulez-I-was-a-bully-Im-not-ashamed.html (December 10, 2008), accessed September 14, 2019.

17 S. Reich, *Writings on Music 1965–2000* (Oxford University Press, 2002), 52.

18 Ibid.

19 I. Stravinsky, *Poetics of Music* (Harvard University Press, 1942), 28.

20 B. Bartók, *Béla Bartók Essays*, B. Suchoff (ed.) (London: Faber & Faber, 1976), 40.

21 Ibid, 41.

22 L. Saavedra (ed.), *Carlos Chávez and His World* (Princeton University Press, 2015), 36.

23 C. Chávez, "The Two Persons," *The Musical Quarterly*, 15 (1929), 153–9.

24 Ibid, 155.

PART IV

Rhythm in Jazz and Popular Music

10 Jazz Rhythm

The Challenge of "Swing"

MATTHEW W. BUTTERFIELD

When we think about the musical features most characteristic of jazz, those that particularize its style and distinguish it from other kinds of music, we almost always think of rhythm first. There are other important features, to be sure – the centrality of improvisation, for example, or the blues foundation of jazz melodic practice. But rhythm has typically been the feature addressed first in most writings on jazz since its origins early in the twentieth century, pride of place signaling its significance to jazz fans, critics, and historians.

The word most centrally associated with the rhythmic component of jazz, of course, is *swing*. The term has a few interrelated meanings today. It is used rather superficially to designate a particular way of articulating eighth notes (understood in contrast to "straight" eighth notes), or to refer to the underlying "groove" of what has come to be called "straight-ahead" or "mainstream" jazz.[1] More substantively, however, *swing* refers to a mysterious but fundamental rhythmic quality historically thought to be the essence of true jazz; absent swing – irrespective of eighth-note articulation or the syntactical features of the rhythm section's groove – one presumably does not have jazz.[2]

And yet, characterizing this rhythmic quality, let alone explaining it, has proven to be extremely difficult, if not impossible. Definitions have varied widely, as have the connotations it carries. Prior to its use with jazz, the term referred to a lively, danceable rhythmic cadence in virtually any kind of music, as well as poetry. It came to be associated exclusively with jazz only in the 1930s, when it acquired an implicit racial meaning that it has never fully shaken.[3] Since then, scholars have taken a variety of approaches to defining swing and explaining its effects. Some have understood swing as the product of timing relationships between the instruments in a jazz ensemble, especially the rhythm section. Others have investigated the "swing ratio," seeking to better differentiate the timing profiles of individual artists or to generalize across instruments or historical periods. Ample data have been gathered, and yet we seem to be no closer to understanding the nature of swing than we were during the Swing Era itself.

Why is swing so difficult to explain? It was intractable by design, a means of establishing a foundational and indisputable criterion of value for jazz as a whole, but also serving as a measuring stick by which to distinguish true jazz from false, good from bad. It emerged in the 1930s as *the* term to describe jazz rhythm, designating a rhythmic quality belonging to no other music, recognizable to those in the know and quantifiable in the sense of less or more, but otherwise, indefinable. As such, it answered a need in jazz criticism of that time as a defense against those who had claimed that jazz offered nothing new, nothing unique, to music.

Prior to the 1930s, discussion of rhythm in jazz differed little from that of its predecessor, ragtime – hardly surprising, since jazz was built on the rhythmic foundation of ragtime. Commentary on both tended to focus on two principal features: (1) the relentlessly steady pulse of the music (what Richard Waterman later famously described as the "metronome sense"), and (2) the extensive use of syncopation.[4] These were indeed the most salient rhythmic characteristics of both ragtime and early jazz, but there was nothing particularly distinctive or original about either one: most kinds of dance music required a fairly metronomic pulse, and syncopation was certainly not unique to jazz or other forms of African American music. Critics of ragtime and jazz frequently seized upon these facts as evidence of the music's lack of artistic merit. The reliance on syncopation was purportedly due to a lack of imagination, and thus the music was about rhythmic excess, not the exercise of good taste, as the anonymous author of an 1899 essay published in *The Étude* makes clear:

> Ragtime music has a respectable old genesis; an old, venerable one indeed. We need not go farther back than to the music of the god-like Beethoven to find examples of ragtime music; though formerly known under a more respectable technical name, that of syncopation. So ragtime music is simply syncopated rhythm maddened into a desperate iterativeness; a rhythm overdone, to please the present public music taste.[5]

David Stanley Smith, Dean of the Yale School of Music, said much the same thing about jazz in 1924:

> What is bound eventually to deaden the inventiveness of the "great American composer" is the fact that jazz is the exploitation of just one rhythm. This rhythm is the original rag-time of thirty years ago. There have been occasional captivating additions to it in the form of elaborate counterpoints in jarring rhythmic dissonance, but the fundamental "um-paugh, um-paugh" and the characteristic syncopation persist through the years. Without these there is no jazz.[6]

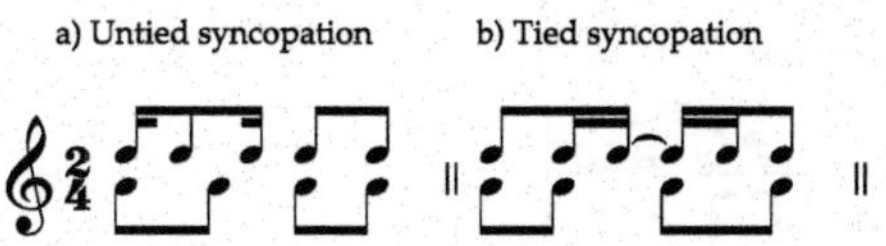

10.1 Conventional ragtime syncopations

Contrary to such criticisms, ragtime historian Edward A. Berlin finds it significant that "these rhythms were used with sufficient consistency to define the ragtime idiom, and that the intent of such rhythms, an intent made abundantly clear from the sheet-music covers and titles, was to reproduce the character of 'quaint' black music."[7] To that end, ragtime composers made extensive use of two specific varieties of syncopation thought to typify black rhythm, which Berlin refers to as "untied" and "tied," illustrated in Example 10.1.[8]

Untied syncopations remain within the separate halves of a measure, and are thus minimally disruptive to the perception of metric regularity. Whatever destabilization of the meter emerges on the weak second eighth-note beat is quickly dispelled through a return to metric congruence on the strong third beat, further confirmed on the fourth. Tied syncopations, by contrast, offer greater potential for disrupting perception of metric regularity over a greater span of time. Here, it is the strong third beat that is destabilized with syncopation; metric congruence returns on the weak fourth beat, and thus the ensuing downbeat is required for further stabilization.

Drawing data from a sample of 1,035 piano rags published between 1897 and 1920, Berlin found that untied syncopations were considerably more common than tied syncopations through about 1900. As the decade wore on, however, tied syncopations came to predominate. In 1900, the ratio of untied-to-tied-syncopation rags in Berlin's sample was 3:1. By 1902, it had flipped to 1:3, and then dropped to 1:7 by 1905 and 1:20 in 1908.[9] The untied syncopation figure was a relic of blackface minstrelsy, a rhythmic convention found in innumerable late nineteenth-century character pieces referencing antebellum black folk dances. The decline of its frequency correlates to the disappearance of "the more flagrantly abusive form of coon song" and a "deracialization" of ragtime song by 1906.[10]

Meanwhile, as the frequency of tied syncopations grew, they came increasingly to be used at the tail end of the "secondary rag" figure, another common feature in early ragtime first identified by Don Knowlton in 1926.[11] Essentially a 3×2 polyrhythm, the secondary rag generates what Harald Krebs describes as a grouping dissonance.[12] The opening measures

10.2 Botsford, *Black and White Rag*, mm. 5–8

of the A strain of George Botsford's *Black and White Rag*, shown in Example 10.2, provide a typical example.[13] In mm. 5–6, a 3-line (1=16th) is superimposed over a 2-line through four iterations over dominant harmony, at which time the pattern breaks with a tied syncopation. This pattern is repeated over tonic harmony in mm. 7–8.

Berlin also reports the growing use of dotted rhythms in the published rag repertory of the 1910s. In the first decade of the century, dotted rhythms appeared in less than 6 percent of published rags. This figure would grow to 12 percent in 1911, 23 percent in 1912, 46 percent in 1913, and 58 percent in 1916. Meanwhile, syncopation remained common in the ragtime repertory throughout this decade, but it was seldom used in dotted-rhythm passages.[14]

This increase in the use of dotted rhythms suggests an effort by ragtime composers to reflect in music notation the performance practices of itinerant black piano players like Jelly Roll Morton. By this time, these musicians were likely making use of what would later be termed "swing eighth notes," a practice hinted at a decade earlier in some of the few extent banjo recordings of rag tunes made in the early 1900s.[15] Dotted notation is simply an early effort to capture in writing the long-short durational patterning of swing eighth notes. Contrary to Berlin, I suggest the absence of syncopations in dotted-note passages is less indicative of a stylistic difference between dotted and non-dotted passages than a consequence of the difficulty of notating (and reading) both untied and tied syncopations in dotted rhythms. Compare, in Example 10.3, the ease of reading the untied syncopations in the passage shown in (a), as opposed to the same passaged rendered in dotted notation in (b). Parts (c) and (d) present a similar passage involving tied syncopations in straight and dotted rhythms, respectively. The notation of (b) and (d) is visually too busy and simply cumbersome. On the other hand, though examples (a) and (c) are notated "straight," as it were, it is easy enough to perform them in swing eighth notes.

Though ragtime and early jazz composers avoided rendering syncopations in dotted rhythms in the 1910s and beyond, they did not hesitate to

10.3 Comparison of syncopated passages using "straight" rhythms and dotted rhythms

10.4 Confrey, *Kitten on the Keys*, mm. 7–10

10.5 Confrey, *Kitten on the Keys*, mm. 11–14

write secondary rag passages in dotted rhythms, as can be seen in the A strain of Zez Confrey's *Kitten on the Keys*, shown in Example 10.4.[16] In notation, this passage appears to involve a very complex grouping dissonance seemingly impossible to define in terms of an intelligible ratio. But if the dotted rhythms are understood as swing eighth notes, it is clear enough that this is simply a durationally embellished version of a simple 3/2 grouping dissonance (1=8th). Confrey avoids writing dotted rhythms for the tied syncopations in the ensuing passage (Example 10.5), but in his recorded performance, the durational relationships of the notated eighth notes are indistinguishable from those of the dotted rhythms in the preceding passage.[17] Confrey was clearly working in terms of swing eighth notes. He used dotted rhythms in non-syncopated passages to convey this, but simplified the notation to plain eighth notes for clarity in the syncopated passages.

10.6 Possible representations of beat division in jazz performance from Waterman's *Piano Forms*

The term *swing eighth notes* would not enter the jazz vernacular for another few decades, but a few astute observers did recognize both the distinct character of beat division in late ragtime and early jazz and the inadequacy of dotted rhythms to convey the long-short durational relationship between downbeat/upbeat pairs. In 1923, Gilbert Seldes observed that the "fixed groups of uneven notes" in Zez Confrey's *Stumbling*, published in 1922, "are really triplets with the first note held or omitted for a time, then with the third note omitted and so on."[18] Seldes seems to be referring to the quarter-eighth (2:1) triplet rhythm that would later become a standard (if inaccurate) way of describing the "swing ratio." Glenn Waterman was more explicit a year later in rendering jazz rhythm explicitly in terms of triplets. In an explanation of how to syncopate a simple quarter-note melody, he describes dotted rhythms as "too jerky." Good jazz performance, according to Waterman, depends on "[t]he exact 'way' of striking these two-eighths (also *written* as dotted eighth and sixteenth). . . . They *must be played* as a triplet with the first note tied."[19]

Another early commentator, Don Knowlton, retained dotted notes in his discussion of jazz rhythm, but emphasized the difference between what he referred to as the "–*um*-pa-*tee*-dle" pattern of "the real jazz tune" and "the old *one-two, one-two* rhythm" of the march, found in much popular music of the day. The "–*um*-pa-*tee*-dle" pattern, according to Knowlton, serves as the real foundation upon which "are superimposed certain alterations of rhythm which are the true components of jazz."[20] Knowlton, like other advocates of jazz in the mid-1920s, recognized there was something truly distinctive about jazz rhythm, something non-jazz musicians, or even non-Americans, found very difficult to produce. Paul Whiteman, for example, found that "only Americans can really play syncopated music. Musicians of other countries do not seem able to get into the swing of it. They fail to accomplish by training what we do by nature."[21] Virgil Thomson, too, felt there was something quite particular about jazz rhythm. In a detailed discussion of the expressive effects of jazz syncopation, he proposed that "the peculiar character of jazz is a rhythm, and that that rhythm is one which provokes motions of the body."[22]

Statements like these, which acknowledge the distinctiveness of jazz rhythm and seek to explain its expressive effects, stand in sharp contrast to the contemptuous writings of those like Oscar Thompson, who found little value in jazz and less still of interest in its rhythms:

> There was never a greater absurdity than the talk of rhythmic variety in jazz. Jazz is rhythm in a straight-jacket. Its so-called "variety" is the apogee of monotonous periodicity. . . . It is this very regularity that gives jazz its propulsively forward movement. Its measures are marked with the deadly certainty of a piston rod. Its rhythm is that of the exhaust of a noisy gas engine. No other music the world has known has so approached the mechanics of driven wheels.[23]

Thompson, like other critics, focused his ire on obvious surface features of jazz rhythm – the relentlessly steady pulse or the overabundance of syncopation. Advocates of jazz, however, felt there was something more to it, something deeper about its rhythm that was irreducible, undefinable, unrepresentable; they simply lacked the vocabulary to talk about it, and thus continued to refer to things like syncopation or the use of dotted rhythms – features that could easily be identified, belittled, and dismissed.

At any rate, Thompson's brand of criticism would largely disappear in the 1930s, at least in the United States. Changes in the jazz rhythm section and a more melodic style of performance less reliant on syncopation led to a music less raucous in its rhythmic effects. Jazz entered the commercial mainstream in the 1930s, as well, and with the repeal of Prohibition, its associations with illicit nightlife largely disappeared. Under these conditions, jazz appeared less of a threat to the social order, and its rhythms were no longer invested with as much anxiety.

Meanwhile, on the critical front, the emergence in the 1930s of the modern concept of swing through the activities of French jazz critic Hugues Panassié and the American impresario John Hammond served to redirect criticism of jazz rhythm from the superficiality of surface features to a deeper, more profound rhythmic core, a generative impulse presumably available and accessible only to a gifted elite.

The word *swing* had been employed in writing about music since at least the 1870s to refer to a danceable rhythmic cadence in styles as widely disparate as Verdi operas and Sousa marches. This breadth of usage continued into the 1930s, but by decade's end, the term had come to be associated exclusively with jazz.

There is evidence the word *swing* had entered American jazz musicians' argot by 1933 (it shows up in spoken passages on a few Louis Armstrong records recorded that spring),[24] but no indication they understood it to be a kind of foundational rhythmic essence, Duke Ellington's "It Don't Mean a Thing" notwithstanding. Though premiered in August 1931, recorded in February 1932, and widely popular by 1933, the "swing" of its subtitle and opening line, belted out with such verve by Ivie Anderson, generated virtually no commentary until well into 1935. Rather, its specialized meaning for jazz came from the efforts of Hugues Panassié to translate it into French around the time of Ellington's visit to Paris in July 1933. Finding no suitable French equivalent, Panassié used *swing* as a technical term, conceptually altering an American colloquialism to serve as a critical filter for distinguishing true jazz from false. His notion of swing was then reintegrated into the American understanding by his colleague and friend John Hammond, who wrote about it repeatedly in his column for the *Brooklyn Daily Eagle* in early 1935, when he was actively promoting Benny Goodman's band. By year's end, "What is 'swing'?" would be the question on everyone's lips.

In truth, no one had a good answer – and no one ever has. The problem of definition started with Panassié, who is most responsible for introducing the term to jazz critical discourse through his book *Le Jazz Hot*, published in 1934. Panassié's conception of swing was built on a constellation of five assumptions. First was the notion that swing was a rhythmic quality foundational to good jazz, what Panassié describes as "that essential element of jazz found in no other music." "All true jazz must have swing," he writes. "Where there is no swing, there can be no authentic jazz." Second, though ultimately undefinable according to Panassié, swing was nevertheless an "entirely objective" property, such that "there is almost always complete agreement among competent critics" regarding its presence and intensity in any given performance. Third, swing is a "gift." It is something innate, something a musician is born with: "either you have it deep within yourself," writes Panassié, "or you don't have it at all." Moreover, it cannot be learned: "neither long study nor hard work will get you anywhere in jazz if you do not naturally know how to play with a swing. You can't learn swing." Fourth, there is no single way to swing: "swing varies according to the instrument played," writes Panassié, but even "on the very same instrument, each musician will have his own ways of getting swing." And finally, for Panassié, *swing* was short for *Negro swing*, a property that "belongs to jazz alone and derives from those Negro musicians who first created it." Swing, in other words, was a rhythmic quality that was ultimately the expression of a black racial essence.[25]

There is plenty to argue with in Panassié's formulation of the swing concept, but by and large, the five basic claims he lays out about swing in *Le Jazz Hot* in 1934, summarized above, continue to serve as the underlying assumptions of our everyday understanding of that concept even today – though most critics wouldn't be so baldly essentialist. This is the modern concept of swing in a nutshell. It crystallized in the popular imagination around 1935, largely as a consequence of Panassié's writings and promotional activities, along with those of his American counterpart, John Hammond.

As an explanation of swing or a guide to how to recognize it or produce it, Panassié's account was an utter failure. But what it made possible was the consolidation of thought about jazz rhythm around a single foundational concept. Swing offered an explanation for the rhythmic particularity of jazz that went beyond surface-level phenomena like syncopation. Swing was not the kind of thing that could be notated and thus co-opted by other forms of music. Syncopation wasn't unique to jazz, of course; it was ubiquitous in the music, to be sure, but not the thing that really distinguished it from other kinds of music. But swing did. It was a deep phenomenon, something rooted in racial essence, and thus something that particularized jazz and explained what made it categorically different from other kinds of music. Never mind that it couldn't be defined; it could be believed. Syncopation was a feature, an effect; swing was an essence, a prime cause.

Panassié's conceptual framework for swing – the five assumptions adumbrated above – served as the critical foundation for discussions of jazz rhythm for decades. Subsequent critics, historians, and scholars repeatedly sought to explain swing and the means of its production, but no one seemed to question Panassié's claim that swing was the essential element of jazz or that it was an objectively real rhythmic phenomenon – or that it was situated in a domain that is difficult, and perhaps even impossible, to access through the intellect. Its power, in Panassié's framework, lies in the mystery of its source and the means whereby it generates its effects, a process hidden from conscious awareness that good musicians can nevertheless actualize without thought or deliberate intention. For Panassié, that source was ultimately to be found in the putative rhythmic effects of race. Countless other scholars have followed his lead in that direction, some more explicitly essentialist than others.

Among the most important post-Panassié critics to undertake an explanation of the swing phenomenon was André Hodeir, who devoted an entire chapter of his book *Jazz: Its Evolution and Essence* to outlining "the five optimal conditions for the production of swing." These included:

1. the right infrastructure
2. the right superstructure
3. getting the notes and accents in the right place
4. relaxation
5. vital drive[26]

The last of these, "vital drive," was Hodeir's most unique contribution to Panassié's conceptual framework, though his explanation of its character and source is as murky as his predecessor's explanation of swing. Hodeir described vital drive as "an element in swing that resists analysis." It stems from "a combination of undefined forces that creates a kind of 'rhythmic fluidity' without which the music's swing is markedly attenuated." It is, moreover, a "manifestation of personal magnetism, which is somehow expressed – I couldn't say exactly how – in the domain of rhythm." Like Panassié, however, Hodeir saw race as a relevant factor in the production of vital drive; white bands, he found, fail to swing adequately because "their vital drive is weak."[27]

In 1966, ethnomusicologist Charles Keil introduced perhaps the most consequential transformation of the Panassié model.[28] Keil abandoned the racial essentialism of earlier writers, but retained the mysterious nature of swing by situating it in a quality he called "engendered feeling," that certain something beyond notation that performers add to music to generate "vital drive." Engendered feeling, Keil proposed, stems not from syntactical processes – i.e., processes that can be represented in standard musical notation, in quarter notes or eighth notes, for example. It emerges rather from musicians' use of expressive microtiming at the sub-syntactical level in sustaining a rhythmic groove, a phenomenon he later dubbed "participatory discrepancies," or PDs.[29] PDs are a form of rhythmic displacement different from offbeat rhythms, syncopations, or anticipations. In the PD framework, engendered feeling (i.e., swing or vital drive) results from the cumulative tension acquired through "pulling against the pulse."[30] Onset discrepancies, typically on the order of less than about 50 milliseconds (about 1/20th of a second), between the pluck of the walking bass and the drummer's ride cymbal taps in their shared articulation of the beat purportedly generate some qualitative feeling of either rhythmic drive ("push") on the one hand, or relaxation ("layback") on the other.

PD theory thus assigns responsibility for the production of swing to the sub-syntactical realm of microtiming and downplays the significance of more tangible and visceral events that take place on the syntactical plane of notatable musical phenomena.[31] Whether or not such discrepancies are robust and powerful enough to drive the groove and generate swing remains an open question, however.[32] At any rate, the belief that expressive microtiming has consequential effects in the realm of jazz rhythm has driven a good deal of scholarship in the last few decades. Studies have concerned two types of timing discrepancies in jazz performance: (1) those within a single instrument or part; and (2) those between the instruments of an ensemble. Research on the former has generally concerned the "swing ratio," whereas research on the latter has addressed the "hookup" between bass and drums in sustaining a steady groove, as well as soloists' timing in relation to the drummer's ride rhythm. Most of these studies, incidentally, have concerned timing in straight-ahead jazz, with the bulk of their data coming from laboratory contexts with currently active professional musicians or from recordings drawn from the hard bop repertory of the 1950s.

The "swing ratio" expresses the durational relationship between the long, downbeat eighth note and the short upbeat that follows it. The conventional assumption that successive swing eighth notes stand in a durational relationship of 2:1, traditionally represented in notation as a quarter-eighth triplet pair, has been shown to be largely inaccurate. In practice, swing ratios vary widely, ranging from an even 1:1 to as high as 3.5:1, varying with tempo and ensemble function (i.e., soloist vs. accompaniment).[33] Soloists tend to play minimally uneven swing eighths, typically ranging from about 1.2:1 to 1.5:1. They often vary their swing ratios over the course of a phrase for expressive purposes, either to drive momentum forward or to dissipate motional energy.[34] Soloist swing ratios tend to be most even in the middle of a phrase, but then frequently increase in value toward the end of a phrase, where what Fernando Benadon has referred to as a "BUR surge" tends to serve a closural function.[35]

By contrast, drummers tend to use relatively large swing ratios, particularly in maintaining time on the ride cymbal. Swing ratios in the "ride rhythm," the standard "ding-ding-a-ding" figure played on the ride cymbal since the bebop era, are typically in the neighborhood of 2:1. They tend to be larger at slow and medium tempos, but approach 1:1 in the fastest tempos.[36] Drummers also sustain remarkably consistent swing ratios in the ride rhythm, especially at moderate to fast tempos.[37]

Studies of timing relationships between instruments have revealed interesting practices also related to ensemble function. The "hookup" between bass and drums, in particular, has received a great deal of attention. Bass players tend to synchronize their downbeat attacks quite tightly with the drummer's ride tap, with generally no more than a 20-ms gap between them.[38] Bass and drums may take turns in the lead, as it were, switching places on occasion for expressive purposes.[39]

Soloists tend to time their attacks with considerably greater flexibility in relation to the drummer's ride tap. They typically lay back on the beat by about 50–80 ms, but then synchronize their offbeat eighth notes quite tightly with the drummer's short tap. Consequently, the degree of delay varies inversely with the swing ratio they employ at any given moment: more delay entails a smaller swing ratio, indicative of more even eighth notes, while less delay entails a higher swing ratio, with greater unevenness.[40]

Eighty-five years have passed since Hugues Panassié published the first comprehensive account of swing in *Le Jazz Hot*. And yet it remains unclear what exactly swing is. Perhaps the most we can say is that it is a word we use to describe an attractive rhythmic quality in jazz, one that is often characterized by a sense of forward propulsion and that presumably has the effect of inducing movement on the part of the listener. However, the fact that no consensus has yet emerged on what exactly swing is or how it is produced suggests that the term has perhaps outlived its usefulness in designating the core component of jazz rhythm. It might be more productive to use Keil's term "engendered feeling," or even Hodeir's "vital drive," to refer to the motional qualities of jazz and other forms of groove-based music – qualities conditioned by the action of "participatory discrepancies." Microtiming studies of both the swing ratio and intra-ensemble "hookup" have begun to clarify at least some of the expressive features of jazz rhythm. But much work remains to be done in integrating the data, most often produced by specialists in music cognition, into a music-theoretical framework of use for music analysis. How do soloists, for example, manipulate microtiming over the course of a single phrase or through an entire solo to expressive effect? How do PDs in the domain of timing interact with those in the realm of timbre and articulation? And to what extent do the data gathered from studies of straight-ahead jazz translate into generalizable features of other jazz styles, or other forms of groove-based music beyond jazz? These and other questions suggest a promising future for the study of jazz rhythm.

Endnotes

1 A "straight-ahead" groove stems from the practices of rhythm-section players from the bebop era through hard bop. It involves "comping" in the piano and/or guitar parts, a walking bass line, and the ride rhythm played on the ride cymbal, with hi-hat snapped closed on beats 2 and 4.

2 For a thoughtful critique of the presumed necessity of "swing feeling" for jazz, see M. Gridley, R. Maxham, and R. Hoff, "Three Approaches to Defining Jazz," *The Musical Quarterly*, 73 (1989), 516–24.

3 M. W. Butterfield, "Race and Rhythm: The Social Component of the Swing Groove," *Jazz Perspectives*, 4 (2010), 301–35.

4 R. A. Waterman, "'Hot' Rhythm in Negro Music," *Journal of the American Musicological Society*, 1 (1948), 24–37.

5 "Ragtime," *The Étude*, June 1899; reprinted in K. Koenig (ed.), *Jazz in Print (1856–1929): An Anthology of Selected Early Readings in Jazz History* (Hillsdale, NY: Pendragon Press, 2002), 51.

6 D. S. Smith, quoted in "Putting Jazz in Its Place," *Literary Digest*, July 5, 1924; reprinted in *Jazz in Print*, 323.

7 E. A. Berlin, *Ragtime: A Musical and Cultural History* (University of California Press, 1980), 106.

8 Ibid., 83. For a catalog of additional rhythmic figures typically found in ragtime, see S. A. Floyd Jr. and M. J. Reisser, "The Sources and Resources of Classic Ragtime Music," *Black Music Research Journal*, 4 (1984), 22–59.

9 Berlin, *Ragtime*, 128.

10 Ibid., 5–6 and 123.

11 D. Knowlton, "The Anatomy of Jazz," *Harper's*, April 1926, 581.

12 H. Krebs, *Fantasy Pieces: Metrical Dissonance in the Music of Robert Schumann* (Oxford University Press, 1999), 31–9.

13 G. Botsford, *Black and White Rag* (Detroit and New York: Jerome H. Remick & Co., 1908).

14 Berlin, *Ragtime*, 147.

15 See, for example, E. Cantrell and R. Williams, "Mississippi River Song – Tapioca," recorded October 2, 1902, originally released as Gramophone 4267; reissued on track 1 of *Ragtime to Jazz, Vol. 3: 1902–1923*, Timeless Historical - CBC 1-085.

16 Z. Confrey, *Kitten on the Keys* (New York: Mills Music Inc., 1921).

17 Z. Confrey, pianist and composer, "Kitten on the Keys," recorded in February 1921, track 3 on *Zez Confrey: Creator of the Novelty Rag*, Folkways RF 28.

18 G. Seldes, "Toujours Jazz," *Dial*, August 23, 1923; reprinted in Koenig, *Jazz in Print*, 248.

19 G. Waterman, *Waterman's Piano Forms: A Course of Invention* (Los Angeles: Waterman Piano School, 1924), 32.

20 Knowlton, "The Anatomy of Jazz," 580–81.

21 Paul Whiteman, quoted in "Say Jazz Will Surely Live," *New York Times*, January 16, 1924; reprinted in Koenig, *Jazz in Print*, 270–71. It is important to note that Whiteman's use of *swing* does not carry the same meanings as the modern sense of the term, as described below. Here, it is synonymous with "get the hang of it."

22 V. Thomson, "Jazz," *Mercury*, August 1924; reprinted in Koenig, *Jazz in Print*, 342–3.

23 O. Thompson, "Jazz, as Art Music, Piles Failure on Failure," *Musical America*, February 13, 1926; reprinted in Koenig, *Jazz in Print*, 452.
24 See the spoken introduction to Louis Armstrong's recording of "High Society," by Porter Steele, recorded on January 26, 1933 (Victor 24232, mx. 74895-1), and the spoken interlude in "Laughing Louis," by Clarence Gaskill, also recorded in Chicago on April 24, 1933 (Bluebird B5363, 75422-2); both titles on *Louis Armstrong: The Complete RCA Victor Recordings*, BMG Classics (09026-68682-2), 1997.
25 H. Panassié, *Le Jazz Hot* (Paris: Editions R.-A. Corrêa, 1934), 4–9.
26 A. Hodeir, *Jazz: Its Evolution and Essence*, D. Noakes (trans.) (New York: Grove, 1956), 197.
27 Ibid., 207–8.
28 C. Keil, "Motion and Feeling through Music," *Journal of Aesthetics and Art Criticism*, 24 (1966), 337–49.
29 C. Keil, "Participatory Discrepancies and the Power of Music," *Cultural Anthropology*, 2 (1987), 275–83.
30 Keil, "Motion and Feeling," 341.
31 For a discussion of the relevance of syntactical pattern in the production of "engendered feeling," see M. W. Butterfield, "The Power of Anacrusis: Engendered Feeling in Groove-Based Musics," *Music Theory Online*, 12.4 (2006).
32 Several studies to date have found no evidence that microtiming variations generate significant impacts on the perceived quality of a rhythmic groove. See, for example, M. W. Butterfield, "Participatory Discrepancies and the Perception of Beats in Jazz," *Music Perception*, 27 (2010), 157–76; G. Madison, F. Gouyon, F. Ullén, and K. Hörnström, "Modeling the Tendency for Music to Induce Movement in Humans: First Correlations with Low-Level Audio Descriptors across Music Genres," *Journal of Experimental Psychology: Human Perception and Performance*, 37 (2011), 1578–94; J. Frühauf, R. Kopiez, and F. Platz, "Music on the Timing Grid: The Influence of Microtiming on the Perceived Groove Quality of a Simple Drum Pattern Performance," *Musicae Scientiae*, 17 (2013), 246–60; G. Madison and G. Sioros, "What Musicians Do to Induce the Sensation of Groove in Simple and Complex Melodies, and How Listeners Perceive It," *Frontiers in Psychology*, 5 (2014), 894; B. Merker, "Groove or Swing as Distributed Rhythmic Consonance: Introducing the Groove Matrix," *Frontiers in Human Neuroscience*, 8 (2014), 454.
33 See especially R. F. Rose, "Computer Assisted Swing!" *Jazz Educators Journal*, 17 (1985), 14–15; M. C. Ellis, "An Analysis of 'Swing' Subdivision and Asynchronization in Three Jazz Saxophonists," *Perceptual and Motor Skills*, 73 (1991), 707–13; A. Friberg and A. Sundström, "Swing Ratios and Ensemble Timing in Jazz Performance: Evidence for a Common Rhythmic Pattern," *Music Perception*, 19 (2002), 333–49; F. Benadon, "Slicing the Beat: Jazz Eighth-Notes as Expressive Microrhythm," *Ethnomusicology*, 50 (2006), 73–98.

34 M. W. Butterfield, "Why Do Jazz Musicians Swing Their Eighth Notes?" *Music Theory Spectrum*, 33 (2011), 3–26.
35 Benadon, "Slicing the Beat," 80–81.
36 Friberg and Sundström, "Swing Ratios."
37 H. Honing and W. Bas de Haas, "Swing Once More: Relating Timing and Tempo in Expert Jazz Drumming," *Music Perception*, 25 (2008), 471–6.
38 Friberg and Sundström, "Swing Ratios." See also Butterfield, "Participatory Discrepancies."
39 J. A. Prögler, "Searching for Swing: Participatory Discrepancies in the Jazz Rhythm Section," *Ethnomusicology*, 39 (1995), 21–54.
40 Friberg and Sundström, "Swing Ratios."

11 Rhythmic Influence in the Rock Revolution

TREVOR DE CLERCQ

Introduction

Following the Second World War, the West – especially the United States – experienced a period of sustained economic growth. In tandem, birth rates peaked such that by the mid-1950s, a strong youth culture began to take shape, fueling a great expansion of mass media. Television, radio, movies, and music became increasingly ubiquitous elements of society as consumers, especially young consumers, sought ways to spend their leisure time and disposable income. This cultural sea change engendered a revolution in musical style, with rock and roll – or simply "rock" as it later became known – emerging as a dominant force in popular music.

The musical characteristics of early rock and roll can be seen as an amalgam of styles prevalent during the 1930s and 1940s, including blues, country, and jazz. The fusion of these disparate styles into a single "super-style" involved importing traits from each, of course, but also a comprehensive streamlining to make the fusion appeal to a broad audience. The rhythm section, for example, became codified into the conventional arrangement of drums, bass, and guitar; meter became distilled into a regular back-and-forth pattern of kick and snare; and song forms began to follow formulaic templates.

But while the norms of 1950s rock and roll can appear to simplify earlier practices, these structures laid the groundwork for decades of stylistic evolution. Indeed, while present-day rock music often involves highly complex rhythmic structures, it grows out of fundamental rhythmic principles already widespread by the 1960s. The current chapter provides an overview of these principles, spanning from the dawn of rock and roll to modern pop/rock.

The chapter is arranged into three main sections. The first, on tactus and tempo, examines what is meant by the "beat" in rock. Although many songs have only one primary pulse layer, others exhibit conflicting levels of pulse. The second section, on meter and measures, offers an overview of the typical organizational schemes for rhythm and meter. Unlike traditional time-signature-based approaches, meter in rock warrants some classification mechanism for swing at various levels and different drum feels. The third section, on syncopation and stress, discusses some of the most common rhythmic patterns in melody and harmony. In particular, the pervasive metric displacement of stressed pitch events away from strong beats creates a rhythmic texture emblematic of the rock style.

Tactus and Tempo

The most central rhythmic element of any musical style is the beat. In traditional understandings, the beat – or tactus – is the most perceptually salient pulse layer, i.e., the steady rate at which a listener will bob their head or tap their foot. Given this understanding, beat is essentially synonymous with tempo, as measured in beats per minute (hereafter, BPM).

In the parlance of rock musicians, though, "the beat" can take on additional meanings. Foremost, it can serve as shorthand for "the drum-beat," i.e., the drum pattern of a song. The standard rock beat, for example, is a drum pattern in $\frac{4}{4}$ with the kick on beats 1 and 3, the snare on beats 2 and 4 (the "backbeat"), and the hi-hat or ride playing some metrically congruent division of the measure into equal parts. This conflation of "beat" and "drumbeat" is no coincidence, since the regular occurrence of the kick and snare on primary divisions of the measure strongly conveys one layer of pulse to the listener.

An even further generalization of "beat" exists as well. Although the drum pattern is an important factor in assessing tempo, other instruments (including the vocal) typically convey information related to tempo perception. For example, when a listener says, "This song has a good beat," they mean at least three separate things: (1) that it is easy to synchronize body motions with the song's primary pulse rate, implying it is not too fast or too slow; (2) that the drumbeat is consonant with this pulse rate; and (3) that all of the instrumental elements facilitate body motions, not only at the primary pulse layer but also other metric levels. In this third sense, "the beat" is somewhat synonymous with "groove" or rhythmic "feel," i.e., the overall rhythmic fabric of a song.

The relationship between body motions and the rock beat is a seminal component of rock rhythm, because a regular role of rock music is something for people to dance to. The goodness of a rock beat thus relates to its danceability, especially the type of energetic dancing that symbolizes youthfulness. Perhaps not surprisingly, average tempos for rock exceed those of other musical styles. Musicologists, for example, posit that tempos

11.1 Beethoven, Piano Sonata in C Minor, Op. 13, II, mm. 1–4

for classical music are most often in the range of 60–80 BPM, corresponding to an adult's resting heart rate.[1] In contrast, average tempos for rock lie within the 110–125 BPM range, corresponding to an elevated heart rate associated with physical activity.[2]

Given that the lower end of the range for typical tempos in classical music (60 BPM) is about half the upper end of the range for rock (125 BPM), it may be that classical and rock musicians will sometimes disagree on the primary pulse layer of a musical work due to different expectations. Which metric level, for example, represents the main beat at the beginning of the second movement to Beethoven's Piano Sonata in C Minor, Op. 13 (Example 11.1)? As a timing reference, consider Arthur Rubinstein's 1962 RCA recording. Despite the $\frac{2}{4}$ time signature that Beethoven indicates, the quarter note cannot be the primary pulse layer, for it is too slow to be a viable beat; in Rubinstein's performance, the quarter-note rate is about 29 BPM, which lies below the 30 BPM threshold for beat perception noted by music cognition researchers.[3] More likely, a classical musician will feel the eighth note as tactus, which in Rubinstein's performance is around 58 BPM, since this rate aligns more closely with tempo norms in classical music.

For a rock musician, however, the sixteenth note may be the preferred tactus, as it engenders a more typical rock tempo. Indeed, it is in this way that the band Kiss conceptualizes Beethoven's theme, which is featured at the beginning of their song "Great Expectations" (1976). In particular, when the Beethoven theme appears at 2:24, the drumbeat implies a tempo of 116 BPM. Note that the pacing of harmonic and melodic content in Kiss's arrangement is almost identical to that in Rubinstein's performance; the opening tonic chord, for example, lasts about two seconds in both versions. The Kiss arrangement thus does not alter the rate at which musical content is disbursed; rather, it offers a different hearing of the tactus, one corresponding better with an upbeat, danceable tempo.

The preference in rock for danceable tempos is so intrinsic to the style that experienced listeners may feel tempos nearer the 110–125 BPM ideal even when the drum pattern gives conflicting information. A good example of this scenario is the song "Human Nature" by Michael Jackson (1983).

If the kick and snare in this song are taken to indicate beats 1 and 2 in $\frac{4}{4}$ the tempo would be 47 BPM. While this tempo lies above the 30 BPM lower limit for beat perception noted earlier, it seems too slow to animate lively body movement. As a result, most listeners will synchronize with a tempo twice that speed, 93 BPM, which comes closer to a typical rock tempo. Indeed, Michael Jackson can be seen in live performances to bounce his leg at this 93 BPM rate. In this song, there thus exists a tension between the tactus more preferred for dancing and the pulse implied by the kick and snare.

What, then, is the tempo of "Human Nature"? Some musicologists suggest that tempo should always be determined by the kick and snare (thus 47 BPM here).[4] But this hard-and-fast rule often ignores the beat rate most listeners prefer. An alternative is to say that the tempo of "Human Nature" is 93 BPM, while the kick and snare alternate at half that rate. Rock musicians refer to this metric organization as a "half-time feel." During a half-time feel, there exists a divorce of the drum pattern from the primary tactus. Thus, while drum patterns traditionally align with the primary beat, the existence of a separate musical layer (the drums) dedicated to rhythmic information allows for a more complex arrangement in which the drumbeat operates on a different level of the metric hierarchy than the tactus.

While some songs like "Human Nature" are in a half-time feel throughout, other songs will change between a normal and half-time feel (and vice versa). For most of the Ne-Yo song "Closer" (2008), for example, the drum pattern is congruent with the song's tempo, 126 BPM in $\frac{4}{4}$ with the handclaps on beats 2 and 4 substituting for the snare. In the last chorus (3:33), however, the hand claps move to beat 3, creating a half-time shift that breaks up the monotony of yet another chorus. Note that this new drum feel at the song's end does not affect the pacing of the harmonic and melodic material, which repeats earlier content verbatim.

In addition to half-time feels, songs may employ a double-time feel, where the kick and snare alternate at twice the primary pulse rate. The song "Should I Stay or Should I Go" by the Clash (1982) provides a good illustration of this scenario. The verse material (0:17) is a variation on the standard twelve-bar blues pattern at a comfortable tempo of 112 BPM in $\frac{4}{4}$ with the normal snare backbeat on beats 2 and 4. In the chorus (1:08), though, the drum pattern changes such that the snare occurs regularly on the "and" of every beat, assuming the same tempo. Admittedly, the increased rate of kick and snare alternations gives the feeling of a faster tempo, 224 BPM. But it is rather uncomfortable to sustain head-bobbing or foot-tapping at this rapid pace. Moreover, the chorus is basically a repeat of the same twelve-bar blues pattern of the verse, with the same pacing of melodic and harmonic content. As a result, it seems more analytically robust to describe the chorus as having a tempo of 112 BPM with a double-time feel – thereby capturing the conflict between the drum pattern and the implied beat based on the unaltered pacing of harmonic and melodic content – rather than to simply say the tempo has increased to 224 BPM, which does not account for the lack of speed change in the harmony and melody.

The notion that the tactus of a song tends to stay close to the 110–125 BPM range may seem overly restrictive, perhaps no less so than the alternative of saying the kick-snare rate always determines tempo. But unlike other musical styles that have primarily instrumental textures, rock texture is almost exclusively based around a vocal melody. Perhaps because the pacing of lyrics is constrained by ideal rates of speech delivery, the pacing of melodic content in rock turns out to be relatively stable. Thus, while music cognition researchers report that the range of tactus perception lies between 30 BPM and 240 BPM (an eightfold increase), the range of variation for the pacing of pitch-based content in rock is much more narrow. As evidence, cover versions of songs rarely shift the speed of the vocal melody more than a small amount, much less than twice or half the original rate. For example, Cream's original version of "Sunshine of Your Love" (1967) has a clear tempo of 116 BPM in $\frac{4}{4}$ with a normal drum feel. In contrast, the cover by Fudge Tunnel (1991) may at first sound extremely slower, but the rate of vocal delivery in Fudge Tunnel's cover is not much slower than the original. The reason Fudge Tunnel's version sounds especially slow is the lumbering drum pattern, which conveys a half-time feel against the more moderate pacing of the melodic and harmonic material. Thus, by referring to the cover as a half-time $\frac{4}{4}$ at 100 BPM, we capture both the change in the drum feel as well as the only moderate change in harmonic and melodic pacing.

Meter and Measures

While the tactus is the most central pulse layer, also of interest is the entire hierarchy of pulse layers, i.e., meter. The meter of a musical composition is traditionally conveyed through its time signature, usually classified into two categories based on (1) the number of beats per measure, usually duple, triple, or quadruple; and (2) the number of regularly occurring, equal divisions of this beat, either two (simple) or three (compound). This scheme results in six standard time signatures: $\frac{2}{4}$, $\frac{3}{4}$, $\frac{4}{4}$, $\frac{6}{8}$, $\frac{9}{8}$, and $\frac{12}{8}$.

Although it is not impossible to classify meter in rock using only this basic system, some addendums are useful to better capture typical pulse hierarchies. We have already seen, for example, that the rhythmic framework of some songs involves conflicting pulse information, such as half-time or double-time feels. Time signatures could be adapted to account for this conflict, such as labeling half-time as $\frac{2}{2}$ or double-time as 8/8. But trying to incorporate drum feels into the time signature becomes problematic in cases other than $\frac{4}{4}$, such as $\frac{3}{4}$ or $\frac{6}{8}$.

The other complicating factor is the widespread use of swing at different metric levels. Swing, which divides the beat into two unequal values, is a common feature of jazz and related styles that predate rock, of course. In jazz, the unevenness of the swing – which primarily occurs between eighth notes – can range from ratios of 1.05:1 to 3.5:1 or higher.[5] In contrast, swing in rock generally conforms to a 2:1 ratio, equivalent to a quarter-note triplet followed by an eighth-note triplet. In this regard, swing in rock represents another standardization of rhythmic parameters from earlier styles.

Because swing in rock typically follows a 2:1 ratio, it can be difficult to distinguish between swing and compound meter. The Elvis Presley song "Stuck on You" (1960), for example, is a rolling twelve-bar blues with a quadruple beat at 132 BPM. It is possible to consider this song as in $\frac{12}{8}$, with the drum fill at 1:04 confirming the division of the beat into three equal parts. But the pervasive "long-short" division of the beat, most noticeable in the hi-hat and piano parts, exemplifies a classic "shuffle" rhythm, which rock musicians understand as a type of triplet division of $\frac{4}{4}$ with the middle triplet missing. The pervasive use of shuffle in rock songs leads to a general trend by rock musicians to conceptualize triply divided quadruple meters not as $\frac{12}{8}$ but rather as $\frac{4}{4}$ with swung eighth notes. Consequently, $\frac{12}{8}$ has become a deprecated meter in rock, even when a consistent underlying triple subdivision exists.[6]

The deprecation of $\frac{12}{8}$ in favor of a swung $\frac{4}{4}$ does not mean that compound meters in rock are deprecated as a rule. To the contrary, $\frac{6}{8}$ is the most appropriate time signature for many songs. In rock, though, $\frac{6}{8}$ and $\frac{12}{8}$ are dissimilar types of compound meter. Although we could think of a $\frac{12}{8}$ measure as twice as long as a $\frac{6}{8}$ measure, the fairly consistent pacing of harmonic and melodic material in rock (discussed above) suggests that it is preferable to maintain consistent measure lengths in terms of absolute time when possible. In other words, given a chunk of time that we are calling a measure, dividing that time into four triply divided beats is very different from dividing that same amount of time into two triply divided beats.

As an illustration, consider two versions of the song "With a Little Help From My Friends." The original version by the Beatles (1967) is a clear $\frac{4}{4}$ shuffle – or $\frac{12}{8}$ perhaps – at a tempo of 110 BPM and measure lengths of 2.2 seconds. In his 1968 cover, Joe Cocker sings the melody at only a slightly slower pace, the same amount of music now lasting 2.5 seconds. If we take bar lengths to be the same between these two versions because the melodic pacing is roughly the same, Cocker's version indicates a $\frac{6}{8}$ time signature, with only one kick and snare per bar. Note that if we consider the Beatles version as in $\frac{12}{8}$, it would be unreasonable to hear the eighth note as tactus, since its rate of 330 BPM lies well above the ceiling for tempo perception. Yet in Cocker's version, the metric level that aligns most closely with tempo norms for rock is the eighth note, at 145 BPM. That said, the kick-snare rate in Cocker's version is around 48 BPM, which still lies within the range of tempo perception. This conflict between an eighth-note tactus and a kick-snare pattern at a slower yet still viable rate is a hallmark of $\frac{6}{8}$ time signatures in rock, paralleling similar conflict between metric layers found in a half-time $\frac{4}{4}$.

Another subtle but important aspect of the rhythmic organization in Cocker's cover is the pervasive swing on the sixteenth-note level, most noticeable in the ride cymbal. Whereas eighth-note swing in $\frac{4}{4}$ can be captured by the time signature (as $\frac{12}{8}$), it is impossible to represent sixteenth-note swing in $\frac{6}{8}$ via some alternative time signature. Because sixteenth-note swing is not possible to designate through the time signature alone, rock musicians typically consider swing overall as a separate aspect of meter than the time signature. Sixteenth-note swing may also occur in $\frac{4}{4}$, as heard in "Rag Doll" by Aerosmith (1987), "Sunday Morning" by Maroon 5 (2002), and "Say You're Sorry" by Sara Bareilles (2010). When sixteenth-note swing occurs in $\frac{4}{4}$, the first and third sixteenth notes of each beat are longer than the second and fourth sixteenth notes, while the eighth notes evenly divide the quarter-note beat. (Eighth-note swing and sixteenth-note swing are thus mutually exclusive.)

In addition to $\frac{4}{4}$ and $\frac{6}{8}$, the next most useful time signature for rock is $\frac{3}{4}$. These three time signatures – $\frac{4}{4}$, $\frac{6}{8}$, and $\frac{3}{4}$ – form the core set of time signatures suitable for classifying meter in rock, since they represent the three most maximally contrasting ways to divide a measure: two parts divided into two subparts ($\frac{4}{4}$), two parts divided into three subparts ($\frac{6}{8}$), and three parts divided into two subparts ($\frac{3}{4}$). Theoretically, it is possible to consider a fourth category that divides the measure into three parts and three subparts, i.e., $\frac{9}{8}$. But potential cases of $\frac{9}{8}$ in rock, such as "A Taste of Honey" by the Beatles (1963) or "Only Love Can Break Your Heart" by

Neil Young (1970), are more commonly conceptualized as songs in $\frac{3}{4}$ with eighth-note swing, since (as with $\frac{12}{8}$) the eight-note layer is typically too fast to be felt as a viable tactus.

Rock songs in $\frac{3}{4}$ are far less common than those in $\frac{4}{4}$ or $\frac{6}{8}$, perhaps because of the difficulty in reconciling a standard drumbeat with the odd number of beats in a measure. The normal drum pattern in $\frac{3}{4}$, for example, is a kick on beat 1 and snare on beat 3, which lacks the evenly spaced alternation between kick and snare found in other meters. As a workaround, drummers can shift the kick-snare pattern to a higher or lower level of the metric hierarchy, akin to a half-time or double-time feel. The song "Take It to the Limit" by the Eagles (1975), for example, has a strong tactus at 90 BPM, yet the kick and snare at the beginning occur every three beats. It is doubtful that the kick and snare distance is perceived as the true beat rate here, given it lies on the threshold of beat perception, so it makes more sense to consider the song in $\frac{3}{4}$ with a half-time feel rather than a slow $\frac{6}{8}$. Further support for the $\frac{3}{4}$ hearing appears later in the leadup to the chorus (1:12), where the drums revert to a normal $\frac{3}{4}$ pattern.

Taking a global view, Figure 11.1 provides a chart of the most common metric parameters found in rock. This chart classifies typical rhythmic organizations via three categories, each of which has three options: (1) the time signature, which is usually $\frac{4}{4}$, $\frac{6}{8}$, or $\frac{3}{4}$; (2) the drum feel, which may be normal time, half time, or double time; and (3) the level of swing, which may be none, eighth notes, or sixteenths. A song could thus be a double-time $\frac{4}{4}$ with sixteenth-note swing, such as "Up from Below" by Edward Sharpe and the Magnetic Zeros (2009); a half-time $\frac{4}{4}$ with eighth-note swing, such as "Grapevine Fires" by Death Cab for Cutie (2008); or a double-time $\frac{3}{4}$ with no swing, such as "Synchronicity I" by the Police (1983). From the standpoint of traditional time signatures, the chart in Figure 11.1 may seem like a radical simplification, but it represents over

Time Signature	**Drum Feel**	**Swing**
$\frac{4}{4}$	**Normal**	**None**
$\frac{6}{8}$	**Half-Time**	**Swung 8ths**
$\frac{3}{4}$	**Double-Time**	**Swung 16ths**

11.1 Chart of common metric parameters found in rock

twenty viable combinations – far more than the six basic time signatures of $\frac{2}{4}$, $\frac{3}{4}$, $\frac{4}{4}$, $\frac{6}{8}$, $\frac{9}{8}$, and $\frac{12}{8}$ – before the consideration of irregular meters.

An in-depth discussion of irregular meters in rock, such as complex or changing meters, is beyond the scope of the current chapter. That said, it seems worth providing one example to model a general approach. The song "Whipping Post" by the Allman Brothers Band (1969) is famous for the odd rhythmic structure of its main riff, which involves some grouping of eleven. This metric irregularity disappears once the vocals enter (0:26), as the verse material settles into a repeated grouping pattern of three at 200 BPM. This fast tempo is somewhat uncomfortable to sustain as a regular tactus, so many listeners may find themselves conflicted between this rate and the slower rate of 67 BPM. This tactus conflict is the hallmark of a $\frac{6}{8}$ meter, and, perhaps not surprisingly, the leadup to the chorus and the chorus itself (0:56) present a standard $\frac{6}{8}$ drum pattern. The song overall, therefore, seems to be in $\frac{6}{8}$, with the verse feeling more energetic due to the surface rhythms of the bass and drum parts. More importantly, we can understand the opening riff not as some long span of eleven beats but rather as a bar of $\frac{6}{8}$ followed by a bar of $\frac{5}{8}$ – this $\frac{5}{8}$ bar resulting from the deletion of an eighth note – which reconciles the riff's 3+3+3+2 grouping with typical metric organizations found in rock. The additional complicating factor arises from the double-time pattern that the drums play against this $\frac{6}{8}$ meter, with the kick on the first of every three eighth notes. In general, irregular meters in rock can be understood as some variation on the strategy seen here, where a beat or sub-beat is deleted from or added to one of the more regular metric organizations shown in Figure 11.1.

Syncopation and Stress

In traditional conceptions of meter, an important distinction exists between strong and weak beats. In $\frac{4}{4}$, for example, beats 1 and 3 are considered strong – i.e., the metric locations that are normally accented – while beats 2 and 4 are weak – i.e., those that are normally unaccented.[7] A similar pattern of strong and weak is understood to continue through higher and lower levels of the metric hierarchy. The first eighth note of a beat, for example, is considered strong while the second is weak. The musical surface typically reinforces these patterns of strong and weak so as to clearly convey the meter; otherwise, metric confusion may occur.

In contrast, meter in rock can appear organized in a somewhat opposite manner. In a standard $\frac{4}{4}$ drumbeat, for example, the snare is almost always louder than the kick, and the spectral energy of a snare lies within a frequency range to which the human ear is especially sensitive. As a result, beats 2 and 4 are arguably more accented in rock on a regular basis than beats 1 and 3. This is not to imply that rock musicians do not recognize the structural importance of the downbeat. Rather, expectations in rock with regard to recurring patterns of stress and accent are often different from traditional norms. (This difference is highlighted by the familiar joke among popular musicians that "friends don't let friends clap on beats 1 and 3.")

Off-beat accents are not exclusive to rock music, of course. Styles ranging from jazz to bluegrass have long traditions of putting stress on what are traditionally considered weak beats or weak portions of the beat. More broadly, syncopation – as a rhythmic pattern that goes against the beat structure – dates back in European music to at least the Middle Ages. That said, certain types of syncopation and non-traditional accent patterns are particularly endemic to rock, as found in its melodic and harmonic material.

Perhaps the most characteristic rhythmic feature of a rock melody is the anticipatory syncopation. In essence, an anticipatory syncopation is an event that occurs prior to a relatively stronger beat but, unlike a regular anticipation, without a new event on that stronger beat. The length of the anticipation is most typically an eighth note, although sixteenth-note anticipatory syncopations are also common. One example can be found in the song "Sweet Caroline" by Neil Diamond (1969). When the title line is sung at the beginning of the famously anthemic chorus (1:02), linguistic stress occurs on the word "sweet" and the first and third syllables of "Caroline." But while "sweet" and the first syllable of "Caroline" are sung on the beat, the last syllable of "Caroline" is sung on an eighth note prior to the following downbeat, without any new melodic content on that downbeat. From the standpoint of traditional text setting, this anticipation by the syllable "–line" may seem odd, since the linguistic stress does not align with the metric stress.

What are we to make of this situation? One view is that rock melodies regularly displace linguistically stressed syllables, typically forward in time, from locations of metric stress. In other words, the third syllable of "Caroline" belongs to the next downbeat on a deeper level, but the musical surface shifts that linguistically stressed note away from the location of metric stress. The reason for this forward shift, we might hypothesize, is perhaps to make the melody more rhythmically interesting. Another view is that rock simply has no priority for aligning linguistically stressed events with strong metric locations. In $\frac{4}{4}$, for example, the metric distribution of note onsets in rock melodies appears to be essentially uniform, with equal probability of a note occurring on any eighth note of the measure.[8] By this view, the last syllable of "Caroline" does not belong to the following downbeat in any sense; instead, it simply belongs where it is. The metric location of melodic notes may be a function of speech patterns. It certainly seems more natural to sing the word "Caroline" as it is in this chorus, rather than evenly spacing out each syllable.

Some evidence for the first view can be found when examining how rock musicians treat traditional melodies. The nursery rhyme "Mary Had a Little Lamb" is a useful case study, since its melody (Example 11.2a) is well known and simple, and has been the basis of more than one rock song. Consider, for example, the version heard on Chubby Checker's 1959 song "The Class" (0:22; Example 11.2b), which hews closely to the original melody. The biggest differences are within the rhythmic domain. In particular, all but one of the rhythmic divergences involve anticipatory syncopation: "lamb" in the second measure, the first syllable of "ev'ry" in the fifth measure, "went" in the sixth measure, "lamb" in the seventh measure, and "go" in the last measure – each has been displaced forward in time by an eighth note. Generally speaking, there appears to be a preference for anticipatory syncopation at the beginning of a phrase but especially at the end of a phrase, similar to the strategy found in "Sweet Caroline."

11.2 Three versions of the nursery rhyme "Mary Had a Little Lamb."
(a) Traditional version
(b) Version from Chubby Checker's song "The Class" (1959)
(c) Version from the Wings' song "Mary Had a Little Lamb" (1972)

The consequent effect is a lack of finality, as the misalignment of linguistic stress with metric strong points thwarts a solid sense of resolution.

A similar strategy can be found in Paul McCartney's version (Example 11.2c), released by Wings in 1972. McCartney significantly changes the pitch structure of the melody, but the rhythmic relationship between his version and the original remains clear. Like Chubby Checker's version, anticipatory syncopations are most commonly found at the ends of phrases or subphrases. But in McCartney's setting, the anticipatory syncopations cascade further back toward the beginning of each phrasal unit. Rather than just syncopating "lamb" in the second measure, for example, McCartney syncopates the second syllable of "little" as well as "lamb." Similarly, each syllable of "white as snow" now occurs an eighth note earlier than in the original version. By enlarging the zone of anticipatory syncopation prior to phrase endings, McCartney's version further increases the sense of being off-balance, thereby avoiding strong melodic closure.

Many melodies in rock employ anticipatory syncopation to such an extreme that almost every note occurs between beats. Examples include the verse material to "Taxman" by the Beatles (1966), "Wrapped Around Your Finger" by the Police (1983), and "Smells Like Teen Spirit" by Nirvana (1991). Similar to how the standard rock drumbeat puts stress on beat locations traditionally considered weak, therefore, rock melodies often put stress on divisions of the beat that are traditionally considered weak. In an unaccompanied setting, such high levels of melodic syncopation might be untenable, causing confusion as to the beat location. Since the metric structure of the song is so clearly conveyed by the drumbeat, though, perhaps there is less onus in rock for the melody to express the meter and more freedom to play against it. In other words, the evolution of typical rhythmic patterns in rock melodies may be the result of having the beat clearly expressed by the dedicated rhythmic layer of the drums.

In contrast to melodic events, harmonic events in rock align fairly closely with traditional rhythmic norms. Generally speaking, chords in rock change every half measure, measure, or two measures. In the overwhelming majority of cases, moreover, these chord changes occur on the beat. Indeed, the downbeat is by far the most common metric location for a new harmony in rock. Because there are so many other counterforces in rock creating stress on traditionally weak beats and weak divisions of the beat, perhaps it is imperative for the harmonic layer to stress the beginnings of measures.

That said, syncopation – particularly anticipatory syncopation – is not uncommon for harmonies in rock. These are sometimes referred to as a "push" by rock musicians, since the chord seems "pushed" forward by an eighth note prior to the beat. In general, anticipatory syncopation in rock harmony tends to occur on weaker portions of the measure or hypermeasure. For example, if a song section has a harmonic rhythm of one chord per measure, the push usually occurs on the harmony in the second and fourth measure, as heard in the verses of "She Will Be Loved" by Maroon 5 (2002) and "Fire Meet Gasoline" by Sia (2014). Similarly, if a song section has a harmonic rhythm of two chords per measure, the push usually occurs on the chord midway through the measure, as heard in the chorus of "Peace of Mind" by Boston (1976) and the verse of "Jesus Take the Wheel" by Carrie Underwood (2005). Note that this more limited approach to anticipatory syncopation in the harmonic domain shows a preference for aligning harmonies with the beginnings of measures and hypermeasures, presumably so as not to overly disturb the underlying metric structure.

Another type of syncopation frequently encountered in the accompanimental pattern of a rock song is the cross rhythm. Typically, cross rhythms involve multiple groupings of three eighth notes in a $\frac{4}{4}$ meter with one or two groupings of two eighth notes that create a repeating one-bar or two-bar unit. A common example is the 3+3+2 "tresillo" rhythm (also found in African and Latin American music), such as at the beginning of "Swingtown" by the Steve Miller Band (1977) and "She Goes Down" by Mötley Crüe (1989). Note that the 3+3+2 cross rhythm is similar to a push on beat 3 in $\frac{4}{4}$, which causes the second chord to enter on the "and" of beat 2. The groupings of threes can also be extended to create a 3+3+3+3+2+2 "double tresillo" pattern, as heard at the beginning of "Shoot to Thrill" by AC/DC (1980) and "Runaway" by Bon Jovi (1984). Rotations of the double tresillo are also possible, such as the 2+3+3+3+3+2 pattern heard at the beginning of "Faithfully" by Journey (1983). Note that in all these cases, the groupings of three do not cut across important structural boundaries, such as the beginning of a hypermeasure or two-bar unit. Instead, the syncopation created by the cross rhythm is regularly resolved on every downbeat or every other downbeat, which helps maintain the clarity of the underlying metric organization within the harmonic domain.

Conclusion

As put forward here, rhythm and meter in rock involve different norms than do other musical styles, especially as compared to classical music.

These differences include expectations about typical beat rates, ways in which the beat is divided, and patterns of stress. Many of these normative characteristics can be traced to earlier popular styles, such as jazz, bluegrass, blues, and gospel. But as a musical melting pot, paralleling similar trends of cultural assimilation in the United States, rock music can be viewed as a homogenization of these tributary styles into an amalgam meant for mass-market appeal.

It would be remiss to close without some mention of the role technology played in this process. Not coincidentally, the birth of rock and roll occurred in tandem with the birth of the multitrack recording studio. Rock musicians were thus able to create arrangements and performances entirely free from musical notation. Other styles – such as folk and blues music – existed primarily as oral traditions prior to rock, of course. But it was in the cauldron of the recording studio where these styles came together. The lack of any requirement to notate the music allowed, arguably, for more complex rhythmic and metric structures to proliferate, most notably in the heavily syncopated melodies of rock. Looking forward, as computer-based digital audio workstations (e.g., Ableton Live, Logic Pro) increasingly supplant the traditional recording studio as the primary setting for music-creation, technological changes will undoubtedly continue to transform the rhythmic and metric organization of popular music in new and revolutionary ways.

Endnotes

1 F. Lerdahl and R. Jackendoff, *A Generative Theory of Tonal Music* (MIT Press, 1983), 73.
2 T. de Clercq, "Measuring a Measure: Absolute Time as a Factor for Determining Bar Lengths and Meter in Pop/Rock Music," *Music Theory Online*, 22.3 (2016).
3 J. London, *Hearing in Time: Psychological Aspects of Music Meter*, 2nd ed. (Oxford University Press, 2012), 30.
4 A. Moore, *Rock: The Primary Text: Developing a Musicology of Rock*, 2nd ed. (Aldershot: Ashgate, 2001), 42.
5 M. W. Butterfield, "Why Do Jazz Musicians Swing Their Eighth Notes?" *Music Theory Spectrum*, 33 (2011), 3–26.
6 K. Wyatt, C. Schroeder, and J. Elliott, *Ear Training for the Contemporary Musician* (Milwaukee: Hal Leonard, 2005), 77.
7 Lerdahl and Jackendoff, *A Generative Theory*, 19.
8 D. Temperley, *The Musical Language of Rock* (Oxford University Press, 2018), 79.

12 Rhythm in Contemporary Rap Music

MITCHELL OHRINER

One can observe two trends in music theory and analysis in recent decades, partly in response to the criticism of New Musicology in the 1990s: increased attention to the topic of rhythm and meter and increased attention to repertoires of popular music.[1] These two trends have been mutually reinforcing. In the 1980s and 1990s, scholars argued that engaging with popular music would push music scholarship beyond its traditional focus on pitch organization. The impetus for this expansion was popular music's distinctive rhythms endowed by the influences (or appropriations) of the musics of the African diaspora. These rhythmic features include pervasive anticipatory syncopation,[2] unequal and often maximally even rhythmic groupings,[3] and a tendency toward metric saturation.[4] Given these trends, it would seem that rap music would hold particular interest to music scholars, and indeed, the study of rap music's sonic organization has also flourished.[5] Yet it still stands somewhat apart, a redux of the relationship of popular music vis-à-vis classical music a generation ago: existing analytic methods (rhythmic or otherwise) are either incompatible with rap music or provide seemingly little illumination. Kyle Adams has documented some ontological reasons for this disconnect: rap music always has a texted component, but the kinds of text-music correspondences analysts find so appealing are scant. Rap music also has an instrumental component (termed "the beat"), but that beat, often with many creators and composed of disparate samples of previous recordings, synthesizers, and programmed drums, would seem not to "work toward a singular expressive purpose."[6]

I would add other hindrances of particular concern for theories and analyses of rhythm and meter in rap music. At the risk of broadly generalizing, recent scholarship on popular music has addressed primarily metric or hypermetric additions or truncations at the macro-level.[7] At the meso-level, it has addressed primarily rhythmic complexities such as non-isochronous meters[8] and durations or groupings with interesting mathematical features such as maximal evenness or Euclidean rhythms at the meso-level.[9] At the micro-level, it has addressed the deployment of swing[10] and minute temporal relationships among collaborating musicians.[11]

Most rap music simply does not partake of these complexities. Instead, rap music has a way of disguising its complexities in aspects of organization that rap discourse presents as simple. In this chapter I will address two such aspects: patterning of the kick and snare streams in rap's instrumental beats and alignment of rap's syllables with the meter. In each case, rap music discourse would suggest little to hear here. As with the backbeat in pop-rock music, the kick and snare in rap music are thought to alternate, with kick events on beats 1 and 3 and snare events on beats 2 and 4. This feature is considered so invariant that the kick and snare of any rap track is given a single, onomatopoeic name, the *boom-bap*. Similarly, the placement of syllables in a rap verse is thought to align with meter in predictable ways, so much so that a rapper who does not align with the meter is delegitimized as "off-beat." In what follows, I will challenge the conventional account of both of these features by discussing selected tracks of a single recent album of rap music, Kendrick Lamar's *DAMN.* from 2017. This album has the distinction of being the only musical work to win both the Grammy Award for album of the year across all genres and the Pulitzer Prize in Music, an award previously given to contemporary classical or jazz composers. My aim in this undertaking is twofold: first, to demonstrate some subtle rhythmic organization in contemporary rap music, and, second, to demonstrate how an engagement with contemporary rap music might refine methods for the analysis of popular music that has, to date, been primarily focused on pop-rock.[12]

Drum Textures in *DAMN.*

Percussive sounds, whether sampled, programmed, or performed, form the rhythmic skeleton of rap music. Some tracks, such as Mobb Deep's "The Infamous" and much of A Tribe Called Quest's "Can I Kick It?," contain nothing else. Existing scholarship on the backbeat, drawing heavily on Christopher Hasty's *Meter as Rhythm*, mostly in reference to pop-rock music, focuses on the quality of motion between successive beats within the meter the backbeat pattern engenders. In Hasty's approach, indebted to earlier theorists like Moritz Hauptmann and Victor Zuckerkandl, each duration experienced in ongoing music conveys a quality of beginning, anticipation, or continuation. Theorists of the backbeat generally conceive of the low-pitch kick events on beats 1 and 3 as beginning a longer duration. This quality of the kick emerges both from a top-down interpretation that beats 1 and 3 are typically "strong" in a four-beat meter[13] and also from a bottom-up perception that the kick is lower and more resonant than the snare. The metric quality of the snare is more contentious. Robin Attas, following Matthew Butterfield, describes the snare as an anacrusis to the kick because its shorter duration and higher pitch contradicts the kick, creating a metric uncertainty that the return of the kick resolves.[14]

While not drawing on Hasty's approach, David Temperley also hears the snare as an anticipatory, syncopated displacement of the kick, a syncopation at the half-note level related to the pervasive displacement of rhythms of pop-rock melodies at the quarter-note level.[15] In a contrary view, Nicole Biamonte argues that the resonance of the kick links it to the following snare, rendering the snare continuational, not anticipatory.[16] Other events in the snare or kick stream might impact the quality of the snare with respect to the kick. If the snare is subdivided (i.e., "boom. . .bap-bap-boom" rather than "boom. . .bap. . .boom"), the relatively longer duration of kick renders the snare anticipatory; if the kick is subdivided (i.e., "boom-boom-bap" rather than "boom-bap"), the relatively longer duration of the snare is continuational. Finally, microtiming variation in the snare might also impact its continuational or anticipatory quality; relatively "late" snares are more anticipatory of the next kick; relatively "early" snares are more continuational of the previous one.[17]

Here I would stress the extent to which discussion of the quality of the backbeat relies on features of pop-rock music that are diminished or absent in contemporary rap music and other genres influenced by it. Rap music only rarely employs sustained displaced-quarter-note rhythms, the hallmark of pop and rock melodies that provides Temperley's frame of "backbeat as syncopation," and, generally, only in sung hooks. And in the era of studio production and digital audio workstations, the backbeat is usually quantized, and thus microtiming has little impact on the character of the snare.[18] Most importantly, the drum textures of contemporary rap music differ from those of pop-rock in their sheer number of events. No track on *DAMN.* has an unadorned backbeat, nor are the ornamentations confined to eighth-note subdivisions. This may be because production of contemporary rap drum textures generally does not require the coordination of skilled drum set players.[19]

At the most basic level, contemporary rap music complicates the description of the backbeat's structure of kick-snare alternation. Figure 12.1 visualizes the snare and kick streams of four tracks on the album, all of which are similar. Each plot represents one measure; thicker gray vertical lines represent beats; thinner gray vertical lines represent sixteenth-note positions. Squares represent kick events; circles represent snare events.

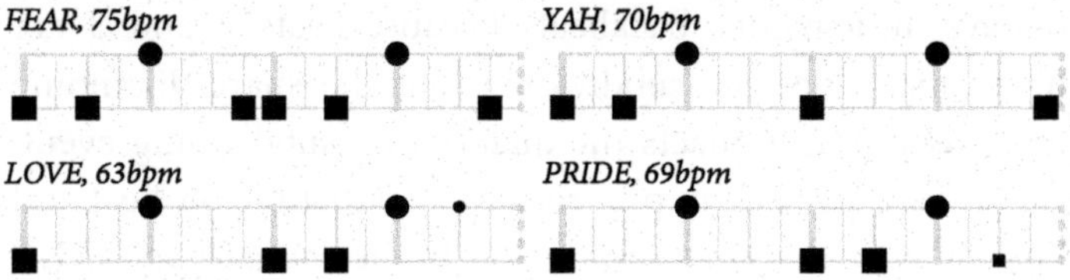

12.1 Kick and snare patterning on "FEAR.," "YAH.," "LOVE.," and "PRIDE." from Kendrick Lamar's DAMN. (2017)

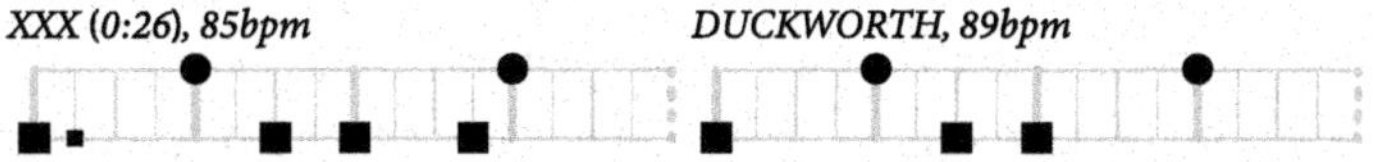

12.2 Kick and snare patterning in "XXX." (starting at 0:26) and "DUCKWORTH." Compare to Figure 12.1.

The size of dot reflects proportion of measures in which the event is heard. Instruments occurring on a particular metric position in only one of each four measures have been discarded. These tracks most closely resemble the typical pop-rock backbeat. They have all the expected events in the kick and snare, but they also have subdividing events in the kick that, according to Biamonte, renders the snare more continuational than anticipatory. Yet none of them exactly repeats the first half of the measure in the second half. Thus, if one argues, like Attas and Butterfield, that the snare of the backbeat is normatively anacrustic, and, like Biamonte, that subdivided kicks render snares continuational, then all of these patterns create one beginning in the measure more prominent than any other. For example, beat 2 in "LOVE." (and also in the nearly identical "PRIDE.") anticipates beat 3 because beat 1 is not subdivided, and beat 4 continues beat 3 because beat 3 is subdivided; thus beat 3 (not beat 1!) is the locus of metric energy. Similarly, in "FEAR." the anticipation of the beat 3 kick on the preceding position again focuses greater attention on beat 3 rather than the downbeat. Only "YAH.," which is the same as "FEAR." two beats later, focuses attention on the downbeat. Indeed, none of the drum patterns on *DAMN.* replicates the first half in their second half. This lends weight to Hasty's view of meter-as-rhythm: the quality of meter differs from track to track. It also undercuts arguments in prior work that the backbeat can be characterized in any particular way if, at least in contemporary rap music, the prototypical backbeat is rarely heard in an actual track.

Figure 12.2 uses the same plotting method to show kick and snare patterning in the first two verses of "XXX." (beginning at 0:26) and the very similar patterning in "DUCKWORTH."[20] These verses of "XXX."

would seem to have anticipatory backbeats because beats 2 and 3 are subdivided, but the kick does the subdividing, not the snare. Biamonte does not address how timbre impacts the quality of a subdividing event, instead assuming (as is reasonable in pop-rock music) that the on-beat and subdividing event will have the same timbre. But in the patterns of "XXX." and "DUCKWORTH.," the snare begins to compete with the kick as the locus of attention. In "XXX.," the longest uninterrupted duration begins with the snare on beat 4, an event that also has an anticipating kick event. Divorced from expectations that beats 1 and 3 are "strong," one could claim that beats 2 and 4 here have more of the features we associate with loci of metric attention: they are predictable, equally spaced, and begin long durations.

Figure 12.3 shows five other patterns that focus attention more toward the snare than the kick and thereby undermine conventional notions of 1- and 3-weighted quadruple meter. All four have typical snare patterns, and none has typical kick patterns. In the first verse of "DNA.," the kick approximates the "double tresillo" rhythm (i.e., 16 divided into 3+3+3+3+2 +2) described by Butler, Biamonte, Cohn, and others.[21] Because this starts on the downbeat, the snare of beat 2 has an anticipatory kick event. A kick fill lends the same to beat 4 in the even-numbered measures. In the last verse of "XXX.," the kick is highly unpredictable, beginning by suggesting a tresillo before placing four events on the weakest parts of the beat in the middle of the measure. The second verse of "DNA." has hardly any kick events at all and none on the expected 1 and 3. Finally, the patterns of "GOD." and "HUMBLE.," which repeat every two measures rather than every measure, similarly have a standard snare and an unpredictable kick.

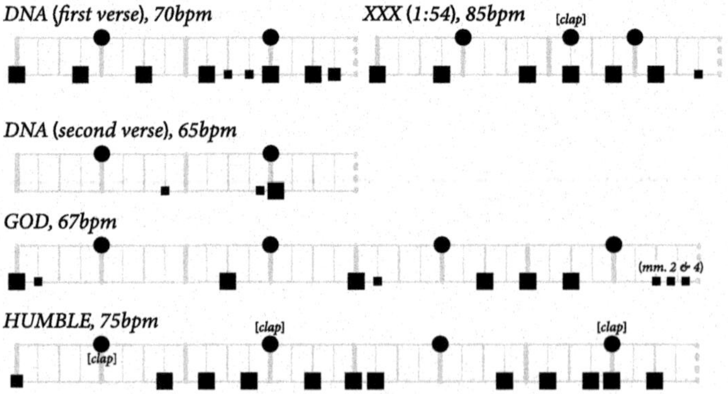

12.3 Kick and snare patterning in the first verse of "DNA.," the last verse of "XXX.," the second verse of "DNA.," "GOD.," and "HUMBLE." The plots for "GOD." and "HUMBLE." show a repeating two-measure pattern.

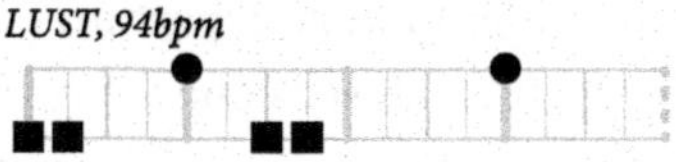

12.4 Kick and snare patterning in "LUST."

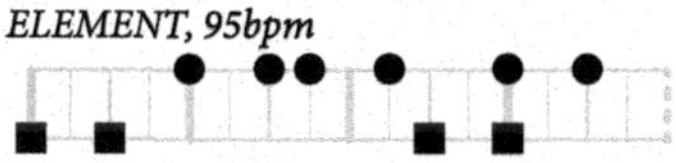

12.5 Kick and snare patterning in "ELEMENT."

All these examples undercut many aspects of the current framing of the backbeat: that the kick is an anchoring presence on 1 and 3, that the low register of the kick implies an uninterrupted resonance, and that the snare either anticipates or continues the attentional energy of the kick. I should stress here that I am not suggesting the cumulative metric experience of these tracks undercuts the $\frac{4}{4}$ meter. Other aspects, especially changes in harmony, bass note, and vocal phrasing, clearly support the meter. What I am suggesting is that contemporary rap drumming does not play the same meter-defining role as in pop-rock music.

The patterns discussed thus far account for less than half of those on the album. The rest, to varying degrees, resist explanation as "backbeats" of any kind. Figure 12.4 shows the pattern of "LUST." Here, the snare is typical. The kick presents two pairs of events, as in a subdivided kick pattern, but the second pair of events is half a beat early, creating an uneven division of the measure, a kind of warped backbeat. Indeed, since neither event is on the beat, it is unclear which takes metric priority: is this a 3+5 grouping in eighth notes? Or perhaps a 7+9 grouping in sixteenths? Figure 12.5 visualizes the streams of "ELEMENT." Like "LUST.," there are two pairs of kick events that do not divide the measure evenly; here the second is a half beat late rather than a half beat early. Mirroring the kick, the snare presents two pairs of events, but these do not alternate with the kick. With neither evenly spaced events nor registral alternation, it is unclear what "backbeat" means in this context.

In summary, the "boom-bap" of earlier rap lives on more in discourse around rap than in contemporary practice. Rap's backbeats have become highly varied in response to changing technologies. Much of the texture is now created in digital audio workstations, and much of the human-generated performance is recorded to a click track, often in different locations. These shifts have seemingly diminished the timekeeping function of the backbeat in pop-rock. I would argue that although prior approaches to the backbeat are not as useful in contemporary repertoires, these changes in drum patterning highlight the utility of Hasty's contingent and affective approach to meter even more so.

Microtiming in *DAMN.*

The rhythm of the rapping voice also calls out for an expansion in analytic approaches to microrhythm. To reiterate, the focus of microrhythmic research in popular music has emphasized swing (where events on weak parts of the beat are delayed) and persistent delays in certain parts of the texture (where events on all parts of the beat are delayed). Because of the widespread use of quantized, sampled sounds, one might expect limited microrhythmic play in the rapping voice. Accordingly, in this section, I will demonstrate Lamar's capacity for near-quantization, but I will also show how his practices can amplify microrhythmic variety and, in some cases, approach the limits of what we understand as musical rhythm.

Alignment in "HUMBLE.," First Verse

Figure 12.6 plots a transcription of the voice in the first four measures of the first verse of "HUMBLE.," the lead single of *DAMN.* Dots in the transcription represent syllables and larger dots represent syllables that are relatively prominent (i.e., accented). I have quantized each syllable to a metric grid of 16 parts per measure (i.e., sixteenth notes); I number these beat classes 0 through 15. As I will show below, this quantization should not be controversial. I consider a syllable accented if it falls on a relatively

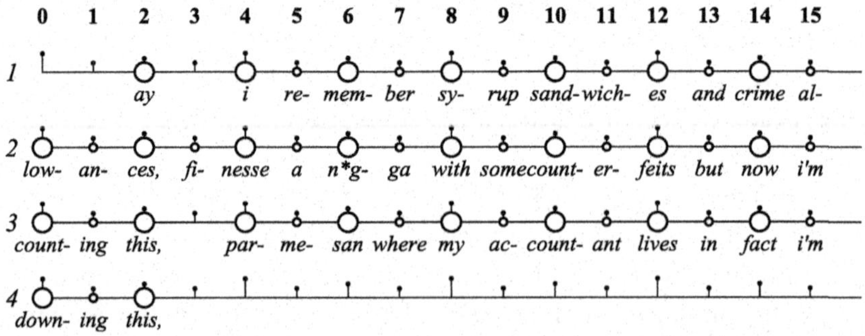

12.6 "HUMBLE.," mm. 1–4, vocal transcription. Each line transcribes one measure. Points represent syllables quantized to the nearest sixteenth note (i.e., beat class); larger points represent relatively accented syllables.

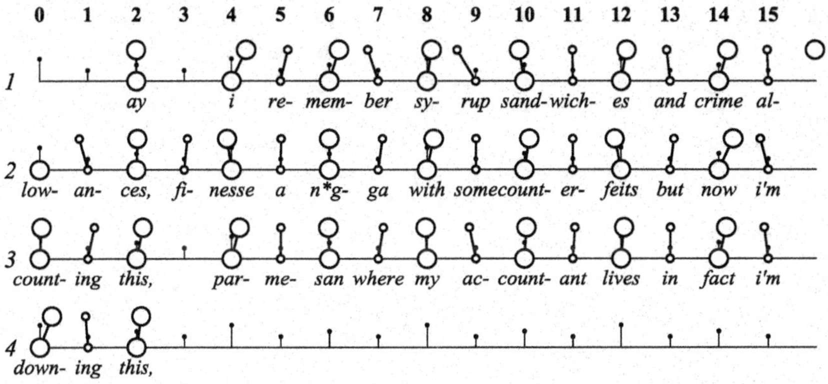

12.7 "HUMBLE.," mm. 1–4, vocal transcription depicting non-alignment. Upper row of points represents the onset of the vowel of the syllable.

strong part of the beat (i.e., an even beat class) or if it is a relatively accented syllable in a multisyllabic word such as the first and third syllables of "sandwiches," "counterfeits," and "accountant." Pitch height and syllable duration also play a role in perceived accent.[22] Notice that every accented syllable falls either on the beat or at the midpoint of the beat; this total alignment of accent to the stronger parts of the beat extends through the entire verse until the statement of the title word of the song as the last word of the verse at the end of m. 16.

Lamar extends his alignment of accent with the beat at the macrorhythmic level by precisely aligning syllables with the beat at the microrhythmic level. Figure 12.7 replots the transcription and adds upper rows of dots reflecting the more precise placement of syllables.[23] And precise they are: in absolute terms, the vowel onsets of syllables differ from the onset of the nearest beat class, on average, by 20 ms; only a fifth of syllables surpass the 30 ms perceptual threshold proposed by Bregman and Pinker.[24] Previous studies can contextualize this degree of alignment with the beat. In a small corpus of thirteen tracks by a variety of rappers, I found an average absolute non-alignment of 89 ms, more than four times that of Lamar's non-alignment in the first verse of "HUMBLE."[25] What is all the more surprising is that in a corpus of thirty-two other verses by Lamar, the average mean non-alignment is 170 ms, greater than other rap artists and much greater than "HUMBLE."[26] (The discussions of "YAH." and "ELEMENT." below will show why Lamar's average aside from this verse is so high.)

It might seem that there is little of rhythmic or metric interest in "HUMBLE." – what more could be said of a verse that places accents on

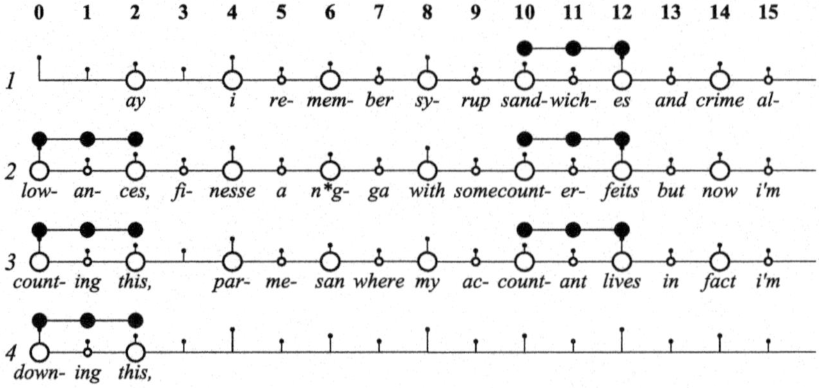

12.8 "HUMBLE.," mm. 1–4, vocal transcription with rhyme. Black dots represent returning three-syllable rhyme.

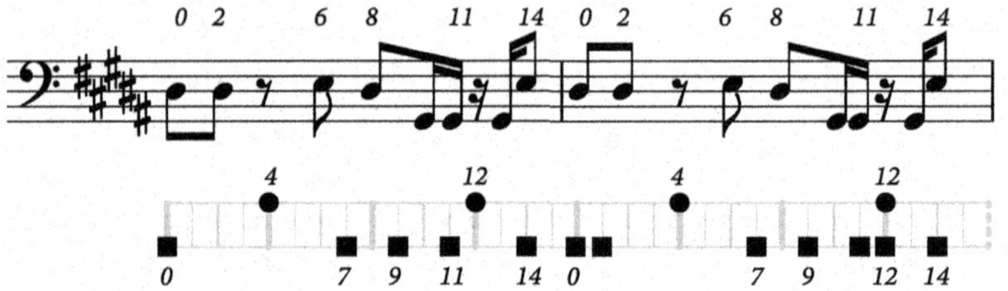

12.9 Piano loop (in conventional notation) and kick-and-snare patterning in the loop of "HUMBLE." Beat class of prominent events also given.

every eighth-note position and places syllables on the beat? Figure 12.8 plots the first four measures again, this time annotating rhyme. This placement of rhyme disrupts the rhythmic squareness of other aspects of the flow. In much rap delivery, if there are to be two instances of rhymes in each measure, they typically align with the snare on beats 2 and 4. Here, Lamar rhymes on 1 and 4 and, moreover, terminates the rhyme at a different part of the beat, ending on beat 4 but at the midpoint of beat 1. This use of rhyme to disrupt the regularity of syllable delivery also serves to permeate the meter with prominent events. Figure 12.9 shows a transcription of kick and snare below as in Figure 12.1, as well as the piano riff, the other stream in the accompaniment. Between these three streams, every eighth-note position of the measure is emphasized except for beat class 10. (There is an event in the piano on beat class 10, the first short duration of the <21212> tresillo-like rhythm of the second half of the measure, but I do not consider that "emphasized.") To saturate the meter at the eighth-note level, Lamar lends prominence to beat class 10 by beginning a rhyme there.

Lateness in "YAH.," First Verse

Much of the commentary on microtiming in Afri-diasporic music has emphasized swing (see Butterfield, this volume), and "YAH." would be a compelling place to look for swing in the voice. In a general sense, Lamar is among the contemporary rappers most associated with jazz. His 2015 release *To Pimp a Butterfly* features collaborations with many noted jazz musicians such as saxophonist Kamasi Washington, pianist Robert Glasper, and bassist Thundercat. More specifically, the kick part of the "YAH." drum pattern includes a swung anacrusis at the very end of every measure.[27] But Lamar's use of swing is very slight, producing a "beat-upbeat ratio"[28] of 1.13:1, far below the typical ratio of 2:1.[29] Instead, "YAH." emphasizes a different aspect of microtiming, that of phase complementarity.

Figure 12.10 shows the last measure of the verse. There is some limited evidence of swing here: the weak parts of the beat do seem shorter than the strong ones, especially the "to-" of "together" and "for-" of "forever," but it is more apparent that each syllable is substantially late, some by an entire sixteenth note. In absolute terms, the syllables of the line sound, on average, 145 ms after their imputed quantized position, and as much as 225 ms late. This degree of delay is far greater than encountered in previous literature.[30] Figure 12.11 shows a boxplot of lateness in the verse, with syllables grouped by measure. The dark line shows the median value of each measure, while the box shows the range of values in the middle half of the data. Here, positive values (in seconds) mean "late" and negative values mean "early." Most measures average significantly above zero. This persistent lateness amplifies the relaxed vibe of the rest of the track; "YAH." is one of the slowest tracks on the album and features a resonant but spare accompaniment of just drums, bass guitar contributing two notes per measure, and some sustained synthesizer. Further, a general trend toward beat alignment in the middle is apparent; mm. 3–5 all move toward the beat, while mm. 14–16 move away from it. This might suggest a formal functionality to lateness, with later syllables more likely at the beginnings and endings of verses.

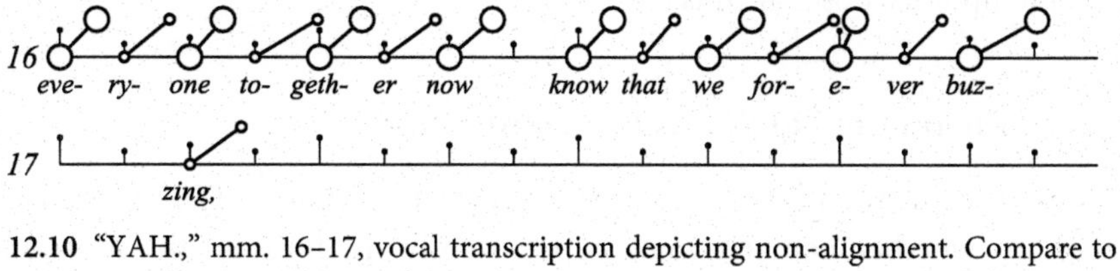

12.10 "YAH.," mm. 16–17, vocal transcription depicting non-alignment. Compare to Figure 12.7.

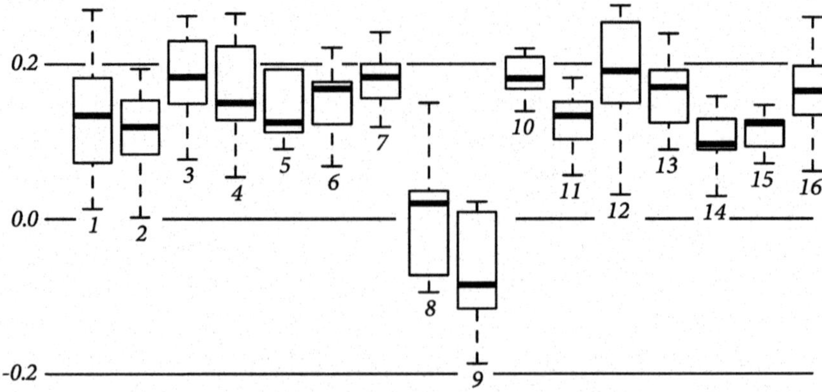

12.11 Boxplot of syllable delay with respect to the meter in "YAH.," second verse, grouped by measure.

The boxplot also reveals an outlier in mm. 8 and 9 that invites interpretation. Much of the verse addresses Lamar's fame, a standard topic in rap's braggadocious lyrics. But mm. 8 and 9 stick out: "I'm a Israelite, don't call me black no more. That word is only a color, it ain't facts no more." These lines could be read as an attempt to escape the United States' persistent racial frame, though I would place more emphasis on the "Israelite" detail. Here, Lamar aligns himself with the Black Israelites movement, whose members see themselves as descendants of the "Lost Tribes" of Israel and typically do not accept the deity of Jesus Christ. Lamar's cousin Carl Duckworth, mentioned in the following lines, is an adherent. Lamar's previous music has included frequent allusions to Christianity, and thus these lines would seem to refute, or at least complicate, his Christian allegiances. That these lines include a sudden alignment with the beat might heighten listeners' attention and inject a note of seriousness in contrast to the relaxed atmosphere of the rest of the verse. Some readers might find this claim ad hoc or unconvincing, but I would argue that whatever its merits, documenting rhythmic structure in this way opens a path to hermeneutic analysis of the interaction of lyric and music (or at least rhythm), topics frequently brought together in analysis of other repertoires but often kept at a distance in considerations of contemporary popular music.

Speech Rhythm in "ELEMENT.," Third Verse

Finally, I turn attention to the last verse from "ELEMENT.," one that questions whether Lamar's voice is persistently rhythmic in the musical sense of the word, that is, a sequence of durations in integral proportions

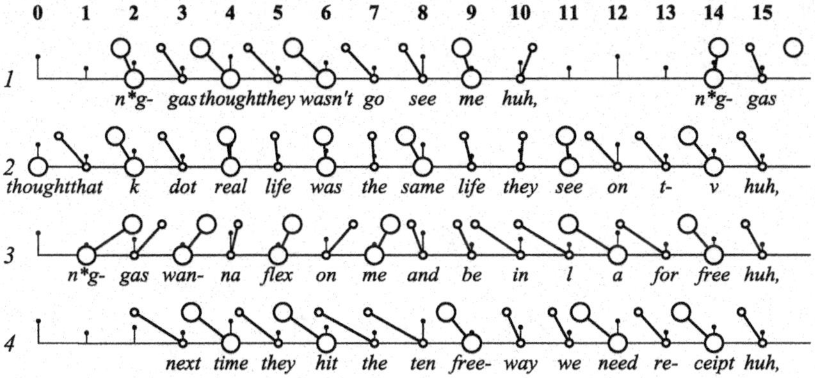

12.12 "ELEMENT.," third verse, mm. 1–4. Compare to Figures 12.7 and 12.10.

aligned with a beat (see Figure 12.12). The first four lines of the verse are epistrophic, each ending in the questioning "huh?"[31] None of these lines aligns with the beat as seen in the first verse of "HUMBLE.," nor are they displaced from the beat in any predictable way as seen in "YAH." Instead, the syllables of each have a distinctive pattern. Those of the first measure fan out away from the beat, those of the second are more aligned, those of the third start late and end early, and those of the fourth start very early and end less so. The ambiguity of Lamar's placement is matched in the reduced beat of these measures, consisting of just the off-kilter kick on beats 1 and 4 (not 3!), with an echo on the "and" of 1 and anticipation on the "and" of 3. The earliness or lateness of a syllable depends on its imputed quantization, which is analytically interpretive. Some readers might dispute the quantization of these measures and thus dispute my characterization of their relation to the metric grid. Here, two simple priorities guide my quantization. The first is to place in a 16-division meter because rappers avow its importance in their practice (Ice-T 2012); the second is to place the last accented syllable of the line (the one before "huh?") on an even-numbered beat class.

These gradations of alignment suggest that the tempo of the accompanying streams does little to organize Lamar's placement of syllables. In m. 3, Lamar rushes 15 syllables in the space of 14 sixteenth notes; in the following measure he drags out 13 in the space of nearly 14. Within the lines, the length of consonants affects the durations of syllables more so than would be expected. The longest syllables of mm. 3 and 4 are those that precede the syllable "free," suggesting that their duration comes in larger part from the necessary time for the fricative "F" and the approximant "R." Lamar demonstrates through rapping like that heard in "HUMBLE." that he can place the vowels of successive syllables on divisions of the beat

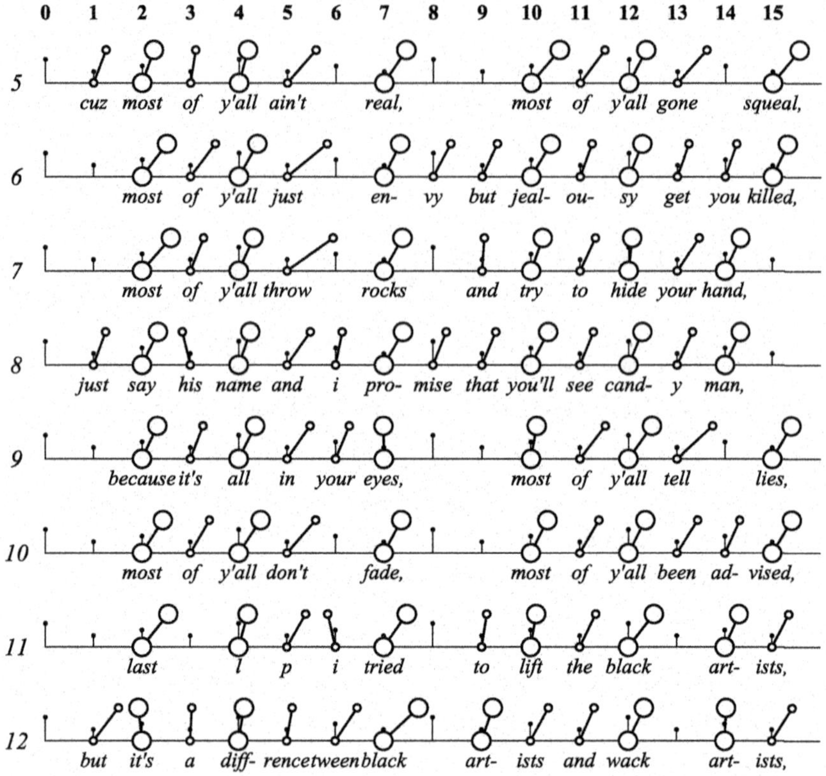

12.13 “ELEMENT.,” third verse, mm. 5–12. Compare to Figures 12.7 and 12.10.

regardless of their initial consonants, but here he seems not to make the effort to do so. Rather than the proportional durations of musical rhythm, Lamar here more closely approaches the rhythms of speech: there is lengthening toward the end of the phrase, but the rhythm of interior syllables is determined more by their phonetic structure and degree of prominence than by an attempt to align with a beat.

Figure 12.13 shows the final eight measures of the verse. Here one sees a gradual return to the kind of rapping evident in “YAH.,” that is, in clear relation to the beat if somewhat behind it. Other aspects of Lamar’s rhythm become more consistent here as well, especially his placement of accent. Figure 12.14 plots all 12 measures of the verse, but shows only the beat classes that receive accents in each measure. While the first four measures are chaotic, the last eight are highly patterned, projecting a kind of groove through accents on beat classes (2, 4, 7, 10, 12, 15).[32] Figure 12.15 maps this groove onto the kick-and-snare pattern of the verse and documents Lamar’s complementarity with the instrumental streams. He answers the

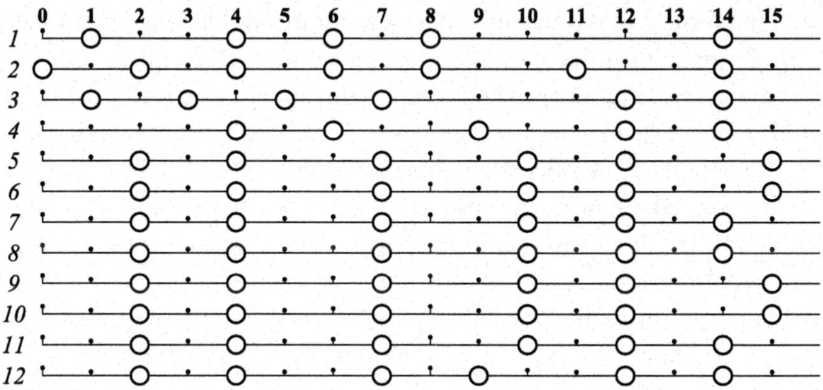

12.14 "ELEMENT.," entire third verse, metric position of accented syllables

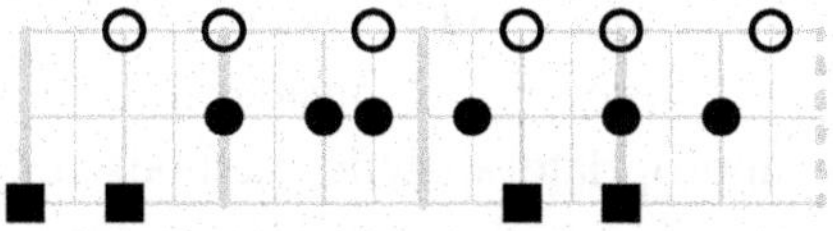

12.15 "ELEMENT.," third verse, mm. 5–12, rhythmic structure of kick, snare, and accented vocal syllables (top)

skewed "boom-bap" with his own patterned groove, while for the most part avoiding beat classes that the instrumental streams also avoid. Taken as a whole, these verses demonstrate the remarkable wealth of rhythmic approaches in the contemporary rapping voice, one that calls for scholarly emphasis beyond swing and phase relationships.

Conclusion

In this chapter I have selected two features of contemporary rap music that distinguish it from conventional approaches to rhythm in popular music – Kendrick Lamar's use of varied backbeats at the meso-level and substantial phase non-alignment and speech-like rhythm at the micro-level. The differences between contemporary rap music and pop-rock music in these regards have their roots in differing technologies, communities, and life histories of contemporary rappers. Yet these distinctions, in my view, are not isolated or marginal. Instead, they have become central to the rhythmic organization of music that extends well beyond rap and hip-hop.

In their study of trajectories and life cycles of music genres, Jennifer Lena and Richard Peterson distinguish between genred and non-genred music; the former is associated with a community and initiated by a small clique of musicians unsatisfied with existing genres.[33] Rock music and rap music are genres. Pop music is not: "At its core, pop music is music found in *Billboard* magazine's Hot 100 Singles chart. . . . Artists making such music may think of their performances in terms of genre, but the organizations that assist them in reaching the chart most certainly do not." Over the past several decades, scholarship on "pop-rock" has made profound contributions to music analysis, not only in the ways that repertoire is understood, but also in the methods analysts bring to the study of many other genres (including "classical" music). But Lena and Peterson's framework suggests that these studies are not of "pop-rock," but rather rock music, much of which was also, for a time, very popular. Since the beginning of the twenty-first century, the genres co-opted by the mainstream music industry as "pop music" have shifted decisively from rock music toward hip-hop and electronic dance music.[34] It is therefore necessary to consider how the influence of these genres impacts the appropriate analytic methods for describing them. This reconsideration, in a sense, is a revival of the impetus for pop-rock scholarship beginning in the 1990s: to describe contemporary popular music on its own terms and see what that project can do for music analysis more generally. I can only hope it will be as fruitful.

Endnotes

1 For one perspective from New Musicology see S. McClary and R. Walser, "Start Making Sense! Musicology Wrestles with Rock," in S. Frith and A. Goodwin (eds.), *On Record: Pop, Rock, and the Written Word* (New York: Pantheon Books, 1990), 277–92.

2 For example, D. Temperley, *The Musical Language of Rock* (Oxford University Press, 2018), 77.

3 For example, D. Traut, "'Simply Irresistible': Recurring Accent Patterns as Hooks in Mainstream 1980s Music," *Popular Music*, 24 (2005), 57–77; and R. Cohn, "A Platonic Model of Funky Rhythms," *Music Theory Online*, 22.2 (2016).

4 For example, J. Pressing, "Black Atlantic Rhythm: Its Computational and Transcultural Foundations," *Music Perception*, 19 (2002), 285–310; and R. Attas, "Meter and Motion in Pop/Rock Backbeats," paper delivered at the Annual Meeting of the Society for Music Theory, 2014.

5 I understand "rap music" as the musical manifestation of the broader aesthetic movement of hip-hop, which also includes manifestations in dance, fashion, art, and literature. When discussing music, I consider "hip-hop" and "rap" interchangeable. Others attach values of authenticity to one term or the other

(e.g., "there's rap music and there's 'real hip-hop'"), but there is no consensus on which of the terms attains these values.

6 K. Adams, "The Musical Analysis of Hip-Hop," in J. Williams (ed.), *The Cambridge Companion to Hip-Hop* (Cambridge University Press, 2015), 120.

7 For example, G. McCandless, "Metal as a Gradual Process: Additive Rhythmic Structures in the Music of Dream Theater, *Music Theory Online*, 19.2 (2013); and N. Murphy, "'The Times They Are a Changin': Flexible Meter and Text Expression in 1960s and 70s Singer-Songwriter Music" (Ph.D. dissertation, University of British Columbia, 2016).

8 For example, J. Pieslak, "Re-casting Metal: Rhythm and Meter in the Music of Meshuggah," *Music Theory Spectrum*, 29 (2007), 219–45; N. Hesselink, "Radiohead's 'Pyramid Song': Ambiguity, Rhythm, and Participation," *Music Theory Online*, 19.1 (2013); S. Hanenberg, "Unpopular Meters: Irregular Grooves and Drumbeats in the Songs of Tori Amos, Radiohead, and Tool" (Ph.D. dissertation, University of Toronto, 2018); and G. Capuzzo, "Rhythmic Deviance in the Music of Meshuggah," *Music Theory Spectrum*, 40 (2018), 121–37.

9 For example, M. Butler, *Unlocking the Groove: Rhythm, Meter, and Musical Design in Electronic Dance Music* (Indiana University Press, 2006); and B. Osborn, "Kid Algebra: Radiohead's Euclidean and Maximally Even Rhythms," *Perspectives of New Music*, 52 (2014), 81–105.

10 For example, M. W. Butterfield, "The Power of Anacrusis: Engendered Feeling in Groove-Based Musics," *Music Theory Online*, 12.4 (2006); and A. Danielsen, "Metrical Ambiguity or Microrhythmic Flexibility? Analysing Groove in 'Nasty Girl' by Destiny's Child," in R. von Appen, A. Doehring, and A. Moore (eds.), *Song Interpretation in 21st-Century Pop Music* (Routledge, 2016), 53–71.

11 M. Doffman, "Making It Groove! Entrainment, Participation, and Discrepancy in the 'Conversation' of a Jazz Trio," *Language and History*, 52 (2009), 130–47; J. Fruehauf, R. Kopiez, and F. Platz, "Music on a Timing Grid: The Influence of Microtiming on the Perceived Groove Quality of a Simple Drum Pattern Preference," *Musicae Scientiae*, 17 (2013), 246–60.

12 By "contemporary," I mean rap music since the end of the era of sample-based hip-hop in the mid-1990s. This distinction is especially pertinent in the second section of this chapter, where the drum textures under discussion are not sampled from previous recordings.

13 F. Lerdahl and R. Jackendoff, *A Generative Theory of Tonal Music* (MIT Press, 1983), 68.

14 R. Attas, "Meter as Process in Groove-Based Popular Music" (Ph.D. dissertation, University of British Columbia, 2011), 51; Butterfield, "Power of Anacrusis."

15 D. Temperley, "Syncopation in Rock: A Perceptual Perspective," *Popular Music*, 18 (1999), 19–40. Temperley's prototypical example of such a melody is the lyric "It's been a long, cold, lonely winter" from the Beatles' "Here Comes the Sun."

16 N. Biamonte, "Formal Functions of Metric Dissonance in Rock Music," *Music Theory Online*, 20.2 (2014), ¶6.1.

17 Butterfield, "Power of Anacrusis," ¶21.

18 Some producers and drum programmers eschew quantization; J Dilla is a notable example. For a sustained consideration of expressivity in non-quantized drums, see Chapter 3 in S. Peterson, "Something Real: Rap, Resistance, and the Music of the Soulquarians" (Ph.D. dissertation, University of Oregon, 2018).

19 In earlier decades of rap music, most drum textures were sampled from funk, soul, and jazz records of the 1960s and 1970s, particularly from instances of solo drum breaks, which, as solos, were more active than typical accompaniment patterns. This practice has diminished substantially in the last fifteen years and is often limited to artists who think they can sample without notice or those like Lamar who can afford licensing fees. Three of *DAMN.*'s fourteen tracks have sampled drums, all from the late 1960s and early 1970s.

20 The pattern of "DUCKWORTH." is similar, but without the kick event just before beat 4 or the occasional one just after the downbeat.

21 Butler, *Unlocking the Groove*, 158; Biamonte, "Formal Functions," ¶3.3; Cohn, "Platonic Model," ¶5.3.

22 For a more complete account of the accent annotation method, see Chapter 3 in M. Ohriner, *Flow: The Rhythmic Voice in Rap Music* (Oxford University Press, 2019). Using Piet Mertens's Prosogram and voice-isolated audio, it can be shown that in the first four measures there are 29 syllables that are both on the beat or at the midpoint of the beat. Of these, 21 are pitched higher than the following syllable, while only two are pitched lower than the following syllable.

23 An account of generating and analyzing this sort of data can be found in M. Ohriner, *Flow*, Chapter 8, and Ohriner, "Rhythm, Lyric, and Non-Alignment in the Second Verse of Kendrick Lamar's 'Momma,'" *Music Theory Online*, 25.1 (2019).

24 A. Bregman and S. Pinker, "Auditory Streaming and the Building of Timbre," *Canadian Journal of Experimental Psychology*, 32 (1978), 19–31.

25 See Ohriner, *Flow*, Chapter 8.

26 These differences in means are all statistically significant with $p < .005$, adjusted through the post-hoc Tukey's Test of Honestly Significant Differences.

27 These final kicks of the measure are 146 ms, much closer to 1/6 of a beat (142 ms) than 1/4 of a beat (214 ms).

28 F. Benadon, "Slicing the Beat: Jazz Eighth Notes as Expressive Microrhythm," *Ethnomusicology*, 50 (2006), 73–98.

29 In absolute terms, at the tempo of 70 beats per minute, the longer events of the beat are only 20 ms longer than the shorter events, a difference that likely does not pass the perceptual threshold.

30 The following measures of delay are representative of the literature: 12 ms in Harvey Mason's drumming on Herbie Hancock's "Chameleon" (Butterfield,

"Power of Anacrusis," ¶50); 10 ms in the rhythm section of a jazz trio performance (Doffman, *Making It Groove*, 139); 75 ms in a selection of Chris Potter's saxophone solos (B. Wesolowski, "Timing Deviations in Jazz Performance: The Relationships of Selected Musical Variables on Horizontal and Vertical Timing Relations: A Case Study," *Psychology of Music*, 44 [2016], 87).

31 Intonationally, Lamar lowers pitch at the ends of each of these lines, signaling not a question but rather a statement – the answer to the question of the first two measures is obviously "no."

32 The accent on beat class 15 is just as often heard on beat class 14.

33 J. Lena and R. Peterson, "Classification as Culture: Types and Trajectories of Music Genres," *American Sociological Review*, 73 (2008), 699.

34 J. Serjeant, "Hip hop and R&B surpass rock as biggest U.S. music genre," *Reuters*, January 4, 2018 (www.reuters.com/article/us-music-2017/hip-hop-and-rb-surpass-rock-as-biggest-u-s-music-genre-idUSKBN1ET258), accessed September 10, 2019. A. Peres, "The Sonic Dimension as Dramatic Driver in 21st-Century Pop Music" (Ph.D. dissertation, University of Michigan, 2016).

PART V

Rhythm in Global Musics

13 The Musical Rhythm of Agbadza Songs

DAVID LOCKE

Introduction

Agbadza and the Alorwoyie Project

Agbadza is a genre of performance art that originated among the Ewe people (Ghana, Togo). The drumming features musical interactions between lead and response drums; in songs, poems are set to tunes that have a variety of call-and-response arrangements between several song leaders and a larger choral group. As discussed here, the rhythm of the vocal music contributes to the overall temporal vitality of an Agbadza performance.

The songs analyzed in this chapter may be heard on a recorded performance by Gideon Foli Alorwoyie[1] and the Afrikania Cultural Troupe of Anlo-Afiadenyigba, Ghana, and are thoroughly documented on an online site (https://sites.tufts.edu/davidlocke/agbadza/).[2] In what might be considered a long work in twenty-five sections, Alorwoyie paired songs with compositions for lead-response drums on the basis of the meaning of a song's lyrics and the meaning of the drum language. Making the point about how it was performed during "the time of our grandparents," Alorwoyie undertook this project to establish a historical baseline for contemporary musicians who would try new ways of playing Agbadza.[3]

Agbadza is generally regarded as the prototypical music and dance of the Ewe people. It began during a tumultuous era (1600–1900) of migration, conquest, and imperialism, including the trans-Atlantic African slave trade. Profound themes of life, death, and warrior ethos make it suitable for performance at funerals, memorial services, and rituals of chieftaincy. In Ewe communities, Agbadza can be heard at wake-keepings and memorial services. If one would posit the existence of an Ewe national dance, it likely would be Agbadza.

Agbadza's instrumental music for drum ensemble features drum language compositions for the low-pitched lead *sogo* drum and medium-pitched response *kidi* drum that are set within a multi-part texture sounded by *gankogui* bell, *axatse* rattle, high-pitched *kagan* support drum, and handclap (*asikpekpe*).[4]

As may be heard on the audio files of Alorwoyie's recording, at the beginning of each drum-dance item of Agbadza music, the song leader freely lines out the tune and text. After this brief introduction, the instrumental ensemble's time parts start the phrases that they continue without variation for the duration of the item. The melo-rhythmic energy generated by this multi-part texture powers the singing and drumming.[5] Guided by the bell phrase, the song leader raises the song in tempo, offering it to the group of singers who reply with gusto. When the song and the time parts are going nicely, the lead drummer plays the drum language phrases on the sogo using his two bare hands. The response drummer answers the leader's call, using two wooden sticks to fashion the medium-pitched kidi drum's recurring phrase. The lead drummer's solo line complements the singers' tune and weaves around the response drum's phrase. In the recorded performance that is our source material, each song recurs with subtle musical variation before the lead drum signals the end of that item.

Author's Preface

Stance

When cultural outsiders do inter-cultural musical analysis, it behooves authors to establish their positionality, especially in the case of Africa with its emotionally powerful histories of the trans-Atlantic slave trade, racial discrimination, and inequality. My stance toward Ewe performance traditions is that of an experienced student who is emboldened to teach and write to the extent of my knowledge and abilities. Compared to expert born-in-the-tradition insiders, I consider myself to be a relatively adept outsider. My authenticity depends on the veracity of information gathered in research, the quality of my ethnographic understanding, the value of my ideas, the clarity of my presentation, and the effectiveness of my pedagogy. Is my analytic apparatus relevant? Does it yield meaningful insight or explanation? Can other musicians make productive use of my publications?

In the text that follows, I position myself as the readers' guide along a path we follow together toward an understanding of musical temporality in Agbadza songs. A discussion of specific songs will precede general conclusions about the full corpus of twenty-five songs in Alorwoyie's Agbadza. This approach mirrors my own learning experience in which clarity emerged gradually from a fog of cognitive uncertainty. I feel that moving from the specific to the general guards the reader against adopting a premature sense of being able to comprehend Agbadza songs at a high level of abstraction and thus to assume control over them.

Analytic Toolkit

I write for all readers who would seek knowledge of music rhythm in Agbadza songs. I do not presume that readers have advanced knowledge of the theory and analysis of any of the world's musics, whether Western Art Music or any of the world's ethnic, folk, or traditional musics. Although I am enculturated into Western culture and have been schooled in Western institutions, I am largely self-taught in music theory and analysis.[6] It may seem enigmatic, therefore, that my scholarly interest lies in transcription, analysis, and aesthetic criticism.

My analytic toolkit, so to speak, grew from direct engagement with Ewe performance arts. In trying to figure out "how the music works," I have used a variety of notation systems and have explored diverse theoretical traditions. My writing aspires toward engaging the most sophisticated aspects of Agbadza's music without either mystifying or condescending to the curious reader. I always try to make available audio files so that readers may also be listeners who do the hard work of bringing together the music itself with its representation in words and graphics.

Pitch

The musical instruments of Agbadza are tuned relative to each other and, as far as I know, no traditional instruments in Eweland are tuned to absolute pitches. The important issue in the tunes of songs is the intervals between pitch classes, not the precise pitches. Singers seem to use a range that is rather high in their comfort zone because this makes them audible in competition with the loud sound of the drum ensemble. The main range of pitch classes in an Agbadza song is an octave, with most songs extending as much as fifth above or below. Like most scholars, I believe staff notation to be adequate in representing the pitch material, even though the actual pitches and their intonation will always be at variance with a strict interpretation. I use simple capital letters to name pitches and assume readers will be able to follow my meaning when I write, "After opening the song with a dramatic relatively wide upward leap (C to G), Leader moves in steps and modest leaps until another large leap (D to A) and final downward step to G."[7]

Because of the patterning of melodic motion, I will argue that pitch class sets in songs, "scales," if you will, are essentially pentatonic in design even when there are more than five pitch classes in a tune. These pentatonic scales are either with or without semi-tones. Tunes sometimes feel organized around one tonal center, but because of their pentatonic structure many songs have more than one pitch class that functions as a place of tonal resolution. Due to their rather brief overall duration and their recurrent nature, the arrival at tonal conclusion on a song's final tone always is short lived.

Rhythmic Mnemonics for Short-Long Time Values

The time values in Agbadza songs overwhelmingly are either short or long, represented here as eighth notes or quarter notes. Because I have found it immensely valuable to vocalize musical time values, I adopt the mnemonic "ti" to represent a short time value and the mnemonic "ta" to represent long time values.

Axiomatic Rhythm Concepts and Basic Terminology

The elapsing flow of musical time will be reckoned by timepoints, which in theory are equidurational but in practice may exhibit consistent non-isochronous microtiming.[8] Elapsing musical time is felt to contain steady temporal marks that will be called beats; beats both divide the time span of the bell and add up to fill the measure. A beat will have one moment that is onbeat and other moments that are offbeat. A beat with three subdivisions is called ternary; a beat with two or four subdivisions is called binary or quaternary. In beats of binary morphology, the midpoint between successive beats is called the upbeat or the "and" of the count; this will be graphically represented with "&," the ampersand. Ternary beats, which are foundational to Agbadza's meter, have an onbeat timepoint (1.1), an afterbeat timepoint (1.2), and a third timepoint (1.3) that may either function as an unaccented pickup if it leads toward a subsequent onbeat tone or an accented offbeat if no note occurs on the subsequent onbeat. The first onbeat in a measure is designated as the downbeat; onbeat three is the midpoint in the measure; onbeats two and four are backbeats.

Accent

Accentuation in songs and drumming, that is, conferring especially strong feeling to particular musical moments, is an important subject in this chapter. Structural accentuation is built into Agbadza's musical meter, the recurring themes sounded on the instruments in the drum ensemble, and the modal/melodic design of tunes. In tunes, for example, modal motion toward arrival on a tonicized pitch is one aspect of a composition's structural accentuation. Notes that are onbeat or onbell will have different accentual valence than those that are offbeat or offbell. Within the polyphonic texture of the full music, notes in unison will have a quality of accentual force that is different from notes not reinforced by other parts. In the analytic system proffered here, each component of the music projects accentual power onto the others. As is true in many of the world's musics, Ewe composers often position a musical note on a structurally unaccented position, which paradoxically gives it special potency for intense musical feeling. In contrast to the features of accentuation that are embedded into the design of an item of Agbadza music, during performance musicians will make spontaneous decisions about timing, pitch, and timbre. The various publications of Alorwoyie and Locke provide ample evidence for study of expressive accentuation, so to speak, but this subject is not addressed here.

Graphic Representation

In prior work I have used staff notation to graphically represent Agbadza's music and will refer readers to these musical examples, which are readily available online. Inevitably, staff notation is regarded by some readers as a sign of a non-African, Western epistemic regime, a semiotic assumption I wish to counteract. Here, I use the Time Unit Box System (TUBS), which is an excellent way to depict temporal relationships. Like staff notation, time moves on the page from left to right, with one graph box equating to one musical timepoint. Readers who would like to see musical examples in staff notation should follow the hyperlink references.

Audio/Visual Documentation

The music discussed in this chapter is available in two ways: a book with audio CD and an online site (https://sites.tufts.edu/davidlocke/agbadza).[9] The online site contains Ewe texts for songs and drumming, various translations into English, lead sheets for songs and drum compositions, complete note-for-note transcriptions of the audio files, interviews with Alorwoyie, and analytic criticism of each of the twenty-five items of Agbadza in Alorwoyie's project.

The Musical Rhythm of Agbadza Songs

Our journey into the rhythm of Agbadza songs begins with the fundamentals of musical time in Ewe dance-drumming. The path begins with the bell part.[10] In genres of Ewe dance-drumming music, the bell part sounds over and over as a recurrent temporal theme that gives to musical time a distinctive pattern or shape.

Learning the Bell

Seven hits with a straight stick on the iron instrument take a player through one occurrence of the bell's theme. The time values are of two types: short notes ("ti") and longer tones ("ta") that are twice the duration of the quicker tones. (The custom in scholarship about Ewe music is to notate these sound events as eighth notes and as quarter notes.) Ewe experts teach the bell part as the sum of two figures: (ta ti ta) + (ta ta ti ta). Alorwoyie teaches that when the music begins, the bell player should strike first on the lower-pitched of the gankogui's two bells and then play all other notes on the higher-pitched bell. The first appearance of the bell theme thus suggests the following pattern of time values – (ta ta ti ta ta ta ti ta) + (ta . . .).[11] To summarize: two grouping patterns of the time values are recognized by culture-bearers as foundational: (1) ta ti ta ta ta ti ta, and (2) ta ta ti ta ta ta ti.

Taking the duration of the short bell tone as a unit for measuring musical time, we observe twelve units within one full occurrence of the phrase. The two fundamental ways of hearing or grouping the bell pattern may thus be rendered numerically as (A) $12 = (2+1+2) + (2 + 2 + 1 + 2)$, and (B) $12 = 2 + 2 + 1 + 2 + 2 + 2 + 1$. Readers familiar with the scholarly and popular literature on African music likely will recognize the second formula, but I emphasize the ethnographic significance of the first formula and suggest its importance for those who would desire to enter what might be termed "an Ewe way of hearing." As a teacher of this music myself, I echo my Ewe teachers who urge students to hear rhythmic shapes in actual musical phenomena rather than counting time according to an abstract mathematical schema (meter, time signatures). Paradoxically, meter is of vital importance.

The Bell in Four: Ternary-Quadruple Time

Agbadza moves with steady tempo that may be felt according to recurring temporal units (beats). Dancers typically step (transfer weight from foot to

Table 13.1 Fundamentals: 12-pulse, 4-beat, bell phrase

12-Pulse	01	02	03	04	05	06	07	08	09	10	11	12	01	02
4-Beat	1.1	1.2	1.3	2.1	2.2	2.3	3.1	3.2	3.3	4.1	4.2	4.3	1.1	1.2
Bell	Ta		ta		Ti	ta		ta		ta		ti	ta	
	1		2		3	4		5		6		7	1	

foot) in unison with these beats.[12] Four beats occur over the time span of one bell phrase. The two-part polyrhythmic duet between the asymmetrically shaped bell part and the steady flow of the equidurational beats is absolutely at the bedrock foundation of Agbadza's musical temporality. Overwhelming evidence suggests that the bell phrase typically is felt "in four." In other words, if and when players or listeners want to reference metric units, they will attend to what I will refer to as "four-feel beats" (dotted quarter notes). The twelve units within one span of the bell phrase thus are structured into four ternary beats: $12 = 4 \times 3$.

How shall bell part, beats, and faster pulses be set within a recurring musical cycle or metric framework? Study of the bell phrase shows that the note played on the low-pitched bell is its main moment of musical resolution and therefore a prominent moment of accentuation in the permanent structure of the music. Furthermore, this is the temporal location in the ever-cycling pattern toward which other parts move for cadence. Even when what the late Ewe scholar Willie Anku termed the "regulative time point" is not accentuated by other parts, the RTP nevertheless serves as a temporal reference point.[13] Despite positing that ONE comes *at the end of the phrase,* I join other scholars of Ewe music who place it at the beginning of measures and assign numbers from there (see Table 13.1). For the sake of simplicity, I will simply use capitalization to denote these crucial time-points in the music's ongoing flow. To summarize our presentation of the bell part: seven short and long tones in two grouping patterns occur over twelve quick pulses that are shaped into four ternary beats.

Meter as a Matrix

Elsewhere, I have suggested that it is productive to think of Ewe meter as a *nexus of temporal fields* that are interconnected in a matrix-like relationship.[14] In genres disciplined by ternary beats, a multidimensional quality arises from the presence of time values in a three-with-two temporal ratio. In staff notation, this can be represented with "dotted notes" and their "undotted" counterparts and signaled through time signature – $\frac{6}{8} : \frac{3}{4}$. This ratio happens between time values of different durations in a multilevel structure that reminds me of a three-dimensional chess board. When the span of the bell phrase establishes a four-beat quadruple measure, the music has the simultaneous presence of metric beats in three time signatures – $\frac{12}{8}$, $\frac{6}{4}$, and $\frac{3}{2}$ – as well as their double-time and cut-time derivatives. Finally, accentuation may be consistently placed on offbeat moments within a metric beat, which multiplies the relationships among metric fields.[15]

In traditional music genres like Agbadza, the flow of metric units is normally experienced as a background part of mental and physical consciousness rather than actively counted as a timing reference. Many African-born teachers instruct students to refrain from tapping their feet as a method of keeping time, for example. To emphasize the phenomenal presence of metric units, I use the word *feel* in my writing as in "four-feel beats" or "six-feel beats." I theorize the constant presence of the "metric matrix" as an implicit and latent resource to inspire creativity, guide timing, shape accentuation, and enhance expressiveness.

The Drum Ensemble Context

The bell part structures musical time for dancers, singers, and drummers. The instrumental ensemble consists of one bell, many hand clappers, many rattles, one high-pitched support drum, one medium-pitched response drum, and one lead drum. Each part in the ensemble establishes its own musical personality and also makes its own distinctive contribution to what Meki Nzewi suggests we call the "melo-rhythm" of Agbadza's "ensemble thematic cycle (ETC)."[16]

Format of Songs

Agbadza songs are sung by a chorus of singers in two parts – Leader and Group.[17] The leader part actually may be performed by as many as three or four people, although one person will be regarded formally as "song leader." The group part, on the other hand, is sung by many voices. Contrast in texture and energy between the few voices in Leader and the many voices of Group is a prominent quality in these songs. In the Alorwoyie's Agbadza project, the song leader began each item with a short, temporally loose rendition of the song without instruments. Once the song was "lined out," the ensemble entered and the full version of the song started.

Selected Agbadza Songs

Let us now consider several songs. General rhythmic characteristics will emerge through discussion of these specific tunes and texts.[18]

Kaleworda (#7)
https://sites.tufts.edu/davidlocke/agbadza-items/

In this discussion of musical rhythm in the twenty-five songs in the Alorwoyie Agbadza project, "Kaleworda" will represent a typical or average song. Its comparatively uncomplicated musical features are a good place to start.

Over the span of four bell cycles, song leader and singing group each sing the same two-sentence lyric about the lonely death of a strong warrior on a distant battlefield (see #7, Song Lyrics).[19] The tune's pitches array within an octave except for the upper A in the Leader's opening motive (see #7, Lead Sheet). Leader works higher in the pitch set, while Group lowers the melody to its final note on the lower G. After opening the song with a dramatic, relatively wide upward leap (C to G), Leader moves in steps and modest leaps until another large downward leap (D to A) and final downward step to G. The group's reply centers on C until it too descends to G with cadential leap-step motion (D–A–G). With the exception of B♭ in m. 4, the tune uses five pitch classes.[20] To me, the song's pitches move toward modal and temporal conclusion on the final G, but C also feels like another, complementary "tonicized pitch," so to speak; this would mean that the song's tonality is a pentatonic scale without half-steps in the modes G–A–C–D–F (2–3–5–6–1) and/or C–D–F–G–A (5–6–1–2–3). Both parts in the call-and-response are of equal duration – two "measures of bell," so to speak – and set the text with the same time values as shown in Table 13.2.

The rhythmic design of its time values contributes to the musical personality of the melody. The words to the song are rendered in four

Table 13.2 "Kaleworda" time values in melody

Bell		5		6		7	1		2		3	4
4-Beats	3.1	3.2	3.3	4.1	4.2	4.3	1.1	1.2	1.3	2.1	2.2	2.3
m. 1	ti	ti	ti	ta								
mm. 1–2						ti	ti	ti	Ti	ti	ta	
m. 3	ti	ta		ta								
mm. 3–4						ti	ti	ti	Ti	ta		

Table 13.3 "Kaleworda" temporal effect of melodic rhythmic patterns

m. 1	▪ Time: Onbeat onsets confer accentuation to four-feel beats 3 and 4. ▪ Bell: Onset on 3.1 makes strong polyrhythmic contrast with bell.
mm. 1–2	▪ Time: Pickup and afterbeat notes soften the accentuation of four-feel beats 1 and 2. ▪ Bell: Pickup and afterbeat notes make the tune rhythmically independent from bell.
m. 3	▪ Time: Omission of an onset on time-point 3.3 adds accentuation to the note on time-point 3.2 (accentuation by duration or agogic accent). ▪ Bell: Omission of an onset on time-point 3.3 highlights tune's unison with bell tones 5 and 6.
mm. 3–4	▪ Time: Pickup-to-onbeat motion gives accentuation to onbeats 1.1 and 2.1. ▪ Bell: Pickup-to-onbeat motion reinforces the bell's cadence on ONE but then the tune extends to 2.1, which does not align with bell.

nearly identical rhythmic figures, each spanning two four-feel beats (see Table 13.2). The idea stated in m. 1, that is, motion in eighth-note values between successive onbeats, establishes a pattern that is slightly modified in the three subsequent rhythmic patterns.

Subtle differences among these four rhythmic figures enable each variant to project its own quality to the flow of time within the span of one bell phrase and each has a particular relationship to notes in the bell phrase (Table 13.3).

Discussion of "Kaleworda" has introduced musical features common in most all Agbadza songs. Call-and-response between the leader and group parts is a foundational aspect of a song's temporal design. The timing of the transfer in vocal action between Leader and Group parts, that is, the rhythm of call-and-response, and the consequent change in musical texture that results is an important component of Agbadza's overall rhythm. Their exchange establishes a before-after temporal structure that provides an opportunity for antecedent-consequent musical logic, which may include aesthetic forces of tension-resolution. The timing of shifts in tonal centers within a pentatonic scale exerts yet another rather large-scale temporal effect. At a more fine-grained dimension, the rhythmic patterns of time values in the melody make polyrhythm with the bell phrase. As if it were another drum in the ensemble, the melodic rhythm may be heard to project musical forces toward other instruments, imparting nuances of accentuation on onbeat and offbeat timepoints to a listener's interpretive experience of the polyphony.[21] Finally, the song's musical form, which is shaped by call-and-response design as well as by melodic factors of tunefulness, so to speak, has impact on a song's rhythm through the comparative duration of its several sections.

Let us review the specific temporal features of this song that are characteristic of most songs among the twenty-five in the Alorwoyie collection. First, Leader was higher in the song's range and had more tonal movement; Group quieted the rhythmic activity of the tune as it lowered the song's pitches toward the finalis.[22] Second, in a straightforward A1A2 form, Leader and Group both set the same text to identical time values; each part made a coherent melodic statement, but the two parts preceded and followed each other according to an Ewe musical logic of melodic gesture, pentatonic tonality, and rhythm governed by bell phrase and meter. Third, time values had a memorable theme – in this case, eighth-note motion through successive four-feel onbeats – that helped unify the tune.

Although I have proposed this song as being prototypical, every Agbadza song is unique. Overall, the genre has characteristic style, but each venerable song was intentionally crafted to convey particular meaning.

Miwua 'Gbo Mayi (#2)
https://sites.tufts.edu/davidlocke/agbadza-items/

Like "Kaleworda," this song spans four bell cycles and has two exchanges between Leader and Group (see #2, Lead Sheet). But the rhythmic design of "Miwua 'Gbo Mayi" is much more asymmetric and the relationship between Leader and Group much more intertwined.

The melody has three phrases with a rounded ABA form in the span of four bell cycles (see Table 13.5). Although the metric structure groups the ternary beats into sets of four (quadruple meter), the pattern of call-and-response confers an asymmetric design: 16 = (3+3) + 5 + 5 (see Table 13.4).

Leader and Group share in the song's dramatic opening lyric, "Brave ones, open the gate. I will go" (see #2, Song Lyrics). Begun by Leader on four-feel beat three (m. 1), Phrase 1 requires a hand-off to Group on four-feel beat two (m. 2). Leader's relatively long Phrase 2 fits neatly within one complete bell cycle: 1–2–3–4–1. As it did in Phrase 1, in Phrase 3 Group

Table 13.4 "Miwua 'Gbo Mayi" asymmetry in duration of melodic phrases

Phrase 1	L: 3-4-1 + G: 2-3-4	six beats (3+3)
Phrase 2	L: 1-2-3-4-1	five beats
Phrase 3	G: 2-3-4-1-2	five beats

Table 13.5 "Miwua 'Gbo Mayi" four-feel of call-and-response

Measure			2				3				4				1	
Beats	3	4	1	2	3	4	1	2	3	4	1	2	3	4	1	2
Phrases	1						2					3				
Form	A						B					A				
c-r	L			G			L					G				

Table 13.6 "Miwua 'Gbo Mayi" three-then-two pattern in melodic rhythm

Bell		5		6		7	1	2		3	4
4-Feel beats	3			4			1		2		
6-Feel beats	4		5		6		1	2		3	
2:3 Accentuation	1			2			1	2		3	
Song text	Mi-	wua		'gbo		ma-	yi	Ka-	lea-	woe	

takes over the flow of four-feel beats from Leader on beat two (m. 4) with another five-beat gesture that extends through the next ONE: 2–3–4–1–2.

The tune adds more intricate melodic rhythm to this motion of metric units. The Leader begins the first phrase with upward and downward pendular leaps of a minor third interval (B–D–B) in a rhythm that aligns with the bell's cadential motion over tones 5–6–7–1 (mm. 1–2).[23] Countering the structural tendency of the music to reach cadence on ONE, the Group quickly continues the melody's rhythmic flow with an upward half-step on timepoint 2.2. Together, the melodic rhythm of the two sub-phrases in Phrase 1 articulates an important metric rhythm in Agbadza's music: the oscillation within the span of one bell cycle between a half-measures "in three" and "in two" (see Table 13.6).[24]

Each part is restricted to two pitches, but the Group part stands out for its long sustained note on C that sets the word with a key semantic image: brave Ewe warriors (see #2 Song Lyrics). Tonally and rhythmically, the melody creates a feeling of anticipation for phrase 2 (m. 3). Into this musical space, the Leader jumps boldly with a dramatic downward gesture that begins in polyrhythmic contrast to bell before aligning with its cadential tones to arrive at G on timepoint 1.1 (m. 4). In the lyric, this powerful melody establishes that the song is about struggle between the Ewes and their prototypical enemies, the Fon people of Dahomey. Although rhythmic motion of Phrase 2 achieves a sense of closure by aligning with bell's cadence to ONE (m. 4), the Group again enters rather quickly (m. 4), this

Table 13.7 "Miwua 'Gbo Mayi" palindrome

Syllable count, number of onsets	3	2	1	2	3
Text	Ka-lea-woe	mi-wua	'gbo	ma-yi	Da-hu-me

time with its own long phrase that arches upward to D before the final plunge to F♯ (m. 5), which to my ear leaves the whole song in an unresolved tonal condition. In a clever feature of the song's text setting, the rhythm of the final word, "Dahomey," imitates the two prior positions of "brave ones" (m. 2, m. 4). I especially enjoy the design of the rhythmic figures in this phrase, which suggest a palindrome: 3–2–1–2–3 (mm. 4–5) (see Table 13.7).

Dzogbe Nye Nutsu Tor (#21)
https://sites.tufts.edu/davidlocke/agbadza-items/

Some Agbadza songs feel especially drum-like (see Items #13 and #21): the sectional form moves quickly between Leader and Group, the melody reiterates only a few pitches, and the rhythms are repetitive and percussive. Compared to the tuneful setting of poetic text in songs like "Kaleworda," these songs seem more like chants to "rally the troops," so to speak. Because the singing functions like drumming, this song provides us with an opportunity to go deeper into the music of the drum ensemble.

The song lyric expresses quintessential warrior bravado: "The battlefield is for men. If I die, bury me there" (see #21, Song Lyrics). To enhance the feeling of urgency, Alorwoyie selected an extraordinarily intense composition for lead and response drums that sets the scene with the insistent statement, "On the battlefield," and/or "The brave place" (see #21, Drum Language). Rhythmic intensity derives from the unusually short time span of the drum parts – only two four-feel beats. Two bounce tones from the response drum align precisely with a similar figure in the high-pitch support drum, thus joining the power of each instrument in a new synthesis (see #21, Full Score). One rhythmic consequence of the fusion of these two drumming parts is accentuation of the fast-moving eight-feel beats, which suggests a "double-time" feeling of tempo. (Compare to the quality of "cut-time" accentuation in "Ahor De Lia Gba 'Dzigo," below.)

The song leader insistently intones the same lyric, "Battlefield-men's place," to a short descending motive (D–C–A) whose rhythm carries the feeling of metric closure – three–four–one motion of the four-feel beats – as well as the bell phrase's cadence to ONE over strokes 5–6–7–1 (m. 1,

m. 3, m. 5). The singing group responds with a sequence of two melodic phrases that end first on D (m. 3) and last on G (m. 5), which conveys a fleeting feeling of tonal and rhythmic stasis before the song's next iteration.

The time values in Group's part have an ingenious impact on the overall polyrhythmic texture. I enjoy hearing this rhythm as two successive occurrences of a four-note motive – ti ta ta ta – that is launched first from the pickup to four-feel beat two (timepoint 1.3) and then again from the onbeat of four-feel beat four (timepoint 4.1). The note with short time value ("ti") functions like a temporal switch that toggles the melodic rhythm back and forth between the upbeats and the onbeats of the six-feel beats (see Table 13.8); the handclapping part gives phenomenal presence to this counter-metric field. The same toggling procedure happens within every cycle of the bell phrase: the short note on timepoint 2.2 shifts the bell's long tones into unison with the flow of beats in the upbeat six-feel until the short note on timepoint 4.3 returns the long bell tones into unison with the flow of beats in the onbeat six feel. In this song, a similar procedure creates two identical rhythmic patterns that make very effective polyrhythmic interaction with bell.

Ahor De Lia Gba 'Dzigo (#17) and *Dzogbe Milador* (#12) https://sites.tufts.edu/davidlocke/agbadza-items/

Songs discussed thus far have illustrated rhythmic dynamism in Agbadza songs. Whether due to factors such as the duration of composed themes, formal design, metric accentuation, or the pattern of its time values, the melodic rhythm of these songs adds to the ever-changing quality of Agbadza's overall musical temporality. The next two songs illustrate a different capacity: the steady and relatively unambiguous accentuation of one kind of metric field, that is, the flow of four-feel or six-feel metric beats. Although the musical rhythm of Agbadza will always be malleable to different interpretations, in these songs we hear and feel strong alignment between a song's accentuation and the foundational time feels of Agbadza.

In many ways, "Ahor De Lia Gba 'Dzigo" is a classic Ewe song. The song lyric heralds a sneak attack on Adzigo, a legendary center for Ewe warriors, a message enhanced by the drum language's command, "Put on your war belt" (see #17, Song Lyrics and Interview). Although more fully developed than "Kaleworda," the design of the call-and-response, the melody's shape, and the song's form are typical for a dance-drumming song (see #17, Lead Sheet): an opening section (A1A1) in which Leader and Group twice exchange relatively long phrases (mm. 1–6); a middle section (B1B2) with

Table 13.8 "Dzogbe Nye Nutsu Tor" toggling onbeat and upbeat six-feel beats

4-Feel	1.1	1.2	1.3	2.1	2.2	2.3	3.1	3.2	3.3	4.1	4.2	4.3	1.1	1.2	1.3	2.1	2.2	2.3
6-Feel	1	&	2	&	3	&	4	&	5	&	6	&	1	&	2	&	3	&
Song			ti	ta		ta		ta		ti	ta		ta		ta			
Bell	ta		ta		ti	ta		ta		ta		ti	ta		ta		ti	ta

Table 13.9 "Ahor De Lia" melodic rhythm of Leader phrase

Measures 1–2												
Beats	2.3	3.1	3.2	3.3	4.1	4.2	4.3	1.1	1.2	1.3	2.1	2.2
Song	ti	**ti**	ta		**ta**		ti	**ti**	ta		**ti**	ta
Measures 2–3												
Beats	2.3	3.1	3.2	3.3	4.1	4.2	4.3	1.1	1.2	1.3	2.1	2.2
Song		**ti**	ta		**ta**		ti	**ti**	ta		**ta**	

faster call-and-response timing (mm. 6–10); and a reprise of Group's phrase from the opening section (A2) (mm. 11–12).

Time values in Leader's melody make a memorable rhythmic topography, so to speak (see Table 13.9, bold shading shows accentuation).[25]

The prominent notes on every onbeat enable a listener to feel the melodic rhythm as conferring accent to the four-feel beats. With long notes initiated from timepoints 3.1 and 1.1 (mm. 3–4), Group's reply reinforces this hard-driving onbeat rhythmic quality.[26] Because it continues with the same text and time values in its B and A2 section, the entire song has an "onbeat four" quality of rhythmic accentuation. This is not the full story, however, as will be discussed below after a brief detour into the theory of Ewe meter.

In Agbadza's musical meter, four-feel beats with ternary subdivision (dotted quarter notes) always are balanced by six-feel beats with binary subdivision (quarter notes). The co-existence of two types of metric units imparts to the music a permanently ongoing three-with-two temporal ratio (3:2 over a half-measure; 6:4 within one bell cycle) that makes patterns in Agbadza's music amenable to different rhythmic interpretations. The timing of the implicit four-feel beats will be so familiar to persons competent in Ewe music that the explicit iteration of the six-feel beats by the hand-clapping part in the Alorwoyie recordings likely makes for a pleasing counterpart. Just as some songs align to the four-feel beats, a song may also "be in six," if I may put it that way.

"Dzogbe Milador" exhibits steady accentuation of the onbeat six-feel beats (see #12, Lead Sheet). Because the time values in the A section (mm. 1–5) tend toward uniformity in eighth notes, they do not suggest a particular accentual pattern in and of themselves. However, the syllabic division of words in the text and the choice of pitches in the tune bring out the "onbeat six-feel," suggested by the bold shading in Table 13.10.

While this quality of rhythmic accentuation is unequivocally present in the Leader's part, in the Group part (m. 2), the consecutive eighth notes on

Table 13.10 "Dzogbe Milador" A section, melodic rhythm accentuation of onbeat six

Measures 1–2; Leader												
Beats	4	&	5	&	6	&	1	&	2	&	3	&
Song	**Dzo-**	gbe	**mi-**	la-	**dor**	Be	**dzo-**	gbe	**mi-**	la-	**dor**	
Measures 2–3; Group												
Beats	4	&	5	&	6	&	1	&	2	&	3	&
Song	**Fon**	ma-	**de**	ma-	**de**	Be	**dzo-**	gbe	**mi-**	la-	**dor**	

Table 13.11 "Dzogbe Milador" B section, melodic rhythm accentuation of onbeat-six in B

Measures 5–6												
Beats	4	&	5	&	6	&	1	&	2	&	3-	&
Song	**L: Tu-**	le a-	**si**		**da-**	da	**glo**		**G: Me-**	yi-	**na**	
Measures 6–7												
Beats	4	&	5	&	6	&	1	&	2	&	3	&
Song	**L: He-**	le a-	**si**		**da-**	da	**glo**		**G: Me-**	yi-	**na**	Be

pitch A present a more rhythmically malleable situation that could be felt in sets of three, i.e., organized within ternary beats three and four.

In the B section (mm. 5–7), Leader and Group combine their incomplete melodic fragments to set one line of text to a full tuneful idea; the melodic rhythm continues to accentuate the onbeat six-feel beats (see Table 13.11, bold shading shows accentuation).

For the first time in our discussion, this song has a C section with important new information in the lyrics. In the A section, Leader and Group both conveyed the message "As warriors, we are prepared to die on the battlefield." In the B section, the song belittled the effectiveness of the enemy's weapons, "Your guns cannot shoot. Your knives cannot cut." The confidence expressed in these lines is tempered in the C section: "Men will die in battle, while women await their own deaths back at home." As if to give the turn in the song's poetry a new musical setting, the melody's pattern of steady accentuation changes dramatically from being "in six" to being "in four" (mm. 7–9). Melodic motion on B♭ and D confers the feeling of grouping within ternary beats onto the long set of nine eighth notes that lead to the onbeat dotted quarter note on G in

Table 13.12 "Dzogbe Milador" C section, melodic accentuation "in four"

Beats	2.3	3.1	3.2	3.3	4.1	4.2	4.3	1.1	1.2	1.3	2.1	2.2	2.3
Song	Be	**nu-**	tsu-	wo	**ku**	me-	Le	**dzi-**	dzi	'fe	**o**		

m. 8, that is, the four-feel groove (see Table 13.12, bold shading shows accentuation).

Then at the midpoint of m. 8 (timepoint 3.1) comes a striking departure from the prior time values of eighths and quarters: a dotted figure followed by highly distinctive duplet motion through beat one of the next bell cycle (m. 9).[27] This is a clear instance of melody dramatizing the meaning of song text. In the closing return of section A (mm. 9–10), Group brings back its opening phrase, thereby ending the song with a return to its accentuation of the six-feel beats.

Multistability is the normal condition of musical rhythm in Agbadza. The primacy of the four-feel beats notwithstanding, the design of tunes usually enables more than one way to interpret the song's rhythmic accentuation and melodic grouping. I suggest that this very quality of temporal dynamism is a reason why traditional genres of music like Agbadza have been popular among Ewe people for centuries. The songs and drumming never will become stale as long as people listen creatively. We return to "Ahor De Lia Gba 'Dzigo" to illustrate.

Above, "Ahor De Lia Gba 'Dzigo" served to exemplify steady accentuation of the four-feel onbeats. Returning again to this song, we can observe how its melodic rhythm also conforms to the resultant rhythm of time values in 3:2 between quarter notes and dotted quarter notes – ta ti ti ta, ta ti ti ta, etc.[28] In this song, the four-note 3:2 pattern is phrased ti **ti** ta **TA**, that is, from offbeat pickup, through onbeat two, toward onbeat one, with the final "ta" aligning to the moment when the two timing streams come together in unison (bold shading and capitalization shows accentuation). From the temporal perspective of the "three side" of 3:2, the melodic rhythm in this song may be said to consistently align with the "ands" of six-feel beats, that is, the flow of upbeat six-feel beats (see Table 13.13, bold shading shows accentuation).

Ewe metric theory reveals another consequence of accentuation on the "upbeat six": moments of unison between upbeat six-feel beats and the onbeat four-feel beats occur on four-feel beats two and four, not one and three. In other words, notes timed to flow of the upbeat six-feel beats tend to accentuate the backbeats, a well-established hallmark of music in the African Diaspora.[29]

Table 13.13 "Ahor De Lia Gba 'Dzigo" accentuation of upbeat six

Measures 1–2												
Onbeat four	2.3	3.1	3.2	3.3	4.1	4.2	4.3	1.1	1.2	1.3	2.1	2.2
Upbeat six	3&		4&		5&		6&		1&		2&	
Song	**ti**	ti	**ta**		**ta**		**ti**	ti	**ta**		**ti**	ta
Measures 2–3												
Onbeat four	2.3	3.1	3.2	3.3	4.1	4.2	4.3	1.1	1.2	1.3	2.1	2.2
Upbeat six	3&		4&		5&		6&		1&		2&	
Song		ti	**ta**		**ta**		**ti**	ti	**ta**		**ta**	

Summary

The foregoing discussion has familiarized us with the overall nature of musical temporality in Agbadza songs and provided opportunity to articulate many of its more sophisticated features of rhythm. Let us summarize.

The bell part establishes the conditions of musical time:

- ever recycling temporal condition
- duration of time span or measure
- distinct pattern of sounded time values and unsounded timepoints using two time values – long and short
- two grouping shapes of full theme: (A) ta ti ta ta ta ti ta, (B) ta ta ti ta ta ta ti
- segmentation into fragments: (A) ta ti ta + ta ta ti ta
- onbell and offbell timepoints
- cadential motion over onsets 5–6–7–1 toward fleeting moment of stasis (ONE)
- strokes 7 and 1 are onbeat in the four-feel
- toggling between onbeat six-feel beats (onsets 1, 2, 3) and upbeat six-feel beats (onsets 4, 5, 6, 7)

Meter establishes duration, subdivisions, and structural accents:

- twelve timepoints within one bell cycle
- ternary-quadruple time or "the four-feel beats" (four groups of three) is foundational
- binary-sextuple time or "the six-feel beats" (six groups of two) is a permanent complement
- three-with-two (3:2) is omnipresent

- the accentual force of four-feel beats ranges from most stabile to most motile as follows: 1–3–4–2, that is, downbeat, midpoint, backbeat, backbeat
- four-feel beats 1 and 4 are onbell; four-feel beats 2 and 3 are offbell
- six-feel beats 1–3 are onbell, six-feel beats 4–6 are offbeat
- three timepoints within one ternary beat: the onbeat timepoint (1.1), the afterbeat timepoint (1.2), and a third timepoint (1.3) that may function as either an unaccented pickup if it leads to a subsequent onbeat tone or an accented offbeat if no onset occurs on the subsequent onbeat
- two timepoints within one binary beat: onbeat and upbeat
- matrix conception: steady flow of onbeats, offbeats, and upbeats in 3:2 ratio at different durational values

Accentuation, heightened feeling of a particular musical moment, is made in several ways:

- structural: resulting from permanent nature of bell, meter, recurring themes of parts in drum ensemble, and scale/mode
- compositional: resulting from design of song and lead-response drum composition
- onbell and onbeat accents: structural
- offbell and offbeat accents: compositional
- agogic accent (relative time value or duration of a note)
- positional accent: first or last note in a group
- pentatonic scales and modes: multiple potential tonal centers
- song finali often is tonal center but not always
- recurrent cyclic nature of music time continuously refreshes accentual patterns of motility and stasis

Song design has impact on musical rhythm in many ways:

- overall duration: from relatively short to relatively long
- organization of motion through metric fields and bell phrase
- moments of beginning and ending on bell and within meter
- timing of transfer between Leader and Group; rhythm of call-and-response; each part may achieve melodic closure or, alternatively, the two parts may combine to make one phrase
- duration of Leader and Group parts: long Leader–short Group; short Leader–long Group; equal duration of Leader-Group
- rhythm of tonal motion: motion toward and arrival at tonal centers; timing of moments of tonal stasis on bell and in meter

- temporal features of musical form (design of melody considered together with design of call-and-response): A sections – tuneful, B-sections – percussive, C sections – tuneful but different and distinctive
- overall before-after temporal/tonal patterns: from temporally busy and high-pitched at a song's beginning to temporally quiet and low-pitch at its end

Melodic rhythm, that is, the design of time values in a melody, projects temporal force just as do the musical instruments in the drum ensemble:

- Duet with bell and each instrument
- Composite rhythm with other parts
- Metric placement of onsets
- Surface pattern: variegated time values make a definite rhythmic shape; unvaried time values have neutral temporal shape and are susceptible to being shaped by the force of other parts (malleability)
- 3:2 as a pattern of time values (ta ti ti ta); melodic rhythm often phrased ti ti ta ta.
- consistent accentuation of a metric field, and/or a metric rhythm such as three–then–two, or three–four–ONE
- musical dramatization of the meaning of song lyrics by a shift in accentual pattern or other means
- non-isochronous timing of two-note, short-long figures when short first note is onbeat
- temporal motion toward accentuation at the end of phrases
- clever design: palindrome; short riff repeated with difference on bell or meter; alignment with instruments in ensemble
- internal references: motivic variation, melodic sequence, recurring rhythmic figures

Conclusion

The onbeat four-feel groove in duet with the seven-note bell theme provides the ultimate temporal logic of Agbadza, but perhaps because this foundation is so well established, a plethora of countervailing forces may be put in play without threatening the music's groove. Agbadza's melodic rhythm might be characterized as iridescent: it resists a one-way interpretation and may be perceived to change depending on its setting in musical context. In Agbadza, everything musical happens within an interactive network of mutual influences: instrumental parts in a multi-part ensemble, meter as a dynamic matrix, and songs with multistable temporal design. Songs are designed to fit with other parts in interesting and musically satisfying ways. Like the other components of Agbadza music, a song acquires its full nature only in relationship to things outside itself.

Endnotes

1 Gideon Foli Alorwoyie has had a long, distinguished career as an expert in traditional African music. Since youth, he has played a leading role in various customs of the Ewe people that entail drumming, singing, and dancing. He has earned his living from performance arts in professional folkloric groups, notably the Gbeho Research Council, the Arts Council of Ghana Folkloric Troupe, and the Ghana National Dance Ensemble. Alorwoyie gathered material for this project during research on Ewe drum language funded by the University of North Texas where he is a tenured professor. As seems fitting for a virtuoso artist, Alorwoyie presented his research results in a sound recording and subsequently invited my help on written documentation.

2 I have published several scholarly articles on the version of Agbadza produced and documented by Alorwoyie. For a comprehensive consideration of musical rhythm, see D. Locke, "An Approach to Musical Rhythm in Agbadza," in R. Wolf, S. Blum, and C. Hasty (eds.), *Thought and Play in Musical Rhythm: Asian, African, and Euro-American Perspectives* (Oxford University Press, 2019).

3 A succinct version of the Alorwoyie-Locke Agbadza Project has been published in the format of book/CD; see G. F. Alorwoyie with D. Locke, *Agbadza: Songs, Drum Language of the Ewe* (St. Louis: African Music Publishers, 2013).

4 The online site uses staff notation for musical examples, which are listed in Critical Edition Figures. Figure 2 shows the polyrhythmic texture of these instruments.

5 Discourses on African music in the scholarly literature tend to use Eurocentric analytic terminology that may be inadequate in conveying the full ethnographic truth of the insider point of view. Terms like *percussion* and *polyrhythm* may minimize the pitched dimension of drumming, for example. Meki Nzewi has been a very effective voice on this subject; see *African Music: Theoretical Content and Creative Continuum: The Culture-Exponent's Definitions* (Olderhausen: Institut für Didaktik populärer Musik, 1997).

6 The excellent and straightforward presentation of analytic concepts and descriptive language for writing about melody in J. H. K. Nketia, *African Music in Ghana* (Northwestern University Press, 1962) had a formative influence on my scholarly writing.

7 Those who listen to the audio files will notice the gradual rise in the actual pitch classes being sung during the recording. This upward drift does not change the intervallic relationships within a tune, however, and is not discussed here.

8 Non-isochronous microtiming of timepoints does not have an impact on the analytic schema I discuss.

9 Alorwoyie with Locke, *Agbadza*.

10 For discussion of this bell part, see K. Agawu, "Structural Analysis or Cultural Analysis? Competing Perspectives on the 'Standard Pattern' of West African Rhythm," *Journal of the American Musicological Society*, 59 (2006), 1–46.

11 This way of grouping the notes in the bell pattern has become standardized in the scholarly literature, which is a bit misleading because it exaggerates the importance of metric structure at the expense of the rhythmic shapes made by the asymmetry in the pattern's time values.

12 For discussion of the Agbadza dance see Locke, "Approach."

13 W. Anku, "Circles and Time: A Theory of Structural Organization of Rhythm in African Music," *Music Theory Online*, 6.1 (2000).

14 D. Locke, "Yevevu in the Metric Matrix," *Music Theory Online*, 16.4 (2010).

15 For my first iteration of these metric concepts, see D. Locke, "Principles of Offbeat Timing and Cross-Rhythm in Southern Ewe Dance Drumming," *Ethnomusicology*, 26 (1982), 217–46.

16 See Nzewi, *African Music*. Although I accept the value of Nzewi's project to interrogate the inappropriate connotations of conventional Eurocentric music terminology, not to mention its colonial history, I continue to favor the internationally accepted vocabulary in many cases. To me, polyrhythm and/or polyphony are helpful terms for Agbadza's drum ensemble music and overall multi-part texture. Furthermore, I disagree with Kofi Agawu's strong position on monometer; I hear polymeter as a constant condition in Agbadza – witness the handclapping part.

17 For a fuller discussion of call-and-response in Agbadza songs, see D. Locke, "Call and Response in Ewe Agbadza Songs," *Analytical Approaches to World Music*, 3.1 (2013).

18 Please visit the "Items" section of the online site and then refer to the item number to find all information referred to here.

19 In our interview, Alorwoyie suspects a "bad death" for which a person is spiritually unprepared (see #7, Interview). The language of the drum composition adds historical detail to the song lyric by calling the name of the place where the incident took place (see #7, Drum Language).

20 I hear the B♭in m. 4 as a special pitch that is added to the pentatonic collection to enable the Group's tune to imitate the Leader's F–G–A upward stepwise motion in measure 2 (see #7, Lead Sheet).

21 Early in my study of Alorwoyie's Agbadza I notated only the time values of songs on a one-line staff to better understand the "rhythm of melody." It proved a helpful step along the path toward understanding the melodic rhythm of songs.

22 Confounding a purely forward-moving sense of time, Group's tune makes reference backward in time through melodic imitation by clever use of the pitch B♭.

23 For useful words to describe melodic motion, see Nketia, *African Music*.

24 This may be understood as a measure in 3/4 followed by a measure of $\frac{6}{8}$.

25 Especially in vocal music, when short-long rhythmic figures are launched from onbeat positions, seldom does the second, longer time value start precisely one-third of the way through the beat. Instead, the onbeat shorter time value is lengthened so that the onset of the offbeat longer time value occurs closer in time to the midpoint between successive onbeats. This is sometimes theorized as "swing," that is, deviation from an isochronous norm for expressive purposes. Challenging this orthodoxy, scholars such as Rainer Polak have discovered West African traditions in which non-isochronous, fast-moving pulses are normative; see R. Polak, "Rhythmic Theory as Meter: Non-Isochronous Beat Subdivision in Jembe Music from Mali," *Music Theory Online*, 16.4 (2010).

26 Group's rhythm also suggests a cut-time interpretation.

27 Rather than use tuplets, I prefer to notate even divisions of the ternary beats with pairs of dotted eighth notes, because in drumming, dotted time values often are handled with two notes – that is, a dotted eighth-note time value often becomes a sixteenth–eighth figure, just as dotted quarter-note time values are traversed with eighth–quarter figures. Maintaining consistency in notation at different temporal "architectonic levels," so to speak, visually communicates the remarkable coherence in the structural design of Ewe dance music. In other words, rhythmic proportions recur at different rates of speed and durational values.

28 First presented by Gerhard Kubik, the term *resultant rhythm* refers to a cognitive process in which a listener combines notes from separate parts into a new composite; G. Kubik, "The Phenomenon of Inherent Rhythms in East and Central African Instrumental Music," *African Music*, 3 (1962), 33–42.

29 Many of the musical features that link music of Africa and the African diaspora are articulated in S. Floyd, *The Power of Black Music: Interpreting Its History from Africa to the United States* (Oxford University Press, 1995).

14 Rhythmic Thought and Practice in the Indian Subcontinent

JAMES KIPPEN

Tala

The remarkable facility in rhythmic play demonstrated by musicians and dancers throughout the Indian subcontinent is as impressive as it can be bewildering for the listener. From local and regional practices, through devotional and popular genres, to the heavily theorized concert traditions of the North (Hindustani music) and South (Karnatak music), rhythmic complexity abounds. A performance may begin without even a pulse, where melodies seem to float unpredictably in musical space. Yet increasing rhythmic regularity leads to the establishment of repetitive sequences of beats, both evenly and unevenly distributed, which provide the frameworks for elaborate melodic and rhythmic compositions, variations, and improvisations. The entrance of drums – also essentially melodic in their subtle manipulations of pitch, timbre, stress, and resonance – is invariably a moment of great visceral as well as intellectual excitement. Together, singers, dancers, instrumentalists, and drummers build their performances around the anchors provided by the beats; they subdivide these beats in myriad ways, playing with different rhythmic densities and syncopations. The thrilling, rapidly articulated sequences with their offbeat stresses can temporarily disorient the listener until all seems to resolve in a triumphant convergence of surface rhythm and target beat. The rhythmic system as a whole and the individual frameworks of beats that serve to organize rhythmic expression are known as *tala*.

The Sanskrit term *tala* (Hindi: *tal*; Tamil: *talam*) is an ancient concept described in treatises close to 2,000 years old, and still today the word carries the same essential meaning of a handclap. Any attempt to summarize what are arguably the world's most complex and virtuoso rhythmic-metric practices must necessarily begin with a definition of *tala*, for it differs from Western meter in a fundamental way. Meter is implicit: it is a pattern that is abstracted from the surface rhythms of a piece, and consists of an underlying pulse that is organized into a recurring hierarchical sequence of strong and weak beats. On the other hand, *tala* is explicit: it is a recurring pattern of non-hierarchical beats manifested as hand

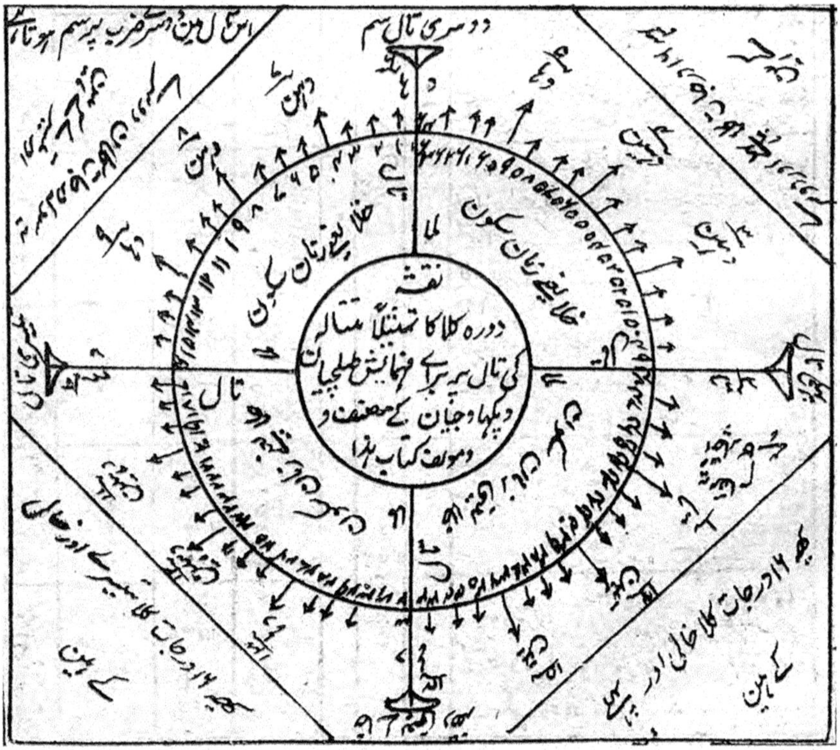

14.1 Cyclic representation of *tala*

gestures consisting of claps, silent waves, and finger counts, or as a relatively fixed sequence of drum strokes.

The repetitive beat patterns of a *tala* are often thought of as cyclic, and certain words describing the cycle (*avartana*, for instance) are based on the Sanskrit root *vrt*, meaning "turning" or "revolving." The circular representation shown in Figure 14.1, taken from an Urdu book published in 1869, maps out *tintal*, Hindustani music's most prevalent *tala* of four beats, with each beat lasting four counts for a total of sixteen: it contains quasi-onomatopoeic syllables for the drum strokes (*dha*, *dhin*, *ta*, *tin*) used to represent the *tala*. Conceptually, the cycle begins and ends on *sama* (Hindi: *sam*; Tamil: *samam* – here, at the top of the dial), which is the beat representing the most common point of melodic and rhythmic confluence.

Throughout this chapter, readers will encounter many examples of clapped beat structures as well as syllables representing the strokes that articulate rhythms. All are encouraged to engage physically with these phenomena by performing the patterns of claps, waves, and finger counts, and by orally expressing the syllables. For it is through physicality and orality that the musical system is taught. Such an embodiment of *tala* is crucial not only for achieving rhythmic competence and engendering creativity as a performer but also for deriving enhanced aesthetic pleasure as an audience. Indeed, audience participation through gestures marking *tala* is prevalent in the concert traditions, especially in Karnatak music, and allows audiences to experience and appreciate more keenly the rhythmic architecture of performance.

Tala in Karnatak Music

As an abstract structure, *tala* finds its most canonical form in the concert tradition of southern India: Karnatak music. We begin with the example of *adi tala*: a series of claps, silent waves, and finger counts that provides the framework for roughly 80 percent of songs and other composed works in this repertoire. In Table 14.1, the eight-count sequence of hand gestures provides both visual and sonic markers that allow performers and listeners alike to know precisely where they are within the *tala* at any given moment. This pattern begins with a clap of the right hand down onto the upturned palm of the left hand on count 1, followed on counts 2, 3, and 4 by taps of the pinky, ring, and middle fingers of the right hand onto the left palm; it continues on count 5 with another clap, and on count 6 with a wave, which is where the right hand turns palm upward and effects either a light tap of the back of the right hand on the left palm or a bounce in the air above it; another clap and wave on counts 7 and 8 conclude the sequence, and the pattern cycles back to repeat from count 1. As stated earlier, the *tala* has no internal accent structure like Western meter, not even on the clap marking count 1. The gestured 8-count pattern functions to provide a solid temporal reference for complex surface musical activity.

Table 14.1 Clapping structure and *solkattu* syllables for *adi tala*

Counts	1	2	3	4	5	6	7	8
Gestures	*clap*	*pinky*	*ring*	*middle*	*clap*	*wave*	*clap*	*wave*
Speed 1	ta	ka	di	mi	ta	ka	jo	nu
Speed 2	taka	dimi	taka	jonu	taka	dimi	taka	jonu
Speed 3	takadimi	takajonu	takadimi	takajonu	takadimi	takajonu	takadimi	takajonu
Triplets	takadi	mitaka	jonuta	kadimi	takajo	nutaka	dimita	kajonu

A musician trained in a Western tradition might well approach the clapping pattern of *adi tala* by doing the hand gestures and counting out the eight counts. Yet this approach is rare in South Asia, where musicians tend to use syllabic sequences to mark time rather than numbers. This results in a qualitatively different way of experiencing one's relationship to the *tala*. The syllabic sequences are based on *solkattu*: a rich vocabulary of drum strokes and sounds that are expressed as onomatopoeic syllables like *ta*, *di*, *tom*, and *nam*. Returning to Table 14.1, we note the presence of eight syllables that should now replace the numbers as one performs the gestures. As a basic exercise, one begins with density level 1, where each hand gesture is accompanied by one syllable. Density level 2 doubles the speed of articulation of the syllables, although one must remember to strictly maintain the original pace of the hand gestures so that now each one is accompanied by two syllables. Density level 3 doubles the speed of articulation yet again, so that four syllables accompany each gesture. These three density levels are known as *trikala*, the "three speeds," and all students of Karnatak music, whether melodic or percussive in form, learn this fundamental technique of changing rhythmic densities while maintaining the original pulse. Students of vocal music, for example, proceed through defined sets of scalar exercises sung to the solfège names Sa Ri Ga Ma Pa Dha Ni Sa, all the while clapping *adi tala* and applying the "three speeds." As can also be seen in Table 14.1, an additional rhythmic exercise arranges the same syllables in triple time.

Adi tala is fundamentally duple in character, and as such it fits into the first of five classes of rhythm. This first class, or *jati*, is known as *caturasra*, or "four sided," and is commonly articulated with the *solkattu* sequence *ta ka di mi* (or *ta ka jo nu*). As shown in Table 14.2, there are four other *jati* of 3, 7, 5, and 9 (this is their traditional order), each with its own pattern. The *jati* are important in several ways: they show how the beat may be internally subdivided into quadruplets, triplets, septuplets, quintuplets, and nonuplets, respectively; they can form the basis for calculating larger units of rhythmic improvisation; and they can serve to modify *tala* structures. This last point necessitates a brief discussion of the *suladi sapta tala* system.

Appearing first in the late nineteenth century, the *suladi sapta tala* (seven primordial *tala*) system quantifies seven basic categories, each with a distinctive gestural structure. The three gestures are *laghu* (symbol I: a clap plus a variable number of finger counts), *drutam* (symbol O: a clap plus a wave), and *anudrutam* (symbol U: a single clap). *Adi tala* belongs to the *triputa* category, which comprises one *laghu* and two *drutam*. The

Table 14.2 The five *jati* "classes," the *suladi sapta tala* system, and some common non-*suladi* structures

Caturasra (4)	ta	ka	di	mi					
Tisra (3)	ta	ki	ta						
Misra (7)	ta	ki	ta	ta	ka	di	mi		
Khanda (5)	ta	ka	ta	ki	ta				
Sankirna (9)	ta	ka	di	mi	ta	ka	ta	ki	ta

I = *laghu*: clap plus finger counts
O = *drutam*: clap plus wave
U = *anudrutam*: clap

	caturasra (4)	*tisra (3)*	*misra (7)*	*khanda (5)*	*sankirna (9)*
Dhruva – IOII	14	11	23	17	29
Matya – IOI	10	8	16	12	20
Rupaka – OI	6	5	9	7	11
Jhampa – IUO	7	6	10	8	12
Triputa – IOO	8 (*adi tala*)	7	11	9	13
Ata – IIOO	12	10	18	14	22
Eka – I	4	3	7	5	9

Rupaka (3) = clap clap wave
Misra capu (7) = wave wave – clap – clap –
Khanda capu (5) = clap – clap clap –

length of the variable *laghu* is determined by one of the *jati* categories: in the case of *adi tala*, the clap is followed by three finger counts for a total of four counts, and thus the *laghu* is "four sided." Another, more cumbersome name for *adi tala* is therefore *caturasra jati triputa tala*. As can be seen in Table 14.2, the combination of seven *tala* categories with the five *jati* results in thirty-five distinctive *tala* structures, from three counts up to twenty-nine. What is interesting is that *adi tala* is not the only structure comprising eight counts, and yet *tisra jati matya tala* (clap pinky ring clap wave clap pinky ring) and *khanda jati jhampa tala* (clap pinky ring middle index clap clap wave) differ markedly in their arrangements of gestures.

In truth, however, very few of the thirty-five structures have been employed in performance practice, though one does occasionally hear uncommon *tala* structures used for exercises and technically challenging showpieces called *pallavi* that are designed to demonstrate technical virtuosity. The vast majority of compositions, including those of the greatest composers from the Golden Age of Karnatak music in the late eighteenth and early nineteenth centuries – the so-called "Holy Trinity" of Tyagaraja, Diksitar, and Syama Sastri – are set in just four *tala*: *adi tala* plus three that do not even belong to the *suladi sapta tala* system. These are also given in Table 14.2 and comprise only claps and waves: *rupaka* (3 counts), *misra capu* (7 counts), and *khanda capu* (5 counts). These structures are very likely to have entered the concert tradition from local or regional practices. *Rupaka* is an interesting and somewhat confusing case, as it shares its name but not its structure (clap clap wave) with one of the seven *suladi* categories (comprising one *drutam* and one *laghu*), and it also appears to be a relatively modern substitute for the ancient *tisra jati eka tala* (clap pinky ring). In practice, *rupaka* and *tisra jati eka tala* are interchangeable, and musicians choose according to the teaching lineage through which they have acquired their knowledge.

Rhythmic Play in Karnatak Music

The performance of a typical piece of Karnatak concert music begins with *alapana*, which is an exposition of the melodic motivic characteristics of a *raga* without *tala*. Although the melodies may seem to be free of any regular sense of rhythm, many musicians insist that they are mindful of an underlying pulse against which melodic expression is measurable. *Alapana* is often quite short, but nevertheless the expanding range of melodic motifs is complemented with increased surface rhythmic density.

Following the *alapana* is the composition, a text set to melody (or an instrumental rendition of one) that is always framed by a *tala* and thus always accompanied by a drum. The great percussion instrument of Karnatak music is the *mridangam*, a barrel drum with two heads made from layers of animal hide, laced together, and capable of being tuned by means of a permanent black compound applied as a low, circular mound in the center of the right head and by the application of a temporary ball of dough stuck and flattened onto the left. While the left head provides a deep, resonant bass, the right produces a variety of timbres depending on how and where the fingers and palm strike it. As the first strains of the melodic composition are delivered, the *mridangam* player must quickly identify the *tala* and the tempo, which then remain constant throughout the piece. The starting point for the melodic composition may occur anywhere in the cycle and could even begin on a half beat. Experienced drummers will likely know many compositions and may even play along with some of the prominent rhythmic signatures of the melody. As an accompanist, the drummer's role is to support the melodic unfolding of the composition, mark the ends of sections of the exposition with rhythmic cadences, and

Table 14.3 *Sarvalaghu* patterns in *adi tala*

	clap	*pinky*	*ring*	*middle*	*clap*	*wave*	*clap*	*wave*
1	ta	din	din	na	ta ka	din	din	na
2	ta	din	ta ka	din	ta	din	ta ka	din
3	ta	din	ta	din	ta ka	din	tom	kita taka
4	ta ka	di mi	ta ka	di mi	ta ka	di mi	ta ka	di mi
5	tam	– ki	ta ka	jo nu	tam	– ki	ta ka	jo nu
6	tam	– ki	ta ka	jo nu	ta ka	tom ki	ta ka	jo nu
7	din din	din tom	– ta	din na	din din	din tom	– ta	din na
8	tom	kita taka	taka din	kita taka	tom	kita taka	taka din	kita taka

contribute to the increasing energy and intensity of sections of improvisation that follow.

The rhythmic patterns played by the drummer fall into two categories: those that structurally maintain the flow of time, and those that disrupt it through rhythmic formulas that are calculated to terminate on a target beat within the *tala*, most commonly *sama*. The first category is known as *sarvalaghu* (from Sanskrit words implying "all short/easy"). Table 14.3 outlines a few simple examples of *sarvalaghu*, each of which the reader is encouraged to read out loud while clapping the structure of *adi tala*. These patterns have a tendency toward internal repetition that subdivides them into two halves and thus reinforces the repetitive groove resulting from the distinctive timbres and articulations. The groove takes on a particularly heavy swing in examples 4–7 (for instance, in example 5 one should sharpen the attack on TAka and exaggerate the weighty resonance of JOnu), and example 8 suggests greater surface rhythmic density, pointing toward patterns that become increasingly complex as pieces develop. Once one has gained familiarity with these patterns, one should double their speed to get a sense of how they sound in performance (yet maintain the original tempo of the clapping pattern – a metronome mark of roughly 84 counts per minute is a fairly typical performance tempo). A drummer will switch between many different *sarvalaghu* patterns according to the flow and rate of activity of the melodic exposition and its development.

The second category is known as *kanakku*, "calculation," which is a vast and complex topic too large for anything but a cursory introduction. We shall briefly look at endings (*mora*), shapes (*yati*), and complex designs (*korvai*). All are configured in such a way as to create temporary uncertainty only to find familiar ground once again by directing our attention to a target beat. The simple examples given in Table 14.4 are borrowed from David Nelson's exemplary *Solkattu Manual.*[1]

Table 14.4 *Mora, yati,* and *korvai*

1. *Mora*

Structure: (statement) + [gap] + (statement) + [gap] + (statement)

Statement: (ta ta kt tom tom ta) = 6 pulses

Gap: [tam – –] = 3 pulses

(ta ta kt tom tom ta) [tam – –] (ta ta kt tom tom ta) [tam – –] (ta ta kt tom tom ta)

clap	*pinky*	*ring*	*middle*
ta – din –	din – na –	(ta ta kt tom	tom ta) [tam –
clap	*wave*	*clap*	*wave*
–] (ta ta kt	tom tom ta) [tam	– –] (ta ta	kt tom tom ta)

2. *Yati*

Gopucca yati	*Srotovaha yati*
6 + 2 (ta ta kt tom tom ta) [tam –]	1 + 2 (ta) [tam –]
4 + 2 (kt tom tom ta) [tam –]	2 + 2 (tom ta) [tam –]
3 + 2 (tom tom ta) [tam –]	3 + 2 (tom tom ta) [tam –]
2 + 2 (tom ta) [tam –]	4 + 2 (kt tom tom ta) [tam –]
1 (ta)	6 (ta ta kt tom tom ta)

3. *Korvai*

a) ta ki ta tom – ta din gi na tom = 10 pulses

b) jo nu jo nu = 4 pulses

c) tom – ta – = 4 pulses

d) tam – – = 3 pulses

ta ki ta tom	– ta din gi	na tom jo nu	jo nu tom –
ta – tam –	– ta ki ta	tom – ta din	gi na tom jo
nu jo nu tom	– ta – tam	– – ta ki	ta tom – ta
din gi na tom	jo nu jo nu	tom – ta –	tam – – jo
nu jo nu tom	– ta – tam	– – jo nu	jo nu (tom –
ta –) [tam –	–] (tom – ta	–) [tam – –]	(tom – ta–)

A *mora* is a rhythmic cadence that ends a section of the music. In its simplest form, it is a sequence of strokes that is played three times: the reason for three statements of a given pattern is important. With just two statements, it would be difficult to anticipate the target beat, whereas with three, the pattern is not only more firmly established in the listener's mind but also the temporal distance from the second to the third can be predicted to be the same as from the first to the second. The *mora* shown in Table 14.4 features the pattern *ta ta kt tom tom ta tam*, which covers

7 pulses (*kt* stands for *kita* and occupies 1 pulse). The body of the pattern is the 6-pulse statement *ta ta kt tom tom ta*, and *tam* is its end point. *Tam* may be followed by no gap at all, or more commonly with a gap of a variable number of pulses. In this case, *tam* is followed by a 2-pulse gap for a total of 3 pulses: *tam* – –. The *mora*, then, comprises (statement) + [gap] + (statement) + [gap] + (statement) for a total of 24 pulses. If the rate of rhythmic action in *adi tala* is 4 pulses per count, then the 8-count cycle will comprise 32 pulses. It follows, therefore, that in order to target the *sama* of the cycle on count 1 the *mora* should start after a gap of 8 pulses (in this case, those pulses are occupied by part of a *sarvalaghu* pattern from Table 14.3, *ta* – *din* – *din* – *na* –); in other words, the *mora* begins on the third count that is marked by the ring-finger gesture.

Yati refers to a series of operations that create shapes in the mind of the listener. The truly interesting ones among them are the cow's tail (*gopucca*) and the river mouth (*srotovaha*), which represent narrowing and expanding operations, respectively. Retaining the same statement used for the first *mora*, we can see in Table 14.4 how elements are subtracted from the original phrase in *gopucca yati*, while the reverse is true in *srotovaha yati*. The gap in each instance is reduced to 2 pulses [tam –], and once again the total number of pulses for each sequence is 24. Therefore, these *mora* also begin on the third count of *adi tala*. By combining these two shapes, one can create two more: *damaru yati* (a small hourglass-shaped drum) with *gopucca-srotovaha*, and the barrel-shaped *mridanga yati* with *srotovaha-gopucca*.

In accompaniment, the *mridangam* player tends toward shorter, simpler *mora* structures. Yet often near the end of a concert piece the spotlight may shift over to the drummer for a solo that can run anywhere from two to ten minutes. This is the *tani avartanam*, and it marks a special moment of great concentration for the other performers on stage who attempt to maintain the clapping pattern of the *tala* as the only accompaniment to the sounds of the drum. Here the rhythmic designs are longer and more complex, and may involve changing the surface rhythmic density from duple to triple time, or even to quintuplets and septuplets. Compound *mora* structures are also increasingly likely, where a *mora* is repeated three times, thus prolonging the tension before a resolution on the *sama* of the cycle. But the *tani avartanam* must also have at least one grand, pre-composed structure: the *korvai*.

A *korvai* may feature all manner of clever rhythmic thinking, but at root it comprises a *yati* plus a *mora*. In the relatively simple example given in Table 14.4, there are four phrases of 10, 4, 4, and 3 pulses, respectively, which create the narrowing shape of *gopucca yati*. The composition repeats phrases abcd three times, then bcd, then b, and finally the *mora* statement and gap constructed from (c)+[d]+(c)+[d]+(c). A *korvai* may in fact be extensive, combining many sections, as long as it ends with a *mora*. They are often difficult to execute, and difficult to follow, but they represent the pinnacle of arithmetic thinking merged with musical aesthetics and technique, and they are quite thrilling to experience.

Finally, one may sometimes find more than one percussion instrument on stage in a Karnatak music concert, most commonly a *ghatam* (clay pot) and a *khanjira* (small tambourine). These are wielded with extraordinary technical skill, and are capable of replicating anything the *mridangam* can do.

A Brief Word on Local and Regional Rhythmic Traditions

There exists an extraordinary diversity of approaches to rhythm in South Asia, yet outside the concert traditions of Karnatak and Hindustani music there is relatively little detailed documentation or analysis of how precisely rhythm works. Certain scholars have unearthed evidence contradicting the notion that rhythm in South Asia is rigidly organized into isometric, that is, unchanging cycles of beats and counts. Jim Sykes[2] has described Sinhala Buddhist ritual music in Sri Lanka where drumming patterns can sound like unmetered speech, where long and short drum syllables set in lines of drum poetry often do not coincide with beats or pulses, and where sometimes the beats may even be stretched to match the durations of drum words. Without an insider's understanding of the rhythmic logic of the drums in these ritual contexts, these irregular cycles and rhythms are difficult or impossible to count. Richard Widdess[3] has noted how in many older repertoires of religious genres – such as Sikh *gurubani* hymns in the Punjab, Sufi devotional *qawwali* songs from Delhi, temple traditions from Lord Krishna's heartland of Vrindaban, and religious and ceremonial music and dance among the Newar of the Kathmandu Valley in Nepal – heterometric rhythmic organization survives alongside isometric structures, and may have been (or indeed may still be) far more widespread that we realize. In a heterometric composition, the *tala* changes from section to section of the piece, unlike the concert traditions where the *tala* changes only if the composition does. In his work with Shi'a drumming groups active during Muharram (the annual period of mourning) in Muslim centers across India and Pakistan, Richard Wolf[4] also documented examples of heterometric structure. Additionally, in his study of Kota tribal drumming from South India,[5] he introduced the important analytic idea of beats as anchor points that act as signposts that are especially important in coordinating group rhythmic practices. The spaces between beats can be flexible through non-uniform inflation, just as they are in the Karnatak system where the variable *laghu* can expand from 3 to 4, 5, 7, or 9 counts. Indeed, the rationale for many of the observations Wolf has made about a wide array of drumming practices focuses on the importance of the number of beats – both as a series of foundational anchors and also as stressed strokes in a surface rhythmic pattern – in the naming and identification of a *tala*. Of course, not all carry the name *tala*: though the term is widespread, others like *cal* (Hindi: "motion; gait") or *ati* (Tamil: "beat") are also found, and some traditions appear to have no word for *tala* at all.

One other very important analytic concept introduced by Richard Wolf is "stroke melody." This resonates with what I wrote earlier about the extraordinary variety of different pitches, timbres, and articulations that drummers can produce on their instruments, either solo or in ensembles featuring several different kinds of membranophones and idiophones (small cymbals, for instance, that have always traditionally marked anchor points). Stroke melodies are prominent throughout South Asia, and are fixed patterns whose combinations of timbres and stresses set up what might best be described as a groove: a repetitive rhythm rooted in bodily movement that often involves offbeat stresses and that conveys a feeling of motion (compare the Hindi term *cal*). They often establish an underlying framework for other musical activity, and sometimes through variation, expansion, and changes in density they can be the focus of the musical performance itself. As we shall see, stroke melodies are also very important in the Hindustani concert tradition.

Hindustani *Tala*

The Hindustani *tala* system in fact harbors two systems that over the past two centuries have become enmeshed to such an extent that few would acknowledge any separation whatsoever. Yet extricating one from the other can prove instructive. The first lies within the domain of *dhrupad*: widely considered to be the oldest genre still performed, a *dhrupad* performance features a substantial unaccompanied *alap* (compare this with *alapana*), followed by one or two compositions set in *tala* and accompanied by a barrel drum called either *pakhavaj* or *mridang* (compare this with *mridangam*, to which it is structurally similar). The second pertains to all other types of concert music: vocal genres such as *khayal*, *thumri*, and so on; instrumental music of the *sitar*, *sarod*, and so on; and the dance form that during the twentieth century came to be known as *kathak*. All these genres are accompanied by the *tabla*, which along with the *sitar* has become a globally recognized symbol of Indian music.

Of the hundreds of *tala* structures that have been listed over the centuries in Sanskrit and Indo-Persian treatises, only four continue to appear with any regularity in the modern *dhrupad* repertoire. Of these, *cautal* and *dhamar* (12 and 14 counts, respectively) dominate slow-tempo compositions, and *sultal* and *tivra* (10 and 7 counts) frame those in fast tempo. *Matra* (etymologically linked to meter) is the commonly used word for a count: in the past, the *matra* corresponded to a healthy human pulse, but it is now conceived as a flexible unit dependent on tempo: *laya*. In the three categories, slow, medium, and fast (*vilambit*, *madhya*, *drut*), the *matra* can range from 12 per minute in the case of slow *khayal* compositions up to 720 in ever-accelerating instrumental climaxes.

Table 14.5 maps the beats of *tala* structures for *dhrupad* using only clap and wave gestures: unlike Karnatak *tala*, finger counts are not generally used, and certainly not systematically so. What *dhrupad* has in common with Karnatak practice, however, is the strict maintenance of the clapping pattern by performers and audience as an external representation of the *tala* in use, which in turn frees the *pakhavaj* player to support the melodic unfolding of the composition, mark the ends of its sections with rhythmic cadences, and contribute to the increasing energy and intensity of the performance – as is precisely the case with the *mridangam* player. Moreover, just as the *mridangam* player may choose from various *sarvalaghu* patterns to fill the *tala* cycle and contribute to rhythmic flow, the *pakhavaj* player too adopts repetitive, groove-like patterns. The first examples were notated in the early 1850s by Wajid Ali Shah, king of Awadh, a lavish patron and practitioner of music at his court in Lucknow. He called them *theka*, "accompaniment." A *theka* is a fixed sequence of drum strokes that, when repeated relatively unchanged cycle after cycle, creates a recognizable representation of a *tala* – an aural symbol of it – and thus its presence largely obviates the need for the clapping pattern to mark time. However, Wajid Ali Shah's *theka* for *cautal* would in subsequent years be interpreted merely as a kind of filler pattern akin to *sarvalaghu*, and was superseded in the late nineteenth century by another pattern that even today continues as the established *theka* representing *cautal*. The paradox is that in spite of the presence of these *theka* patterns, there is still a heavy reliance on external

Table 14.5 *Tala* structures for *dhrupad*

Cautal clapping structure (2+2+2+2+2+2): *clap* *wave* *clap* *wave* *clap* *clap*

. . . *theka* – mid-nineteenth century, Wajid Ali Shah

clap	dha	dhin na	*wave*	na ka	dhet
clap	dhin na	na ka	*wave*	dhin na	na ka
clap	dhad	dhi	*clap*	ghin na	na ka

. . . *theka* – late nineteenth century

clap	dha	dha	*wave*	din	ta
clap	ki ta	dha	*wave*	din	ta
clap	ti te	ka ta	*clap*	ga di	ge na

Dhamar (5+2+3+4)

clap	kat	dhit	ta		dhit	ta	*clap*	dha	—
wave	kat	tit	ta	*clap*	tit	ta		ta	—

Sultal (2+2+2+2+2)

clap	dha	dha	*wave*	din	ta	*clap*	ki ta	dha	*clap*	ti te	ka ta	*wave*	ga di	ge na

Tivra (3+2+2)

clap	dha	din	ta	*clap*	ti te	ka ta	*clap*	ga di	ge na

clapping patterns for *dhrupad* and *pakhavaj* performance. By contrast, clapping in non-*dhrupad* genres is rare. This raises three points: (1) that *dhrupad* and Karnatak performance are less removed from one another than is generally assumed; (2) that the *pakhavaj* accompanist spends very little time playing *theka* but rather quickly shifts gears into filler patterns and compositions, thus creating the need for an external set of markers for the *tala*; and (3) that *theka* is probably not native to the *pakhavaj* but instead owes its presence to the influence of the *tabla*. *Theka* is first linked to *tabla* in texts from the early nineteenth century.

First appearing in the early eighteenth century, the *tabla* was, organologically speaking, a *pakhavaj* split into two parts and played with skins facing up. The substitution of a small hemispherical kettledrum for the bass gave drummers the ability to create extremely active pitch inflections of its resonant sonority, allowing it to replicate not only the rhythmic language of the *pakhavaj* but also that of the barrel drum *dholak*, widely used in local and regional musical genres as well as in the traditions of the Qawwals, who sang Muslim devotional genres as well as *khayal*, among other things. It was this flexibility that led to a growing preference for *tabla* in all genres other than *dhrupad*, but the drum owed its rapid spread throughout northern parts of the subcontinent to the popular songs and dances of female entertainers. Such performances were labelled "nautch" by the British (a corruption of *nac*, "dance"), and were very much the rage in the eighteenth and nineteenth centuries among Indians and foreigners alike.

Three rhythmic patterns dominated the nautch: a compound duple with hemiolic properties called *dadra* (3+3 / 2+2+2), a lilting *ghazal* (3+4), and a duple *kaherva* (4+4). These were articulated on *tabla* with short, fixed patterns – stroke melodies – that likely underwent embellishment and intensification without deviating greatly from the beat pattern other than to end a section of music or dance with a short cadential flourish. As *tabla* began to be used for other genres with longer beat patterns, the grooves largely remained intact, but were played twice in order to fill the extended *tala* structures. A case in point is *ektal*, whose clapping pattern derives from *cautal* for *pakhavaj*, but whose *theka* consists of a *dadra* groove played twice, as seen in Table 14.6. Yet in order to differentiate between the repetitions, and thus ensure that the *theka* marks the *sam* of the cycle, the repeat removes the bass resonance (voiced phonemes *dhin dhin* become unvoiced ones, *kat tin*). This highlights the timbral difference between the opposing polar axes of *sam* at the beginning of the cycle (clapped and marked with an X) and *khali* halfway through it (waved and marked with a 0). *Khali*, the "empty" beat, therefore becomes an

Table 14.6 *Titala* and other *tala* structures

Ektal					
clap	dhin	dhin	*wave*	dha ge	tira kita
clap	tin	na	*wave*	kat	tin
clap	dha ge	tira kita	*clap*	dhin	na

Groove structure of *ektal*

X	dhin	dhin	dhage	tirakita	tin	na
0	kat	tin	dhage	tirakita	dhin	na

Some *theka* structures of *titala*

Dhima titala	X	dhin	kita	dhin	na	na	dhin	dhin	na
	0	tin	kita	tin	na	na	dhin	dhin	na
Tilvara	X	dha	tira kita	dhin	dhin	dha	dha	tin	tin
	0	ta	tira kita	dhin	dhin	dha	dha	dhin	dhin
Addha /	X	dha	ge dhin	– ge	dha	dha	ge tin	– ke	ta
Sattar Khani	0	ta	ge dhin	– ge	dha	dha dha	ge dhin	– ge	dha
Ikvai	X	dha	dhin	—	dha	dha	dhin	—	dha
	0	dha	tin	—	ta	ta	dhin	—	dha
Tintal	X	dha	dhin	dhin	dha	dha	dhin	dhin	dha
	0	dha	tin	tin	ta	ta	dhin	dhin	dha

Some other common *tala/theka* structures

Jhumra	3+4+3+4	X	dhin	– ta	tira kita	dhin	dhin	dha ge	tira kita
		0	tin	– ta	tira kita	dhin	dhin	dha ge	tira kita
Dipcandi	3+4+3+4	X	dha	dhin	—	dha	dha	tin	—
		0	ta	tin	—	dha	dha	dhin	—

Jhaptal	2+3+2+3	X	dhin	na	dhin	dhin	na
		0	tin	na	dhin	dhin	na

Rupak	3+2+2	*wave*	tin	tin	na	*clap*	dhin	na	*clap*	dhin	na

important marker in a bipartite structure. The same process can also be seen in Table 14.6 with the most common of all *tabla tala* structures, *titala*, which in an older form was called *dhima titala* that was adapted from *dhrupad-pakhavaj* repertoire (but that is now rarely heard there). *Dhima* was only one form of *titala*, however, as other stroke melodies appropriate to different song genres were also in common usage. A few of these are shown in Table 14.6, but most are now obscure owing to the almost complete dominance of *tintal* (also represented in Figure 14.1), which was originally used in dance accompaniment. Nowadays, the vast majority of vocal and instrumental genres of concert music accompanied by *tabla* use *tintal, jhumra, dipcandi, ektal, jhaptal,* and *rupak* (this last, a structural anomaly, is representative of an iambic lilt influenced by regional and popular forms of 3+4). These patterns are also given in Table 14.6.

Rhythmic Play in Hindustani Music

In *dhrupad*, a melodic composition is stated several times before undergoing many kinds of rhythmic transformation of text and tune, with the beats being subject to increasingly denser subdivisions. The *pakhavaj* accompanist tries to match these, and can draw on a variety of filler patterns, as noted earlier, or on compositions known broadly as *paran*. Table 14.7 outlines two simple *paran* compositions: the first is known as *sath paran*, *sath* meaning "with; together," suggesting its use in accompaniment; the second is a *mohra* that incorporates a threefold repetition generally called *tihai* in Hindustani music (compare this with the Karnatak *mora*). In these, the typically unbroken stream of stroke phrases in the *sath paran* contrasts with the broken pattern initiating the *mohra* before the *tihai* (*ghege tite kata gadi gena dha –*) directs our attention to the *sam*.

There is no equivalent of Karnatak music's *tani avartanam* in *dhrupad*, but instead the *pakhavaj* may be heard as a discrete solo item in a concert. Here, drummers embark on sets of longer, varied *paran* structures, including the *chakradar paran* that will comprise the threefold repetition of a

Table 14.7 *Paran* and *mohra*

Sath paran						
	clap	dha ge ti te	ga di ge na	*wave*	na ge ti te	ga di ge na
	clap	dha ge ti te	ka ta ka ta	*wave*	ga di ge na	na ge ti te
	clap	kat ti te ta	ge na dha ge	*clap*	ti te ka ta	ga di ge na
Mohra						
	clap	dha ge – na	dhet – ta –	*wave*	dhet – dhet –	ta – (ghe ge
	clap	ti te ka ta	ga di ge na	*wave*	dha –) (ghe ge	ti te ka ta
	clap	ga di ge na	dha –) (ghe ge	*clap*	ti te ka ta	ga di ge na
	clap	dha)				

paran plus a *mohra*, calculated to end on *sam*. *Pakhavaj* players have resurrected many older, obscure *tala* frameworks as the basis for solo performances, many possessing names of Hindu gods: Brahm, Rudra, Lakshmi, and so forth. They also recite and play compositions that blend drum syllables – *bol* – with lines of verse praising gods: the elephant-headed Ganesh, Remover of Obstacles, is a popular subject for an opening piece, an invocation for an auspicious blessing.

The role of the *tabla* as accompaniment to vocal genres differs from *pakhavaj*, because it is confined to a far greater extent to maintaining the *theka*, with very few opportunities for solo flourishes. In instrumental music, the modern trend has moved increasingly toward a collaborative performance where the accompanist is given several opportunities to perform solo, during which time the melodist maintains the *raga* composition as an aural marker of the *tala*. *Theka* and melodic composition become important frames of reference for the *tala* structure in the absence of the clapping gestures of Karnatak music and *dhrupad*. This is true also of *lahra*, a tune specifically designed to accompany the discrete genre of *tabla* solo.

Many different types of composition are available to the *tabla* player, but once again all fall into one of two categories: those that maintain the structure of the cycle and those that are calculated to end on a target beat, the *sam*. As far as the latter category is concerned, *tabla* borrows heavily from the structures of the *pakhavaj*: *tukra* is the equivalent of *mohra*, ending with a threefold *tihai*, and a *chakradar-tukra* repeats that structure three times. A *gat* is a specialized composition of mostly *tabla* material and is prized for its specialized techniques: some end with a *tihai* (*gat-tukra*), and others blend *tabla* material with *pakhavaj* phrases (*gat-paran*).

What truly sets *tabla* apart is the manner in which pieces that maintain the cycle are structured and performed. *Peshkar* ("presentation") and *bant* ("division") are slower, introductory compositions, *qaida* ("base; rule") is the primary vehicle for developing variations on a theme, and *rela* ("torrent") presents a stream of rapidly articulated phrases. There is considerable evidence to suggest that these compositional types emerged from *theka* and its embellishments and variations, particularly those for *tintal*. Crucially, all are subject to transformations dependent on the *khali* of the cycle. Take the popular late nineteenth-century Delhi *qaida* shown in Table 14.8: the 8-count theme (*dhati tedha tite dhadha tite dhage teena kena*) occupies the first half of the cycle, and is then repeated in the second half (*tati teta tite dhadha tite dhage dheena gena*). The right-hand, treble strokes remain the same, but the left-hand bass strokes change from open, resonant sounds to damped ones. As noted earlier with *ektal theka*, the transformation is

Table 14.8 Delhi *qaida*

Qaida theme. . .				
X	dha ti	te dha	ti te	dha dha
	ti te	dha ge	tee na	ke na
0	ta ti	te ta	ti te	dha dha
	ti te	dha ge	dhee na	ge na
. . .doubled				
X	dha ti te dha	ti te dha dha	ti te dha ge	dhee na ge na
	dha ti te dha	ti te dha dha	ti te dha ge	tee na ke na
0	ta ti te ta	ti te ta ta	ti te ta ke	tee na ke na
	dha ti te dha	ti te dha dha	ti te dha ge	dhee na ge na
Dohra				
X	dha ti te dha	ti te dha dha	dha ti te dha	ti te dha dha
	dha ti te dha	ti te dha dha	ti te dha ge	tee na ke na
0	ta ti te ta	ti te ta ta	ta ti te ta	ti te dha dha
	dha ti te dha	ti te dha dha	ti te dha ge	dhee na ge na
Vistar 1				
X	dha ti te dha	ti te dha ti	te dha ti te	dha dha ti te
	dha ti te dha	ti te dha dha	ti te dha ge	tee na ke na
0	ta ti te ta	ti te ta ti	te ta ti te	ta ta ti te
	dha ti te dha	ti te dha dha	ti te dha ge	dhee na ge na
Vistar 2				
X	ti te dha ti	te dha ti te	ti te dha ti	te dha ti te
	dha ti te dha	ti te dha dha	ti te dha ge	tee na ke na
0	ti te ta ti	te ta ti te	ti te ta ti	te ta ti te
	dha ti te dha	ti te dha dha	ti te dha ge	dhee na ge na
Tihai				
X	(dha ti te dha	ti te dha dha	ti te dha ge	tee na ke na
	dha – dha –	dha –) (dha ti	te dha ti te	dha dha ti te
0	dha ge tee na	ke na dha –	dha – dha –)	(dha ti te dha
	ti te dha dha	ti te dha ge	tee na ke na	dha – dha –
X	dha)			

represented by a phonemic change from voiced syllables (*dha, ge*) to unvoiced equivalents (*ta, ke*) as the theme approaches the *khali*, and then by the return of voiced syllables as the repeat returns toward the *sam*. Typically, the *qaida* is then played at twice the rhythmic density, though the theme continues to be subject to the bipartite division of the *tala* into *sam* and *khali* halves. Variations (*vistar*, "spreading") are built from the components of the original theme by repeating, permutating, expanding, and compressing its phrases. *Dohra* ("double"), for example, is a common method of repeating the opening phrase three times. The *qaida* ends with a *tihai* based on the original theme or one of its variations. This Delhi *qaida* with a short sequence of variations and concluding *tihai* (bracketed) can be seen in Table 14.8.

Rhythmic Diversity or Unity?

In a region of the world so obviously socio-culturally diverse, different approaches to musical rhythm are to be expected. Yet as this necessarily brief introduction to rhythmic thought and practice in the Indian subcontinent has tried to show, there is much more that unites the region than divides it, in spite of the tendency of many musicians and scholars to maintain distance between Karnatak and Hindustani music systems, or between elite/concert and local/regional traditions. The fundamental orality of rhythm is ubiquitous, as is the explicitness of *tala* either as gestured, quantitative structures based on arrangements of beats or as qualitative stroke melodies that articulate and represent them. Indeed, it is clear that both Karnatak and Hindustani rhythm combine these quantitative and qualitative approaches to *tala*, and that the rhythmic strategies in their respective performance contexts are really not so different. The all-important beats of a *tala* are anchors that organize the flow of time, frame composition, and coordinate creativity: we have seen that this flow can be maintained with stroke melodies like *sarvalaghu* and *theka*, and through various rhythmic compositions that are bound to and reflective of the structure of the *tala* cycle; and we have noted how the flow may be disrupted by rhythmic patterns and compositions calculated to target a specific beat, most commonly *sama/sam*, the principal marker of creative confluence. One does not need to understand complex theory to sense the sheer excitement of rhythmic performance in South Asia, but an awareness of its beat structures and patterns of maintenance and disruption will most certainly enhance enjoyment of what is one of the world's most thrilling systems of rhythm.

Endnotes

1 D. Nelson, *Solkattu Manual: An Introduction to the Rhythmic Language of South Indian Music* (Wesleyan University Press, 2008).

2 J. Sykes, "South Asian Drumming Beyond *Tala*: The Problem with 'Meter' in Buddhist Sri Lanka," *Analytical Approaches to World Music*, 6 (2018), 1–49.

3 R. Widdess, "Time Changes: Heterometric Rhythm in South Asia," in R. Wolf, S. Blum, and C. Hasty (eds.), *Thought and Play in Musical Rhythm* (Oxford University Press, 2019), 275–313.

4 R. Wolf, *The Voice in the Drum: Music, Language, and Emotion in Islamicate South Asia* (University of Illinois Press, 2014); and "'Rhythm,' 'Beat,' and 'Freedom' in South Asian Musical Traditions," in Wolf, Blum, and Hasty (eds.), *Thought and Play*, 314–36.

5 R. Wolf, *The Black Cow's Footprint: Time, Space and Music in the Lives of the Kotas of South India* (Delhi: Permanent Black, 2005).

15 The Draw of Balinese Rhythm

LESLIE TILLEY

> I began to have a feeling of form and elaborate architecture. . . . The music was rapid, the rhythms intricate. Yet without effort, with eyes closed, or staring out into the night, as though each player were in an isolated world of his own, the men performed their isolated parts with mysterious unity, fell upon the syncopated accents with hair's-breadth precision. . . . As I listened to the musicians, watched them, I could think only of a flock of birds wheeling in the sky, turning with one accord, now this way, now that, and finally descending to the trees.[1]
>
> – Colin McPhee, 1944

Half a century after Debussy's famous encounter with Javanese *gamelan* at the 1889 Paris Exposition, Colin McPhee would decisively catapult the music of neighboring Bali into Western cultural consciousness. Like Debussy before him, the Canadian composer and musicologist saw something novel in the structures, textures, and rhythmic idioms of Balinese *gamelan*. Its "chief strength," McPhee argued, "is its rhythm."[2] He marveled at "highly syncopated passages which . . . upon analysis resolve themselves like mathematical problems" and admired cyclic rhythmic formulae "as yet undreamed of in our world."[3] The Balinese musical soundscape, seen through McPhee's filter, would become source material for a generation of composers from the West, perhaps most notably Benjamin Britten and Steve Reich.

Though their composition styles and priorities differed, each of these men was drawn to similar shades in the Balinese musical palette: textures and structures built from rhythmic complexity, repetition, and precision. But just as the lenses of early observers inescapably shaped conceptions of African music as something fundamentally rhythm-and-percussion-based, ignoring important aspects of melody, for instance,[4] the intellectual frames of these mid-twentieth-century composers cast a picture of Balinese rhythm that, while accurate in part, is also incomplete. As Tenzer observes, whenever Balinese *gamelan* is "reduced to something 'static and nonprogressive,' there is a regrettable ascendancy of convenience over complexity. It is not at all a matter of resisting these juggernauts," he continues, "but of understanding them."[5] This chapter, then, serves a dual purpose. On the one hand, through both Balinese and Western musical examples, it explores those ingenious aspects of Balinese rhythm that inspired McPhee, Britten, and Reich. On the other, it encourages deeper engagement with divergent rhythmic perceptions and priorities by highlighting certain fundamental features that they missed.

Setting the Scene

Just outside the temple gates, a string of hawkers sells grilled saté, peanuts, and suckling pig, while nearby, the fast cyclic melodies of the bamboo *gamelan joged* accompany a flirtatious dance. Passing into the first temple courtyard, I'm immediately enveloped by the bright bronze clangor of the *gamelan gong kebyar*, whose high energy, syncopated rhythms, and tight coordination give the twenty-five-piece ensemble of gongs and metallophones its name: *kebyar* – explosion. Thirty paces away, the members of a small *gamelan geguntangan* accompany a cast of singer-dancers in an *arja* theatrical performance, the intricate interlocking of drums and cycle-marking gongs driving the action beneath long ornamented melodies of voices and flutes. There are other ensembles in the next courtyard, of iron and wood and bamboo, singers and dancers and puppets, short trance-like cycles and slow winding melodies, each sounding independently yet in concert: a truly Ives-ian rhythmic experience.

Unraveling Balinese Rhythm: Cyclicity

An understanding of Balinese rhythm begins with an understanding of Balinese cyclicity. Not all Balinese music is cyclic to be sure. The flashy introductions of *gamelan gong kebyar* works are almost exclusively through-composed, as are diverse practices of sung poetry and much contemporary composition. The extended melodies of the classical instrumental form *lelambatan*, while cyclic, are often so long and elaborate they're unlikely to be perceived as such by the uninitiated listener. And while most *gamelan* works do contain cyclic melodies, their successions accumulate to large-scale forms conveying a sense of forward motion and change.

That said, most of the rhythmic features for which Balinese music is internationally celebrated are made possible through cyclic construction.

Whether the brisk 2-beat vamp of an *arja* fight scene or the slow 128-beat *pengawak* melody of a refined *legong* dance, much Balinese music is built to repeat without ending, the final note of one cycle melting into the first note of its repetition. Important moments in a cycle are punctuated by strokes on a collection of hanging gongs creating a hierarchy of more and less structurally significant tones in a melody. The final note of each cycle is generally marked by the largest hanging gong, often the low-voiced bronze *gong ageng*, or "great gong," while smaller gongs punctuate other important points, typically evenly distributed throughout the cycle.

A common 8-beat gong structure called *Bapang* uses the medium-sized *kempur* (often abbreviated "P") and small high-pitched *klentong* ("t") in a symmetric pattern with *gong ageng* ("G"). Together they create the cyclic structure (G) – P – t – P – G, while the horizontal gong *kempli* strikes a steady beat. A contrasting 8-beat structure called *Gilak* uses just the lower *gong ageng* and *kempur* in an unusual asymmetric pattern of (G) – – – G P – P G. Its dense second half gives *Gilak* the strong feeling that Balinese composers prefer for dance characters like warriors, for instance. Thus does rhythm create feeling – *rasa* – in Balinese music.

While mid-twentieth-century Western composers didn't show particular interest in or understanding of Balinese *rasa*, many were drawn to Balinese cyclic construction. In his opera *Death in Venice*, premiered in 1973, Benjamin Britten employed cyclic melodies and even mimicked cycle-marking gongs. An excerpt from the Act I, Scene 5 beach scene, shown in Example 15.1, sees the tamtam and double bass playing the role of *gong ageng*, demarcating a 9-beat cycle. The dry quarter-note strikes of the tuned drum and repetitive cello *pizzicato* act as *kempli* beat-keepers. Above these structure-marking instruments, the xylophone plays a zigzagging melody that repeats with variation every 9 beats, while the glockenspiel cycles a gently varied melody every 4 or 8 beats, in cross-rhythm to the cyclic structure.[6] Here and elsewhere, only the instruments discussed are transcribed.

Later in the same scene, Britten employs two tamtams of contrasting sizes as well as octave leaps in the cello, bass, and harp to outline a 9-beat cyclic structure with gongs of different pitches, similar in feel to *Gilak*.

Colin McPhee likewise made use of cyclic structures in his celebrated *gamelan*-inspired piece, *Tabuh-Tabuhan: Toccata for Orchestra and Two Pianos*, which premiered in Mexico in 1936. In Example 15.2, excerpted from Rehearsal F of the first movement, McPhee perfectly parallels a *Bapang* structure: low bass and cello *pizzicati* as well as octave Gs in Piano II function as *gong ageng*, while bowed cello and harp fill the role of the first *kempur* stroke. The high *klentong* at cycle's midpoint is marked by a higher chord in Piano II,

15.1 Cyclic structure in *Death in Venice*

doubled on viola, and the harp sounds the final *kempur*. Above these cycle markers, the flutes and clarinets perform an 8-beat call-and-response that, while not strictly cyclic, maintains some consistency of pitch and contour.

A Different Metric Conception: End-Weightedness

One of the most distinguishing features of Balinese cyclicity, yet that does not translate to these Western compositions, is "end-weightedness" – a system of metric organization where the stress is felt not at the beginning of each cycle but at its end. Instead of counting an 8-beat gong pattern with the strongest beat at the start (**1**-2-3-4-5-6-7-8-**1**), Balinese musicians feel the *gong ageng* at cycle's end (**8**-1-2-3-4-5-6-7-**8**). In the preceding discussion, the first "G" of each gong pattern appears in parentheses because it actually "belongs" to the previous cycle; *Bapang* is heard as (G) – P – t – P – G, not G – P – t – P – (G). While this may seem a mere semantic argument, the distinction between front-weighted and end-weighted meter is vital to an understanding of Balinese melodic and rhythmic construction. Melodies are composed to lead

15.2 Cyclic structure in *Tabuh-Tabuhan*

toward strong beats, their grouping structure boundaries ending rather than beginning at these points. Melodic contours and rhythmic patterns often feature increased levels of activity or motion leading up to a gong stroke with more stasis or stability in its wake. Known as *ngegongin*, "leading to the gong," this practice creates an underlying rhythm – somewhat akin to a harmonic rhythm – that densifies over the course of a cycle. End-weighted thinking can thus generate waves of stasis and motion, *ngubeng* and *majalan*, as cycles repeat again and again.[7] At a yet more foundational level, it dictates textural relationships among musical strands in a composition, resulting in a uniquely Balinese-style heterophony.

Heterophony and Stratified Polyphony

> The music, I learned, had its 'stem,' its primary tones . . . from which the melody expanded and developed as a plant grows out of a seed. The glittering ornamental parts which gave the music its shimmer, its sensuous charm, its movement – these were the 'flower parts,' the 'blossoms'.[8]
>
> – Colin McPhee, 1944

Like many traditions across Southeast Asia, most Balinese music could be considered heterophonic: different instruments or musical strands simultaneously perform a single melody, each in their own way. Yet, unlike the relatively un-systematized heterophony of much Indian or Arabic classical music, where diverse instrument idioms and personal improvisatory styles shape subtleties of timing and ornamentation, Southeast Asian heterophony is often highly systematized, characterized rather by differing rhythmic densities across an ensemble. Thus, it is perhaps more accurate to think of such music as *rhythmically stratified polyphony.*

"No voice in the *gamelan* is without its rhythmic function," McPhee wrote.[9] In the internationally renowned *gamelan gong kebyar*, the main melody is generally played by the 10-keyed metallophone *ugal*, whose player uses grace notes, note doublings, and the limited timing flexibility reserved for solo instruments to ornament a simple quarter-note rhythm. Loosely doubling the *ugal* may be a group of bamboo flutes – *suling* – playing the same melody with flexible timing, ornamentation, and pitch shading. A pair of 5-keyed metallophones called *calung* ("*cha-loong*") play a sparser abstraction of the melody compressed into a one-octave range. They track the *ugal*'s contour largely at the half-note density, aligning most importantly with the *gong ageng* at cycle's end. The *calung*'s spare melody is often called the *pokok* or "core melody" and, as we will see, forms the melodic basis for all other strands in the texture, acting as McPhee's "stem." At half or one quarter the density of the *calung*, and one octave lower, is a pair of metallophones called *jegogan*, playing the sparsest version of the melody at the whole (or double whole) note density. These various instruments comprises the second, fourth, and fifth staves in Example 15.3: a 16-beat melody from the dance piece *Oleg Tumulilingan*. Vertical pitch class convergences are circled, and the first note on each staff is parenthesized to indicate end-weightedness.

15.3 Balinese stratified polyphony

The middle staff in Example 15.3 begins to offer insight into the impact of end-weighted thinking on melody-making. A pair of metallophones one octave above the *calung*, and playing at twice their density, the *penyacah* derive their melody from the *calung*'s, anticipating each new *calung* arrival with the tone either directly above or directly below it in the *gong kebyar*'s 5-tone scale (here notated C♯-D-E-G♯-A).[10] Only beats 6–7 show the composer (or player) exercising increased artistic license, temporarily misaligning *penyacah* from *calung* to create a smoother contour in the *penyacah*'s melody. The top staff in Example 15.3 shows an elaborating melody played by an octet of metallophones called *gangsa*. These musicians, too, heterophonically track the *calung*'s tones at the half-note density, in this case filling in the other seven sixteenth notes in an idiomatic elaboration style called *norot*. Characterized by neighbor-note oscillation,[11] *norot* also reflects an end-weighted conception. The *gangsa*'s C♯-C♯-D-C♯ contour, for instance, anticipates the *calung*'s beat-4 C♯; this melodic segment ends on the beat with *calung*. The *gangsa*'s next segment is felt to begin on the weak second subdivision, leading to the following *calung* tone A through the same pitch anticipation technique.

Bali's stratified heterophonic polyphony influenced mid-twentieth-century Western composers in two key ways. First, the simple concept of heterophony allowed composers wishing to divorce themselves from the constraints of functional harmony a fresh organizing principle. Britten, for instance, had a "strong interest in the vertical conflation of linear material" and found kinship in Balinese music where "any 'harmonic' element is a by-product of, and directly related to, the melody."[12] In the orchestral Prelude to Act II of *Death in Venice*, an excerpt of which is shown in Example 15.4, Britten employs the timing flexibility of solo instruments like *ugal* and *suling* to create a close heterophonic texture in the strings, while sustained tones in bassoon, horn, and bass might be said to mimic various gongs.

Even more widespread, however, was the adoption of a rhythmically stratified polyphony. At times, Western composers employed this device without the vertical coincidence of common tones so central to Balinese stratification. In the Prologue to Britten's 1940 operetta *Paul Bunyan*, a simple E-F♯-G-F♯ contour is layered at varying densities: the piccolo cycles it at the sixteenth-note density, the oboe in triplets, the clarinets in eighths, the horns in quarter notes, the trombone in half notes, and so on. As Cooke observes: "There can be no doubt that the polyphonic stratification of this passage, in which rhythmic activity increases as the register rises, was influenced by Balinese music."[13] Somewhat truer

15.4 Flexible heterophony in *Death in Venice*

15.5 Stratified polyphony in *The Prince of the Pagodas*

to a Balinese conception of density stratification is the passage in Example 15.5, excerpted from Act III, Scene 2 of Britten's 1957 ballet *The Prince of the Pagodas*. Two gongs, a larger and a smaller, outline a cyclic structure doubled by Piano II, harp, and low strings (not shown here). Piano I, piccolo, and xylophone perform a stratified polyphonic melody, vertically aligning almost every eighth note and filling in the spaces in their own densities and idioms. The trombones play a more rhythmically diverse melody, only very occasionally stating the same pitch class as the other instruments. Here, Britten may be imitating the freer idioms of *ugal* and *suling*, but is as likely breaking from the Balinese palette altogether.

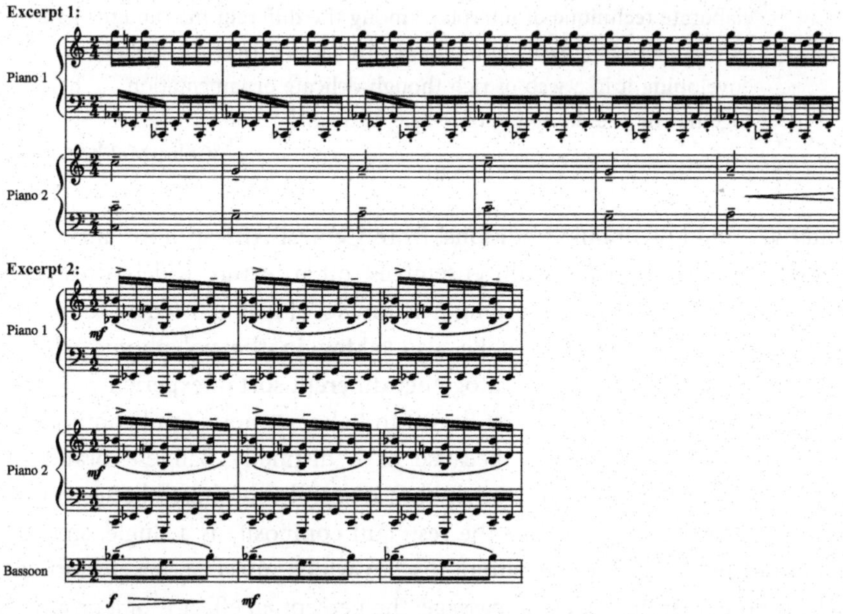

15.6. Stratified polyphony in *Tabuh-Tabuhan*

McPhee, too, used stratified polyphonies in his work. In the first excerpt from Example 15.6, Rehearsal M of *Tabuh-Tabuhan*'s opening movement, a 3-note core melody (*pokok*) in Piano II accompanies shifting sixteenth-note ostinati in Piano I. The ostinati's C-G-A♭ downbeats almost perfectly parallel the C-G-A♮ pitch collection of the *pokok*, allowing vertical alignment at the beginning of most measures. The second excerpt shows just the piano and bassoon parts from Rehearsal G of the piece's third movement, where vertical pitch class convergences outline a 3+3+2 rhythm.

The ostinati in both these excerpts likely grew out of what McPhee saw as the *gamelan*'s "blossoms": fast-moving melodic elaboration styles used on *gangsa* and other instruments. Their distinctive contours, and the playing styles that generate them, bring us to one of Bali's most idiosyncratic musical techniques: interlocking polyphony.

Interlocking Polyphonies

> The iridescent music of Nyoman's gamelan had its roots in a distant past, could be traced to the courts of ancient Java. . . . Successive generations of musicians had recreated it, transformed it, quickening the rhythms and modifying the instruments so that they rang with greater brilliance. An

> elaborate technique of interplay among the different instruments had slowly evolved, a weaving of voices around and over the melody, enveloping it in a web of rich though delicate ornamentation . . . held together by the discipline of long rehearsal.[14]
>
> – Colin McPhee, 1944

Interweaving polyphonic traditions, from Central African horn and vocal musics to West African drum ensembles, often feature widely divergent ranges in pitch and timbre among performers, allowing listeners to follow individual musical strands while also taking in the polyphonic whole. A Balinese performance is an altogether different sort of experience. Many non-Balinese musicians are first drawn to Balinese music (and continue to love and play it for years) because of a distinctly Balinese brand of interlocking, where a melody or rhythm is seamlessly shared between two or more performers such that the resultant composite is a single, smooth strand of music. One often cannot discern which musician has performed which note in an interlocking passage; the perceptual effect is of a group of musicians each playing the entire passage, in perfect synchrony, much faster than humanly possible. As a performer, the embodied experience of playing some notes of a melody while feeling as though one has played them all is equally exhilarating! Whether that melody is blindingly fast and flashy or slower and more subtly constructed, the act of meticulously fitting together jagged rhythmic puzzle pieces to form a perfectly smooth surface texture with one's musical partners is deeply satisfying. And while similar interlocking techniques exist in other Indonesian practices (the Central Javanese *saron*'s *imbal* technique, for instance), in Bali they dominate musical textures.

The 3+3+2 rhythmic patterns in Example 15.6 exemplify a familiar division of eight pulses in a duple metric framework that crosses cultures and continents. One of the most basic Balinese forms of this rhythmic device occurs in the vocal genre *kecak*, often called "the monkey chant" by Western observers due to its incorporation into a twentieth-century simian dramatization of the *Ramayana* Hindu epic. In it, a chorus of dozens or even hundreds of men chant the syllable "cak" ("*chak*") in a thick polyphony of syncopated ostinati, their short, dry shouts grounded by a vocalized *kempli* beat-keeper. Each simultaneous strand is built to rhythmically complement the others and their tight interlocking creates a steady, uninterrupted stream of notes. There are many different patterns in a *kecak* performer's toolkit. One of the most common is a group of three interlocking rhythms together known as *cak telu* ("three"), so named because each rhythmic strand contains three notes; *cak telu* performers chant 3+3+2 rhythms, each offset from his partners by a single pulse. The top left transcription of Figure 15.1 shows *cak telu*'s interlocking texture in end-weighted notation; on the right, the three individual rhythms are transcribed in Western notation, their different rotations circled.

A similar group of patterns is used in the interlocking crash cymbal (*ceng-ceng*) playing of the high-energy processional ensemble *gamelan beleganjur*. Here again, a stream of uninterrupted notes is created by three concurrent 3+3+2 rhythms in different metric rotations, performed against a beatkeeper as in the middle transcriptions in Figure 15.1. Called *kilitan telu*, the slightly denser rhythms of these interlocking patterns ensure no performer has two consecutive rests.[15]

Short, interlocking ostinati such as these were particularly compelling for Steve Reich, whose interest in minimalism favored "a dense, tactile, repetitive, and driving music."[16] As such, he was drawn to the layered polyphonies and "precise rhythmic blending of the ensemble"[17] that he found in Balinese music as well as in drumming practices from Ghana. The middle section of Reich's 1973 *Music for Pieces of Wood* is kin to the *telu* patterns just discussed.[18] The final transcriptions in Figure 15.1 show three adjacent rotations of a closely related 3+2+3 rhythm, played on claves in Reich's piece, with one additional player keeping a steady beat. While the 3+3+2 rhythmic trope is widely used, "phasing [it] to interlock with an audible regulating pulse as Reich does nevertheless points to Kecak [and *kilitan telu*] in its specific arrangement."[19] It seems particularly noteworthy that, while *kilitan telu* patterns fill in extra notes just before the main 3+3+2 onsets, Reich fills in the notes directly following them. I see this as a perfect reflection of end-weighted versus front-weighted metric thinking, with the extra *kilitan telu* notes leading *to* strong onsets in the 3+3+2 construction while, in Reich, they lead *away from* them.

Balinese *melodic* interlocking generally requires two musicians rather than three (though sometimes four are needed), but the principle remains the same: multiple strands of syncopated patterns, frequently rhythmic rotations of one another, together create an uninterrupted melody that can be played very quickly if necessary. Often generically termed *kotekan*, meaning "interlocking parts," this Balinese approach to melody-making comes in a variety of techniques. In each two-person technique, a pair of musicians playing the same instrument type – two *gangsa* metallophones, for instance – shares a melody between them through carefully prescribed roles and rhythmic formulae. One musician in an interlocking pair is the *polos*, "basic" player, whose pattern generally falls more "on the beat" and

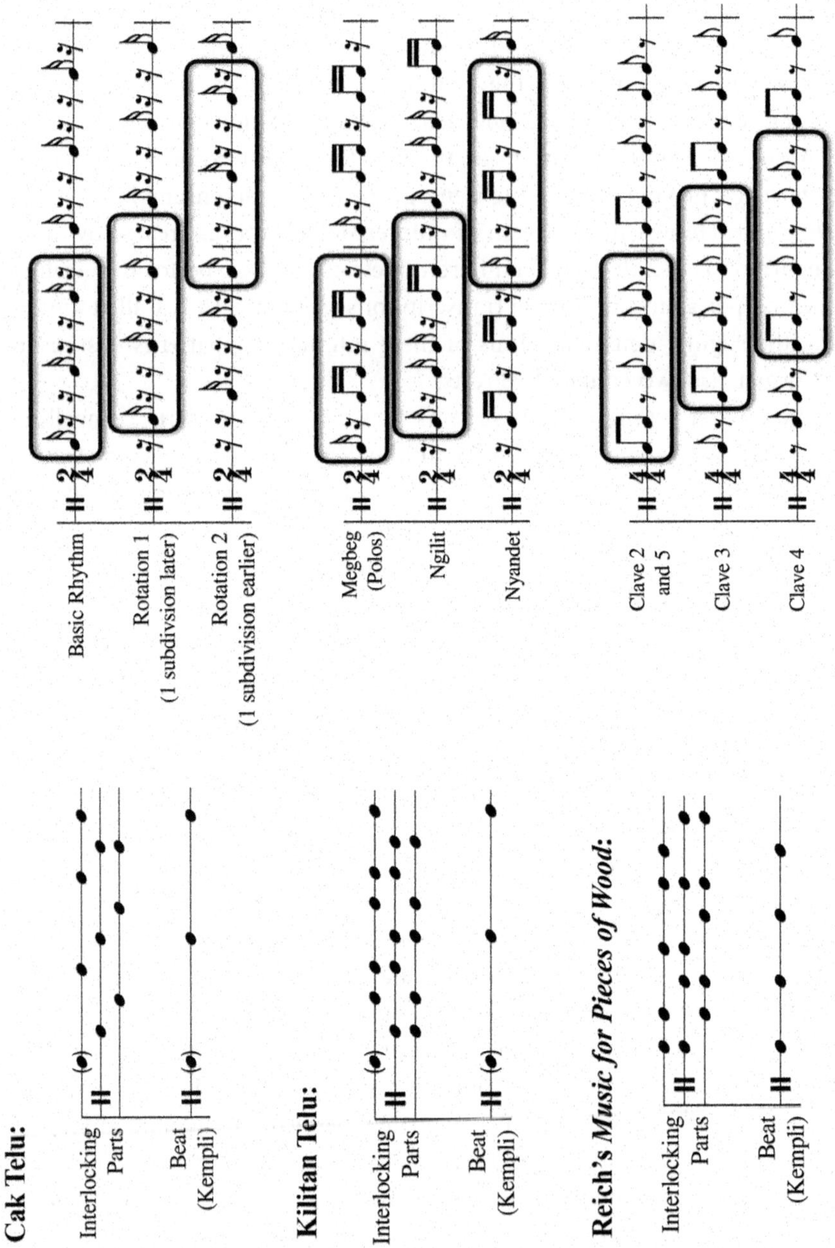

15.1 3+3+2 rhythms in polyphony

15.7 Interlocking *gangsa norot*

whose pitches more closely track the slow *pokok* core melody; her partner, the *sangsih* or "complementary" player, performs a related rhythm, often with more off-beat onsets.

When the *gangsa*'s *norot* melody from the top staff of Example 15.3 is played sufficiently fast, no one player is capable of performing it alone. The melody is then divided between *polos* and *sangsih* partners per Example 15.7.[20]

Here again, interlocking partners play identical rhythms offset by one subdivision. The *polos*, notated stems down, strikes mostly on the beat and sounds just the core melody's tones; the *sangsih* plays largely off the beat and often strikes non-core melody upper-neighbor tones. Each note sounds in at least one of the two strands, resulting in an uninterrupted stream of onsets. Pairs of Balinese hand-drums play comparable interlocking patterns of bass strokes, slap strokes, and various ringing strokes, which find partial reflection in the alternating pitch ranges of Britten's xylophone melody from Example 15.1.

Related to the 3+3+2 rhythms of *kecak* and *kilitan telu* are two styles of melodic elaboration frequently referenced by McPhee. In both, elaborating instruments like *gangsa* anticipate the arrival of new *pokok* core melody tones through repeated three-note ascending or descending gestures at the sixteenth-note density, and here the impact of end-weightedness on grouping structure is particularly salient. If "x" is the current *pokok* tone (irrelevant to the contour of these elaborations), and "1" the upcoming tone (very relevant in this end-weighted music), *gangsa* players in these figuration styles approach a note in a descending *pokok* line with descending contours: (x)-2-1-3-2-1-3-2-**1**; they likewise anticipate a *pokok* tone in an ascending passage (in this case tone 3) with ascending contours: (x)-2-3-1-2-3-1-2-**3**. Both these are considered *majalan*, "kinetic" or "moving" contours. When the *pokok* tone repeats – what Balinese musicians call *ngubeng* or "static" – composers have many more contour options.[21]

There are two quite distinct versions of this three-note elaborating process. In *ubit telu* ("three"), when partners interlock, both *polos* and *sangsih* play the middle of the three tones. *Polos* also plays the upcoming *pokok* tone, either higher or lower depending on the current *pokok* contour,

15.8 Interlocking *ubit telu*

and *sangsih* plays the non-*pokok* tone. Two *majalan* contours – ascending and descending – and two *ngubeng* options for *ubit telu* are shown in Example 15.8. The top staff shows the basic contour; in the second, the two voices are divided, with *polos* notated stems down. The bottom two staves of the example show eight beats of *ubit telu* for a core melody combining motion with stasis.[22] As in *norot* figuration, the melodic idiom itself generates pairs of interlocking rhythms that are identical (or similar) but metrically offset, together creating an uninterrupted stream of notes.

Comparing these contours to McPhee's from the second excerpt in Example 15.6 again draws into sharp relief the distinction between front- and end-weighted metric conception. In *ubit telu*, the 2+3+3 rhythm beginning just after the beat leads the melody smoothly to the following downbeat; in McPhee's writing, a 3+3+2 rhythm starting on the downbeat simply repeats on the next downbeat, without the sense of arrival that end-weighted *ubit telu* engenders.

While *polos* and *sangsih* share the middle of three tones in *ubit telu*, in *ubit empat* ("four"), which is otherwise identically constructed, a higher fourth tone is added instead, always coinciding with the lowest and thus generating an irregular accent pattern. Because minimizing motion across the instrument is prioritized in *ubit empat*, *polos* and *sangsih* interchangeably align with the core melody for this technique. This necessitates a much more varied rhythmic palette for each individual player than does *ubit telu*. Four possible *ubit empat* patterns are notated in the top two staves of Example 15.9; the bottom two staves show *ubit empat* for the first eight beats of a melody from the dance piece *Teruna Jaya*.

The snaking contours and shifting rhythmic accents of *ubit empat* are reflected in the top excerpt from Example 15.6, where McPhee alternates between a 2+3+3 and 3+3+2 accent scheme using virtually identical

15.9 Interlocking *ubit empat*

15.10 Interlocking in *Six Pianos* (top four voices)

contours and pitch collections to the *empat* patterns in Example 15.9. Reich uses a similar technique in his 1973 piece *Six Pianos*, where various rotations of a low-middle-high collection of tones seem to mirror *ubit empat* construction, and alternating right and left hands loosely parallel *polos* and *sangsih* interlocking, per Example 15.10.[23]

The preceding examples show composers largely referencing the composite contours of Balinese interlocking melodies, with only Reich taking advantage of the syncopated rhythms of their individual strands. Because Balinese interlocking is designed to result in a seamless composite, it's not surprising that contour, for these composers, was often more central to the aesthetic than the rhythmic makeup of individual parts. That said, McPhee did sometimes reference discrete *polos* and *sangsih* rhythms in his compositions. Example 15.11 shows an excerpt from *Tabuh-Tabuhan* where two flutes (doubled on clarinet and violin) play an interlocking passage of syncopated rhythms with every sixteenth-note subdivision filled. Other instruments not notated here play at slower densities of eighth, quarter, half, and whole notes, together creating a full stratified polyphony.

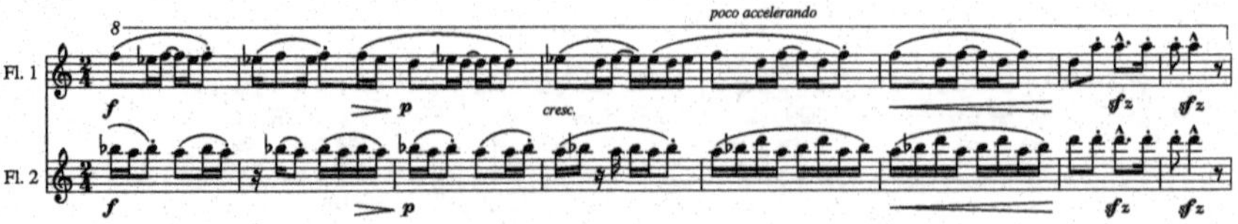

15.11 Interlocking in *Tabuh-Tabuhan*

Complicating the Picture: Balinese Linearity and Malleability

While each of these composers drew inspiration from Balinese stratified and interlocking polyphonies, their music is only a partial reflection of Balinese rhythmic aesthetics, because they were not focused on Balinese feeling, *rasa*. Each broke Bali's rhythmic idioms into two- and four-beat cells of music to be repeated, manipulated, and repeated once more, bypassing the circuitous melodies and expansive structures that make up of so many of Bali's greatest compositions. It is telling that, when played Reich's 1971 composition *Drumming*, the famous Balinese musician Wayan Tembres "smiled and listened politely to part 1 but was unmoved and at last asked: 'Is that all it does? Doesn't it *go* anywhere?'"[24] For Reich, repeating a "static or slowly evolving cyclic pattern at a steady tempo" was "designed to focus listener attention on compositional process. This led him to draw from [Ghanaian] Ewe and Balinese music as though they were canvases of patterns unfolding on neatly ruled tempo grids stretching to infinity."[25] On paper his approach, like Britten's and McPhee's, may seem Balinese; in reality, Balinese rhythm is far more malleable and unpredictable.

Music in Bali *is* very often cyclic, based on formulaic ostinati. Yet within that system, and guiding it, are deep-seated principles of forward motion, variety, and change. The complex, virtuosic patterns of *gong kebyar* introductions, where an ensemble-wide rhythmic unison of fast, unmetered passages embodies the genre's characteristic "explosive" aesthetic, are entirely through-composed. Yet we don't even need to go that far to find a Balinese practice more developed and varied than Britten, McPhee, and Reich present. A *pokok* will as often be a carefully shaped 16-, 64-, or 256-beat melody as a 2- or 4-beat one, and each section in a composition will be linked to the next with contrasting introductory, transitional, and concluding material. Formal organization, then, often centers on progression, not repetition. In *ubit telu* and *norot*, as we've seen, melodic contours move across the instrument as they follow the *pokok*, different for static and kinetic moments; in *ubit empat*, melodic motion in the *pokok* requires ever-shifting shades of 3+2+3 and 2+3+3, ascending and descending, with now *polos* and now *sangsih* on the beat. What's more, each internally cyclic melody is varied through both subtle and extreme shifts in tempo, dynamics, and melodic elaboration to create a forward-directed listening experience. This "temporal and gestural flexibility . . . is obscured once captured within Western staff notation,"[26] reducing a dynamic temporal experience to strict repetition.

In performance, the *Oleg Tumuliligan* melody from Example 15.3 cycles twenty-seven times with virtually no repetition among them.[27] The composition alternates between a higher and lower *pokok*, and transitional high-to-low and low-to-high versions; it moves among different elaboration techniques on the *gangsa* in different cycles; and it features extreme tempo changes that see players shifting between breakneck interlocking polyphonies and slow, languorous figuration where *polos* and *sangsih* perform in parallel contours rather than interlocking parts. On top of that are starts and stops, short inserted *ugal* solos, and accented rhythmic breaks. Such devices are central to Balinese *gamelan* performance. A cyclic melody will frequently be interrupted by an *angsel*: an increase in volume leading to a brief syncopated rhythmic pattern and followed by a sudden stop, similar to the end of McPhee's passage in Example 15.11. This approach to cyclicity shapes waves – *ombak* – of volume and intensity shifts in even the most insistently repetitive passage. More variable and dynamic still are the *ocak-ocakan* rhythms of the *reyong* gong-chime, an elaborating instrument that shifts between melodic and rhythmic roles, alternating interlocking polyphonies with tightly coordinated shots of cluster chords and rhythmic accents. Britten was particularly drawn to these syncopated tone clusters, using them, for instance, to represent the Prince-as-Salamander character in *The Prince of the Pagodas*.[28]

While a Balinese composition may look repetitive on paper, then, experientially it is anything but. Each of these elements brings variability and goal-oriented motion to Balinese music, obvious even to the unseasoned listener. Many expert listeners, though, find their greatest joy in the yet subtler manipulations of collective Balinese improvisation. The works and words of mid-twentieth-century composers cast Bali as a culture of precision and repetition, fostering music that was virtuosic and complex but allowed performing Balinese minimal agency in its creation. Reich unequivocally claimed that "Balinese mallet playing is composed and allows no improvisation."[29] Of course, as Tenzer argues, "improvisation was not Reich's interest. . . . He was not predisposed to envision how improvisation could be integrated into a collectivity, or ponder the possibility that it is not only in 'microvariations' that ensemble musicians 'give life to the music.'"[30] McPhee did acknowledge restricted improvisation on certain instruments, as in the flexible timing and ornamentation of the *ugal* and *suling*, and composers like Britten took advantage of that aesthetic as we saw in Example 15.4. Tadzio's theme in *Death in Venice*, too, has a rhythmic freedom that mimics the Balinese solo instrument *trompong*.[31] But McPhee also maintained that "other than in solo parts there can be no place for spontaneous improvisation [in Balinese music. . . .] Unison in the different parts must prevail or utter confusion results."[32]

These and other Western composers, musicians, and thinkers missed what, to many Balinese, makes their music come alive: the constantly shifting hues of four *reyong* players twisting in and around the *norot* contour, making flexible what on *gangsa* is utterly formulaic; the two drummers of an *arja* theatrical performance simultaneously improvising fast patterns of low bass and high ringing strokes, interlocking with the perfect imperfection that only decades of partnership can bring; the solo drummer stretching her idiom, inventing new patterns in response to a dancer's movements.[33] All this, too, is essential to Balinese rhythm: unpredictable, flexible, creative, constantly evolving. True linearity within cyclicity.

Embracing the Contradictions

Every perspective, Tenzer notes of intercultural fusion and hybrid composition, "is a betrayal of some other perspective."[34] One might wonder whether McPhee, Britten, and Reich, in imitating Balinese rhythm, actually overlooked its most crucial qualities. Improvisation, flexibility, end-weighted thinking, and linear aspects of structure, tempo, dynamics, and figuration are, after all, truly fundamental features. Yet, artistically speaking, these composers never hoped to express themselves in a "Balinese" way; faithful imitation never was the point. Their mishearings instead suggested new creative options, much as Bix Beiderbecke's self-taught fingerings, while technically "wrong," facilitated the jazz trumpeter's innovative musical style.[35] Unlike composer and Bali scholar Michael Tenzer in his 2003 *gamelan* composition *Puser Belah*, or Evan Ziporyn a decade before in his fusion work *Aneh Tapi Nyata*,[36] earlier composers like McPhee weren't looking to problematize tensions between contrasting systems. Rather, they worked like Balinese experimentalist composer Dewa Ketut Alit, who unapologetically draws inspiration from John Adams and György Ligeti, Michael Tenzer and various modern jazz performers, taking their diverse styles wherever his sensibilities lead him.[37] Alit's recent forays into Western idioms, from his chamber works *Ameriki* (2018) and *Simalakama* (2019) to his *Open My Door* (2015) for orchestra, likewise borrow from Western techniques in a piecemeal way, turning the tables to reveal an analogous internationalizing process, but in an opposite direction.[38]

Of course, colonial history and power dynamics necessarily complicate this picture, and we should be wary of too blithely comparing the two perspectives. Western musicians, producers, and listeners have a long history of "put[ting our] Others in (small) boxes"[39] – presuming to delineate "authenticity" for our non-Western counterparts, and to expect it from them, while simultaneously seeing their musics as "a kind of natural resource that is available for the taking."[40] This ideological imbalance reinforces stereotypes shaped by Western discourses, often denying musicians from the Global South the agency to define themselves and their musics – and, by extension, the freedom to truly experiment – but giving Western musicians compositional carte blanche.[41] It may now be incumbent upon non-Balinese composers drawing from Balinese techniques to work toward decolonizing that exchange.[42] There is still plenty of space within such deliberate interactions for radical acts of imagination. Of the inherent tension between tradition and experimentalism, Alit opines: "I think . . . I need both. You need both. . . . It's both good because, for me it gives us inspiration. So traditional thing is good because it's strong root. But new is good because it gives you the future."[43] As Lou Harrison once said of the compositional process, the best results come from "just playing in the sandbox."[44] It was in this creative spirit that Bali's cyclic melodies, specially stratified heterophonies, and rich interlocking polyphonies motivated new approaches to formal structure, vertical relationships, and rhythm for McPhee and his musical descendants. Each borrowed just the things he needed to "create a music based on his fantasies."[45]

Hybrid compositions, Pete Steele argues, "confound simplistic binary relationships, and forge an indeterminate 'third space'"[46] where creative agency balances artistic borrowing. At its worst, such a space embraces only the tropes, reinforcing stereotypes, perpetuating musical and cultural misrepresentations, and ultimately, as Lipsitz warns, "creat[ing] new sources of misunderstanding, misreading, and misappropriation."[47] At its best, though, Steele contends this third space could "embody the gradual destabilization of European and North American hegemony, and serve as [an] exemplary symbo[l] of a more integrated post-colonial world."[48] It may be that McPhee, Reich, and Britten's adoption and creative reinterpretations of Balinese rhythm amount to appropriation, at least by twenty-first-century standards. Unlike Tenzer and Ziporyn, these earlier composers never truly sought to steep themselves in Balinese culture, nor to consciously engage with the experiences of Balinese musicians, yet nevertheless felt entitled to borrow from them without reservation. The act of borrowing, though, came from a place of honest appreciation, curiosity, and respect; their work initiated an exchange, setting the stage for future generations to go deeper. And "without minimizing the very real dangers of cross-cultural appropriations and misunderstandings," as Lipsitz contends, "we must nonetheless be open to the kinds of knowing hidden within some 'incorrect' perceptions."[49] Walking a tightrope between Western and Balinese perspectives, Colin McPhee, Benjamin Britten, and Steve Reich did what innovators have always done: they took elements from disparate ideas and modes of perception and, through their fusion, arrived somewhere new. For them, as for Alit, Tenzer, Ziporyn, and many others, the fusion of Balinese and Western musical elements was and is, unabashedly and experimentally, about embracing the complexity of the encounter and leaping into the sandbox with both feet.

Endnotes

1 C. McPhee, *A House in Bali* (Hong Kong: Periplus, 2002), 40–41.

2 C. McPhee, "The Absolute Music of Bali" *Modern Music*, 12 (1935), 166.

3 McPhee, "Absolute Music," 168.

4 See K. Agawu, *Representing African Music: Postcolonial Notes, Queries, Positions* (New York: Routledge, 2003).

5 M. Tenzer, *Gamelan Gong Kebyar: The Art of Twentieth-Century Balinese Music* (University of Chicago Press, 2000), 434.

6 While 9-beat and misaligned cycles are not traditional, contemporary Balinese composers do employ such techniques.

7 On *ngegongin* in melodic construction, see Tenzer, *Gamelan*, Chapter 5. On rhythmic construction, see L. Tilley, "*Kendang Arja:* The Transmission, Diffusion, and Transformation(s) of an Improvised Balinese Drumming Style" (Ph. D. dissertation, University of British Columbia, 2013), 138–43, 250–62, and Tilley, *Making It Up Together: The Art of Collective Improvisation in Balinese Music and Beyond* (University of Chicago Press, 2019), Chapters 5 and 6.

8 McPhee, *House*, 43–4.

9 McPhee, "Absolute Music," 166.

10 Note, though, that tuning is not standardized.

11 Britten mimics such neighbor-note oscillations throughout his ballet *The Prince of the Pagodas*.

12 M. Cooke, *Britten and the Far East: Asian Influences in the Music of Benjamin Britten* (Woodbridge: The Boydell Press, 1998), 39 and 41.

13 Ibid., 42. That Britten, throughout his career, often used such "exotic" musical references to signal supernatural characters or events – in this case, a blue moon – is a testament to the latent Orientalism of the time.
14 McPhee, *House*, 42.
15 See M. Bakan, *Music of Death and New Creation: Experiences in the World of Balinese Gamelan Beleganjur* (University of Chicago Press, 1999), 66–8. Note that the sparser *cak telu* may also be used in *beleganjur*.
16 M. Tenzer, "That's All It Does: Steve Reich and Balinese Gamelan," in S. Gopinath and P. ap Siôn (eds.), *Rethinking Reich* (Oxford University Press, 2019), 309.
17 S. Reich, "Postscript to a Brief Study of Balinese and African Music, 1973," in *Writings from 1965–2000* (Oxford University Press, 2002), 69–71.
18 See Tenzer, "That's All," 310–12.
19 Ibid., 312.
20 Note that speed is not the only reason to divide into interlocking parts, and such patterns are often used in slow passages to equally satisfying effect.
21 See Tenzer, *Gamelan*, 220–31.
22 For more examples, see W. Vitale, "*Kotekan*: The Technique of Interlocking Parts in Balinese Music," *Balungan*, 4 (1990), 2–15.
23 Though Reich may not have known the details of *empat* technique, the parallels indicate a shared, and likely borrowed, rhythmic aesthetic.
24 Tenzer, "That's All," 316.
25 Ibid., 307.
26 A. C. McGraw, "Different Temporalities: The Time of Balinese Music," *Yearbook for Traditional Music*, 40 (2008), 136.
27 See M. Tenzer, "*Oleg Tumulilingan*: Layers of Time and Melody in Balinese Music," in M. Tenzer (ed.), *Analytical Studies in World Music* (Oxford University Press, 2006), 205–36.
28 D. Mitchell, "Catching on to the Technique in Pagoda-Land," *Tempo*, 146 (1983), 22–4. Britten also drew inspiration from *kebyar* rhythms (see Cooke, *Britten*).
29 Reich, "Postscript," 69.
30 Tenzer, "That's All," 307.
31 Cooke, *Britten*, 237–9.
32 C. McPhee, *Music in Bali: A Study in Form and Instrumental Organization in Balinese Orchestral Music* (Yale University Press, 1966), xvii.
33 On improvised drumming in *arja*, see Tilley, "*Kendang Arja*" and Tilley, *Making It Up Together*, Chapters 5 and 6. On *norot* for *reyong*, see Tilley, *Making It Up Together*, Chapters 2 and 3 and Tilley, "*Reyong Norot* Figuration: An Exploration into the Inherent Musical Techniques of Bali" (master's thesis, University of British Columbia, 2003). On solo drumming, see Tenzer, *Gamelan*, 288–304, and I. W. Sudirana, "*Kendang Tunggal*: Balinese Solo Drumming Improvisation" (master's thesis, University of British Columbia, 2009).

34 M. Tenzer, "One Fusion among Many: Merging Bali, India, and the West through Modernism," *Circuit*, 21 (2011), 79.
35 See G. Lipsitz, *Dangerous Crossroads: Popular Music, Postmodernism and the Poetics of Place* (London: Verso 1994), 165–6.
36 See Tenzer, "One Fusion," and P. Steele, "Split Centers: Gamelan Fusion Post-Multiculturalism," *Perspectives of New Music*, 53.1 (2015), 189–217.
37 Interview September 19, 2017. On the contemporary composition scene in Bali, see A. C. McGraw, *Radical Traditions: Reimagining Culture in Contemporary Balinese Music* (Oxford University Press, 2013).
38 Ida Bagus Madé Widnyana's repurposing of well-known Christmas carols into unusually end-weighted core melodies for interlocking polyphonies shows such selective borrowing in compositions for *gamelan* instruments.
39 T. Taylor, *Music and Capitalism: A History of the Present* (University of Chicago Press, 2016), 93.
40 Ibid., 99. Profit – both financial and social – further complicate this relationship, frequently privileging Western over non-Western participants.
41 That a white, Canadian ethnomusicologist is writing this chapter on Balinese rhythm is perhaps equally problematic. See Taylor, *Music and Capitalism*, on this power imbalance in the "world music" industry.
42 On this effort in music education, see J. Hess, "Decolonizing Music Education: Moving beyond Tokenism," *International Journal of Music Education*, 33 (2015), 336–47.
43 Interview September 19, 2017. My conversations with other Balinese composers and musicians over many years often likewise revealed comfort, satisfaction, and even pride with composers – both in and out of Bali – "playing" with Balinese musical concepts and techniques. That said, not all musicians feel the same way, and composers wishing to borrow across cultures should consider each music culture sensitively and on its own terms.
44 In conversation with graduate students in composition. (Interview with M. Tenzer, September 19, 2017.)
45 Tenzer, "One Fusion," 78.
46 Steele, "Split Centers," 190. On the "third space," see H. Bhabha, *The Location of Culture* (New York: Routledge, 1994).
47 Lipsitz, *Dangerous Crossroads*, 161.
48 Steele, "Split Centers," 190. Steele goes on, however, to reference Tenzer's *Puser Belah*, a piece that "highlights the destructive potential of fusion to further reify polarized notions of cultural difference [. . . and leads to] questions [of] whether truly transcendental fusions can even take place."
49 Lipsitz, *Dangerous Crossroads*, 162.

16 Rhythmic Structures in Latin American and Caribbean Music

PETER MANUEL

For the last century, probably no region has contributed more rhythmic vitality to the global soundscape than Latin America and the Caribbean. More than any other musical element, it has been the uniquely compelling rhythms that have driven the early twentieth-century Parisian vogue of the tango, the transnational spread of salsa and Cuban dance music, and the current global appeal of Jamaican reggae and dance hall. Much of this rhythmic dynamism is a product of the development of syncretic idioms drawing from African as well as European roots. This ongoing and endlessly creative process has generated a great variety of rhythmic styles, and is supplemented by other vital music genres, such as northern Mexican *conjunto* music and Trinidadian tassa drumming, that owe little or nothing to African influence.

Despite the tremendous diversity of the hemisphere's rhythms, many of them, and the music genres associated with them, can be grouped into a few major categories. In this chapter, rather than attempting to provide a comprehensive survey of all these genres, we outline this set of major categories and suggest how each of them is animated by a few distinctive rhythmic generative principles and approaches. The particular categories are (1) neo-African genres, (2) creole $\frac{6}{8}$–$\frac{3}{4}$ hemiola-based genres, (3) urban binary genres, including what we call the "habanera complex" and Latin (Afro-Cuban-based popular dance) music, and lastly, (4) a heterogeneous but still significant grab bag of "miscellaneous" genres.

Neo-African Genres

Most of the best-known Latin American and Caribbean music genres, such as salsa, reggae, and reggaeton, are products of a syncretic process in which musical elements derived from Africa and Europe were creatively combined and reworked over generations, or even centuries, to produce distinctively new entities. However, some of the region's most powerful and rhythmically rich musics are much closer to the African idioms brought by the several millions of slaves transported to the Americas from the early

1500s to the 1870s. Such genres that survive today are best seen as neo-African rather than African per se, in the sense that they have changed and evolved since taking root in the Americas, but along overwhelmingly African-derived aesthetic lines, without any overt European influence or inspiration.

Such musical traditions are to be found primarily in association with African-derived religions, especially since religious musics often tend to be conservative and practitioners are likely to assert the importance of maintaining ancestral continuity. For various reasons, such music genres and their associated religions are strongest in Cuba and Brazil. Spanish and Brazilian colonists, unlike their British counterparts in North America, allowed significant numbers of slaves to purchase or otherwise gain their freedom (in a process called "manumission"), such that they and their descendants could form urban societies (in Cuba: *cabildos*) where they were able to perpetuate, in however modified forms, their African-derived religions and associated songs and dances. Even more important to the survival of these traditions was the fact that the importation of enslaved Africans to Cuba and Brazil continued and even intensified in the 1800s, lasting until the 1870s, unlike in the United States and British colonies, where most slaves were brought in the 1700s. Hence, many black Cubans and Brazilians know the ethnic ancestry of their forebears, and several Afro-Cuban religious songs are still sung across the Atlantic in Nigeria and elsewhere in West Africa.

Perhaps the richest and most vigorous traditions of neo-African drumming are those associated with the Afro-Cuban religion known as Santería, or more properly, *Regla de ocha*. Santería is a sort of streamlined consolidation of Yoruba-derived practices and beliefs, centering on lively ceremonies in which music – especially call-and-response songs accompanied by a trio of *batá* drums – plays a central role, often inducing spirit possession by devotees. For somewhat more festive ceremonies called *bembé*, a set of two or three conga-shaped drums (*cachimbo*, *mula*, and *caja*) are used, together with a cowbell.

Many *batá* and *bembé* rhythms are based on a feature common in much Western and Central African music, namely, polyrhythm, meaning a composite rhythm with two (or possibly more) basic pulses occurring at once. This quintessentially takes the form of a twelve-beat ostinato, with a cowbell providing a syncopated seven-stroke "time-line," while other percussion parts divide the cycle into groups of twos and threes. In several cases, it may be the vocal line and/or the dance moves – typically involving stepping in twos or threes – which set up or reinforce polyrhythms in the vocal and drummed parts. Example 16.1 shows a common *bembé* rhythm, consisting of an ostinato in which the bell plays the standard West African time-line, the high-pitched *cachimbo* plays a rhythm essentially in threes (as in $\genfrac{}{}{0pt}{}{6}{8}$ or $\genfrac{}{}{0pt}{}{12}{8}$), while the mid-pitched *mula* drum pattern is in twos (suggesting $\genfrac{}{}{0pt}{}{6}{4}$).[1] Over this basic polyrhythm, a lead drummer, playing a conga-like drum with a stick in one hand and the bare palm of his other, improvises freely, often alternating between patterns that suggest either the $\genfrac{}{}{0pt}{}{6}{4}$ or $\genfrac{}{}{0pt}{}{6}{8}$ feel.

Aside from Afro-Cuban religious music and dance, such polyrhythms are common in Haitian Vodou drumming, including such basic dance rhythms as *yanvalou.* They are also found in the music of *candomblé,* the Yoruba-derived religion that thrives today in Brazil. In general, the $\genfrac{}{}{0pt}{}{12}{8}$ polyrhythms are most prominent in genres that remain strongly African in character, are associated with African-derived religions, and are typically performed by ensembles of percussion instruments with singing, usually without any melodic instruments such as guitar.

A broader category of percussion-dominated neo-African genres, and especially those that may be associated with secular entertainment dance rather than religion, use predominantly duple meters, which could be notated in $\genfrac{}{}{0pt}{}{4}{4}$ or cut time. In the Caribbean, as well as elsewhere, some of these rhythms, as shown in Example 16.2, are based on particular cells, such as those which, adapting Cuban terminology, could be referred to as

16.1 Polyrhythmic *bembé* ostinato

16.2 Rhythmic cells: *tresillo*, habanera, *cinquillo*, amphibrach, *clave* (3+2 and 2+3)

the *tresillo* (pronounced "tray-see-yo," three-three-two), the "habanera" rhythm (whose related incarnations will be discussed further below), the *cinquillo* ("seen-key-o," a sort of decorated version of the *tresillo*), and the "amphibrach," which could be seen as a displaced version of the *cinquillo*, and/or a slightly elaborated version of the habanera cell.

Thus, for example, in the Afro-Puerto Rican *bomba* genre, in which an individual dances in front of a trio of drummers, while others sing call-and-response songs, the *belén* rhythm is based on the habanera pattern, the *sicá* and *bambulé* are based on the *tresillo*, and the *gracimá* is based on the amphibrach. These patterns also abound in various other predominantly duple-metered Afro-Caribbean genres, such as Jamaican *kumina* drumming, Trinidadian Orisha (or Shango) music (derived, like Santería, from Yoruba roots), Dominican *palo* drumming (which may be either secular or religious in context), and the entertainment-oriented *belé* and *gwo ka* of Martinique and Guadeloupe, respectively.

Another particularly important pattern in "Latin" music – which connotes Afro-Cuban music and its various forms, derivatives, and relatives – is *clave* (clah-vey). In Spanish, *clave* means "key" in a metaphorical sense, as in the key that unlocks a rhythm, but as a musical term it derives more directly from the hard-wooden pegs called *clavija* that could be used in building ships, or to beat the pattern when dockworkers were having informal rumba sessions. *Clave*, as shown in Example 16.2, is usually understood as implying a two-bar pattern of $\frac{4}{4}$ in either "three-two" or "two-three" form, with the "three" side being relatively syncopated and the "two" side not. (The rhythmic jingle "SHAVE and A hairCUT – TWO BITS" coheres nicely with three-two *clave*.)

In some Afro-Cuban music (as in that associated with the *abakuá* brotherhoods), the $\frac{12}{8}$ standard time-line shown in Example 16.1 is often "abbreviated" by omission of the third and final bell strokes, affording a five-stroke "two-three" configuration which itself is referred to as *clave*, and can be seen as a generative source for the familiar $\frac{4}{4}$ *clave* of rumba and popular music.

The $\frac{4}{4}$ *clave* pattern seems to have arisen in connection with Afro-Cuban rumba (and was notated as such in an 1850 composition by Louis Moreau Gottschalk). While the term *rumba* has been loosely used to denote various creole Cuban and Latin genres, properly speaking it refers to an Afro-Cuban dance-music genre in which three conga drums (or *cajón* boxes), a pair of hardwood *clave* sticks, and two other lighter sticks (*palitos*, tapped on some surface, such as the side of a conga) accompany singing and dancing, either by a couple, or else, in the case of *colombia*, by a solo male.

16.3 Rumba *montuno* "Consuélate"

The most common rumba subgenre is the *guaguancó* (wah-wahn-CO), whose basic ostinato, with a typical vocal refrain, is schematized in Example 16.3. (Note that in rumba, the final stroke of the "three" side falls an eighth note later than in the more familiar *son clave.*)

Over this basic pattern, a solo conga (or *quinto*) drummer provides lively improvisations, while the singing takes a two-part form, consisting of an initial section of verses sung by a solo vocalist, followed by a *montuno* section of call-and-response singing, during which dancing occurs. The pre-composed choral response (*coro*) coheres with the *clave* pattern, such that a singer or *clave* player who renders it reversed will generate a jumbled-sounding "crossed" (*cruzado*) effect and inspire glares, scowls, and eye-rolling among the other musicians and knowledgeable listeners. Example 16.3 shows the *coro* of a familiar rumba ("Consuélate"), with *clave* (in this case, three-two, with the phrase emphasis beginning on the second measure shown), a very schematic rendering of the two-conga ostinato, and the pattern of the *palitos.* Note how the main accents in the *coro* coincide with the *clave* strokes.

While we will return to *clave* in discussing *son* and salsa, at this point it is relevant to point out another common feature of duple-metered neo-African and related creole rhythms. Genres like the *guaguancó* and the aforementioned *bomba* styles, being essentially in $\frac{4}{4}$, do not feature classic $\frac{12}{8}$ polyrhythms built into their basic structure. However, the improvisations played by lead drummers (as in rumba) often include syncopated passages that can be seen as temporary introductions of polyrhythms. The most common techniques of achieving this effect involve what could be seen as ternary phrasing of binary beat subdivisions or, conversely, binary phrasing of triplet subdivisions. Example 16.4 shows some examples of these two techniques in the form of high- and lower-pitched drum strokes, such as could be rendered on two congas, or a bongo. In measures two and three, a four-stroke phrase (suggesting duple time) is rendered in triplet

16.4 Rhythmic patterns suggesting polyrhythms

quarter notes (i.e., ternary subdivision), while in measures four and five, a six-stroke phrase (suggesting ternary phrasing) is played in duple eighth notes (i.e., duple subdivision). Any transcription of a conga, bongo, or even piano solo in a salsa performance is going to reveal several instances of this device.

Hemiola-Based Genres in $\frac{6}{8}$–$\frac{3}{4}$

If $\frac{12}{8}$ polyrhythms are characteristic of some of the most distinctively neo-African, percussion-dominated musics, related sorts of rhythmic patterns also undergird a vast category of creole or "mestizo" Latin American genres, in which hemiola patterns are typically rendered on stringed instruments rather than drums. As many musicians know, hemiola implies either the simultaneous or sequential combination of $\frac{3}{4}$ and $\frac{6}{8}$ rhythms. The sequential form quintessentially corresponds to the familiar "I like to live in Ame-ri-ca" pattern (from Leonard Bernstein's *West Side Story*), which suggests a bar of $\frac{6}{8}$ followed by one in $\frac{3}{4}$ (with a constant eighth-note pulse). Vertical hemiola, by contrast, might feature one instrument playing a $\frac{6}{8}$ pattern while another simultaneously plays a $\frac{3}{4}$ pattern.

Scholars and pseudo-scholars have disagreed about the origins of this sort of rhythm in Latin American music, with some musicologists arguing for a Spanish or even Arab derivation. What seems abundantly clear, however, is that these rhythms came into vogue and spread most extensively not in Spain, but in the Caribbean Basin in the sixteenth and seventeenth centuries, as a syncretic product of the interaction of Spanish colonists and sub-Saharan African slaves and their descendants. The hemiola rhythms were of particularly early and vigorous appearance in Mexico (New Spain), where free or enslaved persons of African origin outnumbered Spaniards in the latter 1500s. For their part, many, if not most, of the Spaniards in the region consisted of Andalusians whose own music culture had been shaped by centuries of Moorish rule, which may well have contributed to a fondness for $\frac{6}{8}$ meter, which continues to pervade current-day Moroccan music. It is easy to imagine Afro-Mexicans getting their hands on vihuelas or guitars and coming up with chordal and rhythmic ostinatos in which simple progressions (e.g., D minor–A) would be repeated with quasi-polyrhythmic strumming patterns. Such genres, under names like *guinea*, *zarabanda*, and *cumbé*, were taken up by local Spanish composers and made their way (complete with colloquial Afro-Latin mispronunciations of Spanish) back to Spain, where the "I like to live in Ame-ri-ca" hemiola became a stereotypical icon of Latin American music.

From what may have been the cradle of such rhythms – the area of Veracruz and Mexico City – these sonorities traveled by trade routes to rural Venezuela and beyond, extending to regions, such as highland Colombia, where there were few black people. Despite their evident Afro-Latin origins, these rhythms came to be played by string-based ensembles (especially using variants of guitars and vihuelas) and associated, ironically, with Spanish rather than African heritage. As these infectious rhythms disseminated, they came to animate a vast and diverse set of folk genres stretching from Mexico and Cuba down to the southern cone of Chile and Argentina.

Rhythms in hemiola-based genres (which some Latin American musicologists refer to as the *cancionero ternario*, i.e., the "ternary repertoire") can take different forms. As mentioned, often the hemiola is a sequential alternation of $\frac{6}{8}$ and $\frac{3}{4}$ measures (as in "I like to. . ." etc.), which is generally known in Spanish as *sesquialtera* – from Latin, "six that alters." Thus, for example, in the typical style of Cuban *punto*, as performed by predominantly white Cuban farmers in the central and western part of the island, ten-line *décima* verses sung in free rhythm alternate with instrumental interludes in which guitars and *bandurrias* repeat patterns roughly as shown in Example 16.5.

In vertical hemiola, the $\frac{3}{4}$ and $\frac{6}{8}$ patterns occur simultaneously, constituting a polyrhythm. Such rhythms are structural ostinatos in genres such as the Colombian *bambuco* and are also common in the *música llanera* (plains-region music) of Venezuela and Colombia. Example 16.6 shows a typical ostinato that could occur in a Venezuelan *joropo*, in which the bass pattern is in $\frac{3}{4}$ and the harp and ukulele-like *cuatro* play in $\frac{6}{8}$.

In such *música llanera*, the three instruments typically reiterate the chordal ostinato while jumping back and forth – whether collectively or individually – between patterns that suggest either $\frac{6}{8}$ or $\frac{3}{4}$. The result is as

16.5 Cuban *punto* ostinato

16.6 Venezuelan *joropo* ostinato

intricate, exciting, and richly polyrhythmic as any West African drum ensemble, even though the original fusion with Afro-Latin musicians may have taken place in different regions and as long ago as the sixteenth century.

Genres in the *cancionero ternario* category are too vast to enumerate here, but aside from those mentioned would include the Mexican *jarabe*, *son jalisciense* (together forming the core mariachi repertoire), and *huapango* (in the broader *son huasteco* and *son jarocho* categories), the Ecuadoran *pasillo*, the Peruvian *marinera*, the Chilean *cueca*, and the Argentine *chacarera*. (Oddly enough, the "I like to live in Ame-ri-ca" pattern is conspicuously rare in Puerto Rican music, which Leonard Bernstein meant to evoke in his catchy tune.) Most of these genres today have a folkloric status, with the realm of urban commercial popular music being dominated by duple-metered genres, to which we may now turn.

Urban Binary Genres

For the last century, the vast majority of commercial popular music styles that dominate airwaves and dance clubs throughout Latin America and the Caribbean have been duple-metered, with the *cancionero ternario* genres receding into the realm of traditional folk music, however still vital and valued as national patrimony. This change has occurred on such a broad, hemispheric scale that it begs some grand explanation,[2] although the result has certainly brought the region's popular musics in line with most of the rest of the world.

The Habanera and Cinquillo Complexes

The popularization of syncopated duple-metered genres can be documented in Cuba from around 1800, when the *contradanza* – a creolized version of the European *contredanse (*contra dance/country dance) – became the most popular genre in the innumerable dance halls of Havana and other towns. One factor distinguishing the Cuban *contradanza* from its European ancestors was the use of the habanera bass ostinato (which Cubans musicologists have called the *ritmo de tango*, or tango beat) shown in Example 16.2, which, depending on the nature of the ensemble, could be played on a string bass, on a tuba, by a pianist's left hand, or on the lower strings of a guitar, or possibly on a drum like the timpani. *Contradanzas* were typically instrumental, but in Cuba in the 1840s, a languid, sung version of the *contradanza* called the "habanera" (not "habañera") emerged and became internationally popular, such that outside Cuba its characteristic rhythm came to be known as the "habanera rhythm" – a designation we employ here.

Although simple, the habanera rhythm is in its way quite flexible and protean. If the sixteenth note is stressed, the rhythm shades into the three-three-two *tresillo*, while the addition of an eighth note after the first stroke affords the amphibrach pattern (also shown in Example 16.2). Such mutability may partly explain why the habanera beat and its variants have been adopted in diverse forms as the rhythmic cells of a wide variety of genres, from Afro-Cuban *iyesá* drumming to modern reggaeton. The amphibrach, for example, had become a familiar Caribbean creole rhythm as early as the 1750s, and in the latter 1800s went on to undergird the Brazilian *maxixe* and *lundú*. For its part, the habanera beat subsequently went on to become the underlying ostinato in the early Argentine tango. By the 1920s, the tango had acquired a quite different feel, but the rhythm persisted in the direct descendant of the habanera, namely, the Cuban bolero – like its predecessor, a slow, danceable, sentimental song, often featuring a guitar-based trio format, from the 1940s. The habanera pattern also constituted the standard bass rhythm of the 1950s *chachachá*. In the 1980s, Dominicans effected their own original adaptation of the bolero, and its habanera-pattern bass, in the form of *bachata*; all these basic genre patterns are schematized in Example 16.7. Most remarkable is the resurfacing of the pattern, with a strong three-three-two syncopation, in both up-tempo Trinidadian soca, in the 1970s, and medium-tempo reggaeton, which took its rhythm from Shabba Ranks's 1991 dance-hall song "Dem Bow." While it might not be accurate to say that these genres derive their rhythm from the nineteenth-century *contradanza*, the habanera beat is certainly a common creole Caribbean rhythm that has kept resurfacing over the last two centuries in diverse forms and genres. Example 16.7 also shows the typical rhythm of the *cumbia*, which, originating in Colombia, has become

16.7 Basic patterns of bolero, *chachachá*, *bachata*; *cumbia*

one of the most popular urban dance genres everywhere from Mexico to Argentina.

As mentioned above, another basic creole Caribbean rhythm has been the five-stroke pattern that Cubans call the *cinquillo*. This pattern may have its origins in neo-African and especially Afro-Haitian drumming, as it features prominently in Haitian Vodou rhythms (such as *banda*), as well as Santería *batá* drumming, Martinican *belé*, and the *siká* and *cuembé* styles of Afro-Puerto Rican *bomba*. From the 1870s the *cinquillo* – in a two-bar form in which it is followed by a measure of even quarter notes – became the basic ostinato pattern of the Cuban *danzón* and the related Puerto Rican *danza*. The *cinquillo* also abounds in Trinidadian calypsos, Martinican *zouk*, Haitian *konpa* and popular songs such as "Chouconne" (better known as "Yellow Bird"), and other creole Caribbean genres animated by the colonial-era [Afro-]"French connection." As with the habanera beat, the renderings of the *cinquillo* can vary dramatically in style, ranging from the thunderous pounding of Vodou drumming to the languid rubato of a Chopinesque Puerto Rican piano *danza* by Manuel Tavarez (1843–83). Example 16.8 shows the main theme of the 1893 *danza* "Mis amores," by Puerto Rican composer Simón Madera (1875–1957), in which the left hand plays a characteristically "elastic" version of the two-bar *cinquillo* pattern.

"Latin" Rhythm: Son, *Mambo, and Salsa*

Among the most dynamic, distinctive, and rich forms of rhythm in the Americas is that of "Latin music," which, as mentioned, loosely denotes

16.8 Excerpt of *danza*, "Mis amores"

16.9 Salsa *montuno*, "Maria Luisa"

Afro-Cuban-derived popular dance music rather than "Latin American" in the broader sense. What is understood as Latin rhythm can be seen to have taken its modern shape in the 1940s and 1950s, especially in the contemporary Cuban *son* and big-band mambo, and perpetuated in salsa, the direct stylistic descendant of those genres. The essence of Latin rhythm is a composite ostinato structure created by a set of interlocking conventional patterns played on an ensemble of percussion and melodic instruments. These are typified in Example 16.9, which approximates some of the parts in the basic repeating pattern from the *montuno* section of the 1975 salsa song "María Luisa," sung by Ismael Miranda. (Like traditional rumba and the creole Cuban *son*, salsa songs follow a two-part verses-*montuno* form.)

Several features are noteworthy here. One is the "anticipated bass" pattern, in which the bass, rather than emphasizing the downbeat of each measure, glides over it, sounding the root note of each measure's chord on the quarter-note beat *before* it. Another feature is that while this *montuno* pattern consists, in this case, of a four-bar chordal and vocal refrain, the basic rhythmic ostinato is a two-bar entity cohering with *clave* – in this case, two-three *clave*, in which the "two" side is somewhat less syncopated than the "three" side. Even though the *clave* pattern itself is not being sounded by the hardwood sticks (as it would be in traditional rumba), the pattern still operates as an underlying, implicit rhythm that is ever-present in the performers' heads. Thus, the capitalized syllables in the *coro* coincide with *clave* beats; conversely, if one were to clap the "incorrect" three-two *clave* in this song, the vocal and *clave* beats would miss each other and the sound would be jumbled and *cruzado*. The piano pattern (itself called *guajeo* or *montuno*) follows a two-bar rhythmic pattern that hits the downbeat of each odd-numbered measure (the less syncopated "two" side of the *clave*), and then creates tension by jumping off the rails, as it were, onto offbeats, and skipping the next downbeat (of the even-numbered measures, on the syncopated "three" side), before returning to the downbeat of the third measure. Meanwhile, the lead singer, or an instrumentalist, who is improvising "call" phrases (*sonejos*) in between the *coro* refrains need not slavishly stress the correct *clave* pattern, but must certainly be careful not to perform phrases that would suggest the wrong (in this case, three-two) *clave*. To do so would be regarded by many salsa musicians as a glaring error that muddies and jumbles the otherwise tight and coordinated composite rhythm. In fact, proper rendering of *clave* became a rather cliquish fetish among some salsa musicians, to the point that in recent decades a few prominent salseros have blasphemously defied the "*clave* police" in declaring that they no longer feel bound by such fussy rules.

Another dynamic Latin rhythm is that of the Dominican merengue, whose kinetic drive derives less from salsa-style syncopation than from its insistent, frenetic, four-on-the-floor pounding, articulated by the crisp, tight (*apreta'o*) timbres of the *güira* scraper and the *tambora* drum. In traditional merengue, the essence of the *tambora* pattern is its sixteenth-note roll leading up to the downbeat of each measure – a feature that may derive from Spanish military band music more than any African precedent.

Miscellaneous Rhythms

The categories outlined thus far could collectively be said to cover most of the characteristic rhythms for which Latin American and Caribbean music are known. They do not, however, completely exhaust the vast region's soundscape, such that mention should be made of a few noteworthy genres not accommodated into this taxonomy. The reader, for example, may be wondering by now, what about reggae? The "boom-a-CHUCK-a-boom-a-CHUCK-a" so-called "skank" rhythm of roots reggae is indeed one of the hemisphere's most characteristic and infectious rhythms, and has little structural relationship to the categories presented so far here. The evolution of this rhythm is itself enigmatic, as it came into vogue quite rapidly around 1968, perhaps deriving to some extent from the guitar or banjo strumming pattern of folk mento, and perhaps reinforced by Afro-Jamaican *burru* drumming, and quickly replacing the rhythm 'n' blues shuffle beat of mid-'60s ska.

Other popular genres are relatively independent of the African influences that have directly or indirectly enriched most Latin and Caribbean music styles. An especially substantial and musically fertile region is northern Mexico, together with the Mexican American communities in neighboring border states (and more far-flung but still substantial communities in such sites as Chicago). Here the main musical influences have been those of Germans who settled in the U.S. Southwest and elsewhere in the nineteenth century, bringing with them the keyboard accordion and the favored dances of the polka and waltz. These were adopted as the predominant rhythms of the distinctive Mexican and Mexican-American musics of the region. Most characteristically, the regional polka and waltz have been played on a *conjunto* ensemble traditionally comprising accordion, guitar, and the guitar-like *bajo sexto*, nowadays commonly supplemented by electric bass and drum set. This is the standard ensemble of *norteño* music (*música norteña*) and its Texas-Mexican counterpart, which might be generically called *conjunto*, *música tejana*, or "Tex-Mex." Equally popular in recent decades has been the brass band format called *banda*, or *tecnobanda* if amplified vocals and perhaps keyboard and electric bass are added. Much of the repertoire of these groups, set to polka or waltz rhythm, might be categorized (e.g., on CD labels) as *ranchera*, which coheres with the dandified cowboy spirit reflected in preferred attire. If the songs are narrative and text driven, they may be referred to as *corridos* or, in the case of songs glorifying drug dons, *narcocorridos*. The term *ranchera* also comprises slow ballads (such as Vicente Fernández's evergreen "Volver, volver"), typically employing mariachi instrumentation (with its characteristic violins and trumpets), set to what is essentially a greatly decelerated polka rhythm.

Another musical region little touched by Afro-Latin influences is the Andes, home especially to the Quechua- and Aymara-speaking populations of highland Peru, Bolivia, and, to some extent, Ecuador. The single most popular genre of this region is the *huayno*, a medium-tempo song for solo voice and, typically, stringed instruments such as *charango*, harp, and guitar. A typical *huayno* rhythm may outline a familiar quarter-eighth-eighth ostinato, in which case it can easily be accommodated into a *cumbia* beat, as in urban *chicha* music. Often, however, the first beat of this pattern is slightly shortened, affording a limping "long-short-short" ostinato that is not easily notated. Another distinctive feature of many *huaynos* (such as those by northern Peruvian songstress Dina Paucar) is their irregular and often uneven-numbered phrase lengths, which contrasts with the four-bar phrasings otherwise pervading Euro-American and Latin music.

Finally, another rhythmically distinctive set of genres is that associated with a different set of Indians – not Native Americans, but descendants of the over 400,000 people who came to the Caribbean from India as indentured workers in the period 1845–1917. These Indo-Caribbeans now constitute roughly half the populations of Trinidad, Guyana, and Suriname, and have cultivated their own dynamic music culture. This variously comprises traditional folk genres brought from India, creolized pop "chutney-soca," and a few idioms that, though originally deriving from fragmented genres transplanted by the original immigrants, have over the generations developed – along wholly Indian rather than African lines – into thoroughly distinctive and unique entities. Particularly dynamic is the Indo-Trinidadian genre of tassa drumming, as performed at Hindu weddings, drum competitions, and other festivities by ensembles each consisting of two stick-played, shallow kettledrums (called "tassa"), a large bass drum, and a pair of cymbals (*jhanjh, jhal*).

Tassa drumming has evolved into a highly sophisticated, complex, and dynamic art form, provoking animated dancing and sustaining the interest of connoisseurs who prize virtuosity and creativity as well as adherence to established norms. The latter consist primarily of the repertoire of a dozen or so common "hands," each of which comprises a composite ensemble rhythm (or sequence thereof), and a set of conventional cadences and riff types, which, though standardized, allow room for flashy improvisation ("cutting") by the lead drummer. Tassa drumming is at once disciplined and thunderously loud, exciting, and as "hot" as any African or Afro-Latin music.

Endnotes

1 Adapted from N. Warden, *Afro-Cuban Traditional Music and Transculturation: The Emergence of Cajón pa' los Muertos* (Saarbrücken: VDM Verlag Dr. Müller, 2007), 55.

2 See, e.g., R. Pérez, *La binarización de los ritmos ternarios africanos en América Latina* (Havana: Casa de las Americas, 1986).

17 Indigenous Rhythm and Dance in North and South America

KRISTINA F. NIELSEN

Music and dance are mediums that connect Indigenous communities of North and South America and the social, natural, and cosmic worlds of which they are a part. Despite more than half a millennium of colonization, Indigenous communities sustain Indigenous traditions and practices while simultaneously adapting them to fulfill new communal needs.

The European nations that colonized the Americas left lasting cultural and musical footprints: Starting in the early 1500s in South America and Mesoamerica, Spanish and Portuguese colonizers sought to extract wealth from the colonies to ship back to Spain. Catholicism supplied a moral imperative for Spanish colonial endeavors, and to this day many Indigenous communities in areas colonized by Spain practice syncretic forms of Catholicism that blend Indigenous and Christian beliefs. Following the arrival of the Spanish, rampant disease and the enslavement of Indigenous peoples led to large declines in the Indigenous population. Some towns and communities remained united; in other cases, the Spanish relocated Indigenous peoples to new communities where diverse Indigenous customs, music, and dance melded with Spanish and African influences.

In North America, the 1600s brought an influx of Protestant colonizers who systematically dispossessed Indigenous peoples of their territories. As the nascent countries of Canada and the United States grew, Indigenous communities – also referred to as First Nations, American Indians, or Native Americans – endured broken treaties and genocidal policies. Throughout the twentieth century, the U.S. and Canadian governments ran boarding schools that forcibly removed children from their families and repressed Indigenous languages and practices. Concurrently, government agencies like the Bureau of Indian Affairs (BIA) forbade traditional practices ranging from the potlatches in the Pacific Northwest to the Lakota Sun Dance of the Great Plains. Many Indigenous communities have resisted assimilationist efforts of governments in North and South America and have continued to practice their dance, music, and culture in traditional, syncretic, and folkloric forms.

At the peak of these policies of cultural genocide in the late nineteenth through mid-twentieth century, European researchers extensively documented and recorded Indigenous music in North America. Applying racist evolutionist theories adapted from Charles Darwin, Eurocentric music researchers postulated that music evolved like biological organisms. In their model, European and colonial researchers placed Western European art music at the top of their supposed evolutionary chain because of its use of harmony, melody, and rhythm. At the bottom, European and colonialist researchers put African music and Indigenous music of the Americas, alleging that it was "primitive" in its supposed lack of harmony and melody. Melody and harmony were viewed as secondary to rhythm – or even non-existent – in many early works on Native North American cultures.[1] The racist and simplistic analysis of evolutionism could not be further from the truth: both rhythm and melody are integral components of Indigenous American music.

Colonization and the environmental impact of colonizers on both American continents – ranging from the destruction of salmon runs and traditional migration patterns of buffalo to the destruction of Brazilian forests and droughts in Central America caused by climate change – have caused significant hardship for Indigenous communities. Additionally, academia's complicity in colonial projects, including music research that has archived and catalogued Indigenous music and dance without consent, has caused further harm. With these histories in mind, the music and dance described here have been selected carefully to observe the restriction that the vast majority of Indigenous music and dance traditions are not intended for outsiders; in most cases, only cultural insiders can fully appreciate the meaning of Indigenous music and dance.

Many Indigenous peoples across North and South America continue to practice traditional music and dance; additionally, Indigenous communities use new songs and dances that occasionally integrate other musical styles or genres. These many varieties of Indigenous musics reflect the diversity of Indigenous cultures as well as the range of contemporary urban and rural Indigenous experiences. Today, many Indigenous peoples across the Americas are still resisting colonization, the occupation of their lands, and assimilationist governmental policies; music, dance, language, and ceremonies have been instrumental in these resistance efforts.

Unfolding Sound and Movement over Time

Concepts of rhythm are deeply interwoven with ideas of time, which are not universal between Indigenous communities. Each community has distinct ways of experiencing and marking time and the completion of life-sustaining cycles; for instance, Native American peoples in the Pacific Northwest through California complete community-specific ceremonies that mark the return of the salmon. Similarly, corn-cultivating Indigenous pueblos in Mesoamerica through South America complete community-specific ceremonies at different stages of the agricultural cycle. In many Indigenous communities, ceremonies with music and dance play a vital role in sustaining the delicate balance of these cycles, and humans and their music and dances play an important part in maintaining the natural environment. For this reason, many Indigenous communities only perform songs and dances during specific seasons and ceremonies, following the larger cyclical rhythms that have underpinned the lives of many Indigenous communities in the Americas for millennia.

Music and dance play a central role in the structuring of ritual time in many Native American ceremonies, and repeated rhythms can suspend time and create an experience outside the framework of normal space-time.[2] Layers of intricate repetition and variation in song and dance are integral in achieving this effect. Through song and dance, communities can express complex understandings of the cosmos and humanity's role within it. Glossing these ideas as "religion," however, would mischaracterize the full significance of many Indigenous music and dance traditions; instead, they are widely understood as ways of being in which the boundaries between sacred, social, and life-sustaining activities are kaleidoscopic and permeable.

Language and Rhythm

Most Indigenous American languages do not include a word that translates directly as "music"; for instance, in Nahuatl, one of the many Indigenous languages found in central Mexico, the word *cuica* means to sing whereas the word *pitza* means to play the flute or trumpet: There is no single term in Nahuatl that encompasses both of these ideas or translates to the European concept of "music." Studies of the words used to describe the sounds of dance, instruments, and songs suggests that there is fluidity between language, music, and dance; for instance, in some languages, such as in several Native Alaskan languages, music and dance are synonymous.[3]

Similarly, many Indigenous languages do not appear to have an equivalent to the English word *rhythm*, and instead use other terms to express related ideas. When asked, Indigenous Maya scholar and musician Juan Francisco Cristobal shared with me that in Q'anjob'al Maya the word *tx'olilal b'it* is used to indicate the way sounds are ordered. In Kichwa, the Indigenous language spoken in Otavalo, Ecuador, Jessie Vallejo and Indigenous Kichwa scholar and musician Patricio Maldonado related to me that the word *pacha*, which translates to "time" in English, is the primary word used for rhythm. In addition to *pacha*, Vallejo and Maldonado shared that Kichwa uses emotive words to describe rhythms, including *kushi* for rhythms that are quicker and perceived as happier, and *llaki* for rhythms that are slow and perceived as sad.

Despite some broad similarities in how music, dance, and rhythm are conceptualized across Indigenous cultures in the Americas, each Indigenous nation and community developed its own distinct music and dance traditions. As of the 2000 census, in Mexico alone there were more than sixty distinct living Indigenous languages. When Europeans first arrived in North America, the geographic area comprising Canada and the United States boasted more than three hundred Indigenous languages, and to this day, South America alone is home to more than a quarter of the total language families in the world.[4]

Instruments

Indigenous American music features a wide range of melodic and percussive instruments: from the fiddle of the Métis people of Canada to the marimbas of the Maya and the many varieties of flute in South America, melody and rhythm go hand in hand. Although percussive instruments (particularly drums and rattles) are perhaps among the most widespread and iconic instruments, melodic instruments, including flutes and the human voice, are of equal importance in Indigenous American music. Furthermore, colonizers introduced new instruments that have become fully Indigenized and integrated into Indigenous traditions; for instance, Indigenous communities in South America and Mexico play stringed instruments that are modeled on European instruments but that are distinctly Indigenous. Examples include the Andean charango and the Mexican concha that use armadillo shells as the bodies for small lute-like instruments. These instruments provide rhythmic accompaniment to songs while simultaneously supplying harmony to support the melodic line.

Drums

Drums are of spiritual significance in many Indigenous American cultures, and many traditions feature drums who are powerful living beings and must be treated accordingly. Communities ranging from the Anishnaabeg peoples, whose traditional lands lie in the Great Lakes region, to the Nahua and the Maya-speaking communities of Mexico and Central America acknowledge the spirits of ceremonial drums in their languages and oral histories. For instance, many Indigenous languages, such as Nahuatl, grammatically treat drums as animate beings. Ceremonial and sacred drums also often receive offerings, such as tobacco or food, to nourish their spirits.

The role of drums in accompanying songs and dances varies greatly between Indigenous cultures. In songs from the Haida, located in the Pacific Northwest, drums accompany songs intermittently; in other cases, such as among the Nayara songs of the Shoshone people of the Great Basin region, songs are performed without any accompaniment; instead, dancers must listen for melodic cues and the placement of rests to follow the structure of the song.[5]

Isorhythms, or repeating rhythmic figures, provide a foundation for many songs and dances. One common isorhythm emulates the sound of a heartbeat using a short-long pattern on the drum, where the long stroke is accented. This pattern can become a collective heartbeat for dances, such as round dance songs that are found across the Plains as well as in the Pueblo region of the American Southwest. The drummers and singers play the short-long pattern like a heartbeat that interlocks with the song and guides the collective movements of the dancers around a circle.

Rattles

Like drums, rattles often supply foundational rhythms for Indigenous songs and dances. Alternatively, rattles can accentuate performances and become integrated into choreography as sounding extensions of the dancer. The rattles found across the Americas take many forms and vary in shape, size, and construction. Rattles can be artistically elaborate, further connecting the sounds symbolically to places, animals, and spiritual beings; for example, Tlingit ritual specialists of southeastern Alaska use rattles with sacred images including ravens and killer whales. These ceremonial rattles summon spirits and are only used by cultural experts.[6] Similarly, the ceramic rattles traditionally found in Mesoamerica are made from clay and contain small clay pellets inside. These rattles can be highly elaborate and take the form of spiritual beings, people, or animals.

Many Indigenous cultures use rattles made of gourds or inedible parts of animals, such as turtle shells or deer hooves. With rattles, musicians can create patterns of strong and weak pulses through the movements of their wrists and forearms, or a tremolo effect can be achieved through rapid circular movements. Alternatively, rattles can be wearable; for example, the Yoeme (Yaqui) *ténabarim* consists of moth cocoons filled with small pebbles that are strung together and worn around the legs of dancers.

The Human Voice

The human voice is perhaps the most important and widespread instrument in Indigenous American cultures, and the natural stresses of Indigenous languages contribute to the musical fingerprint of each Indigenous community. Poetry and the rise and fall of poetic language shape the fabric of vocal melodies and rhythms in many Indigenous song traditions. In Native Alaska, poetry typically determines the rhythmic structure of songs, with motifs of three, four, or five notes.[7] Vocal effects can also add rhythmic texture to songs; for instance, in the Great Plains, singers often add rhythmic nuance to melodies by pulsing tones to create rhythmic stresses on a single pitch.[8]

Vocables – or syllables without lexical meaning – are prevalent in many Indigenous songs. Through vocables, singers can invoke ideas that are understood by their intended audience without fully describing them in words. These sounds can be extremely powerful; for instance, in the Pacific Northwest, Indigenous communities including the Kwakiutl peoples use vocables to invoke the spirits of animals. Without mentioning the animals directly, vocables like *Na Na* can invoke a grizzly bear, or *Gka Gka* can invoke a raven.[9] Vocables contribute poetically and rhythmically to the structure of Indigenous songs, and many Indigenous communities use specific vocable patterns with specific song genres.[10] Songs will often repeat vocables using the same rhythms: if the rhythm changes, the vocables usually change accordingly.

The Human Body

In many Indigenous cultures across the Americas, physical gesture and the human body are central to the creation and experience of rhythm. The physical gestures of playing rattles and producing sound are often integral in choreography, and dancers frequently wear regalia designed for both visual and sonic aesthetics. In the case of the Yoeme *ténabarim* mentioned above, the rattles are strapped to the legs of dancers, translating the physical gestures of dance to audible rhythm. In many cases, it is vital to perform steps exactly, both for the sake of choreography and for the musical rhythms that the steps produce. For example, synchronized dances that move in circles or straight lines often require exact steps from dancers to align the rhythms. In other cases, dancers move independently of each other and have significant leeway in their movements: this is often the case in dances where dancers are embodying animals or spirits.

The deer dance among the Tewa Pueblo people of Ohkay Owingeh (formerly identified as San Juan by non-Pueblo peoples) in New Mexico is an example of an Indigenous line dance. The dancers synchronize their steps in a single line to the beat of a drum, moving rattles in their right hand while collectively singing. These dances underscore the semantic blurring of the categories of "dancers" and "musicians": as in many cases, the dancers are themselves vital to the collective sound. The strong rattle pulse created with a downward movement of the arm corresponds with a downward step of one foot, while a smaller and lighter stroke fits with the downward step of the other foot. The Tewa use a rhythmic technique, known as the *t'a*, or pause or rhythmic shift. Responding to the t'a, dancers hold their foot elevated for one extra beat before bringing it back down with the new downbeat: alternatively, dancers momentarily pause for the additional beat.[11]

In contrast, the deer dance of the Yoeme (Yaqui) people in Northern Mexico and the American Southwest integrates independent movements as the spirit of a deer guides the gestures of the dancer. The dance acknowledges human relationships with deer, uniting ceremony with the once important activity of hunting that provided sustenance for the Yoeme people. The deer dance temporarily erodes barriers between the *sea ania*, or flower world, and the everyday, bringing these co-existing worlds into view.[12] The ensemble that accompanies the deer dance comprises three male musicians who sing poetic texts. As they sing, one musician plays a water drum, or a half-gourd floating in water, that provides the flighty heartbeat of the deer. The two other musicians play rasping sticks balanced on gourds that stress the note on the downstroke, creating an alternating pattern that represents the breath of the deer.[13]

The male deer dancer is equally important to the rhythmic texture of the deer dance. With the head of a young deer strapped on his head, the dancer moves in a slightly bent posture with the gait of a deer: In each hand the dancer holds a large gourd rattle that transforms the carefully timed movements of his arms to sound. Adorned in a ceremonial deer hoof belt and the *ténabarim* leg rattles, the dancer creates a range of rhythmic effects. Using combinations of light touches to the heel and the ball of the foot, the *ténabarim* can create vigorous or light sounds with each step. The gourd rattles, *ténabarim*, and the deer hoof belt create layers of rhythmic sound from the gestures of footwork, the larger movements of the hips, and arm movements.

Music and Dance Form

Form is integral to the structure of Indigenous songs, dances, and rituals. Using musically structured time and space, music and dance can depict expansive ideas about the cosmos and humanity's place within it. In many cases, Indigenous musicians and ritual specialists carefully structure rituals, and songs and dances must be performed in a specific order. In these instances, form includes not only the rhythmic and melodic patterns of the songs, but also the broader ways in which songs are conceptualized in ceremonial settings – or even over a longer period, such as a full agricultural cycle.

Indigenous songs vary greatly in their structure, ranging from through-composed, meaning that there are no repetitions, to a strophic structure where the verses repeat the same rhythm and melody. Even if there are repetitions in the music, the dance can vary substantially, as is the case of the traditions of the Yurok, Karok, and Hupa people of northwestern California.[14] In a number of cases, the broader repetitions of rhythms and choreography are determined by culturally significant numbers or by the context of the performance.

Conchero – a syncretic Indigenous dance tradition from Central Mexico – is one example of how culturally significant numbers can inform the rhythmic and melodic structure of music and dance. Although *conchero* is Catholic, it retains elements of pre-Hispanic music aesthetics and blends Catholic and Indigenous cosmologies; for example, it emphasizes the four directions that are each associated with sacred sites while also corresponding with the four directions of the cross. In *conchero*, these four cardinal directions are a critical part of both *conchero* choreography and rhythm. The number four is symbolically represented through the duality of the music and steps: Every step that is completed in one direction must be completed in the other. As a result, the structure of traditional *conchero* rhythms and dances typically follows an AABB format. This form reflects these two overlapping cosmovisions, and music and dance become vehicles for experiencing these broader connections. Through their movements, the dancers travel in the four directions and maintain the balance as they present their gestures and movements as an offering.

Similarly, in the Indigenous Andes, *yanantin* – a vision of the cosmos that views the universe as paired parts that, without both, would be incomplete – shapes musical form, rhythmic repetitions, and dance gestures.[15] *Yanantin* is significant in rituals, including the celebration of the summer solstice that is celebrated across the former territories of the Inca Empire that reached across contemporary Peru, Bolivia, and Ecuador. In the Andean cosmovision, gender figures centrally in these pairings, and seasons, instruments, and geographic features are often ascribed symbolic genders; for instance, the rainy season, which fuels the growth of crops, is considered feminine, while the dry season is considered masculine.[16]

In Otavalo, Ecuador, the music and dance of the summer solstice festival, known as Hatun Puncha-Inti Raymi, serve a central role in allowing humans to communicate with the earth, spiritual beings, and the cosmos.[17] The choreography of the dances in the festival varies between the dancers moving in straight lines or spiraling around musicians while they play short pieces on guitars, conch shells, harmonicas, melodicas, and transverse cane flutes that are made in pairs of male and female instruments. In the spiraling dances, the instruments play repeating phrases to accompany the chanting that uses a call-and-response structure: Each call-and-response pattern occurs twice, while the main melody is repeated three times by the instrumentalists. The stomps of the dancers connect their gestures to the earth and create a steady beat under the instruments and call-and-response vocals.[18] The form of the music and dance movements for the Inti Raymi festival in Otavalo highlight how musical elements of time and collective movement can forge links between humans and their surroundings.

Meter and Beat Patterns

The rhythms of Indigenous music and dances are as diverse as the hundreds of languages found across North and South America, and communities have their own local or regional rhythmic styles that distinguish them from their neighbors. To try to understand relationships between the songs and dances of different communities, music researchers, particularly in the early twentieth to mid-twentieth century, sought to measure and quantify differences in Native North American songs. In an attempt to quantify these differences, researchers compared the number of rhythmic units commonly used in songs to create cross-cultural comparisons. For example, researchers have suggested that the songs of Mescalero and San Carlos Apache typically feature two durational values: one that is half as long as the other.[19] In contrast, Bruno Nettl, who undertook comparative studies in the 1950s, concluded from his analyses that rhythms among the Paiute typically draw on three or four durational values, while Hopi and Zuni songs typically use approximately five or six different durational values.[20] While such categorization has been tantalizing for predominantly European music researchers, there are always exceptions and any broad statements warrant careful consideration.

Furthermore, recent research indicates that European and Indigenous perception can differ in how durational values are heard. Henry Stobart, an ethnomusicologist who has conducted extensive research in the Bolivian Andes, and Ian Cross, a music psychology and cognition researcher, have found that European listeners are likely to mishear the ratios in Indigenous songs. In particular, they found that Europeans are likely to hear ratios of 2:3 as 1:2 in Indigenous Bolivian music; furthermore, they noted that Europeans were likely to hear upbeats at the beginnings of songs where Bolivian performers heard downbeats.[21] These findings point to the challenge of transcribing and analyzing rhythms in ways that do not misconstrue their fundamental qualities.

While many of the musical rhythms across North and South America use duple or triple meters, there are also plenty of examples that use complex meters, changing meters within songs, or added beats. These choices are related to both cultural and aesthetic preferences; for example, in the cases of *conchero* and the Inti Raymi festival mentioned above, symmetry and balance are culturally and musically significant, leading to predominantly symmetric melodies and choreography – and, by extension, symmetric meters. In other communities, asymmetry is a preferred aesthetic, such as in the case of the Yurok, Hupa, and Karok peoples of Northern California: as a result, the meters are often irregular or variations are added to create rhythmic asymmetry.[22]

Across many Indigenous cultures, an underlying consistent rhythm provides the heartbeat for songs and dances, tethering instruments, vocal parts, and dance gestures to each other. Instead of conceptualizing singing and the voice as the musical focal point, the rattles, drums, stomping of feet, or other rhythmic actions provide the framework within which instruments, voices, and dance movements are structured. The songs of the Kwakiutl First Nation underscore this relationship: singing first begins after the drumbeat has been established, since the beat is understood to be of central importance.[23] Similarly, pow-wow songs begin with the drumbeat before the head singer introduces the song, allowing the singer to fit the melody into the grooves of the drumbeat.[24] When the melody moves between the strokes of the drum, it becomes highly syncopated with the drum and the movements of dancers. The composite rhythm of the drum, dance gestures, sounding regalia, and vocal line creates a rich rhythmic texture that cannot be fully grasped through the analysis of any single part.

Transcription

Although Indigenous American music is predominantly learned and preserved through oral tradition, Indigenous peoples in the Americas have long employed pictographs, symbols, and mnemonic devices to assist singers in recalling songs, rituals, and community history. For example, the Anishnaabe-Ojibwe have long used birch-bark scrolls to aid singers in recalling songs and histories.[25]

European and Indigenous researchers have used transcriptions since the early twentieth century to codify the intricacies of Indigenous music and dance rhythms. Researchers transcribing Indigenous music have typically prioritized their research interests, often ignoring components of the performance they deemed extraneous, which in many cases included the sounds of dance steps or the nuances of the performance of instruments like rattles and drums.[26] In recent years, researchers have collaborated with Indigenous musicians to create transcriptions that more accurately reflect performance practices.[27] Since many Indigenous traditions use repetition with subtle variations, many transcriptions mark repeats in lieu of writing out the many iterations and variations of songs and dances. These transcriptions cannot fully capture the nuanced variations that occur in each reiteration. Ultimately, it is worth critically considering the value of analyzing Indigenous music with traditional Western analytic methods, especially in cases where analysis becomes removed from cultural contexts.

Endnotes

1 R. Wallaschek, *Primitive Music: An Inquiry into the Origin and Development of Music, Songs, Instruments, Dances, and Pantomimes of Savage Races* (Aberdeen University Press, 1893); C. M. Bowra, *Primitive Song* (Cleveland: The World Publishing Company, 1962); M. Herndon, *Native American Music* (Norwood, PA.: Norwood Editions, 1980), 37; C. Sachs, *Rhythm and Tempo: A Study in Music History* (New York: W.W. Norton and Company, 1953).

2 A. D. Shapiro and I. Talamantez, "The Mescalero Apache Girls' Puberty Ceremony: The Role of Music in Structuring Ritual Time," *Yearbook for Traditional Music*, 18 (1986), 77–90.

3 M. Williams, "Contemporary Alaska Native Dance: The Spirit of Tradition," in C. Heth (ed.), *Native American Dance: Ceremonies and Social Traditions* (Washington, DC: National Museum of the American Indian Smithsonian Institution with Starwood Publishing, 1992), 167; B. Diamond, M. S. Cronk, and F. von Rosen, *Visions of Sound: Musical Instruments of First Nations Communities in Northeastern America* (University of Chicago Press, 1994), 66.

4 B. Cifuentes and J. L. Moctezuma, "The Mexican Indigenous Languages and the National Censuses: 1970–2000," in M. Hidalgo (ed.), *Mexican Indigenous Languages at the Dawn of the Twenty-First Century* (Berlin: Walter de Gruyter, 2006), 198; M. Mithun, *The Languages of Native North America* (Cambridge University Press, 1999), 1; L. Campbell and V. Grondona, (eds.), *The Indigenous Languages of South America: A Comprehensive Guide* (Berlin: Walter de Gruyter, 2012), 168.

5 I. Halpern, *Haida: Indian Music of the Pacific Northwest* (New York: Folkway Records, 1986), 3; J. Vander, *Shoshone Ghost Dance Religion: Poetry Songs and Great Basin Context* (University of Illinois Press, 1997), 404.

6 A. Jonaitis, "Liminality and Incorporation in the Art of the Tlingit," *American Indian Quarterly*, 7 (1983), 41–68.

7 N. Beaudry, "Arctic Canada and Alaska," in E. Koskoff (ed.), *The Garland Encyclopedia of World Music: The United States and Canada* (New York: Garland, 2001), 378.

8 B. Nettl, *North American Indian Musical Styles* (Philadelphia: American Folklore Society, 1954), 24; B. Nettl, *Blackfoot Musical Thought: Comparative Perspectives* (Kent State University Press, 1989), 44.

9 I. Halpern, *Kwakiutl: Indian Music of the Pacific Northwest* (New York: Ethnic Folkways Records, 1981), 7.

10 C. J. Frisbie, "Vocables in Navajo Ceremonial Music," *Ethnomusicology*, 24 (1980), 375; B. Nettl, "Observations on Meaningless Peyote Song Texts," *The Journal of American Folklore*, 66 (1953), 161–4; D. P. McAllester, *Enemy Way Music* (Cambridge, MA: The Peabody Museum of American Archaeology and Ethnology, 1954), 30.

11 G. P. Kurath and A. Garcia, *Music and Dance of the Tewa Pueblos* (Santa Fe: Museum of New Mexico Press, 1970), 89; A. Garcia and C. Garcia, "Ritual Preludes to Tewa Indian Dances," *Ethnomusicology*, 12 (1968), 241.

12 L. Evers and F. S. Molina, *Yaqui Deer Songs: Maso Bwikam*, vol. 14, Sun Tracks: An American Indian Literary Series (University of Arizona Press, 1987), 52; D. D. Shorter, "Hunting for History in Potam Pueblo: A Yoeme (Yaqui) Indian Deer Dancing Epistemology," *Folklore*, 118 (2007), 285.

13 J. S. Griffith, "Yaqui and Mayo," in D. Olson and D. E. Sheehy (eds.), *The Garland Encyclopedia of World Music: South America, Mexico, Central America, and the Caribbean* (New York: Garland, 2001), 589.

14 R. Keeling, "California," in *The Garland Encyclopedia of World Music: The United States and Canada*, 413.

15 H. Stobart, "In Touch with the Earth? Musical Instruments, Gender and Fertility in the Bolivian Andes," *Ethnomusicology Forum*, 17 (2008), 81; H. Stobart, *Music and the Poetics of Production* (Aldershot: Ashgate, 2006), 120.

16 Stobart, "In Touch with the Earth," 79–84; L. E. "Katsa" Cachiguango and J. Pontón, *Yaku-Mama: La Crianza Del Agua; La Música Ritual Del Hatun Puncha – Inti Raymi En Kotama, Otavalo* (Ecuador: El Taller Azul, 2010), 35.

17 J. Vallejo, "La Música Da Vida a Vida: Transverse Flute Music of Otavalo, Ecuador" (Ph.D. Dissertation, UCLA, 2014), 199; Cachiguango and Pontón, *Yaku-Mama*, 180.

18 Hatun Kotama Escuela de Flauta, and Smithsonian/Folkways Recordings, *¡Así Kotama!: The Flutes of Otavalo, Ecuador*, Compact Disc (Washington, DC: Smithsonian Folkways Recordings, 2013); J. Vallejo, "La Música Da Vida a Vida," 204.

19 Nettl, *North American Indian Musical Styles*, 22; J. R. Haefer, "Southwest," in *The Garland Encyclopedia of World Music: The United States and Canada*, 431.

20 Nettl, *North American Indian Musical Styles*, 16–31; Nettl, *Music in Primitive Culture* (Harvard University Press, 1956).

21 H. Stobart and I. Cross, "The Andean Anacrusis? Rhythmic Structure and Perception in Easter Songs of Northern Potosí, Bolivia," *British Journal of Ethnomusicology*, 9 (2000), 72.

22 R. Keeling, *Cry for Luck: Sacred Song and Speech among the Yurok, Hupa, and Karok Indians of Northwestern California* (University of California Press, 1992), 87.

23 I. Halpern, *Kwakiutl: Indian Music of the Pacific Northwest* (New York: Ethnic Folkways Records, 1981), 6.

24 T. Browner, *Heartbeat of the People: Music and Dance of the Northern Pow-Wow* (University of Illinois Press, 2002).

25 W. J. Hoffman, "The Mid'wiwin or Grand Medicine Society of the Ojibwa," *Annual Report of the Bureau of Ethnology to the Secretary of the Smithsonian Institution*, 7 (1891), 143–300; W. N. Fenton, "The Roll Call of the Iroquois

Chiefs: A Study of a Mnemonic Cane from the Six Nations Reserves," *The Smithsonian Institution*, 111 (1950), 1–73.

26 T. Browner, *Songs from "A New Circle of Voices": The Sixteenth Annual Pow-Wow at UCLA* (Middleton, WI: A-R Editions, 2009), xviii.

27 Notable studies that have transcribed Indigenous rhythm and dance include G. Kurath, "A Problem in Dance Acculturation," *The Journal of American Folklore*, 62 (1949), 87–106; G. P. Kurath, "Panorama of Dance Ethnology," *Current Anthropology*, 1 (1960), 233–54; G. P. Kurath and A. Garcia, *Music and Dance of the Tewa Pueblos* (Santa Fe: Museum of New Mexico Press, 1970); V. L. Levine, *Writing American Indian Music: Historic Transcriptions, Notations, and Arrangements* (Middleton, WI: A-R Editions, 2002); and T. Browner, *Songs from "A New Circle of Voices."*

PART VI

Epilogue

18 The Future of Rhythm

NICK COLLINS

As long as the human race keeps going, there can be no end to rhythm: we will always need to place events in musical time. It is unlikely that a drone music monoculture will hold static sway for future millennia or take over all perpetuity; humanity's hyperactive search for meaning needs more reactionary pacing and diversity. Yet while there should be no dispute that there is a future for rhythm, the contents of that future are inevitably impossible to predict, this being the only accurate prediction in the field of futurology. The present chapter will attempt to extrapolate a few current trends and anticipate interesting and, it is hoped, inspiring scenarios but acknowledges the dangers of dropping a crystal ball on our dancing feet. I proceed by considering the space of possible rhythms, the limits of human production of rhythm, the transformation of rhythm through technological means, and the latest repercussions of artificial intelligence technology on rhythmic practice.

Which Rhythms Haven't Been Invented Yet?

Why didn't early humans beat box drum and bass 100,000 years ago? Although the vocal physiology would have been present, the cultural context was missing. Patterns based on alternation between kick and snare drum timbres make no sense if kicks and snares haven't yet been created, if an enclosing dance culture founded on some particular avenue of high-tempo beats versus half-speed bass within a history taking in Jamaican sound systems, hip-hop, and earlier bombastic rave music is out of scope to daily savannah survival. Thus, there will be future avenues of rhythmic practice that we cannot possibly predict, since we can't live through all the intervening sociocultural steps to reach them.

The best bet is that musical fads over time respect human capability, with a tight coupling of physiology and perception determining the space of plausible rhythms. This position assumes that human physiology stays relatively stable; yet our technology can manipulate the baseline even if evolution is too slow. New eras follow new ears. Neural hearing implants may eventually surpass the number, reaction time, and frequency range of channels in human hearing. Two ears may be too few for some transhumans in futurity, who prefer an array of microphones all around their bodies. The highest timing resolution of the auditory system involves tracking inter-aural time differences in localization, and spatial rhythm may become a site of great future space–time composition and appreciation. Let us not be too side-tracked by transhuman enthusiasm.[1] One way to ask what is left to find is to try to determine how much has been explored already.

We begin with the humble case of the 16-step pattern for a single non-pitched percussion instrument. There are 2^{16} (65,536) possible patterns including the empty pattern of one measure of silence. Now consider a drum kit of three instruments (call them kick, snare, hi-hat, and ignore any current biases in popular music to backbeat construction favouring certain positions in a measure); the possibilities become $(2^{16})^3 = 8^{16}$. Over two measures, there are 8^{32}, over four, 8^{64}. In around 200 BCE Archimedes calculated in the *Sand-Reckoner* that the number of grains of sand in the universe was 8^{63}, the first truly astronomical number considered in human thought.[2] By a strange coincidence, when considering the atoms per grain of sand, this also works out close to the modern estimate of the number of particles in the visible universe at 10^{80}. It is not hard in musical combinatorics to end up with large numbers of possibilities of this order or beyond,[3] and thus it seems that the mathematical space of possible rhythms, which must be enormously greater than just a matter of sixteenth-note patterns, is effectively inexhaustible.

In making this simple case, we have ignored psychological theories of rhythmic similarity that might reduce the size of the space of rhythms by clustering perceptually similar rhythms together. For instance, Desain and Honing investigate perceptual classes of three-onset rhythms, without and with metric priming by an established meter.[4] From sixty-six rhythms presented to experimental subjects, they reduce in a "chronotopic time clumping map" to four primary clusters, a reduction of around 16:1. Similarly, Paul Fraisse's short and long durations[5] would give only two types of durational interval to classify all time gaps, such that a rhythmic sequence of sixteen elements would have 2^{15} possible spacings. Perceptual compression achievable in a reasonable if not high-quality MP3 might be 10:1, so if along with other evidence above we take this order of perceptual compression as a heuristic, it would only reduce the size of the mathematical space by a single order of magnitude.

Such psychological constraints on the population of viable rhythms might be critiqued in turn.[6] Based on a single or double hit on the final beat, surely the following difference in a 16-step pattern is readily spotted:

xxx0xxx0xxx0xx00
xxx0xxx0xxx0x000

It might be contended that it is possible to spot any single bit change in a 16-bit rhythmic pattern and, thus, that the mathematical size of the space at 2^{16} is also the perceptual size for a certain acute level of listening (metric context would influence perception of otherwise rotationally equivalent patterns such as x000x000x0000000 and 0000x000x000x000).

Further, even granting some reduced space of perceptually separate rhythms, the possibilities of varying patterns timbrally, with different instruments assigned to different subsets of onsets, provide scope for variation. Some rhythms may only make sense in a particular multi-stream timbral context.[7] The timbre of rhythm is an underexplored study area, and so the answer to the question of which rhythms are yet to find expands to become also the question of which sounds and enclosing musical contexts remain to find in a perceptual space likely large enough to occupy humanity for quite some time. We turn now to further delimit the space of rhythm, and the interesting gap between production and perception.

The Limits of Rhythm

In a short story written toward the end of his life, the computer music pioneer Max Mathews discussed two options for future music making: that composers become experience architects/game designers for interactive participative systems, and that performers become obsessed with the fastest possible human performance of certain virtuoso pieces.[8] In sports science, the physiological limits of human motor action are examined and asymptotes predicted for eventual world records. At the time of writing, no marathon runner has beaten the 2-hour mark, though the current world record is Eliud Kipchoge's 2 hours, 1 minute, and 39 seconds, and some models predict that the sub 2-hour marathon could happen by 2021.[9] Though less studied, the limits of musical athletes are similarly open to examination. Justin London places the limit on repetitive striking as 10 hertz (Hz) in the absence of any motor system hierarchical chunking of action.[10] The record for fastest talking is just faster, with Sean Shannon's 655 words per minute,[11] placing a limit on the fast elucidation of syllables in singing.

Table 18.1 compiles a set of speeds of musical events within music performed by humans and machines. The speed limits of the human motor system for single actions can be somewhat sidestepped by chunking (hierarchical action trees). Staggered drumming of multiple fingers on a surface or quasi-glissando arpeggiations on a piano rely on subsidiary actions set in motion from a higher-level gesture; some drumming records are undermined by the use of double or triple hits from stick bounces. Yet, if we take individual sample impulses as events, a computer can produce distinct audio samples as fast as the sampling rate of the audio hardware, vastly beyond human haptic rates.[12]

In the course of compiling this table I explored the fastest sequence of button presses achievable in music rhythm video games, and by extension in video games in general. Some websites provide putative video evidence for 16–17 Hz "button mashing," the number of repetitive button presses on a game controller per second. Some online discussions of techniques include shaking the whole arm and shaking the controller to increase trigger rates; there may be accidental double hits enabled by loose buttons and electronics. I have left this evidence out of the table as requiring closer controlled examination.[13]

Positing too close a link of human production and perception might lead to a claim that any machine music that exceeds human physical capability of performance cannot be appreciated; Conlon Nancarrow's player piano studies provide potential counter examples along with innumerable electronic music works. Nonetheless, a continuum operates from form to rhythm to pitch, as noted by Stockhausen,[14] and clear to any fan of drill and bass and breakcore music where fast repetitions enter audio rate to become pitches. Further, spreading events across multiple streams at multiple initial pitch levels or distinct areas of the spectrum can increase the density of events per second without necessarily invoking a wavetable oscillator. The enjoyment of very fast machine music may relate as much to novel timbres as to pure rhythm, though I would argue that much can be found in the work of artists such as Venetian Snares, Squarepusher, and more, where the exciting on-rush of rhythm is clearly perceptible even as it critically depends on computer sequencing.

The perceptibility of complicated new rhythms has been a recurring problem in new art music composition. Xenakis's critique "the crisis of serial music" motivated his introduction of stochastic music as a statistical approach to the organization of musical events, in replacement of the typical perceptual effect of integral serialism.[15] A crisis of successive new

Table 18.1 Comparison of the maximum events per second attainable through various human physiological and machine means

Rate (events per second)	Description	Source
6.87	Alternating hands, pianist Domingos-Antonio Gomes struck a single piano key 824 times in one minute (rate calculated as half this to get rate per hand)	www.guinnessworldrecords.com/world-records/most-piano-key-hits-in-one-minute
8	16th notes at 120 beats per minute (BPM) (500 milliseconds [ms] per beat)	
8.7875	Fastest drummer Siddharth Nagarajan: 2109 drum hits in one minute, but includes bounces. Might be broken down as 35.15 per second, alternating hands, so 17.57 Hz per hand, at least double striking, so actually 8.7875 Hz per hand	www.guinnessworldrecords.com/world-records/most-drumbeats-in-a-minute-using-drumsticks
10	London's limit on single effector human production (without hierarchical control)	London (2012, p. 29)[a]
10.92	Fastest intelligible talking, 655 words per minute (ignoring chunking and counting syllables, 14.37 syllables per second)	*Guinness Book of Records*
12	Peak events per second tabla drumming observed (shortest gap was around 0.08 seconds corresponding to 12.5 Hz)	Clayton et al. (2018)[b]
16	32nd notes at 120 BPM (500 ms per beat) or 16th notes at 240 BPM (250 ms per beat, London's limit for beat perception)	
18	Typing world record: Stella Pajunas in an hour-long test (1946) reached a peak speed of 216 words per minute, rate here calculated assuming an average of 5 characters per word (including spaces)	Listed on multiple sites including IBM electronic typewriter original publicity
18.18	"Trimpin hammer" solenoid striker for robotic musical instruments (maximum rate without failure)	Kapur et al. (2007)[c]
229	Nancarrow Study 37: 15,718 notes in 12 minutes, an average notes per second of 21.83, but peak events per second 229	Calculated from analysis of a Musical Instrument Digital Interface (MIDI) file

Table 18.1 (*cont.*)

Rate (events per second)	Description	Source
25063.94	Black MIDI track *Necrofantasia*: 9.8 million notes over 6 minutes [m] 31 seconds [s]. A number of renders are online varying in rate around the 6 m 20–30 s mark based on attempts to get a clean performance	www.youtube.com/watch?v= UcERJUzQSHo

[a] J. London, *Hearing in Time: Psychological Aspects of Musical Meter*, 2nd ed. (Oxford University Press, 2012).
[b] M. Clayton, L. Leante, and S. Tarsitani, "IEMP North Indian Raga," *Open Science Framework* (2018).
[c] A. Kapur, E. Singer, A. Suleman, and G. Tzanetakis, *A Comparison of Solenoid-Based Strategies for Robotic Drumming* (Copenhagen: ICMC, 2007).

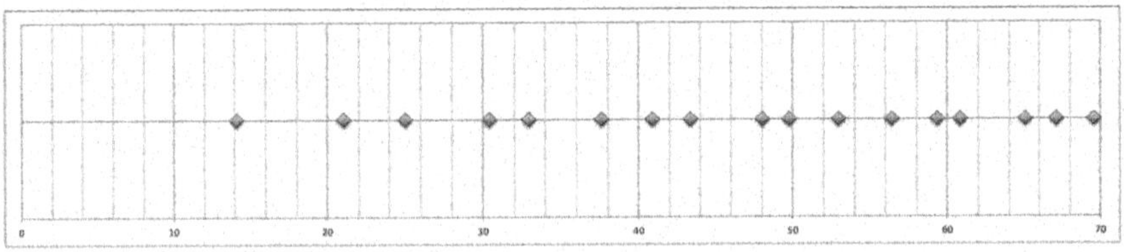

18.1 Riemann zeta function rhythm

complexities has continued on, from such figures as Stockhausen, through Xenakis to Ferneyhough and beyond (see also other chapters in this volume).

As an example of the potential complexity of rhythmic figures, and their perceptual effect, Figure 18.1 plots successive durations based on the spacing of the first seventeen zeros of the Riemann zeta function from analytic number theory.[16]

Numerically, the onset positions (to four decimal places) are:

14.1347, 21.022, 25.0109, 30.4249, 32.9351, 37.5862, 40.9187, 43.3271, 48.0052, 49.7738, 52.9703, 56.4462, 59.347, 60.8318, 65.1125, 67.0798

with corresponding IOIs (including the rest from the beginning to the first event):

14.1347, 6.8873, 3.9888, 5.414, 2.5102, 4.6511, 3.3325, 2.4084, 4.6781, 1.7687, 3.1965, 3.4759, 2.9008, 1.4847, 4.2808, 1.9673, 2.4666

Finding the optimal re-scaling to bring the events close to a grid of 24th notes, leads to the approximate gaps:

1, 0.5, 0.3333, 0.3333, 0.1667, 0.3333, 0.1667, 0.1667, 0.3333, 0.1667, 0.1667, 0.1667, 0.1667, 0.1667, 0.3333, 0.1667, 0.1667

Repeated listening to the original time intervals reveals that the actual spacing is more complicated, but the alternation of fast and slow is relatively well captured by the approximation. The interpretive confound of expressive timing deviation versus intended interonset interval makes accurate reproduction a challenge for human performers, and the finally perceived rhythm of machine music remains contestable. Nonetheless, the charitable listener can hear that this unevenly spaced sequence has a character dissimilar to more obvious constrained rhythms built out of highly related proportions. We now further investigate more deeply the technological influence on rhythmic practice.

Technology-Driven Rhythm

The precision in timing attainable through technological means easily exceeds human biology. An event might be shifted by an individual audio sample (commonly, 1/44100 of a second), multiple synchronized streams can be created that improve upon all possible error bars for human ensemble timing, and humanly impossible rhythms explored from multiple simultaneous tempi to large sets of non-commensurate durations. Electronic and particularly computer music has provided a fertile ground for those seeking absolute control of time.[17] Yet such enhanced sequencing capacity was exhibited first for mechanical musical instruments, most famously in contemporary music circles with the player piano studies of Conlon Nancarrow,[18] himself influenced by suggestions of Henry Cowell.[19] Nancarrow's usage of complicated irrational transcendental ratios such as e/π are essentially impossible for humans to perceive accurately or produce, but make for a neat asymptote to rhythmic striving.[20]

Machine timing is not always absolutely accurate in reality, and there are circumstances where timing errors creep in. Input and output latencies due to digital audio hardware buffers and operating system low-level audio processing loops bring small yet noticeable delays to recording tasks. Modern operating systems can interrupt running processes including audio threads; some holdouts, most famously big beat artist Fatboy Slim, continued to use old Atari ST computers in their studios as reliable sequencers far past the point others had moved on, since the earlier Atari TOS does not support pre-emptive multitasking.[21]

Music making itself may require the navigation of imperfection. The act of live collaboration between humans and computers, or non-realtime computer understanding of human musical action, brings about situations where best-guess prediction of the most likely future events is necessary. Network music is an area of much current investigation,[22] native to the overwhelming rise of the internet, but subject to network timing jitter and latency. Coordinated action over multiple performers who are geographically displaced from one another requires synchronization models for future alignment, including the prediction of future position as if continuing in a straight line ("dead reckoning").[23]

Interfaces in music technology can highly constrain and influence rhythmic choice.[24] The introduction of the metronome had a recognizable impact on musical time in the early nineteenth century,[25] and its descendants continue to influence event timing in digital audio workstations, from the frequent use of metronomes during recording, to the imposition of quantization grids. Step sequencers delimit the possible locations within a measure, as do the list interfaces of tracker programs (even if the tempo and number of steps are definable). Digital audio workstation software projects often default to 120 beats per minute (BPM) and $\frac{4}{4}$, reinforcing the status quo and perhaps influencing the rise in average spontaneous tempo seen in popular music.[26] Future musical options rest in part on the representational decisions of current generation programmers.[27]

Yet some wonderfully innovative, rhythmically complex music has been produced with machines, which could not have been produced otherwise. The capture and repurposing of rhythmic fragments, from strikes and fills to enormous whole beats, is a mainstay of the central role sampling plays in much popular music, and such radical revitalization of past drumming could not possibly have been anticipated by Clyde Stubblefield or his peers at the time of recording their now-classic drum breaks.

There was a charm to early synth pop when acts didn't yet have drum machines or sequencers and had to hand-play parts, sometimes to extremely human effect; witness Orchestral Manoeuvres in the Dark's "Bunker Soldiers" from their first eponymous album (1980). But post-human precision is one of the abiding characteristics of much electronic dance music, for example, the futurist late-1980s sound of Rhythim is Rhythim (or whatever other spellings Derrick May prefers to rhythm) exploring post-funk post-motorik techno. The experimental verges have seen such developments as breakbeats triggered slightly off tempo for rhythmic effect (A Guy Called Gerald, *Black Secret Technology*, 1995) or deliberately wonky loops in juxtaposition (Blectum from Blechdom, *Messy Jesse Fiesta*, 2000). Tracker programs have been used to create highly irregular, fast-paced sequences (Venetian Snares, *Winter in the Belly of a Snake*, 2003). The voice from beat boxing to choral singing has been layered and post-processed to make a fresh approach to the a cappella (Björk, *Medúlla*, 2004). Quantization settings in sequencers have been swapped on the fly to twist rhythms in new directions (Aphex Twin, *Drukqs*, 2001). Manic cascades of Musical Instrument Digital Interface (MIDI) notes as overdeveloped video game music characterize the more recent black MIDI style.[28] There is no reason to doubt that there are many more twists on rhythm to explore through digital means.

One area of live electronic music practice where rhythmic language is under constant active revision is that of live coding, often in the performance context of the algorave.[29] One principal exponent is Alex McLean, who performs as Yaxu in concert, the originator of the Tidal cycles language and its primary developer.[30] Tidal provides powerful shortcuts to rhythmic variety, with generative sequenced patterns redefinable on the fly. An example one-line code snippet will demonstrate the richness of rhythm expressible within the language:

```
d1 $ sound "[bd(7,32) sn*2, hh*15, cp cp [~ cp [cp cp cp]] [mt mt mt]]"
```

The samples bass drum (bd), snare (sn), high-hat (hh), clap (cp), and mid tom (mt) are played back within four simultaneous sequences, sharing a common cycle length (the multiple sequences are separated by commas in the example above). The (7,32) creates a Euclidean rhythm fitting 7 strikes within 32 steps.[31] The symbol ~ is a rest; X*n means to fit n events of type X within the cycle (so hh*15 fits 15 fifteenth notes); [] groups a set of events subdividing a duration, that is, a tuplet, and [~ cp [cp cp cp]] is a nested tuplet, in this case a division of one-quarter of the overall cycle into three (12th notes) consisting of rest, clap, and a further nested triplet of three claps (36th notes, each taking up one-third of a 12th note).

Scoring this complete set of rhythms in conventional notation would lead to a much more awkward representation, and the compact language of Tidal cycles is a beautiful way to approach nested tuplets and polyrhythm, since those rhythmic constructs are fundamental to the language. However, the scope of Tidal is beyond such rhythmic manipulations, which have a heritage back through the Bol Processor language originally intended for cyclic Indian classical music.[32] The Tidal language provides powerful facilities for the manipulation of patterns algorithmically, far removed from conventional sequencing, and where the substance of the music making is more a matter of pattern manipulation ("patterning") than any notion of ordinary sequencing. McLean acknowledges the practice and writing of Laurie Spiegel as a formative influence on the primacy of pattern.[33]

From the general impact of computer music technology on rhythm, we move now to a more specific instance, the appearance of new artificial intelligence techniques in music.

RhythmAIc Practice

Rhythmic practice is currently being transformed through musical artificial intelligences (AI) in what we might denote "musAIc." We discuss here the musicological and creative offshoots of the intensive AI research undertaken at present, which extends from initiatives within big companies, such as Google Magenta, to art projects releasing albums created by deep learning analysis of existing music (http://dadabots.com/). A rough taxonomy of creative projects with music AI, often with a long history in the field of computer music, might mention examples such as:

- Automatic generation of new music for particular use cases in particular styles, based on the statistics of existing music data (beyond imposed music theories)
- New musical interfaces that are highly aware of human musical practice, and seek to extend, complement, train, and even contest human performance
- Sonic transformation and repurposing of existing music based on intensive musical signal processing
- Automatic analysis of recorded music for new musicological understanding of live and studio music projects

An important strand of computer music research here is the better understanding of music by machine, and the creative consequences of this. The transcription problem in computer music to automatically understand musical content within audio files is in no way solved, and dense music with multiple auditory streams provides the most intractable material to analyze. Nonetheless, there are already musicological and creative payoffs to computational analysis. The machine analysis of rhythm, whether or not as accurately transcribed as a human expert listener might achieve, can form the basis for new endeavors and understanding. Even if analysis is rudimentary, the process of automatically extracting musical information can influence new musical practice. Computational models of rhythm, no matter if cognitively implausible, can have an indirect influence on real-world rhythm. For electronic musicians, rhythms arising as a product of psychologically unrealistic models are still "real" in their effect. For instance, an audio file can drive an onset detection algorithm, whose detection mistakes create distantly related rhythms. Mishearing machines influence new composition, such as with David Kant's Happy Valley Band, whose music is scored from the result of inaccurate machine transcription.[34]

An important trend is found in the subfield of Music Information Retrieval (MIR): the analysis of large databases of music, in the form of symbolic score representations, MIDI, or audio files.[35] Corpus analysis allows the examination of historical trends in rhythm, with potential extrapolation to the future. Figure 18.2 is the result of an analysis by automatic onset detection over a large corpus of electronic music from 1950–99.[36] The onset detection is imperfect and is acting on material that has not been split into constituent streams. Nonetheless, the trend over time is noticeable; the best fit line shows an increase of 2.5 attacks per second for pieces over 50 years. This increase can be traced in part to greater incidents of highly percussive electronic dance music and other electronic pop in the corpus, particularly from the 1970s on and especially for the 1990s. The trend might be said to follow "Mathews' Law" of increasingly fast material over time; trends in the 2000s in breakcore and other manic electronica, or contrasting half-speed movements in dubstep or ambient vaporwave may or may not refute the trend. We probably don't expect the line to continue in perpetuity, which would take us outside of the auditory system's capability.

A (generative) model founded on a corpus is not just a musicological tool, but can be a creative tool in new material generation. As a demonstration of this creative application, Example 18.1 plots the original rhythm from Katy Perry's appositely titled "Chained to the Rhythm" (2017), versus one generated from Markovian analysis of the same material.[37] The generated rhythm does not respect the eight-measure structuring of the original, but utilizes similar statistics over inter-onset intervals.

Engineers of algorithmic music systems and powerful new musical signal–processing models may not realize the full influence they have over future musical practice. While I don't expect an AI music takeover for all future music making, the course of music may be highly influenced by the representational decisions for the function space of AI music programs. Only recently have MIR researchers begun to consider ethical issues,[38] and increasingly independent musical AIs are themselves a topic in machine ethics;[39] future copyright law may have to deal with issues around the modeling of the rhythmic style of a given performer from their legacy of recordings, or the ownership by autonomous AI of music it produces. Consider a future AIchestra: each member of the AIchestra is an AI individually trained on

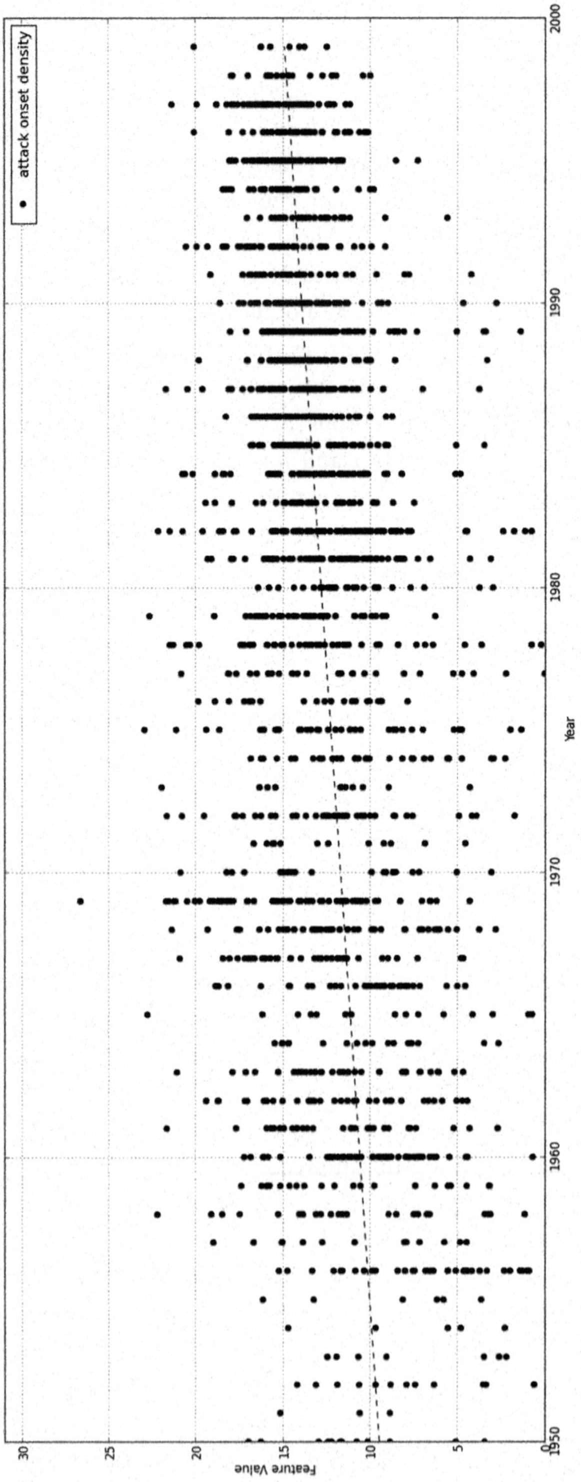

18.2 Corpus analysis of a trend in rhythm from a historical corpus of electronic music (both art and popular works, 1950–1999). The data are from analysis of the mean over pieces of the number of attacks in two-second windows.

18.1 A comparison of Katy Perry's "Chained to the Rhythm" (2017) with chorus rhythm transcribed by a human, versus a rhythm generated by the machine algorithm kAlty perry from Markovian analysis of the same

a particular set of classical music and with their own models of performance practice, having followed a different model of pedagogy. Since rhythmic decisions are intimately coupled to timbre and other musical parameters, the modeling of the AIs is of an order beyond what we might consider the cutting edge right now, but is an aspirational target for musAIc in the coming years.

Conclusions

How will we know when the ultimate rhythm is discovered? The question is ridiculous, since there is no one musical practice, no teleological aim, and music does not have to depend on a single rhythmic pattern! It is clear though that electronic music has opened up new vistas of rhythm; a distant influence would hold even if society turned its collective back on the computer and returned to folk culture.

Forgive a final flourish into long-term futurology. On the grand scale of astrophysics, this book chapter will at best survive only an infinitesimal fraction of time. One of the scenarios for the far future is heat death, where the universe has vastly expanded and cooled to a stable and boring configuration unsympathetic to musicians' union rules as unsupporting of consciousness. At such a point, the uneven clumps of matter will still form an imprint of an interesting rhythm writ large across the skies. Our distant future generations, before the inevitable, may write some wonderful music about it, and physics supply the backbeat.

Endnotes

1 M. O'Connell, *To Be a Machine: Adventures among Cyborgs, Utopians, Hackers, and the Futurists Solving the Modest Problem of Death* (London: Granta, 2017).

2 Archimedes, *The Sand-Reckoner* (translated by Henry Mendell). Available online at https://web.calstatela.edu/faculty/hmendel/Ancient%20Mathematics/Archimedes/SandReckoner/SandReckoner.html, accessed September 18, 2019.

3 As an alternative derivation, consider monophonic 16-step drum patterns, where at each step the four options are silence/kick/snare/hat assuming no simultaneities. There are 4^{16} possible rhythms; over two measures there are 4^{32}, over four, 4^{64}. Allowing a little more variation, if there are nine possible drum sounds and silence, or three dynamic levels for each of three drum sounds and silence, or polyphonic patterns based on none to three hits from three sounds and two alternative sounds, with combinations over five bars, there are 10^{80} possibilities; this number is also an estimate of the number of atoms in the observable universe.

4 P. Desain, and H. Honing, "The Formation of Rhythmic Categories and Metric Priming," *Perception*, 32 (2003), 341–65.

5 E. F. Clarke, "Rhythm and Timing in Music," in D. Deutsch (ed.), *The Psychology of Music*, 2nd ed. (San Diego: Academic Press, 1999), 473–500; J. London, *Hearing in Time: Psychological Aspects of Musical Meter*, 2nd ed. (Oxford University Press, 2012).

6 G. T. Toussaint, "A Comparison of Rhythmic Similarity Measures," *Proceedings of the International Symposium for Music Information Retrieval* (2004).

7 Beat tracking, that is, identification of position within the current metric context, may also critically depend on knowledge of timbral sources relevant to a given musical style. N. Collins, "Towards a Style-Specific Basis for Computational Beat Tracking," *Proceedings of the International Conference on Music Perception and Cognition*, Bologna (2006).

8 M. V. Mathews, "Lektrowsky's Will," *Array* (2008), 110–20.

9 M. J. Joyner, J. R. Ruiz, and A. Lucia, "The Two-Hour Marathon: Who and When?" *Journal of Applied Physiology*, 110 (2011), 275–77.

10 London, *Hearing in Time*, 29.

11 R. Swatman, "Can You Recite Hamlet's 'To Be or Not to Be' Soliloquy Quicker Than the Fastest Talker?" (January 19, 2018), www.guinnessworldrecords.com/news/2018/1/can-you-recite-hamlets-to-be-or-not-to-be-soliloquy-quicker-than-the-fastest-t-509944, accessed October 17, 2019. Syllables per second over the extract of *Hamlet* used for the record I calculated as 342 syllables in 23.8 seconds giving 14.37 Hz, but words per second is probably a fairer measure, given motor system chunking grouping syllables.

12 A further table of musical rates appeared in an earlier publication in the context of examining the border between human and inhuman performance: N. Collins,

"Relating Superhuman Virtuosity to Human Performance," *Proceedings of MAXIS*, Sheffield Hallam University (2002).

13 A selection of web sources includes Takahashi Meijin's 16Hz button mashing record from 1985: https://indie-games-ichiban.wonderhowto.com/news/goodbye-takahashi-meijin-worlds-fastest-button-presser-0127642/a more recent observation of 17Hz button mashing (DrUpauli. How Fast Can Mr. ConCon Button Mash? Published on 30 Dec 2015) www.youtube.com/watch?v=yMJAK4Z5zPo&feature=youtu.beand forum discussion of how to achieve fast button mashing rates: www.reddit.com/r/speedrun/comments/5vefd6/how_do_i_get_better_at_button_mashing/, accessed September 20, 2019.

14 K. Stockhausen, "How Time Passes," *die Reihe*, 3 (1959), 10–40.

15 I. Xenakis, *Formalized Music* (Stuyvesant, NY: Pendragon Press, 1992).

16 On the critical line 0.5 + ti in the complex plane. Given the definition of this function as a convergent infinite sum, this might be said to be a rhythm of a limit as much as any limit of rhythm. B. Mazur and W. Stein, *Prime Numbers and the Riemann Hypothesis* (Cambridge University Press, 2016).

17 C. Roads, *Composing Electronic Music: A New Aesthetic* (Oxford University Press, 2015).

18 K. Gann, *The Music of Conlon Nancarrow* (Cambridge University Press, 1995).

19 H. Cowell, *New Musical Resources* (Cambridge University Press, 1930, reprinted 1996).

20 Human attempts to play Nancarrow's studies are an interesting sideline in the virtuosity of contemporary music performance. The 1993 Ensemble Modern CD containing Yvar Mikhashoff arrangements of the studies is highly recommended (BMG Classics – 09026 61180 2).

21 T. Doyle, "Classic Tracks: Fatboy Slim 'Praise You,'" *Sound on Sound* (January 2017), www.soundonsound.com/techniques/classic-tracks-fatboy-slim-praise-you, accessed September 16, 2019.

22 Á. Barbosa, "Displaced Soundscapes: A Survey of Network Systems for Music and Sonic Art Creation," *Leonardo Music Journal*, 13 (2003), 53–9.

23 C. McKinney, "Collaboration and Embodiment in Networked Music Interfaces for Live Performance" (Ph.D. dissertation, University of Sussex, 2016).

24 T. Magnusson, "Epistemic Tools: The Phenomenology of Digital Musical Instruments" (Ph.D. dissertation, University of Sussex, 2009); C. Nash and A. Blackwell, "Liveness and Flow in Notation Use," *Proceedings of New Interfaces for Musical Expression* (2012).

25 A. E. Bonus. "Metronome," *Oxford Handbooks Online* (2014), www.oxfordhandbooks.com/view/10.1093/oxfordhb/9780199935321.001.0001/oxfordhb-9780199935321-e-001), accessed December 10, 2018.

26 L. van Noorden and D. Moelants, "Resonance in the Perception of Musical Pulse," *Journal of New Music Research*, 28 (1999), 43–66.

27 Particularly where those programmers enthusiastically embrace machine learning technology, abnegating future flexibility for deeply learned but only

speciously creative models, which is not to say that musical artificial intelligence does not have wonderful potential.

28 S. Sutherland, "Black MIDI Songs Will Kill Your Brain and Your Computer," *This Exists*, online video clip (January 16, 2014), www.youtube.com/watch?v=FqjSYtKWyX8, accessed September 16, 2019.

29 N. Collins and A. McLean, "Algorave: Live Performance of Algorithmic Electronic Dance Music," *Proceedings of New Interfaces for Musical Expression*, London (2014). I will try to resist the oft-repeated "algorhythm" pun. Checking the Google word count for the term over the years does not reveal a clear originator, though some earlier 1960s/70s books use it as an equivalent term for algorithm and there was a 1970s company called Algorhythm.

30 A. McLean, "Making Programming Languages to Dance to: Live Coding with Tidal," *Proceedings of the 2nd ACM SIGPLAN International Workshop on Functional Art, Music, Modeling & Design* (2014), 63–70.

31 G. T. Toussaint, *The Geometry of Musical Rhythm: What Makes a "Good" Rhythm Good?* (Boca Raton, FL: CRC, 2016).

32 B. Bel and J. Kippen, "Modelling Music with Grammars: Formal Language Representation in the Bol Processor," in A. Marsden and A. Pople (eds.), *Computer Representations and Models in Music* (London: Academic Press, 1992), 207–38.

33 L. Spiegel, "Manipulations of Musical Patterns," *Proceedings of the Symposium on Small Computers and the Arts, IEEE Computer Society Catalog*, 393 (1981), 19–22.

34 D. Kant, "The Happy Valley Band: Creative (Mis)Transcription," *Leonardo Music Journal*, 26 (2016), 76–8.

35 M.A. Casey, R. Veltkamp, M. Goto, M. Leman, C. Rhodes, and M. Slaney, "Content-Based Music Information Retrieval: Current Directions and Future Challenges," *Proceedings of the IEEE*, 96 (2008), 668–96; A. Lerch, *An Introduction to Audio Content Analysis* (Hoboken, NJ: Wiley, 2012); M. Müller, *Fundamentals of Music Processing* (Cham: Springer, 2015).

36 N. Collins, P. Manning, and S. Tarsitani, "A New Curated Corpus of Historical Electronic Music: Collation, Data and Research Findings," *Transactions of the International Society for Music Information Retrieval*, 1 (2018), 34–43.

37 Technically, a variable order Markov model, Prediction by Partial Match, was used for this analysis, permitting up to order 4 chains. The rhythm of the original contains just six distinct states, the durations 0.25, 0.5, 0.75 and 1 (16th to quarter note), and the rest durations 0.5 and 1.

38 A. Holzapfel, B. Sturm, and M. Coeckelbergh, "Ethical Dimensions of Music Information Retrieval Technology," *Transactions of the International Society for Music Information Retrieval*, 1 (2018), 44–55.

39 N. Collins, "Trading Faures: Virtual Musicians and Machine Ethics," *Leonardo Music Journal*, 21 (2011), 35–9.

Select Bibliography

This short bibliography contains references to books in the English language that might be useful to readers and is not intended to be comprehensive. References to journal articles and unpublished theses will be found in the notes to each chapter.

Adams, J. *Hallelujah Junction: Composing an American Life* (New York: Farrar, Strauss and Giroux, 2008).

Agawu, K. *African Rhythm: A Northern Ewe Perspective* (Cambridge University Press, 1995).

Alorwoyie, G. F. with D. Locke. *Agbadza: Songs, Drum Language of the Ewe* (St. Louis, MO: African Music Publishers, 2013).

Amira, J. and S. Cornelius. *The Music of Santería: Traditional Rhythms of the Batá Drums* (Crown Point, IN: White Cliffs Media, 1992).

Bakan, M. *Music of Death and New Creation: Experiences in the World of Balinese Gamelan Beleganjur* (University of Chicago Press, 1999).

Bartók, B. *Béla Bartók Essays*, B. Suchoff (ed.) (London: Faber and Faber, 1976).

Berlin, E. A. *Ragtime: A Musical and Cultural History* (University of California Press, 1980).

Bowra, C. M. *Primitive Song* (Cleveland: The World Publishing Company, 1962).

Browner, T. *Heartbeat of the People: Music and Dance of the Northern Pow-Wow* (University of Illinois Press, 2002).

Butler, M. *Unlocking the Groove: Rhythm, Meter, and Musical Design in Electronic Dance Music* (Indiana University Press, 2006).

Cage, J. *Silence: Lectures and Writings by John Cage* (Wesleyan University Press, 1973).

Carl, R. *Terry Riley's In C* (Oxford University Press, 2009).

Carter, E. *The Writings of Elliott Carter* (Indiana University Press, 1977).

Chernoff, J. M. *African Rhythm and African Sensibility* (University of Chicago Press, 1979).

Clayton, M. *Time in Indian Music: Rhythm, Metre, and Form in North Indian Rag Performance* (Oxford University Press, 2000).

Cook, N. *Beyond the Score: Music as Performance* (Oxford University Press, 2013).

Cooper, G. W. and L. B. Meyer. *The Rhythmic Structure of Music* (University of Chicago Press, 1963).

Cowell, H. *New Musical Resources* (Cambridge University Press, 1930).

Deleuze, G. *Repetition and Difference*, P. Patton (trans.) (Columbia University Press, 1994).

Diamond, B., M. S. Cronk, and F. von Rosen. *Visions of Sound: Musical Instruments of First Nations Communities in Northeastern America* (University of Chicago Press, 1994).

Fink, R. *Repeating Ourselves: American Minimal Music as Cultural Practice* (University of California Press, 2005).

Gann, K. *The Music of Conlon Nancarrow* (Cambridge University Press, 1995).

Glass, P. *Music by Philip Glass*, R. T. Jones (ed.) (New York: Harper & Row, 1987).

Words Without Music (New York: Liveright Publishing, 2015).

Gopinath, S. and P. ap Siôn (eds.). *Rethinking Reich* (Oxford University Press, 2019).

Grant, M. R. *Beating Time and Measuring Music in the Early Modern Era* (Oxford University Press, 2014).

Hartenberger, R. *Performance Practice in the Music of Steve Reich* (Cambridge University Press, 2016).

Hartenberger, R. (ed.). *The Cambridge Companion to Percussion* (Cambridge University Press, 2016).

Hasty, C. *Meter as Rhythm* (Oxford University Press, 1997).

Herndon, M. *Native American Music* (Norwood, PA: Norwood Editions, 1980).

Hodeir, A. *Jazz: Its Evolution and Essence*, D. Noakes (trans.) (New York: Grove, 1956).

Horlacher, G. *Building Blocks: Repetition and Continuity in the Music of Stravinsky* (Oxford University Press, 2011).

Kapur, A., E. Singer, A. Suleman, and G. Tzanetakis. *A Comparison of Solenoid-Based Strategies for Robotic Drumming* (Copenhagen: ICMC, 2007).

Keeling, R. *Cry for Luck: Sacred Song and Speech Among the Yurok, Hupa, and Karok Indians of Northwestern California* (University of California Press, 1992).

Keil, C. and S. Feld. *Music Grooves: Essays and Dialogues* (University of Chicago Press, 1994).

Kippen, J. *Gurudev's Drumming Legacy: Music, Theory and Nationalism in the Mrdang aur Tabla Vadanpaddhati of Gurudev Patwardhan* (Aldershot: Ashgate, 2006).

The Tabla of Lucknow: A Cultural Analysis of a Musical Tradition (Cambridge University Press, 1988).

Klorman, Edward. *Mozart's Music of Friends: Social Interplay in the Chamber Works* (Oxford University Press, 2016.

Kramer, J. *The Time of Music: New Meanings, New Temporalities, New Listening Strategies* (New York: Schirmer Books, 1988).

Krebs, H. *Fantasy Pieces: Metrical Dissonance in the Music of Robert Schumann* (Oxford University Press, 1999).

Krebs, H. and S. Krebs. *The Life and Songs of Josephine Lang* (Oxford University Press, 2007).

Kurath, G. P. and A. Garcia. *Music and Dance of the Tewa Pueblos* (Santa Fe: Museum of New Mexico Press, 1970).

Lerdahl, F. and R. Jackendoff. *A Generative Theory of Tonal Music* (MIT Press, 1983).

London, J. *Hearing in Time: Psychological Aspects of Musical Meter*, 2nd ed. (Oxford University Press, 2012).

Malin, Y. *Songs in Motion: Rhythm and Meter in the German Lied* (Oxford University Press, 2010).

Manuel, P. *Tales, Tunes, and Tassa Drums: Retention and Invention in Indo-Caribbean Music* (University of Illinois Press, 2015).

Margulis, E. H. *On Repeat: How Music Plays the Mind* (Oxford University Press, 2014).

McAllester, D. P. *Enemy Way Music: A Study of Social and Esthetic Values as Seen in Navaho Music* (Cambridge, MA: The Peabody Museum of American Archaeology and Ethnology, 1954).

McClelland, R. *Brahms and the Scherzo: Studies in Musical Narrative* (Aldershot: Ashgate, 2010).

McGraw, A. C. *Radical Traditions: Reimagining Culture in Contemporary Balinese Music* (Oxford University Press, 2013).

McKee, Eric. *Decorum of the Minuet, Delirium of the Waltz: A Study of Dance-Music Relations in 3/4 Time* (Indiana University Press, 2012).

McPhee, C. *Music in Bali: A Study in Form and Instrumental Organization in Balinese Orchestral Music* (Yale University Press, 1966).

Messiaen, O. *Music and Color: Conversations with Claude Samuel* (Paris: Editions Belfond, 1986).

Mirka, D. *Metric Manipulations in Haydn and Mozart: Chamber Music for Strings, 1787–1791* (Oxford University Press, 2009).

Mithun, M. *The Languages of Native North America* (Cambridge University Press, 1999).

Moore, A. *Rock: The Primary Text: Developing a Musicology of Rock*, 2nd ed. (Aldershot, UK: Ashgate, 2001).

Murphy, S. (ed.). *Brahms and the Shaping of Time* (University of Rochester Press, 2018).

Neff, S., M. Carr, and G. Horlacher (eds.). *The Rite of Spring at 100* (Oxford University Press, 2017).

Nelson, D. P. *Solkattu Manual: An Introduction to the Rhythmic Language of South Indian Music* (Wesleyan University Press, 2008).

Nettl, B. *Blackfoot Musical Thought: Comparative Perspectives* (Kent State University Press, 1989).

Music in Primitive Culture (Harvard University Press, 1956).

Nketia, J. H. K. *African Music in Ghana* (Northwestern University Press, 1962).

Nzewi, M. *African Music: Theoretical Content and Creative Continuum: The Culture-Exponent's Definitions* (Olderhausen: Institut für Didaktik Populärer Musik, 1997).

Ohriner, M. *Flow: The Rhythmic Voice in Rap Music* (Oxford University Press, 2019).

Oja, C. J. *Colin McPhee: Composer in Two Worlds* (Washington: Smithsonian Institution, 1990).

Potter, K. *Four Musical Minimalists* (Cambridge University Press, 2000).

Reich, S. *Writings on Music, 1965–2000*, P. Hillier (ed.) (Oxford University Press, 2002).

Rothstein, W. *Phrase Rhythm in Tonal Music* (New York: Schirmer Books, 1989).

Sachs, C. *Rhythm and Tempo: A Study in Music History* (New York: W.W. Norton and Company, 1953).

Schweitzer, K. *The Artistry of Afro-Cuban Batá Drumming: Aesthetics, Transmission, Bonding, and Creativity* (University Press of Mississippi, 2013).

Stobart, H. *Music and the Poetics of Production in the Bolivian Andes* (Aldershot: Ashgate, 2006).

Stravinsky, I. *Poetics of Music* (Harvard University Press, 1942).

Temperley, D. *The Musical Language of Rock* (Oxford University Press, 2018).

Tenzer, M. *Gamelan Gong Kebyar: The Art of Twentieth-Century Balinese Music* (University of Chicago Press, 2000).

Tilley, L. *Making It Up Together: The Art of Collective Improvisation in Balinese Music and Beyond* (University of Chicago Press, 2019).

Toussaint, G. T. *The Geometry of Musical Rhythm: What Makes a "Good" Rhythm Good?* (Boca Raton, FL: CRC, 2016).

Van den Toorn, P. Stravinsky and the *Rite of Spring* (University of California Press, 1987).

Vander, J. *Shoshone Ghost Dance Religion: Poetry Songs and Great Basin Context* (University of Illinois Press, 1997).

Wallaschek, R. *Primitive Music: An Inquiry into the Origin and Development of Music, Songs, Instruments, Dances, and Pantomimes of Savage Races* (Aberdeen University Press, 1893).

Washburne, C. *Sounding Salsa: Performing Latin Music in New York City* (Temple University Press, 2008).

Wilcken, L. *The Drums of Vodou* (Tempe, AZ: White Cliffs Media 1992).

Wolf, R. K. *The Black Cow's Footprint: Time, Space and Music in the Lives of the Kotas of South India* (Delhi: Permanent Black, 2005).

The Voice in the Drum: Music, Language, and Emotion in Islamicate South Asia (University of Illinois Press, 2014).

Wolf, R., S. Blum, and C. Hasty (eds.). *Thought and Play in Musical Rhythm: Asian, African, and Euro-American Perspectives* (Oxford University Press, 2019).

Index

Printed by Printforce, United Kingdom